The Culture of Addiction

Book 1

The Culture of Recovery

Book 2

*A Travel Guide
for Treatment Professionals*

William L. White

A LIGHTHOUSE TRAINING INSTITUTE PUBLICATION

Additional copies of this publication may be obtained by sending $17.95 plus $2.00 shipping and handling to:

The Lighthouse Training Institute
720 West Chestnut
Bloomington, Illinois 61701
(309) 827-6026

DEDICATION

This book is dedicated to the alcoholics and addicts who have touched my life over the past twenty years. To those whose discovery of freedom has brought me great joy and to those whose continued self-destruction has pained me deeply, you have been my best teachers.

ACKNOWLEDGEMENTS

This book springs from intellectual roots that must be acknowledged. The earliest and perhaps most important roots can be traced to the works of Irving Goffman and Howard Becker whose writings helped me bridge the gap between psychological and sociological perspectives on deviance. Early sociological/cultural perspectives on alcoholism—particularly the work of Howard Bahr, James Spradley and Samuel Wallace—and the more recent appearance of urban ethnographic studies of heroin addiction—to include the studies of Michael Agar, Dan Waldorf, Edward Preble, John Casey, Seymour Fiddle and Harold Finestone—helped shape the theoretical framework utilized to describe the cultures of addiction and recovery. The influence of Stephanie Brown and her work to formulate a developmental model of recovery is also clearly evident throughout the last half of the book. The ideas contained in this book would have clearly remained dormant without the pioneering work of these men and women.

On a more personal level, I must pay tribute to Dr. Ed Senay and Dr. Doug Bey whose early mentorship and personal encouragement sparked the beginning of my professional writing. I am also deeply indebted to my colleagues at the Lighthouse Training Institute for their invaluable support. Russ Hagen and Dr. Mark Godley provided sustained encouragement on the potential importance of the book to the substance abuse field. The thoughtful criticisms and suggestions of Dr. Gene Landrum and Dr. Alan Sodetz have produced a work of far better quality than was present in the earliest drafts. Jo Major, Jim Fraser and Roger Krohe provided helpful critiques on special topics within the book. Brian Cronk provided valuable computer assistance during the printing of the book.

Particular thanks also go to the innumerable institutions that provided me the opportunity to conduct workshops on the ideas found in the book when these ideas were still in an embryonic stage. The dialogue with participants during these workshops did much to assure the clinical specificity and applicability of the work.

I would finally and most importantly like to thank Ms. Rita Chaney for her unflinching support during the more than three years of my life the preparation of this book has spanned.

TABLE OF CONTENTS

BOOK ONE

BOOK TWO

CHAPTER EIGHT: THE CULTURE OF ADDICTION

PREFACE

This is a book written to and for professionals who have direct and indirect involvement in the assessment and treatment of substance abuse disorders. It is written for physicians, nurses, psychologists, social workers, addiction counselors and other interdisciplinary team members involved in substance abuse treatment. It is also written for others, who through their professional roles, have direct contact with substance abusing individuals. It is written for the employee assistance counselors in the workplace, the counselors and social workers in the school systems, the social agency workers, the probation officers and others who need a better understanding of the addiction and recovery process because of the frequency with which they encounter persons with alcohol and drug problems.

This is a book about pilgrimages and pathways. It is a guided tour of two deviant cultures—one which promotes excessive use of psychoactive drugs, the other which promotes radical abstinence from such substances—and how persons can move from one culture to the other. It is an anthropological study of addiction and recovery as cultural phenomenon. It is a manual of both substance abuse program design and a manual of clinical technique in substance abuse assessment and treatment. It is a book which explores how persons who get enmeshed in deviant subcultures can be reclaimed by this society. While the intervention technology described is substance abuse specific, the models and approaches set forth could be applied to other deviant cultures, *e.g.*, delinquency, mental illness, This book is most of all a book of stories about real people who started on the pilgrimage from addiction to recovery and the various pathways and experiences they would encounter on their journey.

To write a book is for me an act of faith that the world and the people in it can be influenced by the power of words and ideas. There is also in most writers—beyond the desire for distinction and some thread of immortality—that revolutionary spirit which seeks to, through the power of thought, reshape the world through their vision. If there is in my words such passion and intensity, I hope

i

it will be viewed as idealism rather than rigidity or arrogance. If there are criticisms of the substance abuse field, they come not from the animus of the outsider but from the love of one who has spent more than two decades in this field. If there is strong feeling expressed related to the future direction of the field, it is because I expect to experience that future within the field. If I have avoided issues that are obvious to the reader, it means either I failed to see them or didn't know what to say about them. If the thoughts expressed in these pages contradict earlier writings, it means I've changed my mind.

The substance abuse field has often failed to capture and carry forward the best within our collective experience. Our direct service emphasis and a strong anti-intellectual tradition within the field have, until recently, discouraged research and writing. Our oral history is regularly bled out and lost through the high staff turnover within the field. While we do much through our written and oral communication to educate and influence persons outside the field, we continue to be remiss in fully capturing and transmitting the best of our clinical work to future generations of substance abuse professionals. I hope this book will constitute at least a minor contribution to filling that void.

I hope this book can be an on-going resource for the reader. A detailed table of contents and index and extensive subtitling have been provided to help the reader return to the book and easily find areas of discussion and recommendations. An extensive bibliography has also been included to assist those readers who may wish to further pursue areas of special interest.

As always, I would welcome the opportunity to receive your comments, your criticisms and your ideas. Correspondence can be sent to:

William L. White
Director of Training and Consultation
Lighthouse Training Institute
720 West Chestnut
Bloomington, Illinois 61701

PROLOGUE

This book portrays the movement from addiction to recovery as a pilgrimage between two social worlds. The reader is invited to share in this pilgrimage by exploring the nature of these worlds and the pathways that lead from one to the other. The purpose of this prologue is to provide an itinerary for the trip and to introduce the language which will be used on this journey.

The illustration on the following page provides a schematic map of this book. There are a significant number of persons within the United States who consume psychoactive drugs with a frequency and intensity that is life impairing. The demographic and personality characteristics of these drug users mirror the great heterogeneity within the total population. The needs, vulnerabilities and influences—the etiological pathways—which lead these individuals to initiate and sustain this person-drug relationship vary widely. Out of the power and primacy of this shared experience, users seek out others like themselves to both facilitate and celebrate continued drug use. The diversity of drug users is meshed and homogenized within a community of drug use, referred to in this book as a "culture of addiction." This culture has but one purpose reflected in its organizing motifs—the promotion of excessive alcohol and drug consumption.

The physiological, psychological, and spiritual transformations which accompany the person-drug relationship occur within and are shaped by the culture of addiction. The progression of addiction is often accompanied by a concurrent disaffiliation from the society at large and an increasing enmeshment in the culture of addiction. This cultural affiliation touches and transforms every dimension of one's existence. What begins as a person drug relationship moves toward an all-encompassing lifestyle. No part of the persona is left untouched by the culture of addiction. Book One (Chapters One through Seven) examines this culture of addiction and the nature of the personal transformations that occur within this society of addicts.

There are many experiences that can trigger opportunities for termination of the person-drug relationship and disengagement from the culture of addiction—pain, exhaustion, boredom, fear, loss, etc. Those seeking such change are inevitably drawn to others of similar inclinations. Over the past century an alternative culture—a culture of recovery—has evolved as a haven for those seeking escape from addiction and the addictive lifestyle. Book Two (Chapters Eight through Fifteen) examines the nature of this culture of recovery and how the movement of persons from the culture of addiction to the culture of recovery can be facilitated. It describes how the culture of addiction must be confronted and stripped from the client as he or she enters the treatment process and be replaced with an equally consuming and well-organized culture of recovery.

The cultures of addiction and recovery are technically subcultures within the United States. The term "culture" will be used in place of subculture both for purposes of simplicity and to reinforce the application of models and tools for studying cultures to the phenomenon of addiction and recovery. For purposes of clarity, the term "culture" as used in this book will always refer to either the culture of addiction or the culture of recovery. When speaking of the American culture as a whole, the term "society" will be used.

The organization of both cultures is explored (Chapters Two and Nine). Both cultures are made up of loosely affiliated social networks or "tribes." These chapters explore how tribes in both cultures are organized and examine in some depth the historical influence of national alcohol and drug abuse policy on tribal organization. They note particularly the organization of tribes around four broad sociolegal drug classifications and the impact drug choice (tribal affiliation) has on one's addictive and/or

A Cultural Model of
Addiction and Recovery

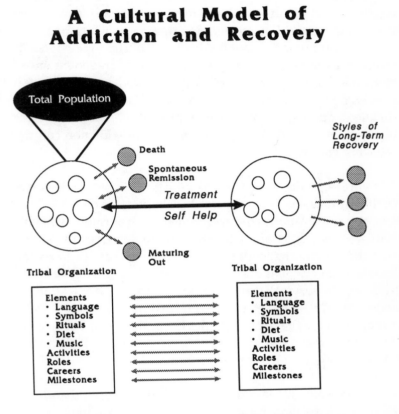

recovery "career." The emerging and future role of the treatment agency within the culture of recovery concludes this discussion.

The core elements within both the culture of addiction and culture of recovery is discussed (Chapters Four and Eleven). Core elements are mediums such as language, symbols, rituals, history, mythology, dress, diet, music, and art, through which both cultures transmit values and shape the behavior of their members. These chapters explore how through the vehicle of treatment one strips elements from the culture of addiction and replaces these with elements from the culture of recovery. These chapters provide detailed guidelines and techniques for enhancing "cultural conversion"—the shift in affiliation from an addiction culture to a recovery culture.

The core activities that drive day-to-day lifestyle for members of both cultures will be reported (Chapters Five and Twelve). Chapter Five examines the evolutionary transformation in daily life rendered by addiction. Chapter Twelve describes the shift from use rituals (hustling, copping and getting off rituals) to abstinence rituals (centering and mirroring rituals, self-constructive behaviors and acts of service) that mark the transition from addiction to recovery. These chapters explore treatment not as a vehicle to simply remove the drug from the life of the client but as a vehicle to remove the client from a lifestyle designed to promote and sustain the person-drug relationship.

The dominant roles within both cultures are identified and described (Chapters Six and Thirteen). In these Chapters, the cast of characters which fill both cultures are introduced. The reader will meet the high priests, the dealers, the elders, the ambassadors, the pseudojunkies, the profiteers, the storytellers, the jailhouse lawyers, the clowns, the pigeons, the martyrs, and others. These chapters explore roles as "job functions" that provide both personal identity and perform tasks crucial to cultural survival. These chapters explore how knowledge and skills implicit in roles in the culture of addiction can be channeled into comparable but more constructive roles within the culture of recovery.

Both addiction and recovery are viewed as "careers" and the career milestones for each are enumerated (Chapters Seven and Fourteen). "Career paths" in both cultures are described, focusing particularly on developmental stages or milestones that mark decision points for disengagement from or intensification of addiction/recovery. Considerable time is given to examining how addicts "do treatment" through self-sabotaging styles designed to escape the experience of treatment and sustain addiction. Interventions are outlined to abort such self-defeating styles. Numerous strategies and techniques for interrupting and terminating the addict career path are catalogued as are guidelines for initiating and supporting the on-going developmental process of recovery.

Both addicts and recovering persons can exhibit divergent styles in the nature of their relationship with the cultures of addiction and recovery. Three such styles will be defined and illustrated (acultural, bicultural, and culturally enmeshed). Implications of these cultural styles of addiction to the treatment process are noted. The book ends with an exploration of the many and varied styles and pathways (both traditional and non-traditional) of recovery.

This book, as the illustration portrays, will address five basic questions:

1. What etiological pathways lead to addiction and engagement in the culture of addiction?
2. How are people transformed through this process of cultural affiliation?
3. What strategies and techniques can help disengage persons from the culture of addiction and provide an alternative career path?
4. What strategies and techniques can help bond the addict to an alternative culture of recovery?
5. What pathways/styles of long term recovery exist for the addict and what roles can the treatment professional play in supporting this developmental process?

Book One addresses the first two questions. Book Two addresses the last three questions.

BOOK ONE

THE CULTURE OF ADDICTION

Junk is not just a habit. It is a way of life. When you give up junk, you give up a way of life.

William Burroughs

Junkie

❦

CULTURAL ASPECTS OF ADDICTION

1.1 *Pilgrims and Pathways*

The addict, regardless of drug choice, is a chameleon. It is little wonder that our understanding of this person is marked by such incongruous descriptions. The addict's self explanation of their status—their story—goes through kaleidoscopic changes depending on the audience. Autobiographical accounts of addiction contain retrospective explanations and justifications that may have little to do with the true dynamics of the person-drug relationship. The addict known and described by family members is often very different than this same person described by others. The plethora of clinical studies, based primarily on the addict's presentation of self in an institutional environment, focus on the personality characteristics shared by addicts. Criminal justice specialists sketch the addict with a special eye on the addict's criminality and exploitative proclivities. Clergy report the overall spiritual abyss and the guilt and shame presented by the addict. Anthropological or ethnographic studies of the addict "in the life" offer very different naturalistic descriptions of the addict operating in their native habitat. Sociologists and social psychologists offer an expanded view of the addict as an outsider embedded within a deviant subculture. And the list goes on, with each discipline reporting that the chameleon is a different color.

Addiction is an infinitely complex labyrinth or maze within which all aspects of one's life are transformed. There are multiple pathways through which one can wander into this maze and yet each pathway seems to pull the pilgrim in deeper. It's as if one wandered into a magical world, but once in became lost amidst the potions and poisons and pleasure and pain. To survive the threats and challenges in this predatory world of twists and turns and paths which lead nowhere, the addict must become a chameleon. The addict has many faces—each a mask that fits a particular drama within the maze. Personæ are created moment by moment in response to the threats and opportunities presented within their environment. There is no character, only context. Any mask, any part, any lines will emerge which allow the addict to sustain their drug relationship within this maze of the addiction lifestyle. How addiction is viewed is often a function of where one encounters addicts within this maze. What we see from our narrow professional roles is not the addict, but the camouflage constructed for our particular drama, which more often than not is simply the addict mirroring to us that for which we are looking. No matter our theoretical bias, the addict will accommodate by playing a role appropriately. This book seeks to integrate multiple theoretical perspectives so that treatment professionals can, by seeing and addressing addiction in all of its dimensions, rewrite the scripts and outcomes of such dramas.

This is a book about the maze and the tribes of addicts that can be found there. It's a story about the pathways into the maze and how one learns to be a chameleon. It is a book about the forces within the maze which begin to transform the pilgrim. It's also, and perhaps most importantly, a story about how the pilgrim finds a pathway out of the labyrinth and how we can serve as a guide in this process.

The following pages are a travel log for a tour through the culture of addiction in the United States. We will explore how this culture is organized, the major elements of the culture, the major activities and roles that exist within the culture and the major developmental milestones experienced by members of the culture.

1.2 *Culture of Addiction Defined*

Drug users seek out and build relationships with other persons whose drug use mirrors their own. They create small groups within which the rituals of drug use can be nurtured. Such groups interact with each other and form loosely constructed tribes which bind groups together around such issues as geography, ethnicity, or drug choice. These tribes overlap, creating a broader social network of drug users who share common goals and attributes. These social networks when looked at in their totality constitute a fully organized culture. From the dyad to the tribe to the culture, the social dynamic within the relationships between drug users constitutes a powerful stimulus for sustained drug use.   The culture has an existence and power that transcends its individual membership. The coming chapters will explore the nature and influence of this culture. The term, culture, as used in this text, will encompass classic definitions that examine customs, traditions, language, artifacts, institutions, religion, social relationships and values shared in common by a group of people. The term will also encompass more expanded definitions (Geertz, 1973) that focus on culture as shared ideas or understandings that guide how individuals perceive themselves and the outside world.   The phrase "culture of addiction" as used in this text can be defined as follows.

Particular concern will be given to how the progressive enmeshment within this culture of addiction redefines personal identity and shapes one's "addictive career." In exploring the sphere of

> *The culture of addiction is an informal social network in which group norms encourage and support shared patterns of thinking, feeling and behaving that promote excessive alcohol and drug use.*

influence of this culture, emphasis will be given to its ability to touch and transform nearly every dimension of the addict's life.

The culture of addiction is a way of life, a means of organizing one's daily existence, and a way of viewing people and events in the outside world. It is a way of talking, walking, dressing, gesturing, believing, mating, working, playing, thinking, and seeing that separates persons who are "in the life" from those who are not. The culture of addiction encompasses values, artifacts, places, rituals, relationships, symbols, music, and art, all of which reinforce one's involvement in excessive drug consumption. The culture of addiction can play a role in both initiating and sustaining substance abuse disorders. The approach to understanding this culture will not be based on retrospective psychological explanations of what personality aberrations led to the deviant behavior of addiction. It will rather try to describe, and to the extent possible, create an experiential awareness of the world of the addict as he or she lives it on a daily basis. Addictive behavior will be examined within the social environment in which such behavior is nested.

1.3 *The Species of Substance Abuse*

Historically, the substance abuse field has been fragmented into various schools, each of which view the etiology of addiction and appropriate treatment interventions from their own theoretical frameworks. Each school, or modality, purported to explain all addiction through its particular theoretical view. The philosophy and methods of each of these schools were based on experience with a highly unique client population and then broadly generalized to fit populations very divergent from those with which the philosophy and methods had proved successful. More recently, multiple pathway theories of addiction have gained in prominence. These theories hold that the onset of addiction may spring from numerous etiologies, producing subpopulations of addicts, each of whom share unique distinguishing characteristics and require significantly different treatment approaches. Multiple pathway theories seek the development of an assessment and treatment paradigm which will encompass both traditionally defined patterns of alcoholism and addiction as well as atypical *patterns of alcohol and drug abuse*. The author, in lectures over the past five years, has proposed a model that looks at distinct patterns or species of addiction/abuse based on varying answers to the following question:

- How do we understand the primary driving forces behind the <u>onset</u> of the pattern of substance abuse in this client?

In answering that question in my clinical work, I have attempted to define the major etiological pathways, identified distinguishing characteristics of each pathway, and outlined treatment interventions most appropriate for each. The major etiological pathways include the following:

- Etiology of biochemical origin. The primary marriage between the drug and the client occurs at a cellular level, vulnerability having been influenced by genetic predisposition, illness or trauma in ways that increase the reinforcing properties of psychoactive substances.
- Etiology tied to diagnosed or undiagnosed medical problems. The onset of substance abuse is linked to a

pattern of self-medication (or iatrogenic use) in which the excessive consumption of psychoactive drugs provides alleviation of discomforting symptoms of a primary medical illness or debilitating trauma.

- Etiology tied to a primary psychiatric illness. Substance abuse is a manifestation of, serves to mask or serves to self-medicate a primary psychiatric disorder.
- Etiology tied to developmental crisis. The onset of substance abuse serves to self-medicate emotional pain resulting from extreme life stressors, *e.g.*, divorce, death of loved one, job loss.
- Etiology tied to a disturbance in the nuclear or extended family system. The onset of substance abuse serves to divert family attention from a much more painful and potentially destabilizing problem, *e.g.*, impending divorce, impending death, sexual abuse.
- Etiology tied to a network of peer relationships. The onset of substance abuse is tied to needs for social identity and acceptance within a peer subculture that promotes excessive alcohol/drug consumption, *e.g.*, adolescent, college, military, organizational or social subcultures.
- Etiology tied to cultural norms. The onset of substance abuse is linked to rites of passage and ongoing member-ship in an ethnic or cultural group.
- Etiology tied to personality disorder. The onset of substance abuse results from a broad pattern of antisocial behavior in which the cultivation of risk and excitement is highly valued.

What is important about multiple pathway theories of addiction for our current discussion is the notion that the culture of addiction can play a role in both initiating and sustaining a pattern of substance abuse no matter which inciting pathway is involved.

The culture of addiction, in late stages of drug dependence, can pose the major obstacle to clients of all species entering the recovery process.

1.4 *Culture as an Initiating Force*

The ritual of psychoactive drug consumption, and particularly excessive consumption with undesirable consequences, may be reinforced initially, not by the euphorigenic properties of such substances, but by the social meanings and rewards derived from participation in such rituals. The culture of addiction offers, as does its drug-specific subcultures, identification with symbols, rituals, relationships and lifestyles that meet significant personal needs of the newcomer. The value of being a smoker to a sixteen-year-old adolescent male, for example, is probably more vested in the personal meanings of testing family boundaries, participation in peer rituals, desire for symbols of manhood, etc. than in an attraction to the pharmacological properties of nicotine. While the cultural trappings and meanings associated with teenage smoking may serve to initiate smoking behavior, other reinforcers, particularly the physiological addiction to nicotine, will develop to help sustain this behavior over time. Persons who are not biochemically high risk for alcoholism may get seduced into a subcultural pattern of excessive alcohol consumption that produces serious alcohol-related consequences in their lives. The emergence of marijuana as the counterculture drug of choice in the sixties led thousands to initiate use more for its symbolic value as a sacrament of political belief than for its value as an intoxicant. The glamour and cultural trappings surrounding cocaine use have been as seductive to many as the effect of the drug itself.

Nearly all psychoactive drug consumption occurs in a social and cultural context. These contexts vary widely but each may serve as an initiating force in the onset of substance abuse for the user who discovers a special magic in his or her participation in "the life."

Waldorf (1973) has suggested that for some persons addiction is a career choice. Career suggests a predictable sequence of activities that require a particular set of skills to perform, that actively engage the major portion of one's life, and that are characterized by predictable milestones or changes common to participants. In Waldorf's study of urban, inner-city heroin addiction, he suggests that the career of the addict can be examined as one would examine the careers of doctor, lawyer, or business executive. Careers connote entrance requirements, knowledge and skills, daily rituals that organize one's life, shared values, a philosophy of living, and, for the urban addict, a way to deal with a hostile society that has provided few other career alternatives. Waldorf's concepts can be utilized to examine the career choice and career progression for addicts with a wide variety of drug choices.

1.5 *Culture as a Sustaining Force*

For many addicts, the culture of addiction does not play a role in the inception of their addiction, but does become a significant force in maintaining the addiction over time. As an individual proceeds from drug experimentation to drug dependence, the search for supports to sustain one's addiction intensifies. This search serves multiple functions, the first of which is simply to be with persons like ourselves. Nicotine addicts feel more comfortable around smokers. Alcoholics feel more comfortable around persons who also drink excessively. For the person addicted to illicit drugs, the culture provides far more than social support for use and reinforcement of denial. In this context, the culture provides needed knowledge and skills on how to use, how to minimize risks, how to avoid apprehension, how to sustain income for drugs, and, most importantly, how and where to sustain one's drug supply.

Involvement in the culture of addiction shapes and reinforces ways of thinking, feeling, and behaving that promote excessive alcohol and drug consumption. As treatment professionals, we may view a particular client as having the "disease of alcoholism." We may attribute the onset of this disease to a genetically transmitted aberration in this client's biochemical response to alcohol. This view does not preclude us from recognizing that adaptation to this disease has shaped every aspect of this client's lifestyle and that all aspects of this lifestyle must be examined in the recovery process. Many addicts have found it easier to break the physiological relationship with their drug than to break their relationship with the culture in which the drug was used. The failure to break the cultural relationship often precedes activation of the disease process via relapse.

1.6 *Styles and Intensity of Cultural Involvement*

Addicted persons exhibit a wide divergence in their degree of involvement in the culture of addiction and in their style of affiliation with that culture. A simple typology is outlined below which describes three basic styles of affiliation with the culture of addiction.

1.7 *The Acultural Addict*

The acultural addict is the person who has initiated and sustained his or her addiction in isolation from other addicts. Acultural addicts may include the physician addicted to Demerol, the person medically addicted to narcotic and non-narcotic analgesics following debilitating and painful trauma, and the alcoholic or Valium addict who has hidden his or her addiction behind the walls of his or her home. Acultural addicts sustain their addiction over time without relationships with other addicts or participation in a licit or illicit drug culture. The isolation and secrecy which maintains this addiction makes detection unlikely until late stages of physiological dependence. It is only through the body's demand for escalating quantities of the drug or through increased drug impairment that the addict becomes visible. Most acultural addicts pride themselves in control and mastery over their drug and do not perceive themselves as addicts. They look with disdain upon alcoholics and addicts as persons lacking in moral strength and character.

Acultural addicts use psychoactive drugs that are medically and/or socially approved. Even when their drug dependence produces severe impairment in life functioning, our culture's stereotypic image of the "drug addict" may result in ascribing impairment to more socially acceptable causes such as medical illness, "medication problems," or psychiatric difficulties. Failure to confront drug use and the consequences produced by such use in the life of the acultural addict is a major barrier to successful intervention. It is this broad pattern of social enabling that allows the acultural addict to escape the consequences of drug use and makes early intervention unlikely. Consider some of the following examples:

- A physician addicted to Demerol and an anesthesiologist addicted to Fentanyl both show a long history of progressive impairment which is confronted only in the latest stages of addiction, the former when he is caught injecting Demerol in the scrub room following surgery and the latter when he passes out during surgery. Their prior reputations of high competence and their professional status would sustain the invisibility of their addictions past the time each posed a major threat to public safety.

• A 47-year-old alcoholic woman is admitted to a local hospital with late stages of liver disease. Her addiction to alcohol has been invisible within her social world and, until this admission, to her physician. Her addiction has been sustained within the upper-class cloistered world of her home. By the time her minimally involved husband would recognize alcohol as a problem and overcome his resistance to exposing such a problem to outsiders, his wife would be at a terminal stage of addiction. Although she would go through treatment subsequent to this medical admission and never take another drink, she would die nine months later from advanced liver disease.

• A highly reputable nurse sustains her addiction to narcotic analgesics for four years using legitimate medical channels and then becomes involved in theft of drugs from the facilities at which she works over the next three years. During this period, there are identifiable signs of personal and professional impairment that are not confronted by her colleagues or supervisors. It is only when the   amount of drugs she needs surpasses the supply available that her addiction would finally become visible through her arrest for forging prescriptions for Darvon and Talwin.

All of the above cases illustrate the isolation of the acultural addict and the failure of the social world to confront the deteriorating performance of these addicts or to consider the possibility that such deterioration might be a consequence of addiction.

1.8 *The Culturally Enmeshed Addict*
Culturally enmeshed addicts have increasingly lost touch with, or never been a participant in, a social world in which abstinence or

moderation are the governing values for psychoactive drug consumption. Depending on whether one looks from outside or inside, these addicts are a member of a deviant subculture or a "fantastic lodge." They are not only addicted to a drug; they are addicted to a way of living that assures their continued member-ship in "the life." It is in this world that they feel alive and at home. It is a world that promises acceptance, status, safety, and, above all, access to the most primary relationship in their life— their drug relationship. Consider the following examples illustrat-ing this style of involvement in the culture of addiction.

- John was born in the culture of addiction and has known no other world. The son of an addicted mother and unknown father, the majority of John's known relatives for three generations have been involved in addictive careers. He was introduced to wine at the age of eight by older family members and to marijuana by his mother at age ten. By twelve he mastered the language of a hardened con, negotiated the streets of his inner-city world with a cockiness known only to those who feel immortal, and learned to live "on the streets" fending for himself during his mother's episodic incarcerations. At thirteen he began selling drugs for an older dealer who would supply the closest thing to a father relationship that he would experience. Over the next ten years he would be absorbed in a world that provided a sense of belonging, status and identity, and enormous amounts of money for one so young. At age twenty-three, his first felony arrest would result in the first of many treatment experiences. He would master the art of "doing treat-ment" just as he would later learn the skills of "doing time" in prison, using each as an opportunity, not to rehabilitate, but to sharpen his repertoire of skills to survive in "the life." By age twenty-six, John presents a living symbol of the culture of addiction—one whose total life is driven by the social world within which addicts have organized themselves. To speak to John of another life is to speak of a world that is both alien and incomprehensible.

• Ellen's social world could not be more different than John's. She was born into a world of wealth and assumed status. The total lack of addiction in the family tree would leave Ellen's parents unprepared for and devastated by the onset of her illicit drug use at age 14. While the forces which propelled Ellen's change in personality and lifestyle are open to speculation, the unquestionable result was a powerful and almost instantaneous marriage between this young woman and the illicit drug culture. As an adolescent who had never felt she measured up and who could never find a niche within or outside her family, Ellen threw herself, like only the new convert in a cult can, into the exclusive society of the addicted young. While drug use was the ticket of admission into this culture, her initial affiliation was with the culture and not the chemical. Where other addicts exhibit elaborate mechanisms of denial and minimization, Ellen would flaunt and exaggerate her drug usage and camaraderie with other users. The next four years would be marked by habitual running from home, extreme conflicts with all authority, escalating drug use, onset and increase in criminal activity, and increased isolation from the "straight" world. After each crisis from which her parents rescued her, she would make promises of change only to return and plunge deeper into "the life." While the outside clinical observer would note the obvious pathology of such a lifestyle, Ellen would experience the early years of this lifestyle as the first time in her life she felt "alive." It would only be at   age 19 that Ellen would present herself at a treatment center, emaciated, disillusioned, and burnt out from her drug experiences and physical and sexual abuse within the culture. In spite of such crises that bring clients like Ellen to treatment, movement back into the culture of addiction is more seductive and less terrifying than finding one's niche in the other world for the first time.

• Andy is the ultimate "good ole boy" and what many treatment professionals would call an old time drunk. Such was not always the case. Until his early thirties, Andy's life and lifestyle varied little from his peers in this rural southern community. He married his high school sweetheart, went to the service and returned to work in a local business. While his early antics while intoxicated were written off as delayed adolescence ("Boys will be boys!"), his drinking would take Andy through his first marriage and two additional short-lived marriages by the time he was 45. As Andy's alcoholism progressed, he began to systematically let go of his other life and absorb himself in the local bar culture. His job, which he had taken great pride in, was his primary link to the world outside the local alcoholic subculture. By his early fifties, and on the brink of being fired for alcohol-related performance problems, Andy was involved in an industrial accident (while hung over) that he was able to manipulate into a large settlement and the status of permanently disabled. His settlement and disability checks would allow Andy to devote his full time to the culture of addiction as his life became an escalating cycle of drunkenness followed by sickness followed by drunkenness. It would only be Andy's third DUI within four years that would bring him to the attention of a treatment professional. While the etiology of Andy's alcoholism may have very likely been genetically shaped, the late stage of his addiction to alcohol was sustained through his daily interactions in a culture shared by others with Andy's disease.

1.9 *The Bicultural Addict*

In contrast to the acultural addict who abhors association with the culture of addiction, and the culturally enmeshed addict who knows no other world, bicultural addicts live simultaneously in the "straight" culture and the culture of addiction. These addicts have two identities and operate in two worlds, each of which serves to meet certain needs but neither of which alone commands total loyalty. Consider the following case histories.

- James was a 37-year-old lawyer who worked for an extremely conservative firm specializing in corporate law. Although James drank socially, there was no history of excessive alcohol use and no history of drug use. In fact, persons who knew James would have considered such behavior unthinkable. More to the point, any behavior outside the bounds of socially approved etiquette would have been unthinkable for James. His life was a model of upper-middle class propriety, down to his selection of the "right" wife, "right" neighborhood, "right" church, and "right" social clubs. When James was thirty-seven, his firm obtained a corporate retainer that would take James from his small midwestern town to Detroit for one week out of each month. During his fourth trip to Detroit,

James had his first exposure to cocaine. No one knows what factors influenced James' decision to use the drug that first night. Perhaps it was because he was with other lawyers and other Republicans and in one of the most exclusive neighborhoods in suburban Detroit and away from the normal environment to which his values were anchored. What is known is that James' first experience freebasing cocaine was love at first inhalation. Detroit became synonymous with the other life—a life of risks and excitement and recaptured adolescence, and always, the intoxicating presence of cocaine. It's as if his old values were suspended when he arrived at the Detroit airport and his other identity began. And at the end of each week he would return home to his wife and neighborhood and church and job and become his old self. The only control James had over cocaine was to leave Detroit. Nine months after James' first experience with cocaine, he was found dead, his body dumped behind a shopping center in an exclusive Detroit suburb. It was only through the investigation into his death that the discoveries would come of his congenital heart defect, his cocaine induced cardiac arrest, and, most surprisingly, his other life. His family would discover that he had withdrawn $27,000 from his savings account during the last nine months of his life.

- A different pattern of bicultural addiction is illustrated through the case of Harry. A middle-class black from Ohio with no history of alcohol or drug abuse, Harry found himself drafted and on his way to Vietnam shortly after his college graduation in 1969. When he arrived at his unit, he was inevitably drawn to other "Bloods" at his base. In this particular case, however, most of his fellow Black soldiers were part of a larger integrated drug subculture. In the alien insanity of Vietnam, drug use seemed to be a small price of admission into a subgroup that offered acceptance, camaraderie, and protection. Harry reports being stoned on marijuana most of his first four months in "Nam," and gradually developing a pattern similar to his chosen peers of smoking heroin in the field and injecting heroin when out of action. Harry recalls recognizing that he was addicted, but such recognition carried little significance given his constant confrontation with death in the war. At the end of his tour of duty, Harry tested positive for drugs and was forced to go through a detoxification program in Saigon before returning to the States. After his return to the U.S. and his discharge from the service, Harry would never again use heroin nor would he substitute another pattern of substance abuse. Like many of his peers studied by Robins (1973), Harry's addiction in Vietnam was a personal and subcultural adaptation to a pathological environment in which old values and ground rules no longer applied. Harry's use was sustained by an artificially created subculture and would stop as Harry exited that subculture and re-entered his culture of origin.

It should be clear from a review of the above histories that acultural, culturally enmeshed and bicultural addicts present different problems in treatment and require significantly different treatment approaches. Chapter Eight will discuss in detail how to assess this intensity of cultural involvement and the treatment modalities appropriate for each style of cultural involvement.

2

ORGANIZATION OF THE CULTURE OF ADDICTION

The "culture of addiction" is used through this text as if there were a single, homogenous entity encompassed by the concept. The fact is that the culture of addiction encompasses a diverse collection of subcultures organized geographically, ethnically, socioeconomically and through each subculture's drug choices. It is only when we look at these cultures in the aggregate that we can begin to identify the shared patterns of thinking, feeling and behaving that revolve around excessive drug consumption. Clinically, it is not enough to understand that a client is extensively involved in the culture of addiction. In addition, we must understand the exact subculture of addiction from which the client comes, the unique characteristics of that subculture and the nature and intensity of the client's participation in that subculture.

2.1 *Tribal Networks* The culture of addiction is organized into a complex confederation of networks, each of which is made up of numerous tribes. A tribe here refers to a voluntary social group of addicts who have banded together out of individual self-interest and the commitment to support each other's addiction. Tribes and networks are tied together through persons who hold membership in and frequently interact with more than one tribe or network. It is through the cross-fertilization of these tribes that the tribes begin to share common characteristics that collectively can be referred to as a culture.

There are a number of dimensions through which one could analyze tribes within a culture of addiction. One could study the organization of these tribes along racial lines. One could study a single geographical region and construct a map of the interconnectedness between tribes from city to city. One could study the assignment of power and status within each tribe and the culture of addiction as a whole. One could study the economic organization of the tribes and the licit and illicit organizations which feed drug supplies into the various tribes. For our purposes, however, it may be most beneficial to study tribal organization based on drug choice.

2.2 *Tribal Selection Based on Drug Choice* Every society makes judgments about the various psychoactive drugs that are available to its citizens. The remainder of this chapter will outline the propositions that:

- The social status and value attached to a particular drug will shape the risks associated with the drug as much as the drug's pharmacological properties.
- The social status and value attached to a particular drug will, more than any other factor, influence the organization of tribes within the culture of addiction.
- The social status and value attached to a drug influences the characteristics of each tribe and the impairment of clients resulting both from the drug and the culture itself.
- By simply knowing a client's primary drug choice(s) and the tribal characteristics associated with such choice(s), one can begin to anticipate client needs, obstacles to successful treatment, and preferred pathways to recovery.

Countries throughout the world generally assign   psychoactive drugs to one of four social designations depending on how, when, and under what conditions, if any, the society prefers the drug to be consumed. These designations include:

- Celebrated drugs
- Tolerated drugs
- Instrumental drugs
- Prohibited drugs

Celebrated drugs within a society encompass those psychoactive substances which have been blessed for social consumption. Such drugs are heavily integrated into the major social rituals of the society. The society often has strong financial incentives for the continued consumption of the drugs *e.g.*, income from production and sales of the drugs, income from taxation on the drug, etc. Therefore, its use is heavily promoted within the society. Our traditional celebrated drugs within the United States have included alcohol, caffeine, and, until recently, nicotine.

Tolerated drugs include psychoactive drugs whose consumption the society is discouraging but not so antagonistically as to prohibit its use. Tolerated drugs often include drugs for which values in the society are being reassessed. Nicotine, for example, has rapidly moved from a celebrated to a tolerated status within the past two decades. While users of tolerated drugs are not punished in a severe manner legally, they are, as any smoker of tobacco today knows, subject to some degree of social stigma and ridicule. Societies also place strict controls on how tolerated drugs can be promoted and, in general, place legal and social controls on the drug in order to make continued excessive use as difficult for the consumer as possible. Again using tobacco as an example, we have seen   restrictions placed on tobacco advertising, increased restrictions placed on where one can smoke, and a growing social stigma associated with smoking.

Instrumental drugs include psychoactive drugs which citizens can access only under very special conditions and for clearly defined purposes. For the more powerful of these drugs, the society will dictate who can use the drug, the dosage and frequency that can be used, the approved method of ingestion, and where use can occur. The best examples of instrumental drugs in our own country are over-the-counter and prescription medications.

Prohibited drugs are substances which a society defines as having highly limited or no utilitarian value and whose presence is seen as potentially disruptive to the society's values and order. Some may have highly limited instrumental use, *e.g.*, cocaine, but are prohibited outside of these narrow channels. Societies expend enormous resources to eliminate the availability of their prohibited drugs. They severely punish use, possession, and sale of the substances, and they create powerful symbols of social stigma in an attempt to deter use of the drugs. Current prohibited drugs in the United States include heroin and most of the hallucinogenic drugs.

There are a few other observations that are important to this introduction to the social designation of psychoactive drugs.

First, the status of a drug is always open to redefinition within a society, particularly during periods of rapid change. During an extended period of such change, for example, a drug may hold more than one designation. Marijuana, for example, was prohibited with the passage of the 1937 Marijuana Tax Act, but emerged as a celebrated drug in the youth subculture during the sixties. By the late 1970s, it was regarded as a tolerated drug as many states radically reduce penalties for possession for personal use. It then became temporarily available as an instrumental drug for the treatment of Glaucoma in the 1980s during the same period which saw increased efforts to restigmatize the drug. Such changes alter both who has access to the drug and the risks associated with use.

Second, the status of a drug and its level of consumption are subject to strong inhibiting and promotional forces within a society. These forces are rarely in balance, resulting in alternating periods of excessive availability and restrictive control. This point can be well-illustrated by examining the status of alcohol over the past 25 years. By 1970, the alcohol industry faced both a difficult dilemma and a golden opportunity. The dilemma was that alcohol consumption had stabilized in the U.S. and there had been only limited success in opening up new populations of users. The alcohol industry was also facing the possibility that an entire generation would reject their product in preference to another drug. (The youthful voice of the sixties: "Alcohol is their (parents') drug; marijuana is our drug!") The opportunity presented to the alcohol industry was that the country was so preoccupied with illicit drug use that alcohol was subject to decreasing scrutiny. The alcohol industry mounted a campaign to dramatically alter alcohol consumption patterns for women and youth. This included the implementation of massive advertising campaigns designed to influence alcohol consumption and engender brand loyalty. The cry, "if you're old enough to die for your country in Vietnam, you're old enough to drink" spread throughout the country, leaving a trail of changes in the age of legal drinking. The alcohol industry also introduced new alcohol products designed specifically for women and youth. For youth, there was the introduction of pop fruit wines designed for both the income and taste buds of a sixteen- year-old. The feminization of alcohol occurred via the introduction of new products whose package size and design, color, texture and taste, alcohol content, and calorie content would be aimed specifically at women. A pleasant surprise for the industry was the number of men who would drink a product designed for women—light beer.

In broad retrospect, the issue of illicit drug use in the 1970s may be viewed historically as insignificant compared to the increased consumption and radically altered patterns of licit drug consumption. The increased number of women and children (many of the latter reporting age of onset of use at 9-12 years of age) entering alcoholism programs in the late eighties is the best testament to the success of the campaigns launched two decades ago by the alcohol industry. The excesses that would grow out of this period have contributed to the social and personal costs that now fuel the backward traverse of the pendulum. This swing of the pendulum resulted in state after state returning the legal drinking age to 21, a heightened visibility and understanding of alcoholism, increased visibility of medical consequences of alcohol consumption such as fetal alcohol syndrome, and a growing intolerance in the society for the drunk driver. These phenomenon support the proposition that broad social and political forces shape the context in which addiction occurs and also shape the nature of the subcultures that support such addiction. The next sections will explore the organization and characteristics of tribes that encompass persons addicted to celebrated, instrumental, tolerated and prohibited drugs.

2.3 *The Celebrated Drug Tribes* A society expends enormous resources to reduce risks associated with the use of its celebrated drugs. The United States, for example, has taken steps to reduce risks surrounding the social consumption of alcohol. Attempts have been made to screen out high risk users. This has been attempted by legislatively postponing the onset of regular alcohol use to adulthood and providing a medical technology that identifies persons to whom alcohol consumption would be particularly high risk, *e.g.*, pregnant women, persons receiving certain kinds of medications, and persons with histories of particular kinds of illnesses. Assurance of quality control over the product itself reduces untoward consequences from contamination or adulteration. Dosage of the drug has been defined and limited through packaging and through shaping social norms that control for most citizens both the hours a day and amount of alcohol that can be consumed without social disapproval. Controlling consumption and consequences of use has also been attempted through limiting the physical settings in which alcohol can be consumed, *e.g.*, prohibitions on alcohol and driving, alcohol in the workplace, drinking in public, etc.

When one looks at just the pharmacological effects of alcohol, particularly its toxicity to body tissue, one wonders how such a substance could be selected as a celebrated drug. In light of this perspective, the surprise is not that roughly ten percent of our population have serious alcohol-induced problems in their life, but that only ten percent of our population experiences such problems. The success of limiting the number of persons affected by such a highly toxic substance hinges on the ability of the society to clearly define who, when, where and under what conditions alcohol can be consumed.

How can one speak of tribes or a culture of alcoholism when discussing a drug integrated into the very social fabric of our country? It is alcohol's status as a celebrated drug that makes addiction to this drug frequently invisible until the latest stages of addiction. During early stages of alcoholism there is little need for tribal supports for alcohol consumption because such consumption is approved in the society at large. It is only when the body's adaptation to alcohol demands ever increasing quantities and the social consequences of consumption occur, *e.g.*, loss of family, loss of job, loss of non-drinking social supports, that alcoholics seek the shelter of a tribal group whose members share the impairment of alcoholism. When the drinking pattern of alcoholics regularly violates the social norms established to control alcohol consumption, they begin the migration toward other persons whose patterns of alcohol consumption mirror their own.

There are shared characteristics that typify celebrated drug tribes and distinguish them from other tribes in the culture of addiction. The most prominent characteristic is the institutionalized denial at all levels of the environment in which celebrated drug addiction occurs. At a societal level, there is a denial that celebrated drugs are "drugs." The society denies both the psychoactive properties of these substances and in particular their addictive potential. There may not even be language within the society to describe addiction to these drugs. There is no generally perceived view or words, for example, to allow perception of tobacco users in our culture as "addicts." Whereas the term "tobaccoism" was commonplace in the late 1800s amid a strong tobacco prohibitionist movement, the concept and the word would disappear from our society as the drug moved to a celebrated status. Where the possibility of addiction to celebrated drugs is acknowledged, the public conception of the addict is an extreme caricature which allows the largest numbers of addicts to go unseen and undetected. Our historical caricature of the "alcoholic" as the skid row wino is a classic example of such institutionalized denial.

The society must maintained the possibility and probability of "controlled use" of any celebrated drug. Saying that alcoholics have a "disease" that doesn't allow them to drink normally allows the drug to continue to be blessed for the majority of society. It lets the society maintain the illusion that problems related to the drug are due to a small proportion of atypical individuals who cannot handle the drug. Think about it. If we completely eliminated alcoholism in this culture today, would alcohol related traffic fatalities disappear? Would the role of alcohol in suicides and homicides disappear? Would the impact of alcohol on business and industry be completely eliminated? The concept of "alcohol abuse" is much more threatening to the role of this drug in our society than is the concept of "alcoholism as a disease."

While the pathway to recovery for celebrated drugs is more accessible and less stigmatized because the drug is within everyone's experience, our extreme caricature of the addict intensifies the addict's denial of his or her status.

Denial constitutes a unique characteristic of most celebrated drug tribes. Drawing sustenance from denial in the society at large, many of these tribes bring together addicted individuals who are drawn into a social contract for the unspoken purpose of mutually supporting one another's addiction, and yet individually and collectively deny the status of addiction. For a tribal member to experience a crisis in which he or she defines themselves as an addict, seeks treatment, and has subsequent contact with tribal members poses a substantial threat to tribal identity and norms. Facing such a threat, the full resources of the tribe are mobilized to redefine the member as a non-addict, *e.g.*, "You can't be an alcoholic, you [a. only drink beer, b. work every day, c. don't drink any more than I do, etc.]" or "Your problem isn't booze, your problem is ...." The implication of this phenomenon to the relapse of addicted clients following treatment is an obvious point to which we will return in great detail in a later chapter.

2.4 *The Instrumental Drug Tribes* The most common instrumental drugs of abuse in our country include licit narcotic analgesics, amphetamines and psychostimulants, barbiturate and non-barbiturate hypnotics, and benzodiazepines (the so-called minor tranquilizers). As this list indicates, instrumental drugs include very powerful psychoactive substances that have a high potential for abuse based on their euphorigenic properties and the seductive

manner in which they endear their presence within human cell
tissue.

How can the utilitarian effects of such substances be made
available within the country while minimizing this potential for
their abuse?   Most societies address this dilemma by providing
explicit legal controls and social taboos that strictly define the
conditions under which these drugs may be consumed.   It was
noted above that the risks associated with celebrated drugs are
reduced by defining who, when, where, how much and under
what conditions each drug can be consumed.   With celebrated
drugs these controls are primarily social and subject to rapid
changes based on promoting and inhibiting forces within the
society.   With instrumental drugs, controls tend to be more stable
and changes are made not by the taste of the masses but by a small
minority entrusted to make such decisions.   Whether this decision
is entrusted to a white witch, medicine man, shaman, priest, or, in
our case, a complicated medical and regulatory establishment;
societies establish extremely precise rules for the manner in which
instrumental drugs shall be used.   Where societies are stable over
time, the use of these drugs outside such proscribed situations is
unthinkable.   By controlling and defining indications and contraindications, drug purity, dosage, frequency of usage, method of
ingestion, duration of use, etc., the society seeks to tap the benefits
of instrumental drugs while minimizing their potential for personal
and social disruption.

There is awareness in our culture of the movement of instrumental
drugs into the illicit drug market.   Law enforcement reports note
arrests for illegal manufacture or diversion or theft of these drugs.
Treatment professionals report increased numbers of clients who
present prescription drug use as at least part of their overall
addiction profile.   Instrumental drug users generally achieve
visibility when their addiction forces them into illegal activity, *e.g.*,

forging prescriptions, or into the illicit culture. Very little is know
about the existence of subcultures of persons who share addiction
to these drugs and sustain such use within socially/medically
approved channels of access. This pattern of addiction, which
dominated nineteenth century America, was hidden then and
remains hidden today.

The fact is that these addicts and their subcultures are almost
invisible within our society. Let's look, for example, at how our
language of addiction fails to encompass these individuals. The
person using amphetamines within the illicit culture is called an
"addict," "speed freak," or "substance abuser." The person using
amphetamines within the framework of a physician's care is called
a "patient," even when the amount used may surpass that of their
illicit counterpart. The drug itself when in the illicit culture is
"dope." The same substance when christened an instrumental drug
within the licit framework is called "medicine" or "medication."
The person distributing amphetamines in the illicit culture is
known as a "pusher." The person (physician/pharmacist) who
distributes amphetamines as an instrumental drug is called a
"healer." In the illicit culture, the need for and use of the drug may
be seen as a "disease." The receipt of the same drug through licit
channels is considered "treatment" for disease. By identifying
instrumental drug addicts as patients suffering from illnesses or
diseases who are receiving medicine from society's designated
healers, we have negated the existence of such addiction through
social fiat.

Addiction to instrumental drugs is so isolated and invisible within
our society, one may be surprised to find that there is any tribal
organization among such addicts. Early stages of dependence upon
instrumental drugs are nearly always typified by an acultural style.
However, as middle and late stages of addiction approach and
surpass the boundaries set for consumption of these drugs, most

users will seek out others whose intense drug involvement parallels their own.

At least two kinds of instrumental drug tribes have been observed. The first is a tribe of persons who were introduced to powerful painkilling drugs to treat debilitating trauma or disease. For many such persons, pain and the random ability of analgesic drugs to provide transient relief becomes the focus of their daily existence. When such pain is extended or chronic, these persons inevitably encounter other persons like themselves through their contacts with hospitals and physicians. The instant rapport created by shared pain and shared drug choices weld relationships together that provide mutual support and justification for continued excessive drug consumption. For many persons who became addicted in the above manner, the reinforcing properties of analgesic drugs had as much to do with self-medicating the fear and anticipation of pain as in the treatment of pain itself. For late stage instrumental drug addicts of this tribe, their identity, which becomes dominated by their physical condition and their drugs, and their social relationships with other instrumental drug addicts pose two of the major barriers to successful recovery.

Another instrumental drug tribe is the real life version of the "Valley of the Dolls" popularized in literature and film some years ago. This tribe is composed of middle and upper class women whose primary chemical choices include benzodiazepines and hypnotic drugs that are superimposed on at least regular, if not excessive, alcohol consumption. These tribes have only transient visibility within the culture usually when one of its members who is a well-known figure either dies from an overdose or, as in the more recent cases of Betty Ford and Kitty Dukakis, publicly proclaims her addiction and efforts at recovery. From such stories, one becomes aware of a world where instrumental drugs play a major role in the daily rituals of social interaction—a world in which addiction is not only an individual affliction but part of a shared lifestyle. It is a world where tribal members measure their daily stress by the number of pills consumed. The Valium addict may be every bit as emersed in a culture of addiction as the urban heroin addict and this cultural involvement must be broken to achieve sustained sobriety.

2.5 *The Tolerated Drug Tribes* Tolerated drugs are often drugs experiencing a major transition in status within a society. They may be drugs that have been celebrated within the society but are now losing favor and approval.   An historical example of this would be the mid 1800s when the early temperance movement was striving not for abstinence from alcohol but moderation in the use of alcohol. They simply wanted to move alcohol from a celebrated to a tolerated drug within our society. The failure of this moderation movement culminated with alcohol prohibition. Tolerated drugs may also include previously prohibited drugs which spill out of the deviant subcultures in which they are usually contained to achieve much wider usage and social acceptance within the society at large. Perhaps the best recent examples of this would be the transition in the status of marijuana between 1960 and 1975 and the status of cocaine between 1980-1990.

The nature of tribal organization that surrounds the use of tolerated drugs is influenced heavily by the nature and intensity of the above noted transition process. Let's consider the currently changing status of nicotine in the United States. First, as a previously celebrated drug, our society has expended enormous resources to reduce the untoward effects of what is clearly a highly toxic substance. We have tried to postpone the onset of use; screen out high risk persons, *e.g.*, pregnant women, from use; introduce filters and low tar and nicotine cigarettes; introduce "smokeless" cigarettes, shape daily dose by defining anything over 20 cigarettes per day as excessive use, and continue our research to develop safer cigarettes and alternatives methods of ingesting nicotine. Twenty-five years ago, smoking was so imbedded within the social structure of the U.S., that no one, man or woman, needed to seek a specific tribal association to support nicotine addiction. Such addiction was supported and made easy by the society at large. Addiction could be sustained without a self-acknowledged or socially identified status of addiction. Such labelling was not possible for a substance we had not even defined as a drug.

In contrast to the above period when smoking could occur without consciousness, the smoker today continues their addiction against growing obstacles. Smokers today face new and discomforting dilemmas. They must declare their status as an addict in every restaurant they enter. They face with growing physical and emotional discomfort a growing numbers of public places, worksites and private residences where they cannot smoke. They can't smoke in company cars; They can't smoke on airplanes. They are bombarded by media proclamations that smoking is not only harmful but stupid. This changing social context is creating new behaviors within the psychodynamics of nicotine addiction. Smokers now feel guilt. Smokers are developing elaborate alibi systems to justify their continued use. Smokers are getting arrogant, hostile and defensive. Smokers are developing surreptitious patterns to sneak cigarettes. Smokers are making and failing to keep resolutions about when they are going to quit. At the social level, we are seeing the first explicit organization of tribal behavior among smokers—smokers actively cultivating relationships with other smokers to avoid stigma and seek unspoken support for continued addiction. If current social values toward nicotine continue their current momentum, we may see the organization of smokers into a deviant and secretive subculture within the next thirty years. As the nicotine addict seeks greater tribal affiliation to sustain addiction, a major obstacle to treatment and a contributing factor to relapse will be, not the physical addiction to nicotine, but the social world constructed by the smoker to sustain that addiction.

2.6 *The Prohibited Drug Tribes* The discussion of the culture of addiction which encompasses the illicit drugs must begin with the question of how drugs get singled out for prohibition. For persons who believe that drug control policies are based on a rational and objective assessment of the potential risks of various psychoactive drugs to humans, a detailed review of how such policies evolve can be quite unsettling. Drugs become celebrated or prohibited based more on who uses the drugs and the political, economic, religious and racial issues and symbols associated with a drug than on the drug's effect upon humans. A society will prohibit drugs whose effects are seen as incongruent with the values of the society. Any drug preferred by persons seen as a potential threat to the order of the society will be prohibited. A celebrated drug in one country may be a prohibited drug in another, *e.g.*, alcohol, opium, coca leaf, etc.

The mere declaration of a psychoactive substance as a prohibited drug automatically increases the risk associated with use of that substance. Where the society applies technology to reduce risks for celebrated drugs, it withdraws technology to increase risks for prohibited drugs. The social designation of a drug is to a great extent self-fulfilling. We prohibit a "bad" drug on the rationale that it is dangerous and then construct social policies that assure high risks related to the drug's use. Let's compare and contrast the technology applied to celebrated and prohibited drugs.

A. **Quality Control** With celebrated drugs, we reduce risks by assuring that substances are free from contamination, adulteration and misrepresentation. The lack of such control for prohibited drugs dramatically increases their risks. Efforts to provide such technology through drug analysis programs have repeatedly come under attack as encouraging use and providing quality control services for users and dealers.

B. **Drug Dosage** With celebrated and instrumental drugs, we reduce risks by packaging the drug in dosages (and matching dosages for special purposes) that provide predictable and desirable effects. We provide social and medical definitions of excessive use. As a neophyte experimenting with prohibited drugs, the products one consumes are of inconsistent dosage and there are no definitions from the society at large as to what constitutes an appropriate or excessive dose. What is an appropriate single dose of LSD? One tab? Two tabs? What is excessive marijuana consumption? Daily use? Three joints a day? Six joints a day? The lack of such definitions, by serving to increase dosages consumed, elevates the risks associated with prohibited drugs.

C. **Screening Out High Risk Users** With celebrated and instrumental drugs, we screen out and discourage use by those persons for whom certain drugs would be a particularly high risk. The Bible of instrumental drugs, the *Physician's Desk Reference*, includes a section for each drug entitled contraindications which in essence says: "don't mix this drug with these kinds of people." For our celebrated drugs we provide a similar service both through our system of medical services and through the popular press. In contrast to the above, there is no such screening process for users of prohibited drugs. The very withdrawal of this technology and information means that we will inevitably have some prohibited drug users unknowingly use substances that may pose particular threats to their health and safety because of their unique developmental and medical history. Another example of this process has to do with the dangers of mixing particular psychoactive substances. The knowledge, for example, that it is dangerous to mix alcohol and sedatives is widely available within the society at large. Consider in contrast the following questions. Is it safe to mix alcohol and heroin? Is it safe to mix alcohol and cocaine? Is it safe to mix alcohol and marijuana? The inability of our culture to provide answers to these questions escalates risks for the neophyte user of prohibited drugs.

D. Withholding Technology That Could Reduce Risks The designation of a drug as prohibited inhibits the exploration of new technology that could potentially lower risks related to its use. Celebrated and instrumental drugs are administered into the human body in a manner designed to reduce untoward conse-quences such as the spread of disease. Elaborate policies of infection control have been   established to assure safety in this aspect of licit drug administration. At the time of this writing, the fastest growing population of HIV positive individuals is IV drug abusers who transmit and receive the AIDS virus through the sharing of needles within the illicit drug culture. Some have suggested that this problem could be potentially addressed through the dissemination of sterile needles and a concentrated educational campaign aimed at teaching addicts how to utilize a sterile technique in their drug administration. Some pilot projects testing the feasibility of this proposal have been implemented amid public criticisms that such approaches encourage drug use. The explora-tion of such risk-reduction programs are constrained by our historical stance of withholding technology to keep risks of prohibited drug use high for its alleged deterrent value. It may be our morality, not just our technological deficits, that will claim young people afflicted with AIDS within the illicit drug culture. Addicted individuals may die from AIDS not as a result of the drug heroin, but as a result of a social policy which prevents us from reducing risks associated with heroin use.

The declaration of a substance as a culturally prohibited drug creates a powerful social stigma which will shape much of the emotional and behavioral patterns of persons using the substance.

To fully understand this point, it is necessary to understand some of the forces which lead to the prohibition of a drug within a society. No matter what rational justification may exist for the need for increased social control on a particular drug, most prohibited drugs achieve this status as a result of a sustained and intense public drive toward criminalizing the drug and its users. In an earlier study of successful prohibition movements (White, 1979), the author noted the following eight themes that characterized such movements.

- The drug is associated with a hated subgroup of the society or a foreign enemy.
- The drug is identified as solely responsible for many problems in the society, *e.g.*, crime, violence,insanity, promiscuity.
- The survival of the society is pictured as being dependent upon the prohibition of the drug.
- The concept of "controlled" usage is destroyed and replaced with a "domino theory" of chemical progression, *e.g.*, everyone who uses will eventually become addicted; marijuana leads to heroin, etc.
- The drug is associated with the corruption of young children, particularly their sexual corruption.
- Both the user and supplier of the drug are defined as "fiends" always in search of new victims; usage of the drug is described as contagious.
- Policy options are presented as total prohibition or total access.
- Anyone questioning any of the above assumptions is bitterly attacked and characterized as part of the problem that needs to be eliminated.

The demonization of the drug through a prohibitionist movement taps powerful fears and shapes images of both the drug and its consumers. Such mythological images provide the rationale for making outcasts of our own children. It is our social policy that created the illicit culture and our society that must reap that culture's unconscious retribution for their exclusion.

All of the above is a prelude to saying that the person addicted to prohibited drugs must sustain that addiction in an alien subculture which day by day detaches them further from the society at large. The worst consequence of prohibited drug use may not be the pharmacological effects of the drugs but the forced extrusion from the society at large that accompanies such usage. The treatment of persons addicted to prohibited drugs must address not only the effects of the drug relationships but also the transforming influence of the illicit drug culture in which this relationship was sustained.

2.7 *Relationship to Other Deviant Cultures* To affiliate with a prohibited drug tribe is to progressively disengage from the society at large or give up the illusion that one could ever become part of that society. To disaffiliate in such a manner not only exposes one to the influence of the drug culture, but to a broad spectrum of deviant subcultures mixed together in the cauldron of the streets. One becomes a tribal member in a world of outsiders. It is within this overlap of deviant cultures that lies the potential intensification of both personal pathology and increased risks to public safety posed by drug consumption.

Psychoactive drugs, through their ability to excite, incite, disinhibit, alter perceptions and alter judgement, have always had the power to intensify personal pathology. It is the social pathology which has changed. Never before have we had such intense cross-fertilization between deviant subcultures. Drugs, and particularly cocaine, have risen to such a role of prominence in the criminal culture in the U.S. as to make the etiology of criminal and drug using behavior almost inseparable. Disinhibiting and mind-altering drugs have been woven into the rituals of deviant religious sects and spill into the headlines through tales of cult violence. The emptying of state psychiatric hospitals, limited and overextended prison capacity, and increased homelessness all contribute to the social mix from which deviant cultures emerge. And within these tribes of the disaffiliated move individual predators who are too impaired and isolated for sustained involvement in even deviant cultures. It is through the increased interaction between such tribes that we see social forces working to intensify personal pathology and its concomitant risk to public safety. It is within this context that we have seen the escalation of incidents in which psychiatrically impaired, drug-influenced and value-depleted individuals commit heinous acts of violence upon the society from which they feel excluded. The concern of this book is not just with pathways that lead into the culture of addiction, but also on the pathways found in this culture that lead to even more extreme patterns of pathology.

3

THE PSYCHOSOCIAL AND TECHNICAL FUNCTIONS OF THE CULTURE OF ADDICTION

The culture of addiction and each tribe within that culture are brought together for one common purpose which is to sustain the addiction of its members. How the culture organizes itself to achieve this purpose differs depending on each tribe's drug choice and other shared characteristics of tribal members. There are, however, common psychosocial needs which members of all tribes generally get met through their participation in the culture.

The culture of addiction, like any culture, is a context or framework through which human needs are met. Although the culture of addiction appears alien to the outsider, it is important to realize that persons participate in this culture and its rituals (drug use) to address the same needs all humans share. It provides an alternative for persons who for whatever reasons have found themselves unable to meet such needs through the society at large. The young person in the drug culture gets the same affiliation needs met that his or her parents do in Kiwanis or a women's social club. The culture provides a purpose and order to daily life. It provides both a world view and a code of values. It provides rituals that govern how and when physical needs for food, shelter and safety shall be met. It provides a context in which sexuality can be expressed.

While persons may be drawn to this culture based on their drug use, it is in this same context that they must progressively meet a broader and broader range of their needs. Each need met forms a tie to the culture. The longer the cultural association the greater the number of ties that lead back to the culture and its rituals of drug use.

This chapter will explore how some of these needs are met within the culture of addiction. How needs for identity and self-esteem are met within this culture will be explored first. It will be followed by an examination of how the special developmental needs of adolescents are met within the culture of addiction.

3.1 *Identity and Self-Esteem* Depending on one's tribe, the culture of addiction can serve to support self-esteem through either nurturing one's special status of addiction, by denying the existence of addiction or by meeting other needs which have been previously unmet.

Celebrated drug tribes, except those whose members are all in the late stages of addiction, present a unique paradox. The activity that binds group members together is their excessive alcohol or drug consumption and yet this bond is never acknowledged. In fact, a major purpose of the group is to help each of its members deny the status of addiction. By affiliating with other addicted individuals and refusing to acknowledge such addiction in themselves or others, members can maintain the illusion that their usage is not different from others and thus not a problem. The alcoholic who retorts defensively, "I don't drink anymore than anyone else around me" or the shared comment between two tribal members, "You're not an alcoholic; you don't drink any more than I do" reveals how one can immerse themselves in an alcoholic subculture while simultaneously denying their alcoholism. A major function of the celebrated drug tribes is to allow their members to maintain the illusion of normalcy and controlled usage. Where acknowledgement of addiction would require a painful redefinition of ones self-identity, the culture supports continued use without the price of such redefinition.

The manner in which the celebrated drug culture supports the self-esteem of its members in the face of assaults from the outside world is quite fascinating. The symptoms of the individual pathology of addiction are organized into group norms that govern member interaction. It's as if members have entered into an unspoken pact in which they proclaim allegiance to mutually support the minimization, projection, intellectualization, rationalization, grandiosity, and aggression that allow members to simultaneously sustain and deny their addiction. Consider the following scenario. The scene is JB's Lounge, and Paul has just entered and taken his traditionally reserved spot at the bar next to John (both of whom are well into the middle stages of alcoholism). Let's listen in.

Paul: Man! You look like you've had it. Hard day in the salt mines?

John: Yeah. I've earned this one. Give me a double of the usual, Bill (Bartender). You know, it's getting crazier and crazier out there.

Paul: That's just what I was telling Bill awhile ago. Is the old man (John's boss) acting up again?

John: Well, Mary (John's wife) started it off last night just because I forgot to run some errands on my way home and then Whitaker (John's boss) was on my case all day about a bunch of piddling junk.

Paul: Sounds like the kind of day I had Monday.

John: Mary was back on her soapbox about my drinking again. Ever since she started seeing that shrink, she's been talking crazy. I don't know if he's making her nuts or it's those pills he's giving her. I think he's trying to convince her I'm an alcoholic.

Paul: That's crazy! You're no more an alcoholic than I am. Hey, speaking of alcoholics, you should have seen Jimmy (the token wino who wanders in and out of JB's Lounge) last night. Now there's an alcoholic. I saw him passed out in the parking lot as I was leaving last night. It's a wonder someone didn't run over him. Now how could anyone who's seen Jimmy talk to you about your drinking? I'd be real careful about what that doc is telling her. Everybody knows most of those guys are crazy themselves.

John: Yeah. You're probably right. You know, women are funny. They complain when a guy has a drink or two after work, but they sure don't complain when the check comes home.

Paul: You can say that again! Hey, is old Whitaker (John's boss) still trying to mess around with his secretary?

John: Yeah. He spends most of his time thinking of excuses to go stand over her desk. I think the old goat fancies himself as some kind of Casanova.

Paul: You know, I'll bet he's on your case because he's jealous of you. Didn't you say his secretary had the "hots" for you for awhile?

John: Maybe he is jealous.

Paul: Well, I wouldn't worry about him too much. We both know that company would be nothing without you. He may be jealous but he still knows you're the best salesman he's ever had. What about the year you topped two million in sales by yourself?

John: That was one helluva year. (John continues a monologue describing his top sales year without reference to the fact that it was ten years ago.)

Paul: You know, one of these days we ought to tell both of our bosses where to go and just take off somewhere.

(The conversation continues indefinitely as both share and elaborate their escapist fantasies.)

The conversation above reveals how interactions in the culture of addiction serve to sustain member identity and self-esteem in the face of increasing negative consequences of their drinking in the outside world.   In this case, Paul has performed an invaluable function for John. He has completed the cultural ritual of helping a fellow tribal member sustain his drinking while denying alcoholism. Through this conversation, we see Paul helping John by:

- Defocusing attention from John's drinking by projecting attention onto the problems of John's wife and the questionable mental status of her psychiatrist
- Supporting John's denial by evoking the wino caricature as proof that John is not an alcoholic
- Refraining from asking what John's boss is upset about (missed days at work) and by projecting other motives to the boss which have no relationship to John's drinking
- Reinforcing John's grandiosity by calling forth John's past episodes of success, *e.g.*, his big sales year, his value to the company, and the secretary's attraction to him, some of which were past glories and some of which constitute alcohol- induced delusions of grandeur
- Cultivating and supporting fantasies of geographical escape when drinking-related consequences begin closing in

Paul is not performing this function out of any altruistic concern for John. He is performing this function because it is part of the unspoken cultural pact. John will be providing this same service for Paul within a matter of days. It is through such mutual pacts that the culture operates to sustain the addiction of its members.

3.2 Transforming Stigma to Status: Identity in the Illicit Drug Culture Where one's addiction to celebrated drugs is sustained through denial, addiction to prohibited drugs requires that one clearly take on the identity of an addict. The illicit culture provides an interesting solution to the riddle of how one can simultaneously accept the identity of an addict and yet sustain one's self-esteem within that identity. To explore the solution to this riddle, we will examine how such terms of disparagement from the culture at large as "dope fiend" and "freak" have been imbued with status within the illicit drug culture.

The term "dope fiend" grew out of the prohibitionist campaigns of the early twentieth century. The term captured the essence of the demonization of certain drugs and the people who consumed them. The term came to represent one of society's most detested and feared persons. To be a "dope fiend" was by social definition a depiction of one who was amoral, criminal, evil, and predatory. To be a "dope fiend" was to be stigmatized and disgraced in society's eyes. Given the above, many persons are surprised to find addicts referring to themselves as "dope fiends" within the elaborate argot of the illicit drug culture. Rather than fighting the societal stigma inherent in this term, the illicit culture embraced the term and turned it into a badge of status. The culture of addiction rejected society's scheme of ascribing status and created one of its own. By turning a term of derogation into one of status and esteem, the straight society and its values could be both ridiculed and rejected. To be known as a "righteous dope fiend" is to have achieved status and respect within the illicit culture of heroin addiction in the United States. A similar phenomenon would occur with the term "freak" in the counterculture of the mid-twentieth century. Described early on as freaks by society at large, the polydrug abusing youth of the sixties and seventies, using the precedent set by their counterparts in the opiate culture, would take on the term "freak" and use it to imbue identity and cultural pride.

The ability of a culture to offer identity and membership provides a powerful attraction to persons who may have already felt excluded from the society at large. An example of this power was illustrated with a drug dependent client of the early seventies. This client had thrown himself into the "psychedelic" culture with the passion of a true believer, adhering to that culture's values, politics, hallucinogen-induced mysticism, language, dress, and excessive drug consumption. In a treatment sessions, he made the following comment: "I love being called a freak. I've felt like a freak all my life and for the first time it means something positive to me. The first time I heard drug users called 'freaks', I felt like that's where I belonged." These comments reflect this young man's lifelong rejection by family and society and his inability to find a "home." In spite of the untoward consequences of drug use for this client, his participation in the drug culture marked the most significant experience of acceptance and belonging in his life.

Taking on the identity of an addict may be a prerequisite for full participation in the culture. Phrases like, "He shoots dope; but he ain't no dope fiend" and "He ain't a freak; he's a fake" illustrate how persons may be denied such identity. These phrases describe individuals who, although they may seek admission to the culture, do not comply with enough of the cultural norms to be considered members.

Some persons, having experienced exclusion from society, wander the subterranean subcultures in search of affiliation. Some may end up in the culture of addiction simply because it was the first or only deviant culture to allow them entrance and full participation.

For prohibited drugs, adopting the identity of user is an important transition into the culture. For many prohibited drug users, this identity meets more needs than does the actual drug consumption. From the outside looking in, one may not be able to fully appreciate the esteem-enhancing powers of the culture of addiction. Although scorned by outsiders, addicts see themselves as part of a special and elite group, as members of a "fantastic lodge." Although an object of scorn, addicts meet challenges and survive every day by their wits in a world most people could never comprehend. The mastery of this world and the drug relationship creates a sense of uniqueness and distinction.

While a major barrier to recovery for the alcoholic is denial of addiction, a major barrier to recovery for the illicit drug user may be difficulty relinquishing an identity which is based on addiction. Whether in a culture of persons collectively denying their alcoholism or in a society of self-identified dope fiends, members are bound to a group through which significant personal needs can be met on a daily basis. A major need for all members is to sustain an identity that provides a sense of both social and personal value. The fact that addiction inevitably eats away at self-esteem suggests that these cultures must provide elaborate mechanisms to sustain the identity of their members. If treatment programs cannot provide an alternate identity and alternate mechanisms to sustain esteem, they have no basis upon which to compete with the culture of addiction.

3.3 *Adolescent Needs and the Culture of Addiction* Once one is enmeshed in the culture of addiction, the culture must provide a framework through which the majority, if not all, of one's needs can be met. The ability of the culture to address these needs

creates multiple ties that reinforce drug use and constitute
powerful sustaining forces for addiction. These principles can also
be observed by examining the manner in which adolescent needs
are addressed in the culture of addiction.

A review of human development literature or a discussion with
someone who works extensively with youth quickly reveals some
of the major developmental needs of adolescence. These needs
include the following:

- developing a sense of personal identity separate from the
  identity of family affiliation, a stage Eric Erikson (1963)
  has referred to as identity versus identity diffusion
- mastery over, and acceptance of, one's body, in the face
  of rapid physiological changes
- exploring growing sexuality to include establishment of
  sexual identity and experimentation with various sexual
  behaviors
- adding abstract and logical thinking to concrete thinking
- formulating one's own values and morals
- charting a pathway toward one's adult role or career, and
- physically and emotionally separating from the nuclear
  family

Any one of the above developmental needs may contribute to an
adolescent's choice to consume alcohol or drugs for the first time.
Any single need may constitute the sole initiating force to the early
stage of drug consumption. If this initial use, however, occurs in
an alcohol or drug-using subculture, additional forces may quickly
come into play to sustain and increase drug consumption over
time. Consider the case of Dwayne.

The onset of Dwayne's alcohol/drug abuse began at age 15. His
peers, typical of the adolescent social world, were organized into

tight cliques that ruled his school through the twin powers of inclusion and exclusion. Lacking the admission requirements for most of these groups, *e.g.*, athletic ability, attractiveness, high intelligence, etc., Dwayne found himself pulled toward the small drug culture which existed at his school. Describing this early period, Dwayne reports: "I wasn't interested in alcohol or drugs; at that point I didn't even like the taste or feel of the stuff. I just wanted to have friends, to be somebody. With my friends that did drugs, that was easy." Dwayne's acceptance in this group was powerful magic. For what he says was the first time in his life, he felt like he belonged. He immersed himself in the culture and its language, dress, rituals and implicitly transmitted values. He further detached himself from family, school and the outside social world. He would establish his first relationship with a female and have his first sexual experience within the drug culture. By age 19, when Dwayne was arrested and subsequently interviewed by the author, he was deeply committed to continued drug use and equally committed to the culture in which such use had been nurtured. Where his early use had responded to a specific need for peer acceptance, his use four years later would serve to not only assure such continued acceptance, but would also touch on almost every other need in his life. The culture had provided Dwayne an identity, which of questionable value as seen by the outsider, would serve as the primary anchor for his self-esteem. His drug use would provide a mechanism for boundary-testing of family limits and would ultimately provide the vehicle for him to leave an extremely closed family which provided college as the only guilt-free pathway out of the family. His sexuality would be discovered and nurtured within the culture. The values of the culture would provide a rationale for him to reject the society from which he felt excluded and provide him an illicit career path from which he could escape the proverbial "what am I gonna be when I get big" question. In addition to the above, the illicit culture would provide continued access to substances upon which he was now physiologically dependent.

Several important principles of that are illustrated in Dwayne's history are summarized below.

- While one need may be dominant during the onset of substance abuse, other needs will be subsequently involved that may provide even more powerful motivators for sustained abuse.
- The number of needs met within the culture of addiction increases with the duration of one's involvement, thus intensifying one's affiliation and loyalty to the culture.
- Treatment of addiction must immediately provide alternative experiences which meet the same psychosocial needs that have initiated and sustained drug consumption.
- Treatment must provide a long-term pathway to another lifestyle within which these same needs can be realistically met by the client.
- Any unmet needs of the client, which were previously met in the culture of addiction, constitute a stimulus for relapse.

If we conceptualize addiction as a career, then there are technical knowledge and skills one must master to take on and sustain the role of addict. A primary function of the culture of addiction is to provide each of its members access to such learning. The remainder of this chapter explores the nature of these skill requirements and how such skills are transmitted within the culture of addiction.

3.4 *How To Use* People who use or who are dependent upon psychoactive drugs are not born knowing how to use such substances nor are they always provided such information from the society at large. Persons who choose celebrated drugs have a distinct advantage here because the culture provides a wealth of information on how to use these substances. One need not find a deviant subculture, for example, to learn how to use alcohol or nicotine. Children practice drinking and being drunk in childhood play, modeling the behavior of adults they have observed. Historically, children have been provided candy cigarettes to practice their technique of use long before they are given access to nicotine. We learn all the appropriate rituals of use, all of which collectively, reduce risks associated with celebrated drugs and provide easy access to the potential consumer. In a similar manner, the culture provides detailed information about the proper technique for consuming its instrumental drugs. A physician, through the prescription ritual, tells how often a drug is to be ingested, how the drug is to be ingested, *e.g.*, orally, any special consumption technique, *e.g.*, taken at meals or with milk, special precautions, *e.g.*, don't drink alcohol or drive while taking the medication, and any unpleasant side effects that might occur from the drug.

In contrast to the above, information regarding prohibited drugs is withheld from the potential consumer. It thus becomes the job of the deviant subculture which has embraced the prohibited drug to convey this technology to consumers. In effect, participation in the culture becomes a requirement for use.

Let's look, for example, at the knowledge and skill requirements of a neophyte heroin user. Such a user is confronted with some of the following knowledge and skill demands.

- If first use is by "snorting," how is it done (assuming the user has never intranasally ingested any drug)? Is there some special technique for using heroin this way?

- If first use is by injection, is it best to inject the drug under the skin ("skinpopping") or into a vein?
- What equipment is required? If one doesn't have a hypodermic syringe, what other equipment can be substituted to make up a set of "works" or an "outfit."
- How is heroin prepared ("cooked") for injection?
- What technique or procedures, are used to inject the drug?
- What does one do if the needle clogs?
- Is there any way to test the purity of the drug?
- How much of the drug constitutes a desirable "dose"?
- If more than one person is using, and an "outfit" is being shared, who uses it first? (Heroin addicts have etiquette too!)
- If sharing, how can the works be cleaned to prevent the transmission of disease?
- How does one know if they have injected too much?
- Are there any unpleasant side effects one should anticipate?
- How long will the effect of the drug last?
- Is there any way to maximize the drug's effects?
- Is there anything one should not do while high on the drug?
- How much time must pass before the drug can be used again?
- If a bruise or abscess develops at the injection site, how can it be hidden and treated (without seeing a physician)?

Most neophyte heroin users would not even know enough to ask the above questions let alone know the answers to them. The idea of someone using this drug in isolation from the illicit opiate culture is almost unthinkable. While the society at large does not provide answers to the above questions for the potential heroin consumer, the culture of opiate addiction does. Whether one is using cocaine, marijuana, LSD, PCP or any other illicit substance, it is within the culture of addiction that one will be taught and apprenticed on the proper techniques, rituals and etiquette of drug consumption.   Mastery of technique and etiquette serve to maximize drug effects, reduce drug risks, dictate status and separate insiders from outsiders.

3.5 *Learning to Experience the Drug* In contrast to the prohibition-ist belief that forces reside within illegal drugs so powerful as to overwhelm the most self-controlled individual at first ingestion, many users experience little or no effects or even dysphoric effects the first time they use (cocaine may be an exception). Many heroin addicts report that they did not experience euphoria when they first used heroin.   In fact, most report experiencing nausea, vomiting and headaches.   While they would later experience euphoria from the drug, this suggests that the user may have to use repeatedly to *learn to* experience the desired effects of the drug. Becker (1963) reports a similar phenomenon in his study of neophyte marijuana users.

The culture of addiction provides, in addition to the techniques of use, guidance for the neophyte on how to recognize and enjoy the drug effects. Frequently first time marijuana users don't even recognize that they are stoned, let alone enjoy the experience. Using their prior experience with alcohol as a standard of compari-son, these individuals may not identify the effects of marijuana. Months later these same neophytes will be creating elaborate arrangements of lighting and music (and snacks) to maximize their experience of the drug's effects. The culture will teach them well.

The role of the culture of addiction in teaching users to experience the euphoric effects of drugs may play a role in the actual inci-dence of addiction. Opiates and opiate derivatives continue to be used frequently within American medicine and yet the incidence of addiction related to such use remains relatively low. While the postsurgical patient or the patient experiencing debilitating pain from trauma or disease may receive substantial dosages of addicting drugs, these users are educated to anticipate the painkilling properties of these drugs, not their euphorigenic properties. Consequently, few exhibit signs of drug hunger or compulsive drug-seeking behavior when their pain subsides and the drug is discontinued. In contrast, the street addict, who may consume smaller dosages of opiates than his medical counterpart, may experience insatiable drug hunger, severe withdrawal and compulsive drug-seeking behavior when access to the drug is lost. In the latter case, the culture of addiction has created an addict by teaching the individual how to increase his or her susceptibility to, and appreciation of, the drug experience.

3.6 *Skills to Sustain Addiction* The culture of addiction also provides its members, in addition to entry skills, the knowledge and skills to sustain addiction over a prolonged period.

Addiction to any drug, prohibited or celebrated, involves substantial risks and the culture must reduce such risks, to the extent possible, for its members. The culture contains a collective body of knowledge that assists one in minimizing risks associated with the following:

- Social consequences resulting from excessive use (What stories can be used to explain one's behavior to persons outside the culture in order to avoid the social identification of addiction? How can other persons be manipulated or hired to assist in escaping such consequences?)

- Misrepresented and adulterated drugs (How do I know that what I am buying is really heroin, cocaine, etc.?

How can I determine the purity and worth of the substance I am purchasing?)

- Acute toxic effects associated with drug ingestion (What dosages, methods of ingestion, procedures for use, settings, etc. will reduce risks of toxic effects or overdose? How can I reduce risks of contracting diseases through needle-sharing? What folk remedies are available if toxic effects do occur?)

- Apprehension by law enforcement officials (How can I spot an undercover agent? How can I spot a "snitch"? What tricks can be used to help one pass a field sobriety test?)

- Apprehension by other authority figures (How can one escape detection through urinalysis programs administered by courts, employers and treatment programs?)

The collective tribal experience in the culture of addiction represents a vast reservoir of knowledge that one can draw upon in shaping the addictive career. To utilize that knowledge, however, requires sifting through both myth and misinformation.

The force that drives daily activity for most addicts is the problem of maintaining adequate and convenient access to a drug supply. This means both access to money and access to the drug. Sustaining a supply of money, while minimal for celebrated drugs, represents a major threat to the addict involved in illicit drugs. The addict's insatiable appetite for the drug requires a regular and substantial supply of money. Obtaining that money often means involvement in criminal activity which requires skills that few persons bring with them to the culture. The variety of such activities will be discussed later but what is important now is to understand the skill requirements of criminal activity and the process by which such skills are obtained.

Confronted with a constant demand for large amounts of capital to sustain addiction, one is forced to capitalize on natural assets and opportunities. One must find a trade or hustle that produces regular income while allowing the time and circumstances to consume the drug. Try to imagine that you, the reader, have acquired a drug habit that requires roughly $90 a day to sustain. You have stretched income from your legitimate career to its limits. You have extended your personal credit to its limits. You have borrowed all possible money from family and friends. And you have sold off those personal possessions most easily converted to cash. How do you now support your continued addiction? You are now at the personal brink in the relationship between addiction and crime. You must assess what options and opportunities you have to generate drug-sustaining income. Options might include embezzlement, forgery, shoplifting, confidence games, burglary, credit card scams, selling drugs, drug thefts, or prostitution. Although society at large does not view such activity as a skilled profession, there is a detailed body of knowledge and skills that must be mastered to successfully perform any criminal activity while simultaneously maintaining one's addiction.

A man who recently attended a workshop by the author argued this point and used prostitution as an example. His rhetorical question was: "How much skill does it take to get paid for laying on your back?" Let's consider for a minute a serious answer to this question by pondering the knowledge requirements of an addict using prostitution to support his or her drug habit. They must know:

- techniques of make-up, clothing selection, talking, walking, gesturing, etc. which will attract customers

- current market prices for the various services he or she is offering,
- how to identify undercover vice cops
- techniques for negotiating the best prices for services
- which services he or she will and will not perform for money
- special techniques to stimulate sexual arousal
- how to bolster the male and female ego through sophisticated acting techniques
- how to listen (Prostitutes are often called upon to play surrogate counseling roles similar to bartenders and hairdressers.)
- how to identify and screen out "johns" who pose risks of physical harm
- techniques for reducing the risk of sexually transmitted diseases
- techniques for producing rapid climax/ejaculation (The goal is the maximum amount of money in the shortest possible time with the least amount of physical exertion. Prolonged exertion also serves to speed drug metabolism and speed the onset of drug hunger.), and
- how to avoid getting "ripped off" by refusals to pay after services have been provided

Our list could go on, but the point is that all hustling activities used to produce income for drugs require knowledge and skill mastery. By affiliating with the culture, one has access to mentors in the "trades."

When the means of procuring money has been addressed, the addict must have ready access to drug supplies. By affiliating with the culture of addiction, one creates a safety net by establishing multiple sources of drug supply. The culture can also transmit information and skills that can assure drug supply. The author worked with four women from one instrumental (Valium) drug culture, in which detailed information had been exchanged about the prescribing practices of local physicians. They knew which physicians would most readily prescribe Valium, which would prescribe in the largest quantities, which would prescribe the largest dosages, and which would prescribe for the longest period of time. These women also knew the exact combination of story line and presenting symptoms that would provide them with the desired prescription from each physician. These women collectively knew a great deal more about their physicians than the physicians knew about them. Their cultural affiliation provided the information they needed to sustain drug supplies indefinitely.

CORE ELEMENTS IN THE CULTURE OF ADDICTION

This chapter examines elements of the culture of addiction as they might be observed and described by a cultural anthropologist. It explores elements found in all cultures—language, values, rituals— —and describes the role of each element in shaping the addict identity and addict career. Each element of the culture of addiction will be depicted as an axis of transformation that serves to disengage neophytes from the society at large and propel them deeper into a closed society of addicts.

4.1 *Language* There are unique problems trying to study and describe language in the culture of addiction. Language in the culture of addiction is a constantly changing kaleidoscope. In addition to such change, there are infinite variations influenced by drug choice, tribal groupings, social class, geography and ethnicity. In spite of such difficulties, we will try to examine the nature and function of the lexicon and conversational themes that characterize "the life."

There is an elaborate argot that one must master during entry into the culture of addiction. From the instrumental drug addict who can sound like a walking *Physician's Desk Reference* to the urban junkie whose language has evolved almost into an art form, culturally enmeshed addicts experience a transformation in language that parallels their progression of addiction. Language changes as one is absorbed into the culture. Language changes reflect the transition to, and confirmation of, one's new identity. Mastery of language confirms one's membership in a secret society and provides cues to separate insiders from outsiders.

When clients in substance abuse treatment are asked how their language changed over the years they were involved in excessive alcohol/drug use, they report increased use of profanity, increased use of addict argot and a unique ritual of verbal gamesmanship that often characterizes addict-to-addict communication.

If one were to spend hours with late stage alcoholics/addicts listening to them converse while intoxicated, a pattern of repeating topics and themes would emerge. These themes include:

- stories about hustling that make virtues of cunning, deceit, quick wits, and being "cold" (poised and merciless)
- stories eliciting euphoric recall of episodes of intoxication
- stories of problems and hassles experienced in "the life"
- grandiose self-presentations that serve to enhance self-esteem
- stories that hold "squares" (non-users) up for ridicule
- often repeated stories (folktales) that transmit cultural values, and
- stories about "cleaning up" (It is a cultural paradox that many addicts verbalize desires to get straight while using but, when straight, are constantly talking about wanting to get high.)

There are a number of clinical implications of the above. First, if one has spent years in these conversational pastimes, what does one talk about other than the life? Every time enmeshed addicts open their mouths, the words form a pathway back into the culture. They have language skills that prepare them for only one world—the world of addiction. If treatment programs are to create an alternate pathway of entry into a different world, then we must provide language skills to prepare one for this new career path. Addicts must relearn how to talk!

Another consideration is to examine the range of human experience not captured in the conversational themes of the culture of addiction. Obviously missing from these themes are both permission for and words for affective expression. To the late stage addict, such words are lines of a script called up as part of a hustle (lines learned to play the game of "treatment") or to extricate oneself from a jam. When we tell late stage addicts shortly after entering treatment "you need to get in touch with your feelings," we might as well be speaking Martian. Such affective expression was extinguished early in their entry into the culture. They have lost the ability to speak of their true selves apart from the roles they have played to sustain addiction. They have become the roles. They will relearn the language of affective expression (because learning lines is easy) long before they relearn how to experience the emotion that goes with such language. We can provide the language tools for affective expression, provide conditions of safety and support, and hope the addict relearns how to feel.

4.2 *Religion, Morality and Values* What happens to an individual's personal beliefs and values, and the congruity between expressed values and behavior, as he or she becomes more progressively involved with psychoactive drugs and the cultures in which such drugs are nested? Are there beliefs and rituals of worship within the culture of addiction that parallel traditional religions? Is there an implicit code of morals and values that members share within the culture of addiction?

When an individual begins a relationship with a psychoactive drug, he or she brings to that relationship a set of pre-existing life experiences that have served to shape values and beliefs. For non-vulnerable individuals, this relationship with the drug may be continued over a lifetime without major untoward consequences in general, and, more specifically, without any drug-related transformation in values and beliefs. A majority of alcohol consumers in our society, for example, use this drug as a social ritual with no significant, enduring problems resulting from such use.   To vulnerable individuals, however, the drug relationship follows a different pathway that will alter the very nature of their identity. This section explores the nature of such transformations.

Alcoholics and addicts present widely divergent religious beliefs at the time their drug use was initiated. Some were devoutly religious. For others, religion played no significant role in their life. And still others had angrily rejected their religious roots lashing out at the emotional pain they felt was produced by their early religious training. If we follow the collective trail of addiction, such differences begin to disappear. The progression of addiction drives a wedge between each person and their pre-addiction values. Addiction doesn't create atheists because atheism requires conscious thought about, and rejection of, God/religion. Addiction doesn't create agnostics because agnosticism also makes the religious question important, if unanswerable. Addiction, until the latest stages, renders insignificant questions of God and religion. Religion isn't consciously rejected as much as just not thought about. Addiction is so consuming there simply is no energy available to raise religious questions, let alone ponder the answers. Addiction becomes one's religion, drugs become one's God, and rituals of use become rites of worship. And yet the same addiction which creates and fills this vacuum, will often in late stages, again create a spiritual void that may leave the alcoholic and addict reaching back wistfully to their childhood religious roots for an escape route from their pain. Treatment programs that do not understand the nature of this void and who don't address spirituality will be unsuccessful with these clients.

The experience of a spiritual void does not always lead to recovery. Addicts, because of this void and because of drug-related psychological impairment, are extremely vulnerable to extreme, and sometimes aberrant, belief systems. Within the broad culture of addiction, there are tribes of highly impaired users that promote such belief systems. Some of these tribes, and particularly the leadership of such tribes, are recruited from the ranks of what are now being called "the dually diagnosed." Such persons experience concurrent patterns of substance abuse and psychiatric impairment. Within a cultural perspective, this constitutes a marriage between individual and social pathology that can have horrifying consequences such as was seen with the Manson family and more recent reports of drug-influenced human sacrifices offered in devil worship.

Addiction is not just a disease of the body. Anyone with substantial experience with addicts can testify that addiction is also a disease of values. Addicts regularly violate, through addiction-related behavior, values to which they still claim adherence. The incongruity, inconsistency and unpredictability of the "Dr. Jekyll/-Mr. Hyde" personality of the addict can be attributed to many factors. Addicts who experience "loss of control" (the inability to control the amount of drug consumption once an episode of use has begun) often experience a metamorphosis of personality while using. These persons, in essence, have two personalities. They become somebody different when they use. The two personalities captured within the body of the addict present an extreme dichotomy in values and behavior. The intoxication-induced personality will commit acts that would be unthinkable to the non-using personality.

While personality transformation may occur in early to middle stages of addiction, the later stages of addiction can bring about additional changes. Toxic drug reactions may precipitate behaviors that mark a radical departure from the addict's normal demeanor. Increased tissue tolerance, and the body's insatiable need for drugs, may also precipitate criminal behavior where no such criminality was previously evident.

The above examples note value changes experienced by the individual through the progression of addiction. There are additional value changes that the addict can experience not as an adaptation to addiction but as an adaptation to membership in the culture of addiction. As an addict becomes more deeply enmeshed in this culture, old values dissipate and new values are absorbed from the cultural milieu. The addict takes on the culture's view of the outside world and internalizes values that will shape his or her interactions within and outside the culture. If we could extract the essence of these values in motto form, they might include some of the following:

- The Drug Comes First
- Everyone's On the Make
- Don't Trust Anyone
- Don't Feel (Feel the drug rather than feel emotion)
- Avoid Responsibility by Projecting Blame
- Every Interaction is a Potential Hustle
- Cultivate Excitement Through Risks
- Violate Taboos
- The Image is the Message
- Cunning Over Conscience

4.3 *Symbols* Culturally enmeshed addicts inevitably begin taking on physical trappings of the culture. Such trappings serve as symbols reinforcing one's identification with the culture. The late stage nicotine addict becomes surrounded by lighters, ashtrays, special filters, and other smoking paraphernalia. The marijuana user begins to collect a broad assortment of smoking paraphernalia. The coke user takes great pride in his ownership of a solid gold razor blade. Increasingly, the culturally enmeshed addict will collect symbols reflected in personal belongings, dress, jewelry, etc., that proclaim his or her identity and allegiance to the drug culture.

Such symbols get integrated into the addict's identity and lifestyle to such an extent that the addict becomes oblivious of their presence. Treatment neophytes fresh from the culture of addiction show up for treatment lectures with T-shirts that proclaim "COKE IS IT," belt buckles with a marijuana leaf design, and hats with "Busch" or "Jack Daniels" emblazoned across the top.

The range of physical objects whose presence reinforces affiliation with the culture of addiction includes:

- the drug itself
- drug containers, *e.g.*, stash boxes, designer bottles, glass vials, etc.
- symbols or logos reflecting drug choice or brand identification
- consumption paraphernalia such as pipes, mugs ashtrays, roach clips, mirrors, or injection equipment
- articles associated with hustling behavior such as beepers, burglary tools, large amount of cash, and money clips
- jewelry, clothes, art objects, etc. which communicate drug/brand choice

- objects which through their presentation communicate special tribal affiliation, *e.g.*, gang colors, logos, graffiti, gang or occult signs, hand signals, presence and placement of one's hat, shoe brand and tying method, and
- markings (tatoos or brands) on the body signalling cultural affiliation or cultural values

Symbols like the above serve to reinforce one's affiliation with a culture which promotes excessive drug use. They also become conditioned stimuli that serve to trigger drug hunger and drug-seeking behavior. The role of such trappings in sustaining addiction is frequently ignored in treatment. A primary role in treatment of the culturally enmeshed addict is the removal of symbols reflective of addiction and their replacement with symbols from the culture of recovery.

4.4 *Rituals* The culturally enmeshed addict has developed elaborate rituals that govern when, where and under what circumstances use will occur. By associating certain events or conditions with use, these events become an integral part of the experience of intoxication and over time will function as independent triggers for use.

Jay has been addicted to nicotine for the past 18 years and is attempting to quit for the first time. If we use the principle above, we should be able to identify those events that are most likely to trigger drug hunger and relapse. Jay routinely smokes one cigarette every 25 minutes through his waking hours. While much of his smoking behavior is random (other than by time frequency), there are some clearly identifiable patterns. By conducting a detailed analysis of Jay's smoking behavior, we discover the following times that Jay always lights up a cigarette:

- Immediately upon waking up

- Anytime coffee is consumed
- Immediately after completion of each meal
- Anytime alcohol is consumed
- When talking on the telephone
- When sitting on the toilet
- When taking a break from any activity
- Immediately after making love, and
- Just before going to sleep

By interviewing Jay, we also find out that the times he is experiencing the greatest cravings for nicotine are after his dinner meal, while drinking coffee or alcohol and after making love. By studying Jay's rituals of addiction we are able to identify triggers to relapse and work with Jay on the development or replacement rituals to link with these triggering events.

Jan and Bill are both middle stage alcoholics just entering treatment. We find by interviewing them that not all drinking experiences are equally reinforcing. There are certain times of ritual use that will be particularly hard to stop. For Jan, it is the drinks she has daily between 2:00 and 3:00, usually her first drinks of the day and her preparation for the children returning home from school. For Bill, it is Friday night, his payday and personal reward for surviving another week. For almost every Friday night for the past eight years Bill has stopped by Roy's Lounge to cash his check and join several buddies from work for some serious drinking. While Jan and Bill have not been plagued the last two weeks of their treatment with cravings or impulses to drink, imagine how Jan will feel at home each afternoon at 2:30 and how Bill will experience his first Friday night. Identifying such rituals and creating alternative replacement rituals are essential steps in the relapse prevention planning process.

Some rituals become so enmeshed in the experience of intoxication that they become sought after in their own right. Perhaps the most extreme example of this can be found in needle-sharing subcultures. It has long been known that many addicts, unable to obtain drug supplies, will go through the ritual of injection without the drug. Studies of the "speed" subculture in the Haight-Ashbury area of San Francisco reveal that needle-sharing rituals meet multiple psychological needs of users apart from the drug experience. (Howard and Borges, 1972) The author is aware of numerous instances in the late sixties in which neophyte marijuana users were sold inert substances (mostly horse manure and oregano) purported to be "Vietnamese Black," a potent variety of marijuana. These same users would report that it was some of the best marijuana they had ever had. The rituals of use must have been particularly reinforcing for these neophytes given that there was to the best of our knowledge no drug experience involved.

4.5 *History and Mythology* Every culture, as part of establishing its identity, articulates and passes on its history and mythology. In the drug culture, this most often encompasses local tribal history. Such history, by the illicit nature of the culture, is passed on through stories and folktales. Most of these stories, which serve as a primary vehicle to transmit values, revolve around significant tribal events and personalities. "Hustling Tales" become a way of transmitting knowledge and techniques to neophytes about various cons. Descriptions of heroes and heroines depicted in these tales become a way of shaping desired personality attributes of cultural members. "Copping Tales" are used to teach neophytes the skills and dangers involving in procuring drugs. "Getting Off Tales" convey a whole body of folklore and folk medicine on how to use and reduce risks associated with use. "Enemy Tales" reinforce cultural paranoia and teach neophytes how to cope with cultural enemies, *e.g.*, undercover agents, snitches, non-smokers, supervisors, dealers who peddle "garbage," "shrinks," and "crazies."

Tribal groups can also reach outside their immediate network for heroes and heroines. Famous personalities who have experiences with addiction play an important role in the culture of addiction. Law enforcement officials for the past forty years have focused apprehension efforts on famous drug users on the belief that their arrest would deter use by non-users and encourage people in the life to get out. Anyone who believes such a proposition understands little about the nature of the addict and the workings of the culture of addiction. Addicts extensively use the mechanism of identification to sustain their self-esteem and to affirm their lifestyle. Every famous personality who is arrested, or for that matter who dies, provides confirmation of the addict's participation in an elite society. Rather than deterring use, such selective enforcement and media attention simply generates more heroes and heroines which affirm the value of drug use. But the reader may ask, what about those impassioned public service announcements against drugs that such public personalities inevitably end up doing? Addicts view such pronouncements with admiration for the heroes skills at extricating themselves from legal difficulties (Such public service announcements are routinely part of plea bargaining agreements). The words spoken by the hero are simply seen as a script prepared by "the Man."

4.6 *Institutions (Places)* There is a geographical dimension of the culture of addiction—physical places that become inextricably bound up in one's addictive lifestyle. For the instrumental drug addict, those places may constitute hospitals, doctor's offices, and pharmacies. For the celebrated drug addict, those places may include taverns, restaurants, liquor stores, and other places associated with drug consumption. For the prohibited drug addict, those places may include neighborhoods, specific streets and street corners, shooting galleries, houses of dealers and other users, pawn shops, houses that were burglarized, stores at which shoplifting regularly occurred, etc. In short, the addiction experience produces a map of often travelled routes and on this map may be hundreds of places whose physical existence calls forth memories that bind one to the culture. Each place has left an emotional imprint that can serve as a trigger for drug use.

For late stage alcoholics, for example, nearly all the places they regularly go are somehow tied to their addiction. If they're not going to drink, where do they go? Does this sound like a silly question? Some years ago a client who had gone through alcoholism treatment a few months earlier came in to see me. He had done very well in treatment and had literally absorbed himself in aftercare and self-help group meetings. He had not had a drink since before he entered treatment but came in to discuss the following disturbing experience.

> *It was Sunday afternoon and for the first time since I left the hospital I was alone without any particular plans till evening. The silence of the house was getting to me so I decided to just go for a drive, something I hadn't done in years. It was a beautiful day and I found myself just driving all around areas of the city I hadn't seen enjoying myself. As I drove past the neighborhood where my office is located, I began thinking about a work project I had coming up next week and continued to drive as I thought through the details of how I was going to handle it. Imagine my horror, when I suddenly come to consciousness and realized that I had just pulled in line to the drive-up window at my old liquor store. My heart started pounding and I broke out in a cold sweat. I practically wrecked the car trying to get out of there. I can't figure out what was going on. Drinking was the furthest thing from my mind.*

This would not be the first client who reported that their car, all by itself, drove them to a liquor store or a dealer's house. As we continued to discuss the client's experience, we identified that for the past eight years the client had driven directly from work stopping by this particular liquor store on his way home. On this particular Sunday, while preoccupied, he drove the exact same route he had made thousands of times, to include the drive-up window at the liquor store. What this client discovered was that there are geographical triggers for drinking in addition to physiological, psychological and social triggers.

Physical places, and the meanings and experiences attached to these places, can constitute reinforcers of excessive alcohol and drug consumption. Substance abuse treatment programs must assist the addict in identifying those places that may trigger impulses to use and substitute other places and rituals that support recovery.

4.7 *Dress/Appearance* Changes in dress and appearance can go in one of two directions as one becomes increasingly enmeshed in the culture of addiction. The most common change reported by alcoholics and addicts is a deterioration in self-care and self-maintenance. In later stages of addiction, most reported that they simply stopped caring about how they looked. This deterioration in appearance is part of a broader pattern of self-neglect that also encompasses hygiene and health. Dentists become a memory. Physical injuries and illnesses are ignored. Cleanliness and personal care become the exception rather than the norm. As increasing amounts of time, emotional energy and dollars are pulled into addiction sustaining activities, self-care becomes an unaffordable luxury. An essential stage in treating the culturally enmeshed addict is to replace self-neglect with self-care. The personal habits that reinforced one's involvement in the culture of addiction must be broken. Bathing, grooming, personal dress, dental care, eye care, and other self-care areas are all treatment issues.

Not all addicts experience a deterioration in appearance. For some addicts, impeccability in appearance is part of their denial of addiction. There are some clients, for example, who enter treatment appearing as if they just stepped off the pages of a fashion magazine. These clients overdress for the treatment setting, change clothes several times a day, and are frequently late for treatment activities due to constant grooming throughout the day. In late stages of addiction and in extreme denial regarding this fact, these clients meticulously maintained their appearances to present a physical refutation of their addiction. Every element of their presentation of self challenges, "How can I be an alcoholic? Look at me!" Their unblemished appearance serves to help sustain their addiction in the same way the extreme lack of self-care serves to sustain addiction for the addicts described above. A major stage in the treatment of these clients is the beginning exploration of personal values and an identity that hinges neither on their drug use nor their personal appearance.

4.8 *Diet/Food* We have all heard the adage, "You are what you eat." If there is truth to this proposition, it is no wonder that addicts find themselves in such serious straits. Very few addicts can get into middle or late stages of addiction without changes in both the quantity and quality of food consumption. What are the eating habits of the culture of addiction? First, there is the irregularity of food consumption. Drinking and drug using, and related behaviors, are not conducive to a regular schedule of food consumption. The drugs themselves also often suppress appetite and result in an overall decreased intake of food. The kinds of foods consumed also change. Most addicts will report decreased intake of protein, fruits and vegetables and an increasing diet of fats and carbohydrates. Poor nutritional habits are part of the neglect of everything not directly related to the drug relationship. If we are to break a client's enmeshment in the culture of addiction, then we must assist the client in altering his/her culturally shaped pattern of food consumption. Clients missing meals and living on junk food is a treatment issue. Such clients may be talking recovery, but they're still eating in the addictive lifestyle.

4.9 *Music* Are the values of the culture of addiction transmitted through song and music in ways that hold special meaning to users? Such values have been captured in words and music throughout our history. New forms of music emerged in the twenties to entertain the patrons of prohibition's speakeasies. The marijuana songs (Cab Calloway's "Reefer Man") of the thirties would reflect this drug's growing visibility in the society—a visibility that would result in the drug's prohibition in 1937. The polydrug revolution launched in the sixties would generate songs to celebrate marijuana ("Don't Bogart That Joint"), hallucinogens ("Lucy in the Sky with Diamonds") and stimulants ("Amphetamine Annie"). The cocaine songs of Jackson Brown and Eric Clapton reflect this drug's dominance of the current period in our history.

Throughout this century lyricists and musicians have created music to celebrate the drug experience. For those legions who share their drug choices, the songs become anthems that support a culture of addiction. By hearing the drug experience captured and promoted in words and music, the drug user's lifestyle is normalized and affirmed. The user also experiences a confirmation of values and beliefs that reinforce addiction and the addictive lifestyle.

Addicts, like Pavlov's dogs, can be conditioned to link the stimuli of music with their experiences of intoxication. If one has consistently listened to particular kinds of music or particular songs while experiencing drug intoxication, then these songs come to constitute triggers or stimuli for use. Let me illustrate. In one of my lectures in an addiction treatment center, clients were asked during a discussion of the culture of addiction if there was a particular kind of music or particular songs that they associated with their alcohol or drug use. After several responses from group members, a man in the back retorted, "C14." Several group members laughed, instinctively understanding to what he was referring. He went on to explain that for the past five years when he was starting a "Katy bar the doors drinkin' night," he would repeatedly play "C14" on the jukebox at his regular tavern. "C14," which was a song by Hank Williams, Jr. entitled "Family Tradition," had become an integral part of his excessive drinking episodes. What do you think this client will experience following his discharge from treatment the first time he hears "Family Tradition" on the radio?

If one function of treatment for culturally enmeshed addicts is to provide a decompression experience from the culture of addiction, then we must either remove stimuli reflecting this culture or neutralize the ability of these stimuli to function as triggers for intoxication.

4.10 *Art* Art has not been a consistently visible component of the culture of addiction during the past century in spite of the visible presence of artists within this culture and the inevitable influence of the drug experience upon their work. Art did exist as a major component during the height of hallucinogenic drug use in the sixties and early seventies. During this period, an entirely new hallucinogenic art form would emerge, illustrated best by the black lights and poster art found within the "head shops" of that period. During this time, art served to both encourage and enhance the drug experience. Art objects would become part of the broad assortment of paraphernalia that would reinforce one's identity as a "freak."

4.11 *Literature* Is there a body of literature that captures the experience and world view of the culture of addiction and supports the culture's goals and values? While such literature is not highly visible in the culture at large, it does exist. In general, such literature can be described in the following categories:

A. *First Person Accounts of Addiction*   These works include biographical novels, topical texts and articles that report personal experiences with various psychoactive drugs. Some, such as the works of Brown (1965), Burroughs (1953), Iceberg Slim (1969), Malcolm X (1964) and Thomas (1967) focus specifically on the addictive lifestyle. Others, such as Huxley (1954), Leary (1968), Wyle (1972), etc., focus more specifically on the drug experience itself. In general, most of the desired literature in the culture is long on description of drug use and addiction and short on the morality of use, the consequences of use and the desirability or the process of rehabilitation.

B. *Technical Books on Drugs and Drug Effects*   These books are obtained and used within the culture to increase one's sophistication as a drug consumer and to learn methods to reduce risks of use. The "folk healers" in the culture of addiction who will be discussed in a later chapter usually serve as the depository of such texts. Their homes are the libraries; they serve as both librarian and interpreter of technical information.

C. *The Recipe Books*   These texts describe the step-by-step procedures for creating, processing, purifying, packaging and testing illicit drugs. A glance through such manuals can provide one the knowledge to hunt and identify hallucinogenic mushrooms, to produce phencyclidine (PCP) in your kitchen, to cook a variety of culinary treats utilizing cannabis as the primary ingredient, and a variety of other skills that would appeal to capitalists and connoisseurs in the culture.

D. *The Law Books*   These texts provide detailed information on drug control laws, how to circumvent drug laws where possible, rights when arrested, how to select a lawyer and other legal issues of interest. Most are billed as survival manuals.

E. *The Promotional Journals* These journals constitute the promotional propagandists of the illicit drug culture. Perhaps best known of this genre are *High Times* and *Head* magazines. To give the reader a feel for the content of such magazines, the June, 1978 copy of *High Times* contains an article on how to grow marijuana in your backyard, an advice column counseling a reader on the best method for extracting and purifying hash oil, the self-confessions of a glue sniffer, and numerous pictorials of, and articles on, currently well known drug users. In the same magazine one can order the following by mail: drug testing equipment, scales for measuring drugs, a marijuana cigarette roller, stash boxes, a wide assortment of bongs, gold razor blades and straws, seeds for growing hallucinogenic mushrooms, coke spoon jewelry, and coke screens.

The above body of literature collectively serves to validate excessive drug use and celebrate one's career in the culture of addiction.

4.12 *Visual Media* There is a pool of visual media in the culture at large from which addicts draw sustenance and support for their continued use of psychoactive drugs. This can include media whose themes communicate acceptance or promotion of drug use or may involve media whose viewing enhances the experience of intoxication. At times, such media are given a special significance in the culture of addiction.

Television and motion pictures both reflect the culture at large and serve as stimuli to shape this culture. To the extent that such media communicate casual acceptance of alcohol and drug use and present addicted people in a favorable or sympathetic light, they serve to affirm values from the culture of addiction. An example of this would include the constant subliminal presence of drinking and smoking in television shows and movies. The presence of such cues can even be used to influence brand preference. A new and insidious form of drug promotion is the placement of identifiable drug brands within movies. Phillip Morris, for example, paid $350,000 to have their Lark cigarettes prominently displayed within the James Bond movie, *License to Kill*. Is it mere chance that the Marlboro logo appears in the movie *Superman* and that shots of Miller Lite Beer appear so frequently and visibly in the movie *Bull Durham*?

Examples of movies with more overt drug themes were obvious during the year which preceded the publication of this book. *Tequila Sunrise* romanticized the life of a cocaine dealer who laments that his financial success will make it hard to leave "the life." *Blind Date* and *License to Drive* both use actors who are very appealing to teenagers to trivialize the risks and consequences of substance abuse. *About Last Night*, *Cocktail* and *Bar Fly* all hold the bar up as the center of social activity. Other movies which convey casual acceptance of drug use included films as diverse as *Crocodile Dundee*, *Dragnet*, *Revenge of the Nerds II*, and *Wall Street*. Such visual communication trivializes and normalizes drug use. It legitimizes and promotes drug use. It creates a camouflage of myth and misconception within which the addict can hide. Have there ever been more lovable characters than Arthur or Norm (on *Cheers*)? Isn't it time we showed what happens to the real Arthurs and Norms?

A special category of visual media encompasses the alcohol commercials regularly seen on television. The intent of these commercials to promote and normalize alcohol consumption helps the alcoholic maintain an illusion of normalcy within the banner, "Everybody drinks." Imagine what would happen to this illusion if the following line was added to the ever-present Lite Beer commercials:

"Lite Beer tastes great!"
"Lite Beer's less filling!"
"Lite Beer can be addicting!"

The group "Science in the Study of Public Interest" recently published an analysis of alcohol advertising in which they suggest that much of this advertising is aimed specifically at alcoholics. While the alcohol industry regularly proclaims they support responsible drinking and that alcoholics give their industry a bad name, there is evidence to suggest that the industry's financial interests would clearly not be served by this position. The above report notes that seventy percent of the alcohol is consumed by fifteen percent of drinkers. The report goes on to contend that the alcohol industry has a clear financial stake in the incidence of this heavy drinking population and protects this interest by directing promotional efforts toward these men and women. Any alcohol advertising, which seeks to extend the timing and frequency of usage beyond current social norms and communicate that alcohol can be used to alter one's emotional state and solve problems, clearly reinforces values from the culture of addiction. Consider the following story.

Several months ago I was out to dinner on a week night at a local bar/restaurant and was seated near the bar where I had the opportunity to observe a highly intoxicated gentleman. I had watched him drinking heavily, randomly watching the TV above the bar and attempting to engage the bartender in conversation. My attention was caught when I heard this gentleman toast the television set and loudly proclaim, "I'll drink to that!" When I looked up an advertisement for Michelob Beer was just ending in which the repeated theme was "Put a little weekend in your week."

I would suggest that the gentleman at the bar received great comfort from this communication. It was as if some great voice was proclaiming, "Hey, I know it's not Saturday night, but go ahead. You deserve it!"

Movies, or more recently music videos, can also be pulled into the culture of addiction to provide special rituals of celebration. How many individuals, for example, do you think have gathered around television sets to watch *Reefer Madness*, *Assassin of Youth* or other anti-marijuana films of the thirties while getting stoned on marijuana? During the height of psychedelic drug use, it became practically an initiation rite for users to gather and watch *Fantasia* while tripping on LSD.

Other visual media from the culture of addiction may include billboards, neon signs, and other advertising paraphernalia. While these objects may hold little significance to the non-addicted person, they may serve as triggers for continued use for the addict. An alcoholic client early in his recovery called me one evening quite distraught. He reported a near relapse experience following a week when he had felt particularly out of sorts. He described a most disturbing event as follows.

> *After that kind of week, I was driving home Thursday night about 10:00 when I looked down the street I was on and saw a large neon Budweiser sign flashing on and off over a bar. I know you're going to think I'm crazy, but it's like I was hypnotized. I couldn't take my eyes off it. It was like that sign was talking to me. You'll never know how close I was to pulling in there.*

A wide variety of visual stimuli can reinforce the addict's involvement in the culture of addiction and can serve as a trigger for relapse during early recovery. The client above was not crazy. He was absolutely correct. The sign was talking to him. It was the seductive call of the culture saying, "WE'RE STILL HERE! WE'VE MISSED YOU! COME BACK!" It was as if the Devil himself had extended a bony finger up out of Hell and beckoned him to return to the dark shadows of his past.

4.13 *Work and Leisure* The worlds of work and leisure are both impacted as the involvement in drug consumption, and the culture which supports it, escalates over time.

Whether as a student, or homemaker or employed worker, the performance of one's role responsibilities are compromised through the progression of addiction. It is not simply that this progression precipitates drug induced impairment of job performance. The very function and meaning of work changes. Work (socially legitimate roles) moves from an arena where one pursues personal and vocational interests and achieves self-esteem to the arena of the "hustle." Work loses all other value except the value to provide capital which assures continued access to drug supply. It is this role which makes the job so important in the life of the addict. We have learned through industrial alcoholism programs that the threat of job loss may serve as a more powerful stimulus to addiction treatment than the threat of loss of health or loss of family. The legitimate job is the ultimate contradiction for the addict. It is often simultaneously the most important, and sometimes last, link to straight society while at the same time it is the major financial link to continued drug use.

The culture of addiction respects legitimate work as a "hustle" and will provide the addict with the collective wisdom of the elders on how to sustain this hustle into the latest stages of addiction. If we were to organize this wisdom into a topical catalogue, it might include the following topics:

- Occupations and job roles especially suited for addict

- The best stories to justify absenteeism and tardiness
- How to use at work without getting caught
- Avoiding detection through frequent job changes
- The best stories of why you left your last job
- Methods of beating your company's drug testing program
- Manipulating your supervisor through tears, rage and blackmail
- Surviving meetings about your job performance
- Avoiding consequences through expertise in company personnel policies and grievance procedures
- The creative use of accidents, medical leave, disability benefits, and worker compensation claims
- What to do when forced to go to the company's employee assistance program
- Resigning in moral outrage before you are fired

The shared experience of other addicts within the culture provides one with the above knowledge and assists the addict in maintaining legitimate employment long past the point of diminished productivity. The real task of work each day becomes getting by—escaping consequences of use and maintaining income (drug supply). When this task can no longer be performed due to the intensity of drug impairment, the culture of addiction offers other avenues to sustain one's drug supply. With the final loss of legitimate job roles, the major umbilical cord to society at large is severed and the addict is inevitably pulled deeper into the culture of addiction in search of alternative "hustles" to maintain drug supply.

The major historically prescribed role responsibility of adolescents in this society is to go to school. For adolescents who are increasingly enmeshed within the culture of addiction, both the nature and duration of school participation is transformed. Time and emotional energy shift from educational to drug-oriented pursuits. Relationships within the school become drug dominated. Rituals of the school day revolve around drug procurement, drug selling, drug using, and drug dominated storytelling. The increased impairment in academic functioning is not simply a matter of drug-related cognitive impairment. It is that directing one's emotional energy toward such pursuits has ceased to have value for the adolescent in the culture of addiction. Where the need for money can keep adult addicts tied to their jobs, this same need eventually pulls many adolescents from the drug culture within the school to the drug culture of the streets. Viewed from the inside rather than the outside of this deviant culture, they have graduated. The adolescent has rejected the work of adolescence—school— and has begun the search for an alternative, and deviant, career path. Like their adult counterpart, the nature and meaning of work has been transformed for the adolescent addict.

How does the use of leisure time change as a result of one's involvement in the culture of addiction? Are there recreational pastimes within the culture of addiction? Many addicts will go through three overlapping stages in their use of leisure time. These stages parallel both the progression of addiction and the progressive involvement in the addictive lifestyle. In the first stage the addict participates in leisure pastimes based on his or her personal interests. Many of the activities at this point do not necessarily involve using or association with other users. During the second stage such activities are continued but alcohol and drug use is almost always integrated into the activity. The addict also begins to exclude non-users from leisure time activities and to stop activities which preclude use. In the third stage, drug use becomes the leisure activity—an activity shared usually with other users. This progression can be illustrated through an excerpt from an interview with an alcoholic client entering treatment.

Author: George, could you describe for me what you do for relaxation and if this has changed as a result of your drinking?

George: You know, I used to be involved in a lot and we also did a lot as a family. When the kids were little, my wife and I still went out together a lot with friends and Sunday was our traditional family day. My drinking eventually stopped all those things. In my sober moments, I would keep saying we ought to do this or that again, but somehow they never happened. Since Sheila (George's wife) left with the kids, I don't do anything but go to work and drink.

Author: Were there hobbies or special activities you used to enjoy?

George: Yeah, I've enjoyed hunting and fishing since I was a kid. I had three or four buddies that used to get away regularly on a hunting or fishing trip. In the last few years, it's just been Skip and I. He's a drunk too.

Author: What happened to the other friends you used to go with?

George: Skip and I used to call them party poopers. They would come to fish and hunt. Skip and I would come to drink. Actually, they just started coming up with reasons they couldn't go with us anymore. Skip and I used to get pretty crazy sometimes too. I'm sure one of them stopped coming out of fear one of us would get drunk and accidentally shoot somebody.

Author: So you have continued to hunt and fish regularly?

George: Well, mostly fishing. But it isn't the same.

Author: In what way?

George: We say we're going fishing. We take our poles and a couple cases of beer but I can't remember the last time we bought bait.

As non-drug-related leisure activities of the addict disappear, the culture of addiction fills the time vacuum. Leisure activities revolve around the institutions, relationships and rituals of the culture of addiction. These rituals become established as deeply imbedded personal habits and serve as powerful triggers for continued drug consumption. Imagine being an addict waking up early Saturday morning the day after you have been discharged from residential treatment. You know what you don't want to do—use. But what do you do? Where do you go? Who do you see? Old Saturday activities mean relapse. Old places mean relapse. Old relationships mean relapse. But what will you do? Where will you go? Who will you see? If these questions are not addressed in treatment through an aggressive program of relapse prevention planning, the culturally enmeshed addict's seduction back into the life is almost inevitable.

4.14 *Sexuality* All cultures provide both explicit (taboos) and implicit (values) boundaries within which members are expected to express their sexuality. Within the culture of addiction, there is wide variance in these boundaries depending on one's tribal group and drug choices. If we look at the culture as a whole, however, there are some observations that may help us understand sexuality issues presented by clients entering addiction treatment.

A. *Sexual Trauma* Research over the past twenty years has noted the significant percentage of women (and increasingly men) who were sexually abused as children and adolescents and would later become involved in an addictive lifestyle. One could posit that this relationship results from a self-medication of emotional pain or that such early sexual trauma aborts normal emotional development and contributes to an increase in high risk-taking and self-destructive behavior that continues one's victim role. An important element in understanding sexuality in the culture of addiction begins with the recognition that many members were victimized sexually prior to their cultural involvement. Treatment must encompass not only the changes in sexuality that occurred through one's addiction, but also the emotional pain related to sexuality and the distortion of sexual development that preceded the onset of drug use.

B. *Sexual Identity* There can exist an important link between the clarity of and comfort with one's sexual identity and alcohol and drug use. The inability to function sexually with the opposite sex or confusion over homosexual experiences are issues that one can bring to one's entrance into the culture of addiction. Additional sexual experiences can also occur within the culture that further diffuse one's clarity of sexual orientation.   The culture itself provides an arena either to avoid or explore such issues of sexual identity. One can become asexual in many tribes without jeopardizing one's acceptance and other tribes within the culture can be found which openly accept, if not promote, bisexuality or homosexuality. If one's sexual identity and behavior have been shaped within the culture of addiction, how then does one address issues of sexuality separate from this world?   If addiction and the addictive lifestyle have allowed one to escape confronting problems related to sexuality, will not these issues surface quickly and painfully as one enters the alternative lifestyle of recovery? If one has sustained a Gay identity through the bar subculture of the Gay community, where will one sustain this identity in recovery? If one entered the culture of addiction as an adolescent and has never over the past twenty years functioned socially or sexually stone cold sober, how will one manage the fear concerning the ability to perform without the aid of drugs and outside the social and sexual rituals of the culture of addiction?

C. *Sexual Values* The disinhibiting effects of many psychoactive drugs, the tolerance and promotion of sexually exploitive behavior in many tribal groups and the use of sex as a vehicle to sustain drug supply can stimulate a transformation in one's sexual values in the culture of addiction. For many, sexual behavior loses its value as a vehicle for achieving physical pleasure or experiencing and expressing emotional intimacy and love. Sexual values also transform within the broader context of values about human relationships. People become objects that either help sustain or get in the way of addiction. In both cases, people are to be used.

D. *Sexual Shame and Guilt* Many addicts exhibit sexual behavior while intoxicated or out of need for drugs that would be unthinkable for them outside the context of addiction. The shame and guilt from such behavior is assuaged both by drug anesthesia and values in the culture of addiction that normalize such behavior. The daily needs of addiction afford little time for reflection and regret. But what happens when a crisis stops this speeding merry-go-round and the addict comes to a stop? How does the addict in treatment look back and make sense out of such experiences? How does one discharge and achieve emotional closure on the shame engendered by such experiences? How does one reformulate values to govern relationships in recovery?

E. *Sexual Dysfunction* A significant percentage of addicts will experience transient, if not recurring, episodes of sexual dysfunction in later stages of addiction. Sexual dysfunction can spring from, or be hidden within, the drug relationship. While the addict may consider such dysfunction as an issue of secondary importance compared with the need to sustain addiction, this same issue may surface as an issue of major importance when the addict considers the alternative lifestyle of recovery. If not addressed appropriately, such dysfunction can serve as a trigger for relapse.

4.15 *Family Relationships* What transformations occur in family life as the addict becomes increasingly involved in this culture of addiction? Changes in family structure and process precipitated by such involvement are first influenced by the nature of family life prior to the onset of substance abuse. While each family constitutes a unique entity upon which addiction can be imposed, there are some general observations which can be made about family life and the culture of addiction.

During early and middle stages of addiction, the family increasingly serves as a safety net for the addict. Wegscheider (1981), Black (1982) and numerous others have graphically described the adaptation of the family to addiction. Such adaptation in family roles, family rules, and family process serve to keep the family in balance while minimizing alcohol/drug related consequences experienced by the addicted member and the family as a whole. As a safety net, family members take on roles and behaviors that divert family attention from the addicted member. They take on excessive responsibility to compensate for the addict's inability to perform family functions and rescue the addict from situations that would provide unpleasant consequences of his or her alcohol and drug use.

The adaptation of the family to addiction does not occur in isolation but within the broader context of the addict's increasing involvement in the culture of addiction. The family is not only in competition with a drug for the addict's loyalty. They are in competition with the culture of addiction for the addict's time, emotional energy, devotion and money. Caught in this competitive dilemma, the family must either wage a seemingly unwinnable battle against the culture or follow the addict into the culture.

At the earliest stages, family members, sensing the emotional distancing of the addict, will identify themselves as somehow responsible for the addict's detachment from the family. The wife of the addict feels that if she were prettier, friendlier, a better housekeeper, a better mother, a better lover, or a better person, the addict would use less and become more involved with the family. Children often feel equally responsible for changes occurring in the addict. If the addict is an adolescent, parents take on feelings of sole responsibility for the child's addiction. All family members begin a series of trial and error transformations trying to find the right thing they can do to control the addict's behavior. The family struggles for perfection, competing against some unseen force which we know to be the addict's drug and the culture which promotes its consumption.

An increasing number of family rituals begin to be shaped by the progression of addiction and the increasingly sophisticated skills the addict is acquiring in the culture. Consider the following scenario.

Dean is sitting at his favorite bar with Joe, his favorite drinking buddy when he realizes that he was supposed to be home two hours ago. He tells Joe not to go anywhere and that he will be back in half an hour. He proceeds to drive home. Entering his home, he gives his wife a breathy 80 proof kiss and the following communication occurs.

Wife: (In frustration and anger) Dean, you promised to be here at six and you're drunk again. The kids...

Dean: (Interrupting with feigned surprise) Drunk? Do I look drunk to you?

Wife: Yes. You know you are. I don't know what...

Dean: (Interrupting now with a tone of righteous indignation) I'm not drunk! You want Drunk? I'll show you what drunk is! (Now heading for door) And another thing. If you'd clean this place up once in a while, maybe I'd feel like showing up on time! (Door slams).

Dean is back on the stool next to Joe in the promised thirty minutes to continue what will now be a night of guilt-free drinking. If we were to analyze the above scenario, we would see a ritual of communication learned from the culture of addiction that has been refined and played out with only minor word changes millions of times. Such rituals serve to justify drinking. They provide communication triggers for escape into the culture of addiction for bouts of alcohol/drug use. As addiction and one's involvement in the life progress, these rituals can begin to dominate marital and family life.

Failing in all attempts to control the addict's drug consumption and failing in efforts to re-engage the addict in family life, the family may take the stance: "if you can't beat'em; join'em." At this stage, family life actually may move into the culture of addiction. The addict's spouse may attempt to join the addict in an addictive lifestyle. Spouse and children may join the addict in use pastimes, *e.g.*, spending evenings at the bar. Other addicts may be moved into the family home. The spouse and older children may take on enabling roles for not only the addict but also for his or her peers in the culture of addiction. The family gets seduced into the culture of addiction and the entire family may begin to emotionally disengage from the outside social world. It is within this context that a child can be born and literally raised within the culture of addiction.

Other families failing in their efforts to control the addict's behavior will themselves begin to emotionally disengage. They may simply disengage emotionally from the addict and sustain family life as best they can under the circumstances or wage war against the culture through angry demands that the spouse stop his/her current lifestyle. It is at this stage that many addicts lose their families.

This emotional detachment of family members grows out of anger, futility, frustration over unmet needs and perhaps most importantly through anticipatory grief. As the addict moves into middle and late stages of addiction, family members repeatedly experience the expectation of death for the family member. Spouses and children lie awake at night wandering if this is the night the addict will not make it home. Every phone call late at night in the addict's absence strikes terror. Family members have buried the addict a thousand times in their emotional experience. They have already begun to grieve the loss of the addict. Is it any wonder that they experience difficulty rekindling emotional involvement with the addict during early recovery? We are asking the family to emotionally resurrect someone they have already figuratively buried. They are being asked to rekindle hope when it is easier to give up, when to hope is to defy the past reality of a thousand broken promises.

When the addict loses his or her family, it is the culture of addiction that must become a surrogate family and take over the function of safety net. This safety net, however, is seriously flawed due to the level of impairment of most members in the culture of addiction. This is why breaks between the addict and his/her family are rarely clean and permanent. The cultural safety net breaks down when the addict is in crisis, and the addict re-engages the family with pleas of assistance. Episodic re-engagement of the family and cyclical reconciliations of marriages all accompanied by promises of change, keep the family on an emotional roller coaster.

4.16 *Social Relationships* Social relationships can be rapidly transformed by addiction as in the case of the adolescent. He or she may suddenly propel themselves into the world of illicit drug experimentation or slowly over an extended number of years as is often the case with alcoholism. Most of us seek out and sustain relationships with others who cherish the same kinds of values and experiences we do. By definition, the addict cherishes the relationship with his or her drug of choice and is inevitably drawn toward others like him/herself.

As one moves from neophyte to committed user, shifting alliances begin to occur in social relationships that serve to reinforce drug consumption. Those individuals who do not share similar drug consumption patterns begin to disappear. It's not as if one makes conscious decisions to no longer associate with these individuals. Such relationships simply fade into nonexistence. Taking their place will be relationships with others who share the user's choices and patterns of drug consumption. It is not just that smokers are more comfortable around other smokers. It is that heavy smokers prefer to be with other heavy smokers. Being with others whose drug use mirrors one's own helps normalize such use and maintain the illusion of control over the drug.

In late stages of addiction, the user's entire social world may be shaped by the experience of addiction. This is particularly true of the person identified in this text as a culturally enmeshed addict. To give up one's relationship with the drug is to give up an entire network of people connected to the drug experience. Every relationship serves as a trigger for use. Every relationship is a pathway back into the life. Every interaction with the old social world constitutes a risk for relapse.

The culturally enmeshed addict who breaks his or her relationship with the drug and severs ties to the drug- oriented social relationships, is left in a void that if unfilled will pull the user back into the life. The systematic engagement of this person in a culture of recovery, as a medium to fill this social vacuum, represents the most critical component of relapse prevention planning for the culturally enmeshed addict.

4.17 *Time Orientation* Time orientation in the culture of addiction is driven by the immediacy needs of its members. One's concept of time is shaped by the relationship with one's drug of choice. For the addict, time is always in the present tense. There is no yesterday and no tomorrow. There is only today and what one must do to maintain supply, sustain use, postpone or medicate sickness, and avoid consequences of use. It was no accident that the fellowship of Alcoholics Anonymous organized its recovery principles around a "one day at a time," 24 hour, program. They simply took the time orientation the alcoholic was already acclimated to and shifted its focus from addiction to recovery.

The past and future may be used by the addict to sustain addiction. Past events become part of the cognitive framework to justify use. History must be rewritten within this framework so that the addict appears as victim rather than active participant. The history must read that the addict was wrongfully and painfully abandoned by his or her spouse. The history of drug-related abuse which led to such separation must be erased. The future can also serve as a tool to fuel continued drug use. Addicts use an interesting technique, shared by some non-addicts, of fantasizing future events, projecting negative experiences into such events, experiencing emotions as if the events were real, and then using these emotions to drive continued alcohol/drug consumption. The addict entering treatment must begin the process of reconstructing a reality-based personal history and restructure the process through which he or she perceives the future.

Part of the time orientation in the culture of addiction is personalized into each member's daily routine—those activities and rituals that have been repeated so often at the same time or on the same day over a long period of time that they now constitute firmly established personal habits. If the working alcoholic has scheduled him/herself to drink Monday through Friday at 12:00 noon and at

5:15 over a period of years, how do you think these times will be experienced during the early months of sobriety? For many addicts in the illicit culture, there may be little consistency as to when such daily activities as eating and sleeping occur. If anything, days and nights may be reversed and eating occurs at happenstance. Is it any wonder that addicts bring such unstructured habits with them when they enter treatment? Issues such as sleeping schedules are not peripheral issues raised to make for more efficient management of a treatment unit. The addict's daily habits constitute a component of the culture of addiction that reinforces an addictive lifestyle. Addicts must learn how to achieve non-drug induced sleep and to do so on a schedule that reinforces recovery rather than addiction.

4.18 *Violence* A discussion of the major elements of the culture of addiction would be incomplete without noting the changing role of violence in this culture. The role of alcohol has been a perpetual theme in studies of victims and perpetrators of violent death. It should not be surprising that a drug such as alcohol which impairs judgment, lowers inhibitions and diminishes impulse control is associated with violence and that such violence is most concentrated in subcultures which drink excessively. Alcohol-related violence—whether by gun, by knife, by fist or by auto—is a constant thread within our society. Many families not only hide alcoholism, but also the violence that so frequently accompanies drinking episodes. Members of the culture of addiction are at increased risk of being both perpetrators and victims of such violence.

In my reading and experience of history, there has been a significant and recent change in the prevalence and intensity of violence in the illicit culture of addiction in the United States. Since the criminalization of addiction in the early part of this century, there has been a complex relationship between the illicit drugs and a broad category of criminal activity. Violence in the illicit drug culture, as a specific type of criminal behavior, however, has been relatively insignificant until recently. Even in the most deviant of the illicit drug subcultures—the urban opiate subculture so known for its predatory crimes—violence is rarely described as part of the junkie profile. One thing has transformed violence in the illicit culture of addiction—cocaine.

Cocaine, cocaine dollars, cocaine turf and cocaine wars have brought an intensity of violence to the culture of addiction that would have been inconceivable only a few years ago. The prevalence of weapons and the toll of victims claimed by these weapons has exploded in tandem with the spread of freebase cocaine and crack. This cocaine-inflamed violence has spread a new form of terrorism, turning drug saturated urban neighborhoods into battlefields.

There are two direct effects of this new violence upon the needs of clients entering addiction treatment. First, clients today are much more likely than in the past to be victims of violence within the culture of addiction. An increased number of clients are reporting having been physically and/or sexually brutalized in this culture. Some are presenting with a form of post traumatic stress disorder superimposed on their addiction, as a result of physical and psychological trauma. Secondly, an increasing number of clients have been desensitized to violence and have learned in this recently transformed culture of addiction that violence is an appropriate method of problem solving. This is not violence which springs from individual psychopathology. This is violence as a form of social pathology. This new violence is a learned, socially approved and rewarded behavior within a deviant culture which has gone mad. These changes will require new clinical approaches specifically designed to address violence. We must strive to heal the violence-induced psychological wounds of our clients. We must strive to confront, re-stigmatize and eliminate the aggressive and violent behavior of our clients.

4.19 *Death* Every human culture and subculture provides beliefs and rituals dealing with death. One would expect exceptionally elaborate rituals surrounding death in a subculture that has a fatality rate as extraordinarily high as the culture of addiction. After all, alcoholics and addicts die frequently from accidents, overdoses, drug-related medical diseases, suicides and as victims of violence. Such elaborate rituals are not the case, however. The reason for this lies partially in the very narcissism of addiction. The experience of loss by the addict is transient at most, and quickly superseded by the daily demands of addiction. The culture of addiction does, however, provide some mechanisms to mourn the loss of members while denying the entire culture's courtship with death.

Many of the young neophytes in the culture, aged 16 to 30, bring with them the belief typical of this age group, that they are immortal. This belief is reinforced by the culture in which they observe phenomenally high levels of risk-taking behavior. They observe people ingesting incomprehensible dosages of psychoactive drugs. They observe people regularly consuming potentially toxic/lethal drug combinations. They observe people conducting activities, such as swimming and driving in states of extreme intoxication. Yet, from their experimental framework, the fatality rate remains low, and their personal risk of fatality seems nonexistent. To reinforce such denial, the culture projects blame for deaths onto individual members or on persons or forces outside the culture. It wasn't the drugs that killed someone. They "ODed" because their wife left them. The wife is to blame. It wasn't the drugs. It was "bad" drugs from a disreputable dealer. It is the individual dealer, not the culture that is to blame. Following a member death, tribal members meet and toast the lost member by using his or her favorite drug. One member is gone; the culture continues unchanged.

Tribal groups and sometimes entire networks of the culture of addiction experience radical transformations over time that change rituals surrounding death. In the late sixties, the polydrug users were highly integrated within a broad youth culture. Marijuana and hallucinogens dominated a scene that was attempting to spark a revolution in cultural values in the U.S. It was the time of Camelot where a new and peaceful world would be shaped out of the values of love and brotherhood. Within a few years that vision would be clouded by transformations in the youth culture itself. A distinct and increasingly destructive drug culture would emerge within the youth culture. Marijuana and hallucinogens gave way to IV use of amphetamines, barbiturates and heroin. Cultural heroes such as Janis Joplin and Jimmy Hendrix, among others, would be struck down by these new drug trends. Medical tents at rock festivals shifted from treating sunburn, cut feet, and an occasional bad trip to treating overdoses and victims of violent assault. The youth culture was burning itself out and fragmenting into a number of self-destructive subcultures. In the midst of such changes, death became more commonplace and more seductive.

When a tribal network within the culture of addiction becomes stagnant through a loss of new members and the increasing progression of addiction of old members, there comes a period in the life of the group when death is almost contagious. Without new members to sustain denial mechanisms surrounding death, the process of the group parallels the collective movement of members into the latest stages of addiction where the distinction between risk-taking and suicidal behavior is lost. When a member is lost and the reality of death strikes close to home, there is almost a desire to merge with and join the lost member. This may be one factor that contributes to the phenomenon of deaths occurring in clusters within tribal groups.

The growing transmission of HIV infection through the practice of needle sharing and unsafe sex within the culture of addiction is testing all the traditional mechanisms through which death has been managed. The growing incidence of AIDS and AIDS-related deaths in the culture first gives testament to the power of addiction. In the face of continued needle sharing, even hardened treatment veterans are struck to see the need for instantaneous contact with the drug transcend even the desire for life itself. AIDS is forcing an intensification of the death denying and death defying defenses of the addict. Unsafe needle sharing practices are sustained through collective denial, open and defiant high risk-taking or through stoic resignation and acceptance of death as one's imminent fate.

With all of the above mechanisms to deal with death, the culture provides an opportunity to reconfirm one's allegiance and commitment to "the life."

5

CORE ACTIVITIES

All cultures have key areas of activity which integrate and almost define the nature of the culture. If we speak of an agrarian culture, we can identify major activities that dominate the life of the culture, such as planting and harvesting. If we speak of a religious culture, we can identify daily and seasonal activities and rituals that define the nature of and dominate the life of this culture. This chapter explores the nature of those core activities that drive life within the culture of addiction. Particular attention is given to those activities that shape the daily lifestyle of addicts within this culture.

5.1 *The Myth of Addiction as an Escapist Lifestyle* The popular notion of addiction for the past century has portrayed the addict as one who lives a withdrawn, passive lifestyle escaping reality and responsibilities through the experience of intoxication. From the images of opium and hashish dreams to the heroin addict on the nod to hallucinogen-induced fantasia to alcoholic Nirvana, we have pictured addiction as an escapist "flight from reality." These images constitute a myth that bears little resemblance to the daily lifestyle of most addicts. Against the backdrop of these popular images, consider the following propositions.

- The addict's consuming need for drugs and the desire to avoid negative consequences related to drug use requires an active, if not aggressive, lifestyle. It is a full-time job: a career that is rigorous, demanding and stress-provoking.

- Addiction is an active rather than a passive process. The addict's body is a living clock imposing deadlines within which drug sustaining activities must be accomplished. No weekends off. No holidays. The clock never stops ticking. The fact that the business person works for money and the addict for drugs does not diminish the rigors of the latter's lifestyle.

- Addiction is not an escape from reality; it is a confrontation with reality. It thrusts one into a reality fraught with risks and challenges that would be inconceivable to one outside the life.

If addiction is an active process, then what are these activities that dominate life in the culture of addiction? For purposes of discussion, Agar's (1973) categorization of these activities will be utilized. In his ethnographic study of addiction, he observed the following core activities around which daily life for the addict was organized.

1. Hustling
2. Copping
3. Getting off
4. Avoiding busts, burns, rip-offs and hassles

5.2 *Hustling* Hustling can be defined in both broad and narrow terms. In the broadest perspective, hustling can encompass a wide range of activities in which the addict uses guile and deceit to sustain their addictive lifestyle. The term "hustling" captures the ability of the addict to manipulate every situation and interaction for his or her own gain. Most addicts experience themselves as being in a world conspiring to impose insurmountable obstacles to their continued drug use. In such a world, the goal is survival (defined as sustaining the drug relationship) and everything is fair game to achieve this goal. The characteristics we often attribute to addicts—dishonesty, manipulativeness, incapacity for intimate relationships, exploitive, high risk-taking—may not be enduring qualities of personality but an inevitable adaptation to the progression of addiction in such a world.

In the addict's world, indefinable forces (which we know to be consequences of addiction) conspire to corner and trap the addict every day. The boss who is about to confront the addict for missed days and deteriorating performance. The probability of chance encounters with persons to whom money is owed. The required assessment interview precipitated by a DUI arrest. Demands from spouse and family. A meeting with one's probation officer. The implementation of a drug screening program at one's worksite. Encounters with persons one has previously "ripped off." An employment physical. The list of obstacles and challenges is unending. Hustling in its broadest terms encompasses the art of extricating oneself from situations that pose a threat to the addictive lifestyle. The addict must be both psychologist and actor, rapidly assessing each threatening interaction and choosing the exact words and emotional tone that can manipulate the situation to their advantage and provide escape.

In a more narrow sense, "hustling" encompasses all activities used by the addict to produce drug-sustaining income. Depending on the addict and the drug of choice, this can include "straight hustles" and "street hustles."

"Straight hustles," or legitimate employment, are considered hustles because the meaning of work has been reduced completely to the need for drug supply. Work equals money equals drugs is the equation for the straight hustle. This equation may have been worked so many times that the newly recovering addicts may exhibit some disorientation in their attempt to redefine why they work. It may take some time to redefine other purposes and needs to which their income can be directed. I recall the case of a recovering cocaine addict for whom money posed such a threat to his continued abstinence that he resigned an extremely well-paying job. While family and friends were horrified by his decision, he instinctively understood that large amounts of cash were an immediate threat to his sobriety until he could redefine the money equals cocaine equation.   The employed addict during early recovery must redefine the meaning of work and money. Discussing with clients how they will spend their money is as important a step in relapse prevention as more traditional discussions concerning the client's emotional life.

The concept of straight hustles can also be extended to roles other than legitimate employment. Many addicts sustain access to income to support their addiction merely by playing a particular role. These roles may include son or daughter, spouse or intimate partner, or parent. Through the process of addiction, other meanings and needs attached to these relationships are lost. They are reduced to the drug supply equation. The marital and intimate relationships of many addicts, both men and women, have been reduced to this drug supply equation by their addiction. Consider the words of Mary, a bright and articulate middle-aged woman, who while in alcoholism treated shared the following observation when asked about her relationship with her husband.

I don't know him and I don't even know if I like him. For our whole marriage, he provided safety and shelter and I guess, most

*importantly, booze. He was always there as a cushion. It's like
I had a blank check to drink myself to death. You know, I was
pretty shocked and snooty yesterday when Ellen and Rene were
talking about prostitution in group. Later I found myself crying
in my room because I realized I felt like a whore. I'm no
different than them. I slept with a man and kept his house and
played his wife in exchange for booze. I can't even picture our
relationship with me not drinking. Will I even need him or want
him if I'm sober?*

Mary's pain and confusion came through the realization that her
marriage had become a straight hustle. Through treatment and
recovery, such relationships are either redefined or, failing to
achieve such redefinition, terminated. The role of treatment in
assisting clients to identify the value of money and people, separate
from the historical issue of drug supply, is a critical one.

The nature and intensity of an addict's involvement in "street
hustles"—criminal activity utilized to sustain drug supply—depend
on geographical location, the addict's drug of choice, the pre-
addictive personality of the addict, and the unique aptitudes of the
addict for various criminal activities.

Street hustling is to a great degree a reflection of social policy
toward psychoactive drugs. While addiction to celebrated drugs
(alcohol) may precipitate criminal behavior due to drug impairment, an intensive involvement in street hustling is rarely required
to sustain supplies of these drugs due to their high availability and
relatively low cost. However, prohibited drugs, particularly those
which are highly addictive (heroin, cocaine), are highly associated
with street hustling. Due to the high price and limited availability
of these latter drugs, there is a marriage between the culture of
addiction and the culture of crime.

Understanding the social designation of various psychoactive drugs is important for understanding the drug-crime relationship. The popular view of this relationship is that an individual becomes drug involved and out of the progression of his or her drug dependence is forced to initiate criminal activity. This view may apply to many, but not all, alcoholics. Both epidemiology and clinical experience validate the notion that many alcoholics, with no pre-addictive criminal histories, will exhibit alcohol-induced criminal behavior. For such persons, criminality emerges out of the progression of alcoholism. In contrast to the above, there is substantial evidence to suggest that criminality in many heroin addicts preceded the onset of addiction. In Finestone's (1957) early ethnographic study of heroin addiction, he found that most addicts had established hustles prior to the onset of heroin addiction. Heroin did not produce street hustling behavior. The street hustling behavior provided the means to incorporate heroin into a lifestyle already characterized by high risk-taking behavior. The subsequent addiction to heroin only altered the intensity and frequency of hustling behavior.

Understanding that there are variations in this drug crime relationship has important clinical implications. Presented with a client deeply involved in street hustles, it is critical to understand whether such criminality is directly precipitated through addiction or whether the criminality has an independent existence separate from the client's addiction. Eliminating addiction in the former will in all likelihood eliminate criminal behavior. Eliminating addiction in the latter, without addressing broader personality issues, may create a more competent and efficient criminal predator.

There is an infinite variety of street hustles. The more notable, such as shoplifting, selling drugs, burglary, robbery, prostitution, "Murphy games," running numbers, selling "hot" goods, credit card scams, forgery, and a wide assortment of confidence games, have been frequently reported by clients and episodically catalogued in the addiction literature. For purposes of this study, it is more important that the reader understand the dynamics of hustling behavior than the detailed variations in hustling games. There are four important principles related to hustling behavior that have important implications to the intervention and treatment strategies that will be discussed later.

Principle One: Hustling behavior, as a major activity within the addictive lifestyle, constitutes a rigorous and demanding vocation, that not only assures continued access to drugs, but also meets a number of other significant needs of the addict.

This first principle is crucial to understanding and treating the pattern of opiate addiction most prevalent in the United States. Waldorf (1973), conceptualizing addiction as a career choice, decries the sparsity of alternative career paths in the urban ghetto. Finestone (1957) describes the desire of inner-city youth to transcend their bleak environment through search for a "kick." He defines a "kick" as "any act tabooed by 'squares' that heightens and intensifies the present moment of experience and differentiates it as much as possible from the humdrum routine of daily life." Prebble and Casey (1969) provide an equally lucid description of this broadened understanding of addiction:

> ...the quest for heroin is the quest for a meaningful life, not an escape from life. And that meaning does not lie, primarily, in the effects of the drug on their minds and bodies; it lies in the gratification of accomplishing a series of challenging, exciting tasks every day of the week.

Heroin and other addictive drugs provide structure and meaning to life. Addiction organizes daily life and reduces existence to a level of concrete need that must be responded to—the body's insatiable appetite for drugs. If this appetite is quelled through treatment, then what will now serve to provide structure and meaning in these clients lives? What alternative career or lifestyle or meaning in life do we offer as the pathway out of addiction? Lacking such alternatives, addiction can and often does again fill the void.

Principle Two: Hustling in the addictive lifestyle depersonalizes human relationships and defines money and physical possessions as chits of exchange for drug supplies.

As noted in our earlier discussion of both straight hustles and street hustles, the addict's world is made up of two groups of people—those who will willfully or through manipulation assist in the maintenance of addiction and those who pose obstacles to continuing drug use. Addiction turns both groups into objects to be exploited or avoided. Addicted clients often require assistance in developing a new framework to both perceive and enter into human relationships. They also need assistance in redefining the value of money in other than drug supply terms.

Principle Three: Hustling does not take place in isolation but within a world of other hustlers and players. To give up hustling is to give up the identity and status one has achieved in this world.

Treatment professionals, drawn mostly from the mainstream of society, perhaps inevitably view hustling behavior in particularly negative terms. We see such behavior as painful consequences forced upon the client because of addiction and are often blind to needs, other than money, that the client meets through hustling behavior. For some clients, their skill and reputation as a hustler may be the most significant status and recognition they have ever achieved. What alternative sustained experiences of achievement do we offer such clients? How does the newly recovering addict achieve the sense of identity and status and belonging that he or she may be forsaking as they cut themselves off from the culture of addiction? Most clients' efforts at treatment are initiated with a short trial and error design—I'll try it on and see how it feels; if I can't handle it, I can always go back. It is a crisis-induced experiment to venture outside the culture, perhaps to discover a niche for oneself in the straight world. Failing to find such a niche, they will be inevitably pulled back to the life. Our job as helping professionals is first to extend the time periods of such experiments and secondly to influence the outcomes.

Principle Four: Identifying the particular skills required for a client's hustles may provide clues to the transfer of such skills to a legitimate career path.

Nearly two decades ago, I was interviewing one of the first heroin addicts I had ever counseled in a residential setting. This particular client had been extensively involved in the opiate culture for more than ten years and had minimal education and no legitimate work history. He had, in fact, supported a very comfortable lifestyle during these years by selling drugs. I opened this particular interview with the comment that we needed to talk about the kind of work John could do when he was discharged. Looking me straight in the eyes, he deadpanned the comment, "I have an extensive background in sales." Following the outburst of laughter from both of us, I reverted to my straight role and naively prepared a vocational plan for John which, if successful, would result in his earning in one month what he often took in from drug sales in one day. Plans such as the one I prepared for John may comply with any number of regulatory requirements governing treatment agencies, but they have no relationship to the realities from which John came or to which he would return. Who knows, if I had taken John's comment seriously, he might own a whole chain of car lots today.

By understanding the nature of a client's hustling behavior, counselors may be able to isolate and extract areas of knowledge and skill that can be transferred to a legitimate career, or at least a legitimate transitional role that can be held until other vocational aptitudes can be developed. Rather than negate all of the hustling skills which the client brings to treatment from his/her experience with addiction, we may wish to validate and shift the focus of such skills.

5.3 *Copping* Copping—the planning, procuring, and protection of one's drug supply—is the second core activity within the culture of addiction.

As the person-drug relationship intensifies, there is a growing preoccupation with drug supply. There is more time spent thinking about the drug, worrying about the adequacy of one's drug supply, and fantasizing about huge quantities of the drug.

In spite of such preoccupation, there are unplanned episodes of loss of supply, often resulting from a misperception of the pace at which the drug is being consumed. The sudden realization that one's drug supply is depleted and not immediately accessible engenders panic and compulsive drug-seeking behavior. The phenomenon of the nicotine addict, suddenly realizing he has smoked his last cigarette, frantically searching through clothing and furniture and vehicles offers a convincing image of such intense drug-seeking behavior. The image of this same person fishing cigarette butts out of the waste basket and smoking them is dynamically parallel to the heroin addict who, finding himself in a similar position, strains minuscule amounts of heroin from used cottons. Surreptitious use also leads to hiding drug supplies, often while intoxicated, and later failures to remember where such drugs were concealed. The tragic caricature of the addict storming through her home unable to find the drugs she knows are concealed there offers an additional image of this panic over drug supply.

It doesn't take too many episodes of such panic to stimulate hoarding behavior. The "pack a day" nicotine addict always carries an extra pack. The amount of alcohol required for regular home consumption or a party is always overestimated. Similar hoarding behavior can be seen with prohibited drugs, although the cost of such substances often makes hoarding less possible for many users.

The actual mechanics of procuring drugs is dictated primarily by the social status of one's drug of choice. The open and acceptable purchase of celebrated and tolerated drugs makes access and hoarding of these drugs a matter of ease. Access to instrumental drugs, on the other hand, requires more sophistication and skill in the manipulation of medical professionals. Here the hustling equals money equals drugs equation is often reduced to hustling equals drugs. The rituals to procure drugs are themselves hustles. With prohibited drugs, it is the need for reliable drug supplies that most ties the addict to the culture of addiction. Within the prohibited drug tribes, rituals of procurement are extremely elaborate and most accessible to those most deeply enmeshed in the culture. This phenomenon, in and of itself, pulls the addict deeper into the life.

It important that treatment professionals understand the nuances of such copping rituals within the culture of addiction. First, such knowledge offers a vehicle for assessing the frequency and intensity of a client's drug seeking behavior and thus the progression of his or her addiction. Secondly, many clients will bring drug seeking behaviors with them into treatment. Third, and perhaps most important, there are important issues related to copping behavior that if ignored constitute an obstacle to the client's treatment. Regarding the latter, some of the most frequent questions we fail to ask clients entering treatment include the following.

- Did you bring any drugs of any kind in with you?
- Do you still have supplies of drugs in your home or at other locations? (If so, an issue in treatment is: What do you intend to do with them?)
- Do you currently owe anyone money for drugs or related hustles? If so, are they looking for you?
- Which individuals are most likely to bring you drugs while in treatment?
- Have you been involved in drug transactions (buying or selling) with any other clients currently in treatment?

5.4 *Getting Off* Getting off—the ritual of drug ingestion and the experience of drug intoxication—is the third core activity within the culture of addiction. It is this activity which drives all other activities and rituals within the culture of addiction.

The periods of initial and regular substance use almost always occur in a social context. It is then an interesting irony, given our emphasis on social and cultural influences, that the experience of getting off, for many, becomes an increasingly solitary activity in late stages of addiction. This shift reflects the physiological transformation that occurs with most drugs of abuse. No matter what etiological pathways initiate use, in the later stages of addiction, issues of physiology—the drug relationship at the cellular level—begin to dominate all other factors in shaping the addiction experience. The social context of use is the courtship leading to the marriage between the drug and the human body.

The repetitive and compulsive consumption of psychoactive drugs is founded on a special magic between the drug and the user. This magic from its earliest stages may differ from user to user. It may be the magic of physical ecstasy. It may be the magic of risk. It may be the magic of emotional tranquility. It may be the magic of acceptance from the social context. Whatever the source of such magic, it leaves an indelible imprint. It is the imprint of this magic to which the user seeks to return again and again. Even though social contexts change, risk taking needs escalate, and euphoria becomes fleeting and unpredictable, the obsession to recapture the imprinted magic drives continued use. Dying alcoholics and addicts can still, even in their sickness, bring forth euphoric recall of that special magic.

The deeply imprinted memory of this magic, once established, lies forever like a sleeping giant within the psyche of the addict—a tinderbox that can ignite with unquenchable fire. An essential element of successful addiction treatment is understanding the nature of this magic for each client. Treatment to a great extent consists of teaching each client how to live his or her life so as not to disturb this sleeping giant and how, if aroused, how to put this giant back to sleep.

There is in the culture of addiction a competition for the most supreme drug experience. One learns to seek out the highest high, to create the most exotic experiences while intoxicated. There is pressure to act and use in excess. The outrageous and bizarre are highly valued. This competitive celebration of excess pushes risk-taking behavior to extreme limits and initiates the addict's beginning courtship with death. Perhaps nothing illustrates this competitive zeal for the highest high more than the response to a "hot shot" within the community of heroin users. A "hot shot" is an heroin overdose, death having been allegedly caused by heroin of uncharacteristic strength and purity. When the news of the "hot shot" spreads, it sparks an intense inquiry into the source (dealer) of the heroin involved. Such inquiries occur not out of desire to avoid the heroin supply but out of a desire to find heroin of such potency. That's right. Demand for a dealer's product may increase rather than decrease following the heroin overdose of one of his or her customers.

5.5   *Avoiding Busts, Burns, Ripoffs and Hassles*   Hustling, copping, and getting off are all fraught with roadblocks and hazards. The final category of core activities within the culture of addiction includes a wide assortment of protective behaviors designed to avoid these hazards.

Forces from outside and within the culture of addiction pose obstacles to the addictive career. The most dominant threat looming from outside the culture is that of the bust—one's arrest for alcohol/drug-related activities. Within the prohibited drug tribes, this event takes on enormous significance by fueling individual paranoia and driving tribal life into greater closure and secrecy. It is the social policy prohibiting these drugs and the omnipresent threat of arrest that creates a much more deviant career path for the heroin addict than for the alcoholic.

For the heroin addict, the very status of addiction is a crime. Addiction by definition requires both possession of the drug and possession or access to a set of "works" (hypodermic syringe or other injection paraphernalia). The daily challenge is to "score" one's drug supply and use it within an elaborate social context of "cops and robbers." The addict wins the game each day if he or she is able to sustain drug supply and drug use while avoiding apprehension.

There are also threats imposed from within the culture of addiction. While we have depicted the culture of addiction as organized around a set of deviant values and closed off from the society at large, each addict within this culture is essentially alone. Honor among addicts is rare. It is a culture marked by an "every person for himself or herself" mentality and morality. Loyalty to one's own addiction is the driving value and all other persons and considerations are sacrificed to that reality. It is a predatory and cannibalistic culture.

In the prohibited drug tribes, the addict must constantly be on guard against "burns" and "ripoffs."

Burns are drug transactions in which addicts themselves become the victims of a hustle. The burn can involve an addict giving money to a dealer with the agreement to pick the drug up at a designated location. When he or she arrives at the location, there is no dealer and no drugs. The addict has been burned for his or her money. Other burns revolve around the misrepresentation or adulteration of purchased drugs. The drugs purchased may contain only inert substances, may contain only a small quantity of the desired drug, or may contain psychoactive substances other than the desired drug.

Ripoffs encompass a variety of events in which the addict is forcefully deprived of either money or drugs by other addicts or street hustlers. The addict dealer is particularly subject to such ripoffs given the quantity of drugs and money he or she usually possesses. While the need for the addict to maintain a relationship with the dealer as a source of future supply works to diminish this threat, there are times when this consideration is ignored. The author can recall a period in one community when a subculture of IV amphetamine addicts were repeatedly ripping each other off for drugs and money. Within this particular subculture, the drug-induced paranoia and increased incidence of violence made the sawed off shotgun as much a symbol of this culture as the hypodermic syringe.

Hassles constitute any event which poses an obstacle to the addict's routine rituals of hustling, copping and getting off.

5.6 *Core Activities and Personality Adaptation* In the earlier discussion of hustling the notion was introduced that many of the personality characteristics associated with the addict are not enduring traits, but adaptations to the realities confronted in the addictive lifestyle. This chapter on core activities within the culture of addiction will conclude with an exploration of how the conduct of these activities over time begins to shape a set of predictable personality adaptations. Colin Wilson (1956), in his classic study, *The Outsider*, made the following observation about personality adaptation within deviant subcultures.

> *Then I came to realize that men build themselves personalities as they build houses—to protect themselves from the world. But once they have built a house, they are forced to live in it. They become its prisoners.*

The remainder of this chapter explores the nature of the house in which the addict is imprisoned. It examines several core personality traits and the extent to which such traits are induced or magnified by life within the culture of addiction.

Paranoia Addicts who believe people may be watching them and that forces in their environment are conspiring against them are not experiencing delusions but an accurate perception of reality. Paranoia is a natural and protective adaptation emerging out of the progression of addiction. It is a style of perceiving the self-world relationship learned within the culture of addiction.

Depression The addiction literature abounds with references to the incidence of depression in addicts. While there are undoubtedly some addicts who initiated a pattern of drug use to alleviate this condition, depression for many addicts is a consequence of, not a stimulus for, the addictive lifestyle. Depression is an inevitable consequence of both biochemical changes that occur in addiction and the real losses experienced through the progression of addiction. Nearly all drugs of abuse induce chronic depletion of both endorphins and catecholamines, a process that often produces endogenous depression. The depression of the addicted client entering treatment is also a normal reaction to real life losses and the earliest stages of grief and mourning related to the loss of the drug relationship. The danger (via relapse) is that the culture of addiction has a consistently proscribed method of treatment for such depression—self-medication with psychoactive drugs.

Narcissism The addict is consistently, and appropriately, described as being self-centered. Whether such narcissism predates the onset of addiction is a matter of debate. What is not debatable is that the addict's physical relationship with the drug will begin to dominate all other relationships and concerns. This is both a physiological and psychodynamic consequence of addiction and a value learned through participation in a culture which worships self-gratification. One's natural empathy, altruism and other-directedness are quickly extinguished in the culture of addiction and replaced with values that affirm self-centeredness and grandiosity. To expect anything other than such an orientation is to fail to grasp the very essence of the addictive lifestyle.

Intimacy The addict is consistently characterized as one who is incapable of initiating or sustaining intimate relationships with others. The addict who maintains such capability does so in defiance of cultural norms which place great value on coldness, cunning and emotional detachment. What as professional helpers we would describe as openness for emotional and interpersonal exploration, the culture of addiction would describe as vulnerability and stupidity. The values of the culture of addiction become self-prophetic on this point. The addict who is open and vulnerable is quickly victimized in a world of users and hustlers. To ask the addict entering treatment to experience trust, to care for peers in treatment, and to disclose areas of emotional pain is asking the addict to defy some of the most sacred norms within the culture of addiction.

Manipulation For the addict to manipulate social situations to his or her advantage is as natural as breathing. For most, the daily existence of their drug relationship hinged on this ability. For most, it was these very skills that achieved respect and status within the culture of addiction. Such manipulation may or may not reflect the premorbid personality characteristic of the addict. It is unquestionably a culturally approved behavior without which most addicts could not sustain their addiction.

Risk-taking Risk-taking behavior is highly valued and rewarded among most tribal groups within the culture of addiction. The intensity of risk-taking behavior often parallels the intensity and progression of drug involvement. Such risk-taking thus becomes a set of learned behaviors that are increasingly necessary to sustain addiction. The movement from a high risk-taking to a low risk-taking lifestyle may be one of the greatest transformations we are asking the recovering client to make. For some, relapse may be triggered by their experience of the drug-free lifestyle as boring and devoid of either excitement or enjoyment.

Authority Folk wisdom in the addiction field is replete with observations that addicts have problems with authority. For some, such defiance may serve as the primary initiating factor in their involvement with a deviant, drug using subculture, while for others this may be an acquired, learned behavior within the addictive culture. The culture of addiction holds almost all authority up for ridicule and disdain. One's willingness to test and cross boundaries established by authority is the very essence of one's experience as an "outsider." Authority symbolizes every force in the world that has posed an obstacle to continued drug use. It should not be surprising that the treatment professional is viewed within this rubric of authority along with parents, police and employers.

Morality Addicts are often depicted as amoral human beings devoid of compassion and conscience in their interaction with others. Addicts are often described as having a striking incapacity for shame or guilt related to their predatory and anti-social behavior. As with the other characteristics, there is debate over whether the impairment of moral values precedes or is a consequence of the addictive lifestyle. It is my experience that it can be either, although I believe the vast majority of addicts experience a transformation in morals as their addiction progresses. It is easy to be moral when one's needs are met. Addiction superimposes both an intoxication-induced impairment in moral judgment and the cellular demand for drugs which often supersedes personal morality. Expediency in the service of addiction replaces personal morality.

Most of the personality characteristics listed above have been identified as part of the psychopathology of drug addiction. They have been characterized as part of the constellation of traits that make up the "addictive personality" and predispose one to alcohol and drug dependence. It is my view that such observations are based on descriptive studies of addicts that examine addiction in isolation from its social and cultural context. Many of the personality traits associated with addiction may not be permanent traits of personality but rather traits of the social pathology of a deviant subculture. For many, these traits can more accurately be described as adaptations and defenses necessary to sustain oneself as an addict within the culture of addiction.

6

KEY CULTURAL ROLES

Societies evolve key roles that promote stability and sustain cultural values as well as perform activities crucial to the society's continued existence. The society of addicts, here referred to as the culture of addiction, has evolved roles in a similar manner. This chapter explores some of the roles which affect the styles with which addicts present themselves for treatment and other roles which often serve to sabotage treatment efforts by culturally enmeshed addicts.

6.1 *The Dealers* Dealers play a central role in the culture of addiction by providing a consistent source of drug supplies for cultural members. There is a complex organizational structure and hierarchy governing dealing for both the licit and illicit drugs. The role of dealers in the illicit culture has been extensively studied by Blum (1972) in his classic work, *The Dream Sellers*, and is recommended to readers wanting a more in-depth understanding of this area. The work of Blum and others explodes the myth of the dealer's role in aggressively initiating non-users into drug use for the financial gain of the dealer. The fact is that most users are initiated into drug use in social situations with friends in which there are no financial transactions involved. The dealer's role begins only after the neophyte user desires to maintain his or her own drug supply. There is such a high demand for the products of the dealer that the idea of "pushing" drugs is probably a misnomer.

Many dealers are also addicts, particularly those at the lowest levels of drug distribution. As addicts, many of these dealers may eventually present themselves for treatment due to arrest or other consequences related to their addiction. An important treatment dynamic often overlooked is the fact that the dealer addict may have reinforcers holding them in the culture of addiction other than their drug relationship. A minority of addict dealers will be wedded to the culture because of the large amount of profit from dealing and the comfortable lifestyle such a role provides them. Most addict dealers do not make large profits, but may be particularly enamored of the power and status achieved by the dealer role. They quite simply deal not only to support their own addiction, but to pursue an activity which they enjoy and which brings them a great sense of identity and esteem. Some may have a more difficult time letting go of the dealer role than letting go of their addiction to drugs.

A major treatment issue for addict dealers is how to convert the illicit role of dealing into a legitimate, and equally rewarding, vocational role in the recovery process.

Treatment professionals can facilitate this process if they can set aside their moral judgement about dealing, and examine this role in terms of its skill components and how such skills can be transferred to alternative career paths. Casanave (1980) conducted a fascinating study of the transformation of such career paths within the early days of the Illinois Drug Abuse Program (IDAP). In the early days of this state program, thousands of heroin addicts were engaged in a broad range of treatment modalities. As the program grew, large numbers of recovering addicts assumed responsibilities and roles at all levels within this program.

Casanave studied a comparison between the roles which these recovering addicts held within IDAP and the roles which they had held within the culture of addiction. What she found was a direct transfer of status and roles from the illicit drug culture to one's status and role within IDAP. Those persons drawn into treatment from the highest ranks of the addict dealers who successfully recovered went on to assume the highest staff positions within the treatment programs of IDAP. The concept of skill transfer was well illustrated by the fact that the best predictor of one's role in recovery was one's role while addicted.

6.2 *The High Priests* High priests are the champions of drug consumption. High priests articulate specific values of drug use and values of the drug culture. In contrast to the dealer, high priests derive special pleasure in introducing neophytes to drug use. They view such initiation as a conversion experience and work passionately to recruit new converts. Timothy Leary is probably the most nationally visible high priest over the last half century. In his lectures, writings, and films, he championed the "Tune In, Turn On, Drop Out" philosophy of the psychedelic era. He promoted LSD as a sacrament and "tripping" as a religious experience. Less notable and famous high priests can be found within most tribes in the culture of addiction. Functions performed by the high priests within the culture of addiction include:

- recruiting and indoctrinating new members
- providing addicts with philosophical, political or religious rationalizations to support drug use
- identifying or creating outside enemies in order to sustain the closure and cohesiveness of the culture
- re-instilling faith in wavering members in the life

High priests have a fairly high casualty rate. Their visibility makes them high risk for arrest. Their excessive drug use often begins to produce a deterioration in their functioning. The passion of many high priests is sometimes fueled by personality disturbances that may culminate in a drug-induced suicide (committed psychodynamically as an act of self-induced martyrdom). High priests periodically end up in treatment programs.

High priests are not usually responsive to treatment until their addiction, in later stages, produces serious impairment in functioning including their ability to perform their role of high priest within the culture. In earlier stages, high priests usually present in treatment with an elaborate structure of rationalizations and political and philosophical underpinnings for their drug use. Their presence in treatment due to arrest merely adds weight and intensity to their prolonged monologues on their role as victim and martyr within an oppressive system. This cognitive structure is extremely difficult to penetrate. Early stage treatment of high priests often does little to impact drug-using behavior in spite of the effort given and frustration experienced by the treatment staff. The high priest in early stages of addiction may pose a major threat and source of disruption to any residential treatment milieu.

High priests are skilled. They are generally quite intelligent, articulate and, in many cases, personally charismatic. They are particularly skilled in the art of verbal persuasion and often have reasonably good skills in interpersonal support. They often possess both leadership and organizational skills. It is perhaps ironic that the high priests, who are so skilled in converting others, are themselves susceptible to conversion experiences in late stages of addiction. A number of these individuals have experienced such a conversion in values and gone on to become leaders within the recovering community. They move from the role of high priest within the culture of addiction to the role of high priest within the culture of recovery.

6.3 *The Story Tellers* Story tellers are the oral historians of the culture of addiction. They are addicts who have a knack for telling and embellishing stories of real and mythical events within the culture. The stories are a medium of socialization for new addicts and usually convey important cultural values through the mediums of folklore and humor. The story teller's role in the culture may transcend the time span of his or her own addiction. I have seen such individuals, too old to "cut the mustard" in the lifestyle of opiate addiction, sitting on a porch step drinking wine while weaving colorful stories to young addicts about their glory days of "rippin' and runnin.'" Story tellers can be found in any bar frequented by middle and late stage alcoholics. The story teller provides an important pastime that enriches the shared intoxication of cultural members.

Story telling is a skill that, when mastered, assures one's social status. Much of the esteem of the story teller comes from the desire of others to seek them out for conversation and inclusion in social activities. The skills of the story teller provide a pathway of esteem both in treatment and long-term recovery. Some of the most popular and sought after speakers at AA and NA meetings earlier in their lives performed the role of story tellers in the culture of addiction. Those same skills, and the social acceptance achieved by those skills, help sustain their involvement in the culture of recovery. Our task is not to treat only the story teller's addiction, but to help transfer his or her unique skills into a similar role in support of recovery.

6.4 *The Medicine Men/Midwives* Medicine men and midwives practice folk medicine within the culture of addiction. They know how to treat hangovers. They know how to treat overdoses. They have folk remedies for infections and needle abscesses. They are sort of a walking *Physician's Desk Reference* for illicit drugs. They have remedies for the heroin addict's constipation and the alcoholic's diarrhea. They are often the first point of consultation for the addict experiencing any physical problems. Some can even support their own addiction from these skills. It is the medicine men and midwives that often run the "shooting galleries" frequented by urban heroin addicts. It is not just that they offer a safe house and drug paraphernalia for drug use in exchange for money or drugs. The safety comes with the knowledge that these individuals possess enough knowledge of folk medicine to provide assistance if some untoward drug reaction should occur. Some such medicine men and midwives have developed special reputations for their ability to inject addicts with burned out veins. The ability of many of these individuals to find and hit a vein with a hypodermic needle will equal, if not surpass, the abilities of their legitimate medical counterparts.

Medicine men and midwives can enter treatment due to the same problems and consequences experienced by other addicts. They often pose a threat to treatment personnel due to their close scrutiny of medical and treatment protocol, their obvious sophistication about illicit drugs, and their proclivity for continuing to offer advice and counsel to other clients in treatment. It is important for treatment professionals to recognize that separate from their addiction, these individuals performed a role from which they derived a great deal of status and personal satisfaction. This role can be reinforced and transformed into a pathway to recovery rather than confronted as inappropriate treatment behavior. To confront, deny access to, and impugn this role is to strip the client of self-esteem and drive them back into the culture which values them. The treatment of medicine men and midwives from the culture of addiction can be greatly enhanced when their skills are acknowledged and guided into an alternative career path within the culture of recovery. The roots of many recovering persons in the addiction treatment field can be traced to their early roles as medicine men and midwives in the culture of addiction.

6.5 *The Jailhouse Lawyers* Jailhouse lawyers are addicts who
have developed a special knowledge of law and who have special
concerns about procedural rights, due process, and the appropriate
or inappropriateness of all procedures to which they find themselves subjected. Most of these skills emerged from their own
experiences with arrest and/or incarceration or through the
discovery that such concerns quickly placed representatives of
"straight" society in a highly defensive position. Within the culture
of addiction, such skills are highly valued and provide the
jailhouse lawyers with identity, esteem and social acceptance.
Many jailhouse lawyers use their skills at manipulating the letter
of the law to sustain their addiction through suits, grievances, and
regulatory appeals. Their addiction may be supported by accident
settlements, wrongful injury suits, or disability claims.

Many jailhouse lawyers are highly institutionalized, even though
the source of such institutionalization may vary from the criminal
justice system or psychiatric or addiction treatment settings, to
systems of outside financial support. Their primary identity may
lie not within the culture of addiction itself, but within societal
institutions that contain addicts. A major barrier to their treatment
is a lack of identity outside of their adversarial relationship with
institutions. Relapse is often precipitated by crises in self-esteem.
Facing such a crisis, jailhouse lawyers will exhibit behaviors which
will bring them back into the criminal justice or treatment system
where they can once again activate their skills.

The jailhouse lawyer is a nightmare to treatment professionals.
One treatment program director, describing her experience with an
addicted jailhouse lawyer, reported that it was like having a Joint
Commission on Accreditation of Hospitals survey team living in
your program for 30 days. The client presented scathing indict-
ments of the program on a daily basis, constantly requested
changes in counselors, filed numerous grievances, regularly wrote

letters to the agency's board of directors, presented an unending list of special needs, and episodically threatened to sue everyone associated with the program. The pathway to recovery for the jailhouse lawyer takes one of two pathways. The first, like the other roles we have described, involves transferring skills from the illegitimate role to a socially acceptable role outside the culture of addiction. Such a transfer may be necessary to sustain the esteem of many jailhouse lawyers through the early recovery process. The key is to shift the use of such skills for oneself to use of the skills to assist others. Some of these clients have sustained themselves through early recovery working as volunteers or as staff in client advocacy programs dealing with youth, the aged, the homeless, or Vietnam veterans. A critical component of such a transfer of skills is the ability of the client to let go of the jailhouse lawyer role to the extent that he or she can actually experience treatment, rather than continue to use this skill as a diversion from treatment. A second pathway, usually available only in long-term residential treatment, is to strip the client of this defensive style and rebuild an identity and interpersonal style congruent with a non-institutionalized lifestyle.

6.6 *The Ambassadors* Ambassadors are addicts that hold affiliation with numerous tribal groups within the culture of addiction. They have high needs for social approval and may maintain superficial relationships with hundreds of other addicts. Their addiction is often initiated and sustained over time by the need for peer acceptance and affiliation. Unlike the story tellers who are prized for their verbal skills, ambassadors are prized for their listening skills and their value as sources of information. The ambassador is a walking news report of what's happening everywhere. They are the illicit counterpart to the evening news, the newspaper and the yellow pages. Ambassadors are highly valued by the police and, once known, are subject to intense police pressure to serve as informers.

Ambassadors in treatment perform the same role as on the streets. They will establish contact with every other client and every staff member and can tell you at any point in time what is going on with each person as well the client or staff groups as a whole. Their high need for social support tends to dictate their course of treatment. Whether a particular client group is well motivated or poorly motivated for treatment, the ambassador will adapt a style compliant with the majority or with whatever subgroup he or she happens to be in at any point in time. The personality and interpersonal style of the ambassadors tend to be fairly fixed and are not amenable to enduring change through short term treatment experiences. The key to long-term recovery lies not in immediate changes in personality but changes in the social network within which the ambassador can experience identity and acceptance.

Those ambassadors who have experienced some pain and conse-quences from their involvement in the culture of addiction show a remarkably good prognosis when their affiliation is shifted to an active and large recovery network. While involved in a recovery process that will eventually lead to a strengthening of identity and self-esteem, they are still able to perform their role of ambassador moving within the different tribes of the recovery network.

6.7 *The Gangsters* Historically, the culture of addiction posed risks for its users, but mostly of a non-violent nature. Violence has always been more associated with the alcohol tribes. In the illicit culture of addiction where guile and deceit were highly valued, brute force was viewed as a sign of ineptitude. With the exception of hustling roles that called for violence or the threat of violence, *e.g.*, as a method of control by the pimp or to save one's reputation when ripped off, addicts usually eschewed the use of violence. In the past several decades, larger numbers of new types of addicts have emerged that bring a particular penchant for violent behavior. The prototype of this new addict is the gangster—the individual who presents both a pattern of addiction and a pattern of planned and unplanned violence that is unrelated to the addiction. The gangster is a reflection of the destabilization of the illicit drug market, competition for this market between groups of organized criminals and an increased number of independent, unaffiliated dealers at the street level. Perhaps it is not so much that new types of persons are coming into the existing drug culture as it is that the drug culture has permeated outward to encompass a larger segment of the criminal subculture.

Gangsters constitute a type of client that has not been traditionally seen in addiction treatment programs. The gangster will usually resist access to treatment even when such treatment is an alternative to incarceration. The preference for jail constitutes one more step in building the gangster's reputation. Lawyers attempting to defend such individuals for criminal acts are increasingly calling on the defense of drug impairment and calling upon treatment professionals to assess these individuals. The current substance abuse service system has only limited assessment technology and treatment technology appropriate for these clients.

6.8 *The Non-addicted Hustlers* There are large numbers of alcohol and drug using, but non-addicted, hustlers who operate in and out of the social world of addiction. They are part of the panorama of the addict's world, but are neither addicted nor enmeshed in the culture of addiction. They were involved in a criminal lifestyle long before the initiation of their alcohol/drug use and the nature or frequency of their criminal activity has no relationship with their alcohol or drug consumption. Addicts most frequently interact with these individuals as part of their own hustling behavior.

With prisons overcrowded and the growing judicial acceptance of addict diversion into treatment, an increased number of non-addicted hustlers are fabricating addictive histories to escape incarceration. Such individuals present a particular dilemma to treatment programs. When initially assessed to determine their eligibility for diversion into treatment, these individuals grossly exaggerate the extent of their alcohol and drug use and its consequences. When found eligible for diversion and referred to treatment (usually residential), they begin to minimize the extent of their problem and present elaborate arguments for their referral to outpatient services or simple participation in self-help groups. When such efforts fail, these individuals take on enough play-acting behaviors to comply with treatment as if they were "doing time," often continuing their criminal activity while in treatment. The inclusion of non-addicted hustlers in treatment not only violates the integrity of the treatment process but also seriously damages the reputation of treatment agencies in the eyes of the criminal justice system.

6.9 *The Addict with Money and Fame* There exists a self-identi-fied elite within the culture of addiction. These individuals because of money, fame or professional status set themselves above other addicts, and yet in later stages of addiction, are drawn toward the larger membership of the culture of addiction. It is at this point that a unique symbiotic relationship begins. The "slumming" behavior of the elite confirms their superiority, allows them to deny their status of addiction, and allows them to feel a sense of esteem they can no longer feel in the presence of their more usual social peers. In exchange for such benefits, cultural members are provided access to money or free drugs and perhaps also some validation for their own addictive lifestyle.

Money, fame and professional status can all serve as a major obstacle to recovery for the elite. These very characteristics often serve as a powerful buffer preventing these individuals from experiencing the consequences of their addiction. Money, fame and position can provide unlimited supplies of drugs and a social network, to say nothing of lawyers, physicians and other professional rescuers, that prevents the elite addicts from "hitting bottom." By the time they reach treatment, they are often in later stages of addiction than their less blessed counterparts and present an elaborate armor of defenses that must be gently but consistently stripped for them to begin the addiction recovery process.

6.10 *The Working Class Addicts* The working class addicts make up the majority of the addicted population. The pathway for each into the culture constitutes a personal and unique story. They perform no specialized roles or hold no special status in the culture. They are the citizens in a society of addicts. They create relationships with each other, share common values, and a common language all reflective of the common bond of addiction. They do what most working stiffs do—struggle each day to get by and make the best of their life, the only difference is that getting by for them hinges on maintaining their relationship with powerful psychoactive drugs.

6.11 *The Weekend Players* Weekend players are individuals who episodically abuse alcohol and drugs, often with minimal consequences, but who have a particular affinity and fascination for life in the culture of addiction. Earlier described as bicultural addicts, the forays of these individuals into the culture of addiction constitute not a lifestyle but a recreational activity and an exciting diversion from an otherwise straight lifestyle. Depending on the drug choices involved in such forays, such diversions can provide an entryway into a more full time commitment to addiction.

Contrary to most popular writing on addiction, there are a number of such weekend players who continue to episodically use these psychoactive substances over an extended number of years without experiencing either addiction or serious consequences related to use. That such episodic use can include heroin and cocaine (by intranasal ingestion) clearly violates popular folk wisdom about the power of these drugs. There has been in fact a powerful "no-talk" rule and taboo about openly acknowledging the existence of such persons. To state that such users exist is to open oneself up to charges of promoting drug use.

Zinberg (1982) is one of the few researchers who has studied this population. He notes that such persons, from the beginning of their use, have established non-negotiable standards governing acceptable and unacceptable drug choices, control over drug quality and dosage, method of drug administration, and frequency of use. Persons who fail to set and keep such standards because of their physiological or psychological vulnerability to addiction are inevitably drawn into the web of addiction.

Both the small population of controlled users and the early stage bicultural addicts play an important role to the culture of addiction. The presence of such persons entering the culture from the straight world both legitimizes the addict's lifestyle choice and helps maintain an illusion of control over drug consumption. The dynamics should be familiar to any nicotine addict. As a chronically relapsing smoker through much of my early adult life, I liked discovering that people I perceived as intelligent and successful also smoked. It helped affirm my addiction and deny my stupidity.

6.12 *The Pseudo-Junkies* Pseudo-junkies are individuals who are deeply enmeshed in the culture of addiction, who take on nearly all the trappings of an addict but are, in fact, not addicted. They may present themselves for treatment during an emotional crisis and report vivid details of their addictive history. It is only from other addicts that we eventually learn that their addiction is for the most part a fabrication. For these individuals, addiction constitutes not a drug relationship but the performance of a role within a cultural context they find comfortable. For some of these addicts meandering in and around the culture of addiction and various treatment settings, their first actual experience of addiction can occur through their inappropriate admission for methadone maintenance.

Pseudo-junkies are individuals who for, whatever reasons, have found themselves unable to find any special niche in life but who have discovered a certain identity and acceptance within the culture of addiction that is more satisfying than their experiences outside this culture. Often lacking in social skills and any clear sense of personal identity, they can easily latch on to more powerful individuals within the culture of addiction. Such identification provides safety, reduces the need for personal decision-making and provides a modicum of social approval and acceptance. These individuals often develop elaborate rituals to obfuscate or obscure their lack of drug consumption, although under certain conditions they may actually be forced to use enough to acquire a habit in order to prove their status as an addict.

Given the context in which they feel most comfortable, the addiction treatment setting may be the most appropriate setting for the pseudo-junkie to change the direction of his or her life. Rather than confront the pseudo-junkie with evidence of non-addiction, it is more clinically appropriate to accept this identity as presented and begin shifting that identity from "addict" to "recovering addict." Some pseudo-junkies are able to transform their lives into a much more productive and personally satisfying status through their affiliation with a network of recovering individuals and through personal application of key concepts of addiction recovery. All this, in spite of the fact that they have never been addicted.

6.13 *The Pledges* Pledges are the neophytes in the culture of addiction. They constitute a population toward which older addicts hold great ambivalence. On the one hand, pledges validate the life pathway of the older addict. The pledge's honeymoon period in their drug courtship strikes longing in the older addict of a period that can never be recaptured. On the other hand, older addicts are saddened by the blindness of the pledges who are so confident they are smarter and slicker and can therefore avoid the pitfalls of their elders. Older late stage addicts spend a surprising amount of time advising pledges to get out of the life, even though as they speak there is the wisdom from their own life that such words will go unheeded.

Pledges often present themselves in treatment because of neophyte stupidity. Few pledges enter the culture with the sophistication to sustain regular drug use without detection. Those with the greatest level of incompetence perform their addict role with embarrassing ineptness that provides a source of humor to both police and more experienced addicts. It is often the less sophisticated pledges whose behavior precipitates some crisis which leads them to the doors of a treatment center. This earliest stage of courtship with drugs is perhaps the most difficult point of intervention for treatment professionals. Neophytes have not yet experienced any drug-related consequences that, within their world view, are worthy of note. They feel immortal and in total control of their drug use. Regardless of the nature of treatment interventions, many pledges will continue their entry into the culture of addiction until more serious consequences force them to reassess this commitment.

6.14 *The Crazies* There are a number of individuals in the culture of addiction who present both identifiable histories of substance abuse and symptoms of psychiatric impairment or illness. Many such individuals have found that psychoactive drug consumption can serve to self-medicate symptoms of psychiatric illness while others have discovered that such illness can be easily masked behind drug use in the culture. Many treatment providers would be surprised to discover that these professionally labeled "dually diagnosed clients" are not considered crazy in the culture of addiction. There are many tribal groups within the culture of addiction whose threshold for deviant behavior is so high that the aberrant behavior of such individuals is hardly acknowledged. To be judged crazy in the culture of addiction is to be measured not by DSM-IIIR standards, but by standards of normalcy within the culture. Only a small proportion of dually diagnosed individuals would be considered crazy in the culture of addiction.

Crazies in the culture are those individuals whose behavior is so outlandish that it poses a threat to other cultural members. Such a designation usually requires behavior ranging from the grossly psychotic to more typical patterns of either extreme risk-taking or unpredictable and uncontrollable rage. Nearly all addicts experience some episodes of fear of insanity. The presence of crazies in the culture provides a stabilizing function. By even the grossest comparisons, the addict's behavior appears quite sane. Some crazies come to the attention of treatment agencies because their behavior has become so extreme that they are rejected by the culture.

The more traditionally defined populations of psychiatrically impaired or developmentally disabled clients may also be embraced within the culture of addiction. The more vulnerable of these individuals are particularly subject to exploitation. They may be exploited sexually or financially or they may be used as players in certain high risk hustles, e.g., drug deliveries to new clients. While we may view such behavior as viciously exploitive, it is particularly sad to discover that the alleged victims have received more affirmation and attention in the culture of addiction than they have from the society at large and in fact may wish to continue their involvement in the culture of addiction.

6.15 *The Marks* Marks are not addicts but they play a significant role in the culture of addiction. Marks are the victims upon which the addict culture feeds. As the term will be used here, they include the "johns" that frequent addict prostitutes, the victims of addict theft and burglary, and the victims of various addict scams or cons. While the usual picture of the mark is some anonymous person who has come within the prey of the addict subculture, it is surprising to some that the most frequently victimized marks include the addict's family and friends.

As addiction progresses, the number of marks in each addict's life multiplies into an army of ghosts. Each day the addict must seek out new marks while keeping a wary eye to avoid face-to-face contact with old marks. When the addict stops using for any period, the ghosts of these old marks may be quite haunting as the addict, in a state of sobriety, is forced to look back on those he or she has victimized.

The early founders of Alcoholics Anonymous instinctively understood the danger of such ghosts from the past and the ability of guilt and shame to trigger relapse. It is not accidental that three of the twelve steps of Alcoholics Anonymous provide a framework to make amends to past victims and allow the alcoholic a vehicle to expiate guilt over past harm to others. This process of making amends may extend over a lifetime of recovery. What is important for treatment professionals is the recognition of our role in assisting the addict in treatment to identify and bury the most powerful of these ghosts through a process of confession and restitution.

6.16 *The Man* "The Man" is a phrase from the culture of addiction that encompasses another role that has a significant effect on the culture, even though it is outside the culture. The Man encompass-es a wide assortment of law enforcement officials ranging from the beat cop to undercover narcotics agents. The Man is the most direct symbol of the outside enemy—the forces the society at large has placed in opposition to the culture of addiction. The existence of The Man justifies the paranoia of the addict and helps fuel the closure of the addict culture into a secret and deviant society. The Man, as the pivotal point of contact between the culture of addiction and the criminal justice system, also plays a key role in precipitating crises that engage addicts in a treatment process.

6.17 *The Snitches* Snitches constitute a particular class of addicts that work for The Man. Snitches may serve as a source of information to police and may make controlled buys with marked money for the police and testify or provide evidence to convict dealers. The motivation of snitches varies from providing informa-tion in exchange for escape from arrest to providing information for drugs or money. While there is a strong cultural taboo against the role of snitch, there is also an unspoken recognition that most addicts, when sick in jail, would snitch on their mother to gain freedom and access to drugs.

The existence of undercover agents and snitches drives the daily dictum of the culture that "you can't trust anyone." Given the intense socialization around this dictum, it is little surprise that addicted clients present themselves as wary and distrustful of treatment professionals. Distrust is a learned behavior that has served to protect the safety and security of the addict.

Known snitches, or persons suspected of being snitches, often present themselves for treatment as doorways within the culture of addiction suddenly become closed to them. Having supplies of drugs shut off and access to routine hustles blocked, snitches may escape into treatment to buy time and re-plot their addictive career.

This is a particularly difficult dilemma for snitches. They may have few skills to begin entry into a legitimate career path and yet have been rejected by the deviant culture of which they were a part. This crisis of isolation may actually serve as a stimulus to begin an addiction recovery process. Snitches may be particularly overwhelmed with guilt at the time they seek treatment. They have broken society's rules and hurt any number of people whom they care about and, in their addiction, have broken the implicit oath of the culture by trading their freedom for the arrest and incarceration of others.

6.18 *The Protectors*   The protectors are volunteers and paid professionals who protect the addict from the consequences of their addiction and, through such assistance, allow the excessive alcohol/drug consumption of the addict to continue unabated. They are the rescuers used by addicts, not to overcome addiction, but to sustain addiction.

Family members, particularly the parents and spouse of the addict, are often engaged in such protection roles. Wegscheider (1981) and others have described in detail the role of these "chief enablers" and the impact of such enabling behaviors on the addict. Protective behaviors of family members often encompass such diverse practices as:

- organizing family life around the unpredictable behavior of the addict
- establishing and perpetuating "no-talk" rules within the family that prohibit direct mention or confrontation of addiction
- hiding the addictive behavior from other relatives and persons outside the family
- making excuses for the addict, thereby feeding the addict's already elaborate alibi system

- helping the addict sustain drug supply
- calling in "sick" and lying on behalf of the addict
- failing to involve authorities to address criminal behavior, *e.g.*, theft of property or money, perpetuated against the family by the addict
- making promises and threats to the addict that are never carried out
- overcompensating for the addict's deteriorating performance by taking over the addict's role responsibilities within the family
- bailing the addict out of legal difficulties and using family influence to minimize societal consequences experienced by the addict

In addition to the family, there are non-addicted members of the culture of addiction whose primary role is to rescue the addict in crisis. These individuals sustain their own identities through their nurturing and rescuing behaviors with addicts. Many of these individuals come from addicted families in which they performed a similar role as a child. They may have spent their entire life in primary relationships with addicts. Many will eventually marry one or more addicts over the course of their life. Their protective behaviors include those listed above for family and may additionally include "lending" money to the addict, providing shelter and hiding, and meeting the sexual needs of addicts.

In addition to the volunteer protectors, there are professionals helpers who also serve to protect the addict from the consequences of their behavior. These protectors often include health and human service professionals and lawyers. Health and human service professionals may play protective roles through the following behaviors:

- failing to assess and openly confront the addiction of their clients
- failing to identify addiction as a causative agent to presenting problems of clients, *e.g.*, addiction-related medical disorders, marital discord, depression, errors in judgment, legal problems, or financial problems
- rescuing clients from the criminal justice system without ongoing external controls to assure client follow through with treatment
- complying with a client's request for a treatment regimen that is of insufficient intensity or duration to abort the client's pattern of addiction
- failing to appropriately monitor client abstinence, *e.g.*, through urine testing, where a client's chronicity of use and prior treatment failures would dictate such monitoring
- mistaking a client's compliance with a short term treatment regimen for permanent enduring changes in behavior and lifestyle

Given the propensity of addicts to become engaged in the criminal justice system, lawyers play an important role in the culture of addiction. The protection of an addict's rights to civil and criminal due process is a legitimate and desirable role for the lawyer advocate. The lawyer can, however, overstep these protections and take on a role which becomes supportive of his or her client's addiction. There are a number of lawyers, for example, who will assist their clients arrested for Driving Under the Influence by helping them avoid alcoholism treatment recommendations. This is done by explaining the nature of the required alcoholism assessment process (which is quite appropriate) and then showing them the assessment instruments and instructing them how to answer the assessment questionnaire to avoid detection of one's drinking problem (which is professional enabling).

6.19 *The Cultural Rejects* Cultural rejects include addicts who for a variety of reasons are no longer in good standing within the culture and thus shunned by other addicts. This category includes known snitches and other addicts whose behavior has gotten so outlandish as to pose a threat to other cultural members. Also included in this category are a number of late stage addicts whose physical and mental deterioration no longer allow them to withstand the rigors of the addictive lifestyle. These late stage addicts make up a significant proportion of the revolving door clients in publicly funded substance abuse programs.

Cultural rejects often require intense, long-term residential rehabilitation. They are increasingly becoming the forgotten addict population as the field migrates toward more "preferred" treatment designs for the early and middle stage addict. Having lived outside society at large and having been rejected by the culture of addiction, these individuals will increasingly become the homeless and the helpless meandering in their isolation from institution to institution.

6.20 *The Profiteers* The profiteers are "good citizens" who deplore addiction but are part of the financial chain that supports addiction. They buy stolen goods from addicts and may even put in special orders. In spite of their verbalized attitudes, they reap quite direct benefits from addiction. They purchase food, clothes, stereos, Tvs, etc., for a fraction of their value, even though they may themselves become victims of such predatory addict behavior. They hate addiction, but will readily purchase the services of an addicted prostitute. They worry about drugs their kids may be exposed to, but they appreciate the drug money which sets in the bank they manage. They feel dealers should be locked up forever, but they will gladly take the real estate commissions that come from drug money. They are the multitudes of non-addicted persons who play unseen and unacknowledged supportive roles within the culture of addiction.

6.21 *Summary: Cultural Roles and the Treatment Process* There are a number of principles or observations that can be extracted from our discussion of roles within the culture of addiction. The following have particularly significant implications to the treatment of culturally enmeshed addicts.

- Many of the roles performed by addicts in the culture of addiction require a significant level of knowledge and skill mastery.
- These roles, while stigmatized by society, may have provided the addict enjoyment, excitement, personal identity, social acceptance and status and are valued for those reasons.
- Some areas of knowledge and skill from roles in the culture of addiction may be transferable to legitimate careers outside the addictive culture.
- Understanding a client's role within the culture of addiction may provide the treatment professional with an understanding of those career paths to recovery most congruent with this past role.
- The roles of non-addicts within the culture of addiction can serve either as supports for addict recovery or as major sources of sabotage to the recovery process.

7

CAREER MILESTONES
IN THE CULTURE OF ADDICTION

If one accepts Waldorf's (1973) notion that addiction can be conceptualized as a career, then it should be possible through careful study and observation to identify milestones that most addicts share who pursue such a career. Studies from Crothers (1893) to Jellinek (1960) have attempted to construct the sequential steps of the addiction process. These studies focused primarily on the individual addict's physical and psychological adaptation to increased drug dependence. This chapter focuses on the metamorphosis in the addict's interaction with the outside world and how such interactions influence the course of the addictive illness.

In the space below, twelve milestones are identified and described that the author feels constitute major stages in the life cycle of addiction. There are numerous factors that influence the career progression of the individual addict. There is first of all the drug chosen by the addict—its pharmacological properties, the dosage and purity of the drug, and the method of drug administration. There are secondly, those unique characteristics of the user—physical, psychological and socioeconomic vulnerabilities that influence the intensity and consequences of the addictive career. Finally, there is the social status of the addict's drug of choice which for the prohibited drugs, dictates a particularly deviant career path. Most of the career milestones described below are shared by most addicts, regardless of drug choice, although the intensity of the addict's transformation will be much more visibly pronounced for the prohibited drugs.

The particular points identified for discussion are called milestones because they represent major points of decision-making. While there are potential pathways out of the addictive career at each milestone, each progressive milestone diminishes the addict's ability to seek alternative career paths. The milestones are marked by increased intensity in the addict-drug relationship and increased absorption into the culture of addiction.

7.1 *Joining the Culture: Initiation Rites* Addicts are drawn from the total population of persons who have had exposure to psychoactive drug consumption. The context of this initial exposure is the same for nearly all of the popularly abused psychoactive substances. Contrary to popular "dope fiend mythology" which posits the existence of unscrupulous money hungry pushers searching out and inducing new victims into drug use, nearly all initial psychoactive drug consumption—whether heroin or alcohol—is characterized by the following:

- Initial use takes place in a social context, usually with one's peers.
- Initial use is an experience sought after by the user more often than an experience foisted on the innocent by the experienced.
- The neophyte's initial drug experience occurs in a social context of drug availability; neophytes rarely ever pay for their initial drug experiences as drugs are provided as a token of friendship and inclusion.
- Initial use occurs in a social situation in which the mood is hospitable to compliant social behavior, making the

decision to use drugs seem natural and of no great consequence.

The population of persons who have experienced such initial exposure to psychoactive drug experiences is indeed large. Studies conducted by the National Institute on Drug Abuse suggest that persons in the United States who have experienced such initial exposure in their lifetime constitute the following proportions of the total population.

Estimated Number of American Users of Various Substances		
Drug Category	Percentage of the Population with Exposure	Estimated Number of Users
Alcohol	86	164,360,000
Cigarettes	76	144,510,000
Marijuana and Hashish	32	61,940,000
Cocaine	12	22,240,000
Non-Medical Use:		
Stimulants	9	17,610,000
Tranquilizers	8	14,750,000
Analgesics	7	12,620,000
Sedatives	6	11,540,000
Inhalants	7	12,940,000
Hallucinogens	7	12,880,000
Heroin	1	1,930,000
Source: National Inst. on Drug Abuse, *National Household Survey*, 1985.		

A comparison of these figures with epidemiological data on addiction clearly suggests that the vast majority of persons who have initial exposure to psychoactive drugs do not proceed into more regular drug use or at least not into addiction.

What occurs at this initial exposure that dictates a pathway into controlled use or non-use versus a pathway into addiction? The initial exposure may be different for susceptible versus non-susceptible populations.

Among the non-susceptible populations are individuals for whom the initial drug experience was dysphoric rather than euphoric or for whom the initial drug experiences provided little personal meaning. Lacking any physiological, psychological or social rewards, the behavior is discontinued.

There are also non-susceptible persons for whom the drug experience was not dysphoric who may progress into a more frequent pattern of socially approved drug experimentation. The drug experience for the latter group still does not hold forth special rewards or significance. Both groups have the ability to cast off drug experimentation for alternative behaviors that provide greater meaning and rewards. For these individuals, the initial drug experience has simply not been a powerful enough event to drive them toward more sustained and regular use.

The susceptible population is very special. It is composed of persons for whom the initial drug experience has tremendous meaning and power. They are individuals whose unique physiological and psychological characteristics make the drug experience particularly rewarding. While the nature of these rewards differs from individual to individual, there is a special bond established between the drug or drug using context and the susceptible user. One or more of the following statements typify initial use by the susceptible population and distinguish their experience from their less susceptible counterparts.

- There is a special magic of initial intoxication that is physically and emotionally imprinted making the event subject to detailed recall.
- Initial use is marked by extreme physical pleasure and a feeling of emotional well-being.
- Initial use creates a feeling of "specialness."
- Use frees the user from physical or psychological discomfort creating the feeling of "normalcy."
- The user discovers that he or she can do things, *e.g.*, communicate with self-confidence, while intoxicated that have been previously unachievable.
- The ritual of use and intoxication creates a feeling of social acceptance and closeness previously unobtainable.
- The act of using holds great symbolic meaning, *i.e.*, as a rite of passage into adulthood, risk-taking, or defiance of family/social boundaries.
- Initial use is followed by preoccupation with the event (exhibited in thought and conversation).
- Initial use is followed by a strong attraction to affiliate with those most associated with the drug.

The factor which distinguishes susceptible from non-susceptible neophytes is the existence and intensity of rewards experienced from initial drug use. At the highest end of this reward continuum, initial use, in and of itself, may be so powerful as to propel the susceptible individual into an addictive lifestyle and validate the often heard phrase from clients: "I was an alcoholic from my very first drink." There are later events and decisions that can lead the non-susceptible population into an addictive pathway by in fact altering and increasing their susceptibility, but it is unlikely that such events will create a pattern of addiction with the chronicity and intensity as those vulnerable from their point of initial use.

Drug use, in and of itself, does not always constitute a pathway into addiction or a rite of initiation into the culture of addiction. Non-susceptible individuals may experience their first drug exposure within the culture of addiction without such use constituting an initiation rite into the culture. The experience may, in fact, decrease the odds of repeating drug ingestion and lead to disaffiliation from those with whom the initial experience was shared. It is not the ritual of consumption, but the meanings attached to such use that are pivotal. For susceptible individuals, the rite of initiation comes not from just the drug ingestion but from their affirmation of the experience as desirable, from their attraction to those who most symbolize the drug experience, and from their expressed desire to "join" as a regular in the drug experience.

7.2 Chipping: The Period of Controlled Use The second milestone involves the movement of the drug user from neophyte to accepted and established member of the culture of addiction. One again finds both susceptible and non-susceptible populations involved in this period, although both drug usage and cultural identification are greater for the former.

Understanding the difference between those persons who can initiate and sustain non-problematic drug use from those who cannot rests on a concept of susceptible and non-susceptible populations. The notion of susceptibility is not a static concept. It is not a clear black-white issue that one either is or is not vulnerable to addiction. Susceptibility is dynamic. There is a continuum of susceptibility and one can move, within certain ranges, back and forth on this continuum from increased to decreased vulnerability. Some individuals may be so far at the high susceptibility end of this continuum that they will always be high risk for addictive behavior. Others may be at the other extreme and constitute a population almost invulnerable to addiction. The middle of the continuum constitutes a large population of persons whose susceptibility to addiction is subject to change based on changes in physiology, changes and crises in their emotional lives, changes in intimate and social relationships and other life changes. Susceptibility is the axis upon which the outcome of regular drug use will be determined.

When drug use continues past initial use, one can begin to plot changing behaviors that differentiate episodic or occasional use and regular use. There are a number of behaviors shared by most users during this period.

- The first untoward consequences, *e.g.*, hangovers, occur here if they were not experienced on initial use.
- Preferred dosages (tolerance) are established and the user learns how to regulate levels of intoxication by amount and frequency of intake.
- The first regular purchases of the drug are made.
- There is beginning preoccupation with drug supply.
- One begins to expect the availability and use of the drug during designated social rituals.
- There are a growing number of stimuli associated with drug use that serve as "triggers" for use.
- One begins to "sound out" the values of one's existing social network on the issue of drug consumption.
- One learns, from more experienced users, the basic "etiquette" surrounding rituals of use and learns desirable precautions related to use.

- One establishes personal rituals that will initially dictate when, where, how much and under what conditions use will occur.

The above tasks are shared by susceptible and non-susceptible users. Differences begin to appear that distinguish people who can use psychoactive drugs in a controlled manner over an extended period of time, versus those individuals who will migrate toward a pattern of compulsive drug use and addiction with regular use.

Nearly everyone is aware of persons who use alcohol and prescription psychoactive drugs regularly or episodically without experiencing any of the characteristics, problems and consequences associated with addiction. There are also individuals, documented in the professional literature (Zinberg, 1982; Chein,1964) who use illicit substances, including heroin and cocaine (intranasally), without experiencing the addictive characteristics and problems associated with such drugs. Looking at these populations of controlled users collectively, what patterns characterize such control? How is their use distinguished from that of the addict? The hallmarks of such control for these individuals include the following.

- The frequency and dosage of drug ingestion is established on a schedule that minimizes the building of tissue tolerance.
- High risk methods of drug ingestion (freebasing of cocaine) are eschewed for lower risk methods of drug ingestion (intranasal ingestion of cocaine).
- Personal ground rules preclude use in high risk situations, *e.g.*, drinking and driving.
- Use is limited and restricted to certain situations chosen by the user.

- There is frequent exercise of one's choice and right to abstain or minimize use in social situations.
- Personal ground rules preclude or minimize use in times of heightened vulnerability (*e.g.*, physical weakness or impairment), periods of excessive stress or emotional turmoil.
- Drug supplies are either minimized (maintained in small quantities) or not regularly kept in one's residence.
- Drug ingestion is always viewed as a peripheral experience secondary to one's major activities and commitments.
- One's social relationships are marked by great variety and not restricted to drug consumers (use without commitment or significant involvement in the culture of addiction).
- One is in such circumstances that episodic use does not disrupt family or other intimate relationships. (Congruency of values on controlled use.)

Controlled users drawn from the non-susceptible population, by using guidelines like the above, may sustain drug use over a lifetime without experiencing significant problems or consequences related to such use. There are conditions, however, under which non-susceptible individuals can violate such standards and progress into an addictive lifestyle. There are case histories from the addiction literature dating back more than a century which describe non-susceptible individuals who after years of controlled drinking experienced some crisis which propelled them into the ranks of those susceptible to addiction. In other words, under the proper conditions nearly all humans are at least susceptible to addiction. Stimuli which can precipitate such vulnerability can include physical trauma or disease that alters the body's sensitivity and response to psychoactive drugs. Emotional trauma and psychiatric illness can lead an individual to discard prior guidelines on use and initiate an intense pattern of self-medication. Guidelines for controlled use are also anchored to particular familiar environments and social networks which reinforce drug use values. Disruption of such anchors and placement of the non-susceptible individual in an alien environment, *e.g.*, Vietnam, can stimulate a shift from controlled to compulsive use. Any event which stimulates an increased frequency and quantity of drug consumption engages the mechanism of tissue tolerance and results in greater vulnerability to addiction.

What characteristics of the susceptible population make it impossible for them to sustain controlled use over time? The earliest period of regular use for susceptible individuals is often referred to as the honeymoon period in their relationship with the drug. It is the period of greatest rewards and least consequences achieved from drug consumption. Yet, if we examine use during this period, there are already signs that distinguish this pattern of consumption from that of persons less susceptible to addiction. In contrast to the guidelines that characterize controlled users, the drug use of susceptible individuals is undisciplined and unpredictable. Early use is characterized by a lack of guidelines and such guidelines will only appear later as the individual, in middle stages of addiction begins to test his or her personal control and power over the drug. The intensity of needs met by drug use for susceptible individuals precludes the development of guidelines which minimize frequency and quantity of use. The special magic uniquely experienced from drug use by susceptible individuals inevitably drives such use toward a compulsive and addictive pattern.

Both susceptible and non-susceptible individuals can cycle out of this period of regular use, although the reasons for such shifts tend to differ for the two groups. Reasons given for moving toward episodic use or abstinence by non-susceptibles might include the following.

- "I got bored with it."
- "It wasn't worth the money."
- "I met my wife and she didn't use. I just gave it up."
- "I decided it was stupid. Every time I drank, I got a headache. People spend millions getting rid of headaches every day and I was paying money to get one. That's nuts."
- "After a while, I just didn't like the way it made me feel."
- "I think I just grew out of it. You know, you do a lot of crazy things in college. After I got out, it just didn't seem to fit in with my lifestyle."

Susceptible individuals can also cycle out of regular use into abstinence while at the earliest stages of what for them could have been an addictive lifestyle. When we listen to their reasons for stopping use, we discover their early recognition of both the magic and dangers of continued drug use.

- "I didn't stop using because it was bad. I stopped using because it was too good. The first time I used cocaine, I used for three days straight. I was so into it, it scared the _____ out of me! I haven't used since."

- "I used to take great pride as a kid that I could drink everybody under the table. I think my wife understood that I could easily become an alcoholic. She would marry me only under the condition I never drank. Well, we've been married a long time and I haven't drank, but sometimes I still miss it."

- "I was one of those heroin users who was convinced he would never be addicted. I was young and cocky and couldn't believe the drug could control me. The first few times I was junk sick, I wrote it off as flu. Then I was too sick to go to work. I hated admitting that I had a habit. I hated myself. That was the end of my heroin use."

- "I don't know if I was an alcoholic or not. It wasn't like I drank every day. But when I drank, I got drunk and I got crazy. I was horrified one morning to wake up and see the black eye that I had given my wife and couldn't even recall getting home let alone hitting her. I haven't had a drink since."

- "I grew up with an alcoholic father. I hated him and alcohol and swore I would never be like him. When I was 24 I woke up in an alcohol stupor and almost puked in disgust when I realized the bed was wet. All I could remember was how many times I had helped Mom change the sheets because Dad had come home drunk and _____ in his sleep. I quit because I knew I was becoming the worst of what I hated in my father."

The individuals mentioned above did not go through a treatment program nor did they participate in self-help groups. They didn't even necessarily define themselves as addicts. They did, however, recognize warning signs of their susceptibility at a time when they were still able to abort what would in all likelihood have been an addictive career.

For those susceptible individuals who proceed from regular use to compulsive and addictive patterns of use, other transformations begin that further cement the drug relationship and one's affiliation with the culture of addiction.

7.3 *Justifying Usage: Ideological Beliefs* A third milestone in one's involvement in the culture of addiction involves the development, through interaction with other addicts, of a cognitive defense structure to justify excessive alcohol and drug consumption. This defense structure involves the use of ideological beliefs and defensive maneuvers that serve to maintain the addict's self esteem by justifying and normalizing excessive drug use.

This milestone involves the amount and nature of time the regular user spends thinking about alcohol/drug consumption. Drug consumption plays a minor and insignificant role in the life of the controlled user and, as a result, engages a minimal amount of the time and emotional energy from both use and thoughts about use. For the controlled user, drug consumption is one of numerous pastimes that can be chosen or avoided at whim. In contrast, use for the addict becomes a profession that engages significant amounts of emotional energy.

Preoccupation with drug use is the first hallmark of this period of regular and increasingly compulsive use. Such preoccupation is evident during periods of non-use and is often reflected in the conversational themes of the user. This growing mental obsession begins to push out other areas of cognitive and emotional concern and leads the user to disengage from activities and relationships that are incongruent with excessive drug consumption. The user also must develop beliefs about drug use and the world that are supportive of his or her drug consumption pattern. User values begin to shift toward those values which were identified in Chapter Four as being core beliefs from the culture of addiction.

The compulsive user is experiencing a transformation and must either develop a rational justification for such change or must minimize or somehow normalize this change. In the former, one takes on elaborate rationalizations to make excessive alcohol or other drug consumption appear appropriate and desirable. One drinks in celebration and in disappointment. One drinks because it's hot and because it's cold. One drinks because of the job and because one doesn't have a job. One drinks because of the wife and because she left. Normal drinkers use without the need for complex justifications. The compulsive user, in contrast, must develop elaborate beliefs which can maintain self-esteem and at the same time provide permission for excessive drug consumption. In the latter style, the user denies that use is excessive, and by shifting social affiliations, can in fact truthfully say that they do not use any more than anyone else around them. By shifting primary relationships to persons inside the culture of addiction, one's excessive drug use is normalized.

7.4 *The Change in Identity* The increasing cognitive and emotional preoccupation with drug use is also reflected in the changing identity of the addict. As noted earlier, the nature of this identity may vary. The following summarizes the two major styles of adaptation in identity. The styles are not mutually exclusive and, in fact, often present as sequential or alternating patterns.

A. *Preoccupation with Denial* Many addicts are able to deny the existence of addiction long after they have embraced an addictive lifestyle. To achieve such denial, the addict must utilize a number of defense mechanisms that allow one to continue excessive alcohol/drug use while avoiding detection of one's addiction by others and avoiding self-detection. The addict's armor is buttressed by embracing a number of societal myths about addiction. The alcoholic, for example, can carry on internal and external dialogues of denial such as the following: "I can't be an alcoholic because...

- I only drink beer.
- I don't drink every day.
- I can quit any time I want.
- I haven't missed a day of work in my life because of drinking.
- I've never had DT's.
- I've seen what alcohol has done to others and I won't let that happen to me.

To the extent that public education undermines these myths, the alcoholic has increasing difficulty utilizing such beliefs to sustain denial. What helps addict denial is the fact that such denial is rarely done alone. Through association with other addicts at similar stages of addiction, there is a shared denial within the social group. The shared patterns of use and shared beliefs about use help normalize addictive drug consumption.

Emotional preoccupation with the drug experience is evident even in the presence of denial. Addiction-denying addicts begin to live for the drug experience. They begin to organize their life around this experience. When they are not using, they're thinking about using. Emotional well-being is increasingly tied to drug access and supply. Stress is provoked by any conditions which impinge on this preoccupation and access to the drug.

B. *Preoccupation with Acceptance* Whereas some addicts deny addiction to sustain self-esteem and identity, others embrace the role of addict to achieve self-esteem and identity. The discovery that the identity of user or addict can meet significant psychological and social needs can be an important, and, for some, the most crucial milestone in the addictive career. Where the emotional preoccupation of the addiction denying group is hidden, the addiction accepting group exhibits such preoccupations visibly and, at times, flamboyantly. With the former group, the primary relationship is with the drug and social relationships are sought to buttress the drug relationship. With the latter, one's primary affiliation may be with the cultural context in which the drug is consumed.

7.5 *Letting Go of the Other World* Throughout this text, it has been suggested that addiction often involves a progressive disengagement from the society at large and an increasing engagement in the culture of addiction. The process of detaching oneself from society at large—the severing of non-drug relation-ships—is a crucial milestone in the addictive career. This detach-ment removes those forces which have served to inhibit drug use and sets the stage for one's total absorption into the addictive lifestyle. Once detached, the intense socialization begins with what have earlier been described as the core elements of the culture of addiction.

7.6 *Developing Status and Reputation in the Culture* As the addict becomes more enmeshed in relationships within the culture of addiction, he or she must reforge a role and identity within their new social world. For some addicts the status and acceptance they achieve within this context may far surpass whatever status they were able to establish in straight society. Each addict establishes a persona—an image and reputation—reinforced through interac-tion with other addicts. These social interactions serve to anchor the addict to the culture and reinforce excessive drug consumption. These social interactions and the ability of the addict to meet needs for esteem through such interactions can serve as a major obstacle to addiction recovery.

7.7 *Learning to Hustle* For those addicts whose hustling behavior does not predate their addiction, the onset of hustling behavior marks a milestone in the addictive career. It marks the transition from leisure drug taking to confirmed entrance into the addictive career.

By reviewing our earlier discussions of hustling behavior, we can isolate some aspects of this milestone that have particular implications to how addicts present themselves for treatment.

- Hustling eats away personal morality and values leading to what is experienced in late stages of addiction as a spiritual vacuum or spiritual hunger.
- Hustling leads to emotional detachment, habitual manipulation in relationships, and predatory thinking and predatory behavior.
- Hustling creates victims, leaving the addict haunted psychologically by "ghosts" and physically vulnerable to retribution.
- Hustling for the addict with an intact conscience creates a backlog of unexpiated guilt and shame.
- Surviving in a world of hustlers creates a world view of "everyone on the make" and "every person for himself."
- One's "hustle," separate from its ability to sustain drug supply, may meet significant needs for the addict, that have been unmet in other arenas.

7.8 *Kicking: The Testing of Control* During early and middle stages of addiction, addicts may utilize a number of psychological maneuvers to re-assert control over the drug. Such maneuvers are attempts to deny or minimize the increasing loss of control they are experiencing in their relationship with the drug. These efforts to control consumption, and the failure of such controls, constitute a crucial milestone in the addictive career.

Most efforts to control seek to minimize or deny the increasing power of the drug over the person. Consider, for example, the following control mechanisms commonly used by alcoholics:

- Short periods of abstinence, *e.g.*, "I'll prove to you I'm not an alcoholic; I won't take a drink for thirty days."
- Control of drug choice, *e.g.*, "My problem's whiskey. When I drink whiskey, I get crazy. As long as I drink beer, I'm O.K."
- Control of location, *e.g.*, "My problem's not drinking; it's where I drink. I'll be O.K. if I just drink at home and stay out of the bars."
- Control of context, *e.g.*, "My problem's not drinking; it's who I drink with. Nobody could stay sober with those guys. If I stay away from them, I'll be alright."
- Control of drug quantity, *e.g.*, "I'm just going to have three drinks and then I'll quit and go home."
- Control of time, *e.g.*, "I'm just going to drink from Friday night when I get off work till after the last football game on Sunday."

Perhaps the ultimate test of control occurs when the addict experiences withdrawal sickness. The earliest episodes of such sickness are marked by continuing denial as sickness is attributed to flu, a cold or other medical disorder rather than to the absence of the drug. Even when the addict recognizes drug sickness, he or she is able to reframe the experience in such a way as to allow continued drug consumption. Most addicts will self-acknowledge that their use "got a little out of control" and that they need to be more careful when they resume use. Most will believe they have sufficient control to regain the period of controlled use where they experienced maximum drug reward and minimal consequences from use. It is a testament to the strength of addiction when we

examine how many times these myths of control must be dispro-
ven before the addict accepts their powerlessness over the drug.

7.9 *Escaping and Reframing Consequences* Efforts to control the
frequency and quantity of drug consumption are usually tied to
consequences the addict is beginning to experience as a result of
drug use. The progression of such consequences makes the use of
minimization and denial inadequate, by themselves, to protect self-
esteem and sustain drug use. The addict must, at this milestone,
find enablers to protect him or her from drug related consequences.
He or she must also develop additional defense mechanisms to
support continued drug use.

The importance of enablers in sustaining addiction has already
been discussed in earlier chapters. We have not yet focused on the
skills of the addict necessary to manipulate people into such roles.
Such manipulation grows out of the new defense mechanisms
required to sustain addiction.   When reality begins to break
through the mechanisms of denial and minimization, the addict
must develop ways to reframe experiences so that consequences
are attributed to factors other than drug use. Some addicts will
refine the mechanisms of intellectualization and rationalization to
develop elaborate explanations for irrational addictive behavior.
Others will develop a more aggressive stance by projecting blame
for their difficulties, not on their drug use, but on persons and
forces outside themselves. Such projection allows the addict to
assume the victim role and manipulate others into rescuing
behaviors. Such projection says, in essence: "I am not responsible
for my condition, and since I am a victim of circumstances over
which I had no control, then you have a responsibility to help me."
The implicit communication is that somehow the potential helper
is responsible for the addict's condition and must therefore atone
by rescuing them.

7.10 *Getting Busted and Doing Time* Arrest and incarceration as a milestone in the addictive career is determined to a great extent by the social status of one's drug of choice and one's socioeconomic status. For the Black or Hispanic urban opiate addict, arrest and eventual incarceration may be almost an inevitable milestone of the addictive career. The White, upper class alcoholic is much less likely to experience this milestone. Money and social status often provide protection from such consequences. For many addicts, however, mastery of the profession of addiction entails handling the arrest event and, when necessary, "doing time."

Knowledge of law and lawyers, arrest procedures, rules of evidence, plea options, sentencing options, and the nuances of doing probation are essential for opiate addicts. Their participation in the culture has prepared them for the eventuality of arrest, how to reduce the probabilities of arrest, and what to do when it occurs. It is little wonder that most jailhouse lawyers have backgrounds in addiction. Survival for an addict often required skills inherent in the jailhouse lawyer role.

One would think that such a serious consequence as incarceration would lead many addicts to rethink their decision to pursue the addictive career path. Unfortunately, the evidence is quite the contrary. Prison does not disrupt the addict's affiliation with the culture of addiction. If anything, it intensifies that affiliation. To understand this phenomenon, we must explore how addicts "do time."

Prison is the Ph.D. program of the drug culture. Here addicts of all varieties are brought together in a way that not only fails in a rehabilitative sense but actually enhances the knowledge and skills required to pursue the addictive career. The drug culture exists unchecked inside most penitentiaries. Even when drugs are unavailable, the addict lives in a daily environment that carries forth the values and many of the rituals of the culture of addiction. Every interaction reinforces one's identity as an addict and expands the range of knowledge and skills which can be utilized to proceed with the addictive career.

Judges and parole boards sometimes have a particularly difficult time recognizing the role prison has in sustaining the addictive career. Until recently, most of these professionals could not understand why a person who had spent four years in prison, and allegedly had not used drugs in that time, needed addiction treatment prior to entering the community at large. It was their belief that if the person was no longer addicted with a physical habit, there was no need for treatment. It was hard to articulate for these professionals that a particular addict may be in greater need of treatment upon leaving prison than when he or she arrived. Such need springs, not from the physical relationship with the drug, but from the constant reinforcement of values and a lifestyle that makes relapse to active addiction almost inevitable. Residential treatment programs have also sometimes been adverse to taking individuals straight from prison, preferring to have such persons placed in the community and seek treatment only in the event of relapse. Such exclusion almost dooms the individual to relapse, and once the addiction is physically reactivated, reduces the probability of voluntary entrance into treatment.

7.11 *Doing Treatment* Addicts can "do treatment" like they "do time" in prison. The challenge for the culturally enmeshed addict is to "do treatment" under such external pressure as threat of incarceration while sustaining one's identity and affiliation with the culture of addiction. One goes about the business of "doing treatment" as just one more hustle or role to perform in order to sustain the addictive career. Since the focus of this study is on the treatment implications of the concepts of culture of addiction and culture of recovery, the milestone of "doing treatment" will be explored in great detail.

This section explores how the natural career path of many addicts propels them into treatment, not to end this career, but to sustain it. It explores those behaviors and teachings from the culture of addiction which dictate how the addict responds to the treatment milieu. The discussion begins with the premise that those behaviors and styles of "doing treatment" shaped by the culture of addiction are incongruent with addiction recovery and must be altered as part of the treatment process.

A. *Gambits to Avoid Treatment* Addicts usually enter treatment because of an externally induced crisis that threatens their continued relationship with their drug. The addict is cornered by family, friends, employer or by the criminal justice system and given the choice between treatment or an undesirable alternative. The task of the addict is to escape from this crisis while sustaining the drug relationship.

The first gambit is to avoid treatment altogether by formulating promises and commitments that, if accepted, buy the addict some time and allow the crisis to pass. This can be achieved by:

- Convincing others that one has achieved some new insight or resolve and now has the strength to alter his/her past behavior without the need for treatment.
- Redefining the problem and accepting an action plan that poses less threat to addiction, *e.g.*, going for marriage counseling rather than addiction treatment.
- Making counter-threats to test the resolution of those inducing the crisis, *e.g.*, "If you force me to do this, our marriage is over."

When this initial gambit fails, usually because of an established history of past failures, the goal then becomes finding an action plan that poses the least threat to one's addiction. When treatment becomes unavoidable, the addict will seek to achieve the treatment with the lowest frequency of contact, the shortest duration of contact and the least intensity required from the treatment experience.

- "I'm telling you, I'll go to some AA meetings. I don't need any shrink!"
- "Look, I've agreed to see a counselor. I don't need to go into a hospital."

The final gambit in the crisis is to postpone the initiation of treatment.

- "I've agreed to go to treatment. It's just that now isn't a good time."
- "O.K., I'll go (to a program); I just need a few weeks to take care of loose ends."

The above descriptions do not deny the fact that there is a part of every addict that wants to cast off addiction nor that there are times in the career of addiction in which the pain of addiction creates a genuine openness and acceptance of treatment. They do reinforce that the very definition of addiction connotes a passionate desire to continue the drug relationship and to escape any situations which threaten this relationship.

The treatment crisis is a chess game played for the highest stakes, and the game involves a host of players. On one side are the forces inhibiting addiction. The family is increasingly calling on addiction intervention specialists for assistance. The supervisor is now frequently provided with highly skilled employee assistance professionals. The courts are utilizing outside addiction experts for assessment and intervention. While the inhibiting forces are becoming increasingly aggressive and sophisticated, it is important to recognize that addicts in the game of "Enter Treatment; Avoid Treatment" are not playing the game alone. Through their relationship with other addicts in the culture of addiction, addicts have a large pool of collective experience to draw upon to formulate their game plans. The culture can assist addicts with the above gambits, and when treatment is unavoidable, help prepare the best approach to "do treatment."

Interventions designed to engage the addict in treatment can be best constructed under the following conditions:

- The addict, to the extent possible, is isolated from contact from the culture of addiction during the period of intervention.
- The intervention must be focused on the alcohol and drug use of the addict and the consequences of such use. The goal of the intervention is addiction treatment, not psychiatric evaluation/treatment, budget counseling, stress management, marital counseling or other services that may, as a diversion, allow drug consumption to continue.
- Treatment resulting from an intervention should reflect an intensity and duration commensurate with the intensity and chronicity of the pattern of addiction.
- Entry into to treatment should, where possible, be immediate. It is desirable that treatment entry occur at a time when the defenses that have supported addiction are at their weakest. By delaying, we provide time to reorganize and strengthen these defenses resulting in avoidance of treatment or an altered course of treatment.

B. *Scoping Out the Program*   Culturally enmeshed addicts often know a great deal about treatment long before they ever enter their first treatment program.   The culture of addiction is filled with numerous individuals who have relapsed following various treatment experiences.   It may be a difficult scene for some treatment professionals to visualize, but the cultural pastime of sitting around getting high talking about various treatment programs is quite common.   There is also a substantial amount of treatment paraphernalia, *e.g.*, addiction literature, program descriptions, etc. that relapsed addicts bring into the culture.   The scene of an alcoholic drinking a beer while skimming through the "Big Book" of Alcoholics Anonymous or a group of adolescents smoking reefer while looking over literature one of the members got while in treatment is not at all unusual.   Through normal contact within the culture, one begins to acquire some general knowledge about various treatment modalities and treatment programs.

To the addict about to enter a treatment program due to some external pressure or crisis, such general knowledge is not enough. By polling other addicts who have been through the program, one can begin to construct an overall scheme to get through treatment with one's addiction intact.   As soon as the addict enters the treatment program, a process of intelligence gathering begins in which the addict both observes and questions fellow addicts about the ground rules required to "do treatment."

C. *Demonstrating Motivation*   To get into a treatment program usually requires that the addict exhibit some degree of motivation toward rehabilitation.   By asking other addicts, "what kind of changes do you have to go through to get in that place," the addict seeking treatment usually has a pretty good sense of the story line, level of verbal commitment and level of emotion that will assure their acceptance into a particular program.

This notion of playacting is not to suggest that the addict entering treatment is without pain. The pain is often quite real and intense. Until the addict recognizes "powerlessness" and experiences "acceptance," however, the pain is a pain of consequences. The motivation is a motivation to escape consequences and continue the drug relationship. It is the struggle to find that one loophole or gimmick that will allow one to continue the drug relationship without pain and consequences.

D. *Hustling Medication* For many addicts, the crisis of treatment is most intense during the period their relationship with the drug is severed through detoxification. The cellular hunger for the drug can drive a number of manipulative behaviors that seek to sustain some drug relationship. Addicts who experience this drug hunger most intensely and fear the loss of the drug are likely to exaggerate their drug consumption, *e.g.*, every heroin addict entering treatment has a $200-300 a day habit. Such individuals often exaggerate withdrawal symptoms and discomfort and strive to sustain access to medication long after the period such medication is physically needed. Addicts in treatment compare dosages of medications received, and in some cases, enter into competition on who can receive the best and largest dosages of medication. In an unsophisticated program, an addict may manipulate access to higher dosages of drugs than they used on the streets, *e.g.* heroin addicts getting a higher dosage of methadone for detox than the equivalent dosage of heroin used prior to treatment.

E. *Assessing Your Counselor* The addict entering treatment is psychologically vulnerable and this vulnerability reaches its apex in the relationship with the primary counselor charged with the addict's care. To reduce this vulnerability, it is imperative that the addict conduct a discrete but thorough psychological evaluation of his or her primary counselor. They must tease out the counselor's background, interests, theoretical beliefs and biases, favored therapeutic techniques, blind spots, weaknesses, and overall operating style. Based on this data and data gathering on the overall program structure, the addict can determine the most appropriate style with which to play out the treatment experience.

It is an obvious but disquieting proposition that we (as substance abuse treatment professionals) are being assessed in the exact situations we construct and utilize to assess the addict in treatment. There are times in which the addict-client's assessment activities may be even more rigorous and thorough than our own. I remember with great humility an assessment interview conducted during my early years in the substance abuse field. The purpose of the interview was to assess the individual's need for treatment as part of an upcoming probation hearing. The client entered my office with an air of detached hostility, established no eye contact during the first ten minutes and responded with only short cryptic answers to my questions. Suddenly making eye contact, he informed me that the only other time he had seen a counselor, the counselor "squealed" on him resulting in his being sent to "reform school" and that he wasn't sure I could understand his "story" because I was white. I can still remember how important it was for me to convince this client that I was not like the other counselor and that, in spite of my color, I could understand and empathize with his situation. Out of defensiveness, I began talking some about myself and responding to questions and challenges presented by the client. As the interview progressed (and I talked more), the client seemed to slowly warm by making more eye contact and becoming more relaxed in the situation. When the hour was up, I concluded the interview feeling I had met the challenge of a particularly difficult interview. It would be a few hours before reality would set in and I would realize that I still knew almost nothing about this client and his potential need for treatment. It was even more embarrassing when I realized that this client, by hooking my defensiveness and need for acceptance, could write a much better psychosocial assessment of me than I could of him.

The addict "doing treatment" picks and chooses from his or her personal history and presents those elements that fit the interests and biases of the counselor. Treatment responds then not to client reality and client need but to the client's perception of what the therapist desires. The client who does the best job responding to the therapist's own biases thus becomes viewed as "responsive to treatment" and as having a "good prognosis." Rather than knowing the addict, the counselor has come to know a reflection of themselves. They have encountered only the milieu-shaped color of the chameleon.

F. *The Best Rationalizations for Why Past Treatment Didn't Work* For some addicts, treatment becomes a familiar sanctuary and escape. They have become institutionalized to the nuances of various treatment programs and seek the shelter of such programs when crises arise in their addictive career. Treatment is sought, not to end this career, but to assure its continuation. Such clients are presented with a dilemma not faced by the neophyte. They must articulate why treatment did not work before and why this treatment episode will be different.

The answer to this question will differ according to the addict's style of doing treatment and the amount of contact they have had with other "professional patients." The addicts with more compliant styles of doing treatment will exhibit intense self-deprecation in their explanations of prior treatment failure.

- "When I was in treatment before, I wasn't there for myself. I was doing it for my wife. I know now that that doesn't work."

- "I was stupid. I really believed I could go back to some of my old haunts and not drink. I was too confident."
- "I said I was an alcoholic before but I don't think I really believed it. I just had to keep testing it."
- "I guess I really hadn't hit bottom. Maybe I had to lose everything before I could get sober."
- "I was O.K. until my wife left. I just couldn't believe she would leave me after I had tried so hard. When that happened, I just gave up."

The "poor me" demeanor and pleas for another chance trigger rescue fantasies and usually result in a quick re-admission to treatment. The difficulty is that the client quickly reverts back to the same style with which he or she did treatment previously. Even when their explanations of prior treatment failure hold some truth, their treatment demeanor replicates the old style rather than stimulating a new openness to the treatment experience.

Clients with more aggressive styles of doing treatment usually project blame for prior treatment failure onto the prior treatment programs or prior therapists. Such projection is calculated to hook the biases of the current treatment program which the addict is trying to enter. Playing to such biases is quite easy. Seeking admission to radically abstinent programs, one can hook the intake worker with stories of over-medication, advocacy of controlled drinking, and analytical approaches to counseling. Seeking admission into an AA/NA oriented program, one can deride the previous program's failure to actively involve AA/NA, utilize step work as part of treatment, establish sponsorship, etc. Seeking admission into psychiatric models of treatment, one can condemn prior treatment programs for their lack of professionally trained staff, their failure to address one's emotional problems, and their denial of mood-altering medication.

Treatment professionals frequently get hooked and manipulated through such communications. We all want to believe that we have the best program and that we are the best counselor. When addicts present themselves criticizing prior approaches to their treatment that are consistent with our own beliefs, one can get easily hooked into the belief that the client has been victimized by "bad treatment" but through our approach will undoubtedly achieve success. As an addict describes their prior unsuccessful treatment experiences, it is somewhat humbling to wonder: "If this client's history of treatment failure continues through the current experience, how will he or she describe this program and this counselor at the time he or she enters the next program?"

When counselors get hooked into such projections, they allow the addict client to continue the belief that responsibility for recovery lies within a treatment program rather than within the client. These clients are committed foremost to their continued drug use, will willingly enter treatment during a crisis, and will continue both the pattern of drug use and episodic treatment until someone does something "to them" to alter the pattern. To alter the career path of the "professional patient," one must first alter and reframe the conditions and beliefs under which he or she enters the treatment process.

G. *Yassa Boss: The Art of Compliance*   There are a number of compliant styles addicts can take on to minimize their treatment involvement.

1. **The Miracle Cures** are clients who present a superficial conversion reaction almost the second they enter treatment. They are the treatment Pollyannas. The program is wonderful. Their counselor is wonderful. They have seen the light. They gush with praise for everyone around them and mouth superficial slogans and platitudes. They are filled with bold but vague resolutions

about their future life in sobriety. The problem is that the miracle cures present themselves as having completed treatment before they start it. Upon close examination, one finds that their participation is verbal and not behavioral. They talk about the importance of meetings, but they don't go to meetings. They talk about the importance of expressing feelings, but they don't express feelings. The miracle cures are mirrors who, to reduce personal vulnerability in treatment, utilize the defense mechanism of introjection to absorb and reflect back the values of whatever environment they are in. Their compliance is an escape from the experience of treatment. Upon discharge, the continued style of introjection usually dictates rapid relapse as they return to the environment which previously supported their alcohol and drug consumption.

2. **The Invisible Clients** are addicts who escape the treatment experience by seeking invisibility within the treatment environment. They adhere to all rules within the treatment milieu, meet all minimal expectations set for them, but initiate nothing related to their own treatment. They create the illusion of involvement while remaining emotionally detached from the treatment process. They are quiet and socially isolated within the treatment environment and use their withdrawal from interaction as a way simply to mark time until they can resume their addictive career.

3. **The Instant Counselors** are addicts who spend most of their time in treatment focusing on the problems of others. They externalize the recovery process. Often coming from medicine men, midwife, or high priest roles from the culture of addiction, they apply new learnings in treatment to other addicts. They may offer deep insight into the addictive patterns of their peers. They can be quite supportive. They can offer sound advice based on recovery principles absorbed from the treatment milieu. What they have great difficulty doing, however, is personalizing these

principles to themselves. Their preoccupation with others is a defensive posture that allows them to escape the pain and consequences of their own addictive career. Failing to achieve such personalization in treatment, they often quickly revert back to both their helping roles and addictive lifestyle within the culture of addiction.

4. **The Professional Patients** are addicts who may have reached a point in their addictive career where they are spending more time in treatment than actively addicted. They are often outcasts from the culture of addiction, who, failing to achieve a role in straight society, and no longer able to function in the addictive culture, utilize treatment programs as a shelter or alternative lifestyle. No longer able to adequately sustain the addict role and lacking skills to pursue an alternative career, they do what they do best—they do treatment. They often become highly institutionalized to addiction treatment settings and have learned all the appropriate role behaviors for a client in treatment. They know recovery literature backwards and forwards—sometimes better than the staff. They could give most of the lectures commonly presented in addiction treatment settings. They do wonderful written assignments while in treatment. They can articulate elaborate plans for their ongoing recovery following discharge. What they can't do is stay sober outside of an institutional setting. Without radically altering the nature of the treatment experience for these addicts, they will perform their well rehearsed role while in treatment with little personalization and no alteration in behavior and lifestyle following their discharge from treatment. Their expertise at "doing treatment" is actually an escape from treatment.

H. *The Best Defense is a Good Offense* Not all clients present compliance as a style of doing treatment and continuing their addictive lifestyle. Some will present a much more aggressive posture as they present themselves for treatment. Several variations of such aggressive styles are presented below.

1. **The Intimidators** are addicted clients who enter treatment daring the treatment staff to remove the chip on their shoulder. They are resistive to most of the program structure and equally resistive in entering into relationships within the treatment milieu. Their overt hostility is quite functional as it drives treatment staff into a posture of emotional distancing and allows them to escape the vulnerability that would come from normal therapeutic relationships. Intimidators quickly hook that part of professional helpers that needs to be liked and appreciated. Staff are kept in such a defensive posture that most treatment time is spent on forcing behavioral compliance with basic program rules. The intimidator style is encapsuled within a world view that is self-fulfilling. They expect to be disliked and rejected and present behaviors that assure such an outcome. When their behavior results in rejection, they can continue their addictive lifestyle, defiance intact, with their view of the world having once again been confirmed.

Because intimidators are so disliked by treatment staff, the staff can be manipulated into rather untenable and absurd positions. Many years ago a particularly skilled intimidator was unnerving an entire staff of a residential treatment program. He was testing every program boundary possible: refusing to go to self-help meetings, constantly demanding a change in primary counselor, violating numerous rules, etc. A staff meeting was called regarding this client in which staff ventilated their frustration and rage at this client in language couched both in professional jargon and unprofessional expletives. The decision was made that after informing the client, we would administratively discharge him the next time he refused to obey any of the rules. That very night the client was so discharged when he refused to go to bed at the required time. We all felt piously justified in the decision and, to be honest, were quite happy and relieved that this particular client was gone. Everything was fine until the judge who had placed him in the treatment facility called. I remember these final words before the judge hung up on me. "Let me get this straight. You take a man who has been addicted to heroin for fifteen years. A man who we both know has committed every kind of unspeakable crime. A man who has not lived in what we would call human society for the past two decades. A man who has lived like an animal on the streets. And you throw him out of treatment because he won't go to bed at 10:30! I sent him to you for addiction treatment, not for charm school!" I still feel sheepish about that phone call.

Treatment of the intimidator is a game of conflicting world views. The intimidator's world view is one of anticipatory rejection which provides part of the cognitive defense structure that fuels self-destructive behavior. The treatment team is positing a world view based on human potential set free from debilitating illness. When we throw intimidators out of treatment, they win.

2. **Splitting the Staff** Another aggressive style of doing treatment, one which involves considerably more charm than the intimidator, is the splitting of staff. The purpose of this gambit is to create friction within the treatment team and thereby reduce the intensity of focus on the client. Splitting pits doctor against nurse, nurse against counselor, recovering staff against non-recovering staff, first shift against second shift, black staff against white staff, etc. The strategy of splitting is actually quite simple. The addict client through a campaign of misinformation stimulates resentment and suspicion within the staff team. The following scenarios are typical.

- A client in treatment with a deep abrasion on his arm communicates the following to his doctor during daily rounds: "I'm really confused. You told me to keep it covered but the nurses keep telling me to keep it exposed to the air. When I told them what you wanted, they said to just do what they say." The physician storms into the nurses station and shouts before quickly leaving that he will not have his orders countermanded by a nurse. The nurses, following the doctor's rapid exit, look at each other in pained confusion.

- A client communicates the following to two evening nurses in a substance abuse unit: "You two have meant a whole lot to me. It seems like the day nurses never have time to talk to us. When I mentioned this to Betty (the Head Nurse), she said it was because the evening shift had it a lot easier than the day shift. I don't think you have it easier, I think you just care more."

- A client communicates the following to a counselor: "Listen, is there a way that I could ask for you to be my primary counselor? Jim (the assigned counselor) is O.K.; it's just that you seem to be tougher and I think that's what I need. Besides, I think I'd do better with a counselor who has also been addicted."

The "splitters" are quite intuitive and will pick up any areas of latent conflict within the staff team and magnify and exploit such differences for their own advantage. This could be described as a "divide and conquer" approach to self-protection in treatment. The functioning of treatment teams can disintegrate under the skill and influence of the sophisticated splitter. While the team is torn by the emergence of conflict, the splitter is setting back observing the chaos and escaping the treatment experience.

3. **The Program Evaluator** The treatment role that most parallels the role of "jailhouse lawyer" is the program evaluator. Like the intimidator and the splitter, the goal of the program evaluator is to place treatment staff on the defensive and to decrease the intensity of the treatment experience. The evaluator questions the rationale for every program procedure and enters as if he or she were there to assess rather than experience the program. In its most aggressive form, the evaluator will demand numerous changes in program structure, question the professional competence of every staff person, file numerous grievances and threaten to sue everyone at least once per week. When this style is successful, staff will be so defensive and preoccupied with the Evaluator's demands that little treatment will take place. By evaluating the treatment experience, the evaluator escapes treatment and is thus freed to continue pursuit of the addictive career.

I. *Creating Diversions* Another style of doing treatment that addicts bring from the culture of addiction involves the use of diversions to escape the treatment experience. Some variations of this style are catalogued below.

1. **My Real Problem Is...** The pain and consequences the addict experiences from drug consumption often reach an apex in the crisis that brings the addict into treatment. The very admission into treatment however, may reduce the experience of such pain, and allow the addict to quickly reframe the pain in ways that provide a loophole for continued drug use. Such reframing is often seen in the various forms of denial and minimization that may intensify shortly after the treatment admission. One of the most common types of reframing involves a shift in the addict's definition of his or her primary problem. Such reframing can constitute a powerful diversion. Through this gambit, the addict presents the treatment team with significant life problems to shift attention away from addiction. The addict providing token

acknowledgement of substance abuse, tantalizes the treatment team with secondary issues. In the addict's own words: "There is no question that my drinking/drug use got out of hand, but my REAL problem is...

- my wife. If I could just get her to see a psychiatrist."
- my unhappy childhood."
- my marriage. If I could just get my marriage back on track."
- my upcoming court date."
- my financial problems."
- my supervisor at work. If I could just get her off my back."
- my depression."
- my sexuality. If I could just come to grips with being Gay."
- this town. Nobody could stay sober in this place."

It is only natural for a therapist to pick up on some of these issues that the client reports as disturbing. The danger is that we get seduced into addressing not the primary addictive disorder, but the consequences of that disorder on other areas of the client's life. By getting seduced out of our primary role, we not only fail to provide addiction treatment, but inadvertently patch up the drug-related pain and crises in the addict's life so that he or she can resume the addictive career.

2. **Playing Crazy** Another diversion that can be offered up by the addict is playing crazy. "Playing crazy" does not refer to clients who present a genuine organic or functional psychiatric illness. It refers to a gambit used by an addict to minimize the intensity of, or escape from, addiction treatment. By presenting bizarre ideation, the addict forces substance abuse treatment staff to immediately disengage and reconsider their diagnosis and

treatment plan. Such a gambit not only provides a temporary reprieve from the pressure of the treatment process, but may also provide a pathway out of treatment. The author has known a number of addicts who were quite comfortable entering inpatient psychiatric treatment programs during addiction induced crises. This setting provided temporary escape and shelter with much less threat posed to their addictive career than entry into an addiction treatment setting.

3. **Cultivating Chaos and Crises** Another style of diversion is exemplified by the client who presents a new crisis each day in treatment. There is an emergency with the family. There is a crisis related to the job. A best friend is sick. A great uncle just died. The family is gone and there's no one to feed the pet. The client just found out he has a court appearance in 45 minutes. The client has just discovered that they are in love with another client. Therapist begin to think they are conducting therapy in the middle of a hurricane. It is not so much the individual events as the total pattern of crises that must be confronted as a diversion from treatment. Left unchecked, the addict will escape the treatment process and will be left to create new crises through the continuation of the addictive career.

4. **The Treatment Elite** Another style of diversion can be seen in those addicts who self-identify as the treatment elite. Such status can be self confirmed based on personal wealth, professional position, public fame, physical beauty, or one's drug of choice (cocaine). The grandiosity and "specialness" of the elite are confirmed through numerous behaviors that serve as an escape from treatment. The doctor in treatment plays doctor and the professor plays professor, both refusing to ever get "out of role." The famous hold court with staff and other clients. The beautiful ones prepare for treatment activities not in meditation or reading, but in front of a mirror. The cocaine addicts spin cocaine tales and

remain aloof, seeing themselves above and different from the common lot of addicts with whom they are forced to share treatment. Such specialness must be therapeutically manipulated and eventually removed if the elite are to experience treatment. Left unchecked, the same images and behaviors that helped them sustain their addiction will help them escape treatment.

J. *The Self-Help Critic* Most addiction treatment modalities in the United States involve exposure of the client to such self-help groups as Alcoholics Anonymous or Narcotics Anonymous. The addict "doing treatment" faces substantial risks through self-help participation. They enter a closed society of other addicts—sober and drug free addicts—who see through the neophyte's posturing and gambits. These men and women are intimately acquainted with the chameleon's many colors. The neophyte inevitably feels an affinity and pull toward these individuals. Seeing former addicts healthy and vibrant and articulate can precipitate a crisis of hope. They, who came to treatment to get out of a jam, may actually find themselves seriously considering the prospect of recovery. To continue their addictive career, they must develop a cognitive defense that allows them to distance themselves from this self-help experience. In short, they must become a self-help critic. They must stay detached or face the risk of giving up their drug relationship.

The intensity of the threat that AA and NA can pose to the addictive career can be easily understood if we closely examine the most common "reasons" cited by addicts in treatment as to why they don't like meetings.

- I can't stand drunkalogs. (cited by persons who have spent decades sharing hustling tales, copping tales, and getting off tales within the culture of addiction.)

- I refuse to expose myself to all that smoke. (cited by health conscious individuals who have poisoned their bodies with innumerable varieties of toxic psychoactive substances.)
- I can't handle all that God stuff. (Cited by individuals who have prayed to all manner of gods to extricate them from drug-induced crises.)
- I can't stand some of the people. (Cited by individuals drawn from a culture in which members are not known for their warmth and charm.)
- I get tired of hearing people say the same things at every meeting. (Cited by individuals whose affiliation with the culture of addiction was questionably related to the sparkling variety and stimulation of the conversation found there.)

The early resistance of the addict to AA and NA may actually be a positive sign. Most addicts find it easier to "do treatment" than to "do AA/NA." Resistance is a signal that continued contact poses a significant threat or crisis in continuing one's addictive career. It is precisely that crisis which successful treatment attempts to precipitate for the addict.

K. *Doing Treatment; Sustaining Addiction* For some addicts, the treatment experience does not provide an interruption in their addictive career. They attempt to do treatment while continuing their drug relationship. Long before they enter treatment, most addicts have heard tales from other addicts that acknowledge both the fact of drug use while in treatment as well as how such use was conducted to avoid detection. Every culturally enmeshed addict is therefore presented with the choice of whether they will attempt continued use during their treatment experience. Sorting out this decision taps the addict's ambivalence about the drug relationship. A part of the addict desperately hopes that something will happen to break the addictive pattern—a desire to get well in spite of themselves. Another part wants more than anything else to sustain their drug relationship.

Addicts who continue use during treatment must devote significant energy toward such use—energy that cannot then be used to focus on themselves and their treatment. The addict is going through rote behaviors of treatment, but his primary attention is diverted to such issues as drug supply, drug concealment, and identifying the best times and places to use to avoid detection. Because of the ambivalence associated with this behavior, the addict will often seek one or more collaborators to share use while in treatment. By engaging others in such use, the decision of the addict to continue drug use is again culturally affirmed. Perhaps this is why drug use in treatment is rarely done alone, but in dyads and triads that constitute a shared conspiracy to sabotage treatment.

Imagine two addicts in residential or outpatient treatment who have entered into such a conspiracy. Imagine them participating in group knowing they are going to get high afterwards. Imagine them sitting next to each other at an AA/NA meeting. Imagine their conversations when alone. Imagine the careful planning that must be involved. Imagine the intensity of their efforts to find loopholes in the treatment structure which they can exploit to avoid detection. Imagine the duplicity required to get through individual counseling sessions. They are in a treatment environment but they brought the culture of addiction in with them and that culture remains alive and well.

Avoiding detection requires substantial effort when the addict is involved in a program that conducts random urinalysis. The culture of addiction does, however, provide assistance to an addict in such a situation. If the procedures used for urine collection by the treatment program are not highly refined and rigorous, the addict can escape detection. The culture provides information on how long various drugs can be detected in urine. The culture teaches "flushing" techniques designed to lower drug concentrations below detectable levels. The culture provides information on medications/foods that may trigger false positives, thus providing rationalizations for test results. The culture provides paraphernalia that can be utilized to surreptitiously substitute clean urine for one's own. The culture has even gone so far in some areas as to provide guaranteed clean urine that can be purchased by the addicts for such substitutions. The above is not to suggest that escaping detection through urinalysis programs is easy. It does suggest that the addict wishing to continue use through treatment without detection does have some cultural assistance in achieving this feat.

A more common phenomenon occurs when the addict gives up the primary drug choice during the treatment experience but clings to secondary drugs of abuse through this same period. Secondary drugs provide a buffer to sustain the addict until, with passage of the crisis that induced treatment, he or she can resume use of the primary drug.

There are a number of implications for treatment programs that emerge from the above descriptions.

- Abstinence during treatment must be assessed and monitored rather than assumed.
- Monitoring of abstinence, to include urinalysis, must be rigorous and reflect an understanding of those means generally used by addicts to escape detection of use.
- Review of client treatment history should include questions related to prior use while in treatment.

- Questions of use while in treatment must be confronted immediately and directly, not to expel the individual from treatment, but to initiate treatment.
- Cultural influences make use during treatment contagious. Discovery of use by one client should be followed by the identification of cultural alliances that may indicate drug use by other clients.
- The use of secondary drugs should be addressed aggressively to prevent the use of such substances as a buffer during treatment.

7.12 *Pathways Out of the Culture of Addiction* If we conceptualize addiction as a career with predictable initiation rites and career milestones, we should also then be able to identify various pathways through which one can exit such a career. This section will describe some of the pathways out of the culture of addiction. The next chapter will examine the motivations and conditions under which the more desirable alternative careers are chosen.

A. *Death* For many addicts, the addictive career is sustained until death. Whether due to lack of internal resources or the existence of external obstacles or the whim of fate, such individuals were not able to avail themselves of alternative career paths. Most persons in our culture readily acknowledge the risks and dangers associated with addiction, and yet the mortality associated with addiction is grossly underestimated.

Addiction-related deaths are usually thought of in terms of heroin addicts dying of overdoses or alcoholics dying of cirrhosis of the liver or other alcohol-related disease. The incidence of such deaths, while significant, probably constitute only a small portion of addiction-related deaths in the United States. Such incidence pales in comparison to the number (if we could determine it) of addicts who die in accidents, who die as victims of violence, and who die by their own hand.

Addiction is a progressive condition, which when left unchecked, results in premature death. While the instrument of death may vary widely, the fact of premature death is assured for those addicts who cannot find and sustain alternative career paths. With the advent of new and more powerful drugs (designer fentanyl) and new diseases (AIDS) transmitted within the culture of addiction, even the neophyte or transient user faces increased risks of death.

Perhaps the largest category of unseen deaths from addiction are those involving suicide. Death is a constant companion of the addict appearing at times as a demon to be fought off and appearing at other times as a seductive lover to be embraced. When we combine organic impairment, high risk-taking behavior, chronic depression resulting from losses experienced during the addictive career, the increasing fear of insanity, escalating feelings of shame and guilt and the continued consumption of drugs that lower inhibitions and impair judgement; death appears more and more frequently in the form of the seductive lover.

Most addicts have encountered what are referred to as "near death experiences." Perhaps these experiences explain why many addicts carry a morbid fear of death into their early recovery. It is as if they have narrowly cheated death so many times that death will seek its revenge by taking them once they are finally sober. For some addicts, it will be the sharing and looking back on those near death experiences that will bring the beginnings of their spiritual awakening.

B. *Psychiatric Impairment*   One pathway out of the culture of addiction is to move from an addictive career to a psychiatric career. Severe psychiatric impairment, which preceded and was exacerbated by addiction, or which was caused by drug consumption, may impair one's ability to sustain the addictive lifestyle. Such impairment demands alteration in one's career path. One drifts toward those tribes within the culture most populated with "crazies." Drug choices shift toward those that require less money and less skill to sustain and toward those drugs which can either self-medicate or mask the psychiatric symptoms. One begins to disengage from the mainstream of the culture of addiction and move toward more deviant fringe groups. Institutional affiliations begin to shift from substance abuse treatment centers to psychiatric units. One's identity begins its transformation from that of addict to that of psychiatric patient.

The above shift may be a stage, or an intermediate step in the recovery process, or it may involve an alternative long term career path. For some, the pathway will mark the beginning of a long history of acute episodes of psychiatric impairment and psychiatric hospitalization. Their concurrent drug use and psychiatric impairment may be particularly disabling given the probability they will find themselves shifted back and forth from addiction to psychiatric treatment settings, with neither setting equipped to deal with a client who presents multiple disorders.

Clients on this pathway present unique characteristics and treatment needs. Treatment approaches designed to help these clients discover the recovery pathway must bring together, in the assessment and treatment planning process, the best technology from both the field of substance abuse and the field of psychiatry.

C. *Criminality* Those addicts whose pattern of substance abuse is associated with criminal behavior may be diverted from a primary addictive career to a criminal career. Through repeated arrest and incarceration, their primary institutional affiliation becomes the prison rather than the treatment center. The pattern of drug consumption shifts to less intensity and frequency or may stop altogether, but the involvement in criminal activity (and the culture which supports it) continues. For those users whose antisocial and criminal behavior predated the onset of their addiction, this is a very predictable career path.

The criminal career path may represent a permanent career choice or can also be an intermediate stage on the way to one of the career paths described below.

D. *Spontaneous Remission* Is it possible that an addict can simply cease being an addict without aid of treatment, self-help groups or other recovery framework? Is it possible that one engaged in the ongoing use of psychoactive substances can simply stop using such substances and go on with his or her life, leaving such history completely behind? There is growing evidence that the answer to this question is in the affirmative. In fact, until the recent proliferation of treatment centers and the dramatic increase in the number of addicts exposed to treatment, this group may have composed the largest group of non-using addicts.

There are really two such groups of non-using addicts. The first group contains addicts who instinctively recognize their potential vulnerability during the early to middle stages of their drug addiction. They experience early consequences which lead to a complete cessation of drug consumption. These cases are described here as "spontaneous remission." A second group of addicts, who also stop drug consumption without treatment or self-help involvement, include those addicts who cease drug consumption in the latter stages of addiction because of the wear and tear of years struggling to sustain the addictive lifestyle. It is these addicts whom we will refer to as "maturing out" in the late stages of the addiction life cycle. The distinction between the two groups is an arbitrary one imposed by the author as there is little objective research that has been conducted on such non-treated, non-using addicts.

A study by Tuchfield at Texas Christian University involved detailed analysis of 51 cases of spontaneous remission. The cases studied involved persons who had past histories of serious drinking problems who quit drinking without the aid of self-help groups, substance abuse treatment or other professional assistance. The decision of Tuchfield's respondents to stop drinking was influenced by such factors as:

- Experiencing a personally humiliating event as a result of intoxication.
- Experiencing an event that precipitated a crisis in values related to drinking behavior *e.g.* one pregnant respondent, drinking beer to get rid of a hangover, felt her baby quiver and was so overwhelmed with shame that she poured out the beer and never drank again.
- Experiencing a serious alcohol-related medical problem.
- Experiencing a religious conversion.

The persons in Tuchfield's study who successfully stopped drinking did have significant social influences to support their decision. Many cited the important role of family and friends in helping them sustain their decision to no longer drink. Other studies have described similar factors influencing spontaneous remission in persons addicted to drugs other than alcohol.

The phenomenon of "spontaneous remission" is an important and historically neglected aspect of addiction research. By more extensive study of such individuals it may be discovered that there is a significant population of addicts who stop using without the aid of self-help groups or treatment. It may also be discovered that this population differs from those addicts who require treatment and self-help support. Understanding which species of addiction are most likely to utilize spontaneous remission as a pathway out of addiction and understanding at which stages such spontaneous remission is possible will be an important new areas of knowledge for the addiction treatment field. It may be discovered in retrospect that spontaneous remission is both a possible pathway out of addiction and, for some addicts, the preferred pathway. Spontaneous remission may provide a pathway to sobriety and health for some addicts whose unique personality characteristics or life circumstances would make success through treatment and self-help involvement unlikely.

E. *Maturing Out* Winick (1962, 1964, 1972) and Vaillant (1970), in their long term studies of heroin addiction, have posited the existence of a "life cycle" or "natural history" of heroin addiction. Winick described a phenomenon through which perhaps as many as two-thirds of addicts stopped using heroin in a process he describes as "maturing out" of narcotic addiction. Such drug cessation appears to be a function of age rather than a function of treatment. Prior to these studies, it was generally believed that addictions in the form of alcoholism, heroin addiction, etc., were self-accelerating. Winick's studies confirm that, for at least a large percentage of heroin addicts, addiction is self-limiting.

Winick's studies raise a number of fascinating questions about the addictive career. What differences exist between addicts whose addiction continues along a self-accelerating pathway versus those addicts who are likely to mature out of addiction in their thirties? Are there persons addicted to drugs other than heroin who also experience the maturing out process? Is maturing out a function of cumulative insight or cumulative pain and consequences from addiction? Are there actual physical adaptations occurring in the body of some addicts that inhibit continued addiction? Are there outside interventions that could speed up the maturing out process? Could factors that we know to be associated with maturing out be integrated into the addiction treatment process? How do the lives of maturing out addicts differ from the lives of treated addicts in the years following cessation of drug use?

Maturing out—the cessation of drug use in late stages of addiction without the aid of treatment—is one pathway out of the culture of addiction that is poorly understood. Perhaps by more openly acknowledging the existence of this pathway, the field can come to a better understanding of which clients this pathway is most accessible to and explore ways to accelerate this maturing out process.

F. *Getting Religion* Considering that many branches of modern substance abuse treatment spring from distinctly religious roots, it is somewhat surprising that the field remains suspect of alcoholics and addicts who utilize religion as a pathway to sobriety. Religious and spiritual experiences have been the genesis of sobriety long before the founding of Alcoholics Anonymous and modern addiction treatment. Religious organizations such as the Salvation Army were selflessly dedicated to the care of alcoholics decades before such care became popular or profitable.

The fact that addiction treatment professionals constantly see addicts for whom religious belief could not or did not serve as a sufficient stimulus for sobriety does not discount the ability of this pathway to provide a framework for lifelong sobriety for a considerable number of addicts. The spiritual abyss so characteristic of late stage addiction can create both the need and susceptibility for the religious conversion experience. What follows this spiritual crisis will determine whether the religious pathway is a sustained road to recovery or merely a rest stop on the continuing addiction pathway.

Many addicts and alcoholics report unusual religious or spiritual experiences during their addiction. When such experiences happen in isolation from a religious movement, relapse and continued addiction reduce the power of such experiences to sustain recovery. When the addict experiences the crisis and has sustained contact with a religious movement, the prospects of religion providing a medium for long term recovery are greatly enhanced. Conversations with numerous addicts who achieved sobriety in this manner reveal what seem to be the crucial influences.

- The conversion experience provides a powerful emotional stimulus to initiate sobriety.
- The framework of religious beliefs provides a framework to justify radical abstinence.
- The religious conversion is immediately followed by disengagement from relationships in the culture of addiction and saturation in new relationships within the church.
- One's new identity facilitates shedding language, dress, music, symbols and other triggers from the culture of addiction and provides for replacement of each element from the culture of addiction via the religious culture.
- Such concepts as "forgiveness," "redemption," "reborn," etc. provide anchors that allow the addict to begin fresh, creating a line of demarcation between the old life and the new.
- Religion provides rituals of confession that help expiate the shame and guilt of the addict.
- The status of "reformed addict" allows escape from stigma, offers significant social rewards in the new

setting, and provides living proof to other believers of the power of their faith.

- The religious conversion provides a new social network and opens up doors for further career conversion *i.e.* housing, jobs, and education.

Rather than look askance at religious pathways to recovery that share the above characteristics, treatment professionals might explore the distinct parallels between these characteristics and very similar characteristics that typify recovery via substance abuse treatment. Perhaps in the future it will be possible to develop an understanding of which pathway—the religious pathway or the broader spiritual pathway found in addiction treatment—is most appropriate for which addicts.

G. *The Super Ex-Dope Fiend Folk Hero* The "super ex-dope fiend folk hero," "reformed smoker" and "reformed drunk" represent other conversion experiences that lead to at least short-term abstinence. The addict, in this case, utilizes the defense mechanism of reaction formation to construct an anti-drug/alcohol facade to sustain sobriety. The style is marked by extreme proselytizing— the attempt to convert other addicts to non-use. The addict fights off impulses to resume addiction by exaggerating an anti-drug stance.

The super ex-dope fiend folk hero role can represent a style of entry into recovery but it does not provide a sufficiently solid foundation to sustain long term recovery for most addicts. Rather than disengaging from the culture of addiction, this role provides a way to sustain involvement in this culture minus the drug relationship. One's reformation can become simply a new hustle to be played for self-advantage. Unless there is a transition in this role toward a more stable basis of recovery, many addicts in this role will revert to active addiction during an episode of emotional crisis. Their conversion back into addiction can occur as rapidly as their earlier conversion out of addiction.

One reason that this style is so fragile is that it continues the addict's struggle for power and control over the drug. Rather than experience the unconditional surrender to the power of the drug, the folk hero role is one more effort to use one's will to fight the drug and win. Rather than seeking strength outside himself to support recovery, the folk hero continues the belief that he alone can gain mastery over the power of drugs in his life. The style reflects an effort of willpower that can rarely be sustained over time.

The super ex-dope fiend folk heroes have played a visible role in the substance abuse prevention and treatment field. In the 1960s and 1970s, such persons could be found on the soap boxes of high school auditoriums and various community forums preaching the horrors of drug addiction through exposure of their personal histories. They could also be found working as counselors in many substance abuse treatment programs. Many would assume such roles with frighteningly short periods of sobriety. For many, their jobs would be indistinguishable from their sobriety. The substance abuse field would become a haven from the culture of addiction while keeping them dangerously close to this culture. Their sobriety would become tied to their job.

As a field, we often mistook the passion and commitment of these individuals for competence. Their charisma blinded us to their fragile hold on sobriety and their lack of a program for long-term recovery. The long line of casualties (relapses) of such heroes working in the field has, in retrospect, helped us develop a more reasoned approach to the appropriate use of recovering addicts in the field.

The passion of the recently "reformed" addict can mark the initial stage of recovery or a short leave of absence from the addictive career. Our job is to work with this style and facilitate the transition to a more stable, long-term framework for recovery.

H. *Treatment/Recovery* The most visible pathway out of addiction today is through involvement in self-help groups and addiction treatment. This pathway is more open today than it has ever been in our country's history. Major strides have been made in decreasing the stigma of addiction. Public awareness about addiction and treatment resources for addiction has dramatically increased. Self-help groups have proliferated beyond the wildest predictions that could have been made twenty years ago. And addiction treatment has become increasingly professionalized and legitimized through its integration into the broad stream of health care in the United States.

I. *The Question of Controlled Use* Nearly all of the pathways out of addiction described above imply the shift from addictive drug use to total drug abstinence. In concluding the overall discussion of pathways out of addiction, it is appropriate to address the following two questions:

1. Is there a pathway out of addiction that involves the shift from addiction to a particular drug to controlled and non-consequential use of this same substance?

2. Is there a pathway out of addiction that involves abstinence from the primary drug of abuse but continued controlled and non-consequential use of other psychoactive substances?

Given the current state of knowledge, is it appropriate for us to *advocate* controlled alcohol/drug use for even a selected minority of our clients? The advocacy of client experiments in controlled drinking cannot be justified based on current clinical research. Such advocacy could also not be defended ethically given the lack of data to determine which substance abusers, if any, can return to controlled use of primary or secondary drugs. Given our current state of knowledge, the advocacy of controlled use would propose an experimental method of treatment that would pose grave and potentially life-threatening risks to clients.

Is it possible to condemn advocacy of controlled drug/alcohol use for clients while aggressively supporting research into the controlled use question? This position seems to the author to be both defensible and desirable.   Given the growing recognition of multiple etiological pathways to addiction and the increased technology to intervene at early and middle stages of addiction, it is particularly important to the future of substance abuse treatment that we develop definitive answers to the controlled use question.

It is important to recognize that there is a new context within which the question of controlled drinking and controlled drug use can and must be addressed. Historically this question has been applied to one population of addicts—male alcoholics in the latest stages of progression of alcoholism. A body of limited research and folk wisdom within the substance abuse treatment field emerged to suggest that these alcoholics could not return to any type of controlled drinking and that they would be equally high risk to addiction to other central nervous system depressants. New patterns of drug consumption and a more heterogeneous population of users entering treatment force the formulation of new positions or rationales in response to the controlled use question.

The dialogue on this issue stirs primitive passions among treatment professionals and within the recovering community. The passions are well-founded and rest on our understanding of the propensity of addicts to seek any loophole or glimmer of hope that can restore control over the drug that has dominated their life. The fear is that the controlled drinking dialogue may stimulate addicts to continue field research with deadly consequences.

The controlled use question today is not a treatment issue; it is a research issue. It is sound research that must provide a basis for the future education of clients. This research cannot come from contrived experiments in which we subject clients to the risks of controlled drinking techniques on the grounds of expanding scientific knowledge. Much of the research on controlled drinking can begin by rigorous long-term follow-up studies on treated and untreated addicts. Such research could address some of the following questions:

- Is there a population of persons who can move from an abusive or addictive pattern of drug consumption to a pattern of controlled non-consequential use? If there is such a population, how do they differ from those persons who exhibit continued self-accelerating patterns of abuse or addiction? What is the size of this population in relationship to the total pool of addicts?
- Is there a critical period or stage of drug consumption past which controlled use is impossible? If so, what physiological or behavioral markers signify this critical period? Is the issue of controlled use different when intervention occurs at an early stage of use as opposed to late stages of addiction?
- Does the ability of an addict to move to controlled non-consequential drug use require a period of sobriety to break the cycle of abuse before controlled use commences? Are there other factors that are identifiable pre-conditions that must be present to support controlled use?

- Is the risk of addiction drug-specific or specific to a pharmacological category of drugs or to all psychoactive substances? If the cocaine addict cannot use alcohol in a controlled non-consequential manner, is this failure a function of physiology, psychological attributes or environmental factors?
- If the risks of controlled drinking are variable for different species of addiction and different stages of addiction, as this author believes, then what is the varying nature of such risks?

Research on such questions can help us answer which, if any, clients can return to controlled use and, perhaps more importantly, provide clearer and stronger rationales for radical abstinence for those who cannot.

7.13 *Summary: The Culture as Cult* The culture of addiction is not a cult in the traditional conception of such groups. There is no single charismatic, authoritarian leader of the culture of addiction. Membership is more a function of voluntary choice than aggressive recruitment or deceitful manipulation. The loose, almost chaotic organization of the culture of addiction defies comparison with the rigid structure of most cults. Yet, there are striking similarities if we compare one's experience in a cult to one's experience in the culture of addiction.

- Both involve disengagement from society at large and involvement in a closed, secretive subculture.
- Both require fanatical attachment and devotion, one to a person, the other to a drug and the social network in which it is found.
- Both result in a resocialization of basic values and beliefs and adherence to group "doctrine."
- Both involve a transformation of personal identity.

- Both radically re-shape daily rituals and personal habits in ways that reinforce continued membership.
- Both utilize conscious altering mechanisms, one with ritual and the other with drugs, to alter emotional experience.
- Both tend to undermine traditional values of marriage and family and are often associated with the abuse or neglect of children.
- Both involve what becomes allegiance to a total lifestyle shared only by other members.

The cult analogy is made here to emphasize the power of the culture of addiction to command allegiance, and also to underscore the power of the techniques that may be required to disengage addicts from the culture of addiction. The disengagement of the addict from the drug itself may be the easiest task; the task of disengaging the addict from the culture of addiction may prove to be the most difficult.

BOOK TWO

THE CULTURE OF RECOVERY

"We have not even to risk the adventure alone; for the heroes of all time have gone before us; the labyrinth is thoroughly known; we have only to follow the thread of the hero-path. And where we had thought to find an abomination, we shall find a god; where we had thought to slay another, we shall slay ourselves; where we had thought to travel outward, we shall come to the center of our existence; where we had thought to be alone, we shall be with all the world."

Joseph Campbell

The Hero With A Thousand Faces

❦

8

THE CULTURE OF ADDICTION
AND THE TREATMENT PROCESS

The seven chapters of Book I have described the culture of addiction and how enmeshment in this culture provides powerful anchors to sustain excessive alcohol and drug consumption. The forthcoming chapters which make up Book II outline strategies and techniques that can disengage addicts from this culture and guide them into an alternative "culture of recovery."

This chapter details how the substance abuse treatment professional can assess the intensity of a client's involvement in the culture of addiction, enhance the client's bonding to the treatment milieu, and weaken self-defeating styles of "doing treatment." Particular emphasis is given to how client contact and engagement with the culture of addiction is broken and how the initial relationship with the culture of recovery is established.

8.1 *Culture of Addiction as an Assessment Component* There are varying styles and intensities in each client's historical involvement in the culture of addiction. A major premise of this book is that treatment professionals should assess, not only the intensity and chronicity of the client's relationships with drugs, but also the intensity and chronicity of his or her involvement in the culture of addiction. Presented below is a model for assessing cultural involvement.

A. *Cultural Assessment at Intake* Given the amount of data that needs to be collected from a client during the intake interview, it is important that there be a vehicle to rapidly assess the client's intensity of cultural involvement. As we shall see shortly, such assessment may help determine the most appropriate treatment modality for the client. For many clients this level of cultural involvement will be obvious. Where the level of such involvement is unclear, the following questions can quickly identify cultural enmeshment.

YES NO 1.   Do most of your leisure activities involve alcohol/drug use?

YES NO 2.   Have you procured alcohol/drugs from more than five locations in the past 3 months?

YES NO 3.   Do most of your friends consume alcohol/drugs in the same frequency and quantity as you do?

YES NO 4.   Are there others with whom you regularly share alcohol and drugs?

YES NO 5.   Have you stopped seeing friends who don't use alcohol/drugs the way you do?

YES NO 6.   Do you own alcohol/drug-related paraphernalia? (contrivances for use, brand symbols, etc.)?

YES NO 7.   Have you been involved in criminal activity related to your alcohol/drug use (other than possession) or have close friends who have?

YES NO 8.   Do you feel that through your association with others that you know a great deal about alcohol/drugs?

YES NO 9.   When you are with your friends, do you find yourselves telling "war stories" about your alcohol/drug escapades?

YES NO 10.   Do you feel your whole lifestyle has changed as a result of your alcohol/drug use?

Questions like those above begin to elicit the client's degree of cultural involvement. A greater the number of "YES" responses, the greater is the intensity of cultural enmeshment. Clients in denial or who are generally resistive to treatment may minimize yes responses to the above questions at the point of intake. Where such denial or minimization occurs, the following method may be helpful.

B. *Collateral Interview* The use of collateral contacts is particularly helpful in assessing the client's degree of involvement in the culture of addiction. The following questions directed to family members, friends, or other collaterals can quickly validate or alter the data obtained from the client at intake.

YES NO 1.   Does (client) spend considerable time with other alcohol/drug users?

YES NO 2.   Has (client) become more and more detached from family and friends who don't drink/use drugs?

YES NO 3.   Have you seen dramatic changes in (client's) language, values, appearance, and eating/sleeping habits as a result of his/her drug use?

YES NO 4.   Do you feel (client), through his/her association with other users, is transforming into someone you no longer know or can reach?

YES NO 5.   Do you feel there are other alcohol/drug users who are a particularly bad influence on (client)?

"YES" responses to questions like the above confirm the existence of cultural enmeshment. Confirmation of cultural enmeshment is also indicated by other data from the intake interview which would indicate performance of a key role within the culture of addiction (*i.e.* dealing, preoccupation with key cultural activities such as hustling, or the existence of numerous career milestones from the culture such as arrest or incarceration.

C. *Self-Assessment Techniques* Once the client has settled into the treatment milieu and begun to build some trust in the treatment relationship, it is helpful to return to the area of cultural assessment in more depth. It is preferable to use a method for structuring this assessment so that client defenses are not fully aroused. Asking the client to complete Exhibit A, the "Self-Assessment Inventory," displayed in the Appendix, in the quiet of their room or at home in between outpatient interviews can be a useful treatment assignment. With defenses lowered, it may be possible to detect a much greater level of cultural involvement than was indicated at intake. The "Self-Assessment Inventory" expands upon the intake questions to assess the total number of areas of the client's life that have been transformed by addiction.
The greater the number of "YES" responses, the greater is the intensity of cultural involvement.

D. *The Social Network Diagram* Another helpful assessment technique is to have clients diagram their social network and then assess the extent to which this network supports continued addiction or recovery. Using the instrument on the following page, ask clients to place in each of the twenty-five circles the name of a person with whom they have frequent contact. Then ask them to identify those persons in the diagram who will support their continued addiction by using with them, providing them alcohol/-drugs, bailing them out of trouble, etc. These persons are indicated by placing a minus sign beside the circle with their name in it. Then ask them to place a plus sign beside the circles containing the name of those persons who will be most supportive of their recovery. With culturally enmeshed clients, nearly all the network is marked with minus signs. The comparison of minus and plus scores provides both good assessment data, a powerful visual message to the client on the forces (people) promoting either continued addiction or recovery, and an excellent entry point for the counselor to begin discussing reconstruction of the client's social world.

An extension of the above process can be utilized with adolescents by presenting the diagram as a game of conflicting forces. The additional steps are added to the above.

1. Pick out up to five persons whom you see very frequently and who have been very important to you. Place the number 5 beside each of their circles.
2. Place the number 2 beside all other circles.
3. Add up the numbers on all the minus circles to get a total score.
4. Add up the numbers on all the plus circles to get a total score.

The side with the highest numerical score wins. It is explained that this game is played for exceptionally high stakes. The clients are given the assignment of identifying and comparing the prizes offered by each side. One-to-one sessions explore what the adolescent can do to change the score and by so doing tip the scales toward continued addiction or recovery. The

SOCIAL NETWORK DIAGRAM

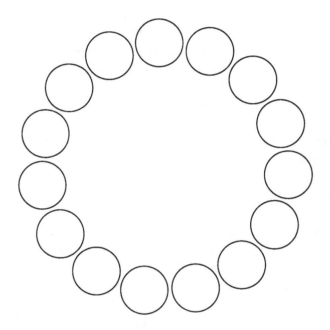

message is that the outcome of the real life version of this game is a result of choices and decisions over which they have control.

The social network diagram provides important assessment data but can also be used as a tool in treatment and as a component of relapse prevention planning.

E. *Identifying the Bicultural Style of Addiction* Once a client has been assessed to be heavily involved in the culture of addiction, it is helpful to delineate whether the involvement represents an enmeshed or bicultural style. As will be seen shortly, such distinction is relevant to the choice of treatment modalities.

A relatively easy way to identify bicultural addicts is by using the assessment interview to identify the pattern and conditions under which drug use occurs. Bicultural addicts will generally answer in the affirmative such questions as the following:

YES NO 1.   Is your alcohol/drug use generally restricted to particular times and particular settings?

YES NO 2.   Do you tend to move in and out of excessive alcohol/drug use depending on the group you're with?

YES NO 3.   Do you feel like you have two identities—one taken on with other users, the other taken on with non-users?

YES NO 4.   Do you feel equally comfortable with users and non-users?

YES NO 5.   Have you had sustained periods of minimal or no alcohol/drug use?

8.2   *The Culture of Addiction and the Choice of Treatment Modalities* The style and intensity of involvement in the culture of addiction dictates the kind of structure an addict requires to initiate the recovery process. The principle involved is one which suggests that the intensity and duration of a treatment modality must be commensurate with the intensity and chronicity of cultural involvement.

Acultural addicts sustain addiction without cultural supports. When a crisis related to addiction precipitates involvement in treatment, they often enter this involvement with significant social supports for their recovery and minimal social forces that will work to sabotage treatment. Such addicts are much more likely to enter the recovery process through the vehicle of outpatient treatment or short inpatient treatment than their more culturally involved counterparts. Other factors may enter in to indicate inpatient treatment, such as the need for medical detoxification, concurrent psychiatric illness, or prior outpatient treatment failures; but their social network increases the possibility of successful intervention using shorter term and less restrictive treatment modalities.

Culturally enmeshed addicts are rarely appropriate for traditional outpatient and the more recent intensive outpatient treatments. Addicts that present extremely intense and chronic patterns of cultural enmeshment may also receive only limited benefits from the 21-28 day short term addiction treatment model that now dominates the field. If the above treatment models are examined closely, it will be seen that they are generally designed as rehabilitation models. For persons who have achieved some level of social competence and productivity but who have had that functioning deteriorate as a result of addiction and who also maintain significant social supports for recovery, the above modalities are the treatments of choice. These models do not provide habilitative services. They possess neither the intensity nor the duration to break cultural involvement and rebuild the life of the culturally enmeshed addict. They are particularly inappropriate for the increasing population of addicts in their twenties and thirties who have no history of adequate social functioning and who have been deeply involved in the culture of addiction throughout their adolescent and adult years.

What is ironic is that the treatment settings of twenty years ago may be more appropriate for culturally enmeshed addicts than the treatment programs of today. In our search for the new higher functioning, earlier stage and well insured addicts, we may have become less capable of meeting the needs of the clients we have historically served—late stage addicts who are deeply enmeshed in the addictive lifestyle and incapable of functioning outside the culture of addiction. Long term residential treatment (more than 30 days), for example, is rapidly becoming the historical artifact that halfway houses have already become in many areas. The result of these changing resources and changing treatment models is that the lowest functioning of the culturally enmeshed addicts become part of the chronically relapsing treatment population entering and re-entering the doors of treatment centers which possess neither the power nor the duration to disengage these clients from the culture of addiction.

A number of practical implications emerge from the above observations.

1. We must stop blaming and punishing (*i.e.* refusing continued services) culturally enmeshed clients for failing to achieve sobriety through treatment modalities that by design and duration have little chance of supporting such achievement.
2. Clients with chronic and intense levels of cultural involvement should be referred to treatment resources such as long term residential programs where treatment methods and treatment duration are capable of breaking cultural affiliation, restructuring value systems, reformulating personal identity,

and reconstructing personal lifestyle. Failing to provide referral to such resources when they exist constitutes a form of professional enabling—providing a message to the client that diminishes and devalues the seriousness and morbidity of their condition.

3. Where such resources do not exist, and for clients with less intense levels of cultural involvement, the intensity of available treatment must be increased to strip the culture of addiction and the duration of treatment must be extended to assure client engagement in the culture of recovery. Inpatient treatment, for example, can be followed by outpatient treatment which can be followed by an exceptionally intense regimen of aftercare contact.

4. We must become client advocates—even to the point of advocating against our own internal systems. Arbitrary definitions of "medical necessity" for continued inpatient care and utilization review "continued stay reviews" must not become the basis for expelling the culturally enmeshed client into what is almost assured relapse. Fiscal integrity and procedural efficiency cannot take precedence over the needs of a client we have already agreed to bring into our treatment system.

5. Lacking comprehensive, long-term treatment resources, we must engage the full resources of the health and human services network to complement our efforts to guide the culturally enmeshed addict in rebuilding a new life.

Bicultural addicts are often appropriate for traditional outpatient treatment, intensive outpatient treatment, and short-term residential treatment. They differ from the culturally enmeshed addicts in their ability to sustain abstinence with less treatment structure and surveillance. They have past periods of minimal or no drug use, and they usually possess a much higher level of social functioning than culturally enmeshed clients. Bicultural addicts often have significant supports in their family and social network who will provide comfort and encouragement during the early recovery process.

8.3 *Methadone and the Culture of Addiction* Before discussing the placement of opiate addicts in Methadone maintenance, it is helpful to provide some background for readers who are unfamiliar with this treatment modality and the profile of the clients usually served by it.

Methadone is a synthetic narcotic developed in Germany during the Second World War. The approach of maintaining opiate addicts on dosages of methadone while providing rehabilitation services to alter the addictive lifestyle was pioneered by Dr. Vincent Dole and Dr. Marie Nyswander during the middle sixties. Treating late stage heroin addicts living within some of the most impoverished areas of New York City, they found this program capable of dramatically reducing illicit drug consumption and drug related criminal behavior. Social productivity increased as well, as measured by employment, involvement in school, and increased involvement and performance in family role responsibilities. Methadone maintenance would become the first modality that was capable of voluntarily bringing large numbers of opiate addicts into a rehabilitation setting.

Methadone maintenance would emerge as a major social policy strategy in the late sixties, not as a vehicle to address the needs of narcotic addicts, but as a vehicle to reduce urban crime. The goal of this policy would have great influence on the design of methadone maintenance programs as they were rapidly set up in urban centers throughout the country. Many of the early programs constituted little more than methadone filling stations staffed by too few persons with too little training to recreate the model of rehabilitation pioneered by Drs. Dole and Nyswander. More than twenty-five years after methadone maintenance was pioneered, many such programs are just now approaching the rehabilitative intensity of the original program design.

A full discussion of methadone maintenance is beyond the purpose and scope of this book. It is, however, important to address what types of addicts are most appropriate for this modality and whether the application of the concepts of "culture of addiction" and "culture of recovery" can be utilized to enhance the effectiveness of this treatment modality.

For culturally enmeshed opiate addicts, methadone maintenance and methadone detoxification can serve as important mediums of transition between the addictive lifestyle and long-term recovery. By bringing the addict's metabolic craving for opiates under control, we at least provide a foundation upon which further rehabilitation efforts can be based. The culturally enmeshed opiate addict is not generally appropriate for outpatient abstinence-oriented modalities and methadone maintenance and detoxification are the only modalities that these addicts will voluntarily seek, in the absence of strong external controls such as the threat of incarceration. Methadone can also be an important aid in initiating sustained recovery for acultural and bicultural opiate addicts with chronic histories of failure in abstinence-oriented modalities.

The most vociferous critics of methadone modalities have focused on the addictive properties of methadone. I offer no such criticisms and would suggest that it is the very addictive properties of the drug—its ability to reduce metabolic drug hunger without producing euphoric effects—that are the key to altering the life style of late-stage heroin addicts. Clinical experience suggests that there are clients for whom methadone maintenance is the only modality that has successfully eliminated the abuse of opiates and other secondary drugs and allowed such clients to construct a socially productive and fulfilling lifestyle. Criticisms of methadone maintenance might best focus not on the use of methadone but on the lack of rehabilitative services that accompany the use of the drug.

When the only significant service provided by methadone programs is the drug methadone, the culture of addiction continues to flourish both in the lives of most of the clients and within the treatment milieu of the program. Methadone has provided the foundation for change, but in such programs, nothing is built on this foundation. The momentum of the addictive lifestyle of clients in such a program will be reflected by episodic heroin use, frequent abuse of secondary drugs, continued criminal activity in spite of the altered need for heroin, and the lack of social productivity. The methods and approaches outlined in the coming pages are particularly appropriate to methadone programs. What methadone does for the body of the heroin addict, these methods do for the lifestyle of the heroin addict. These methods provide a framework for disengaging the addict from the culture which has fed and reinforced drug hunger and they provide a means of providing the addict a new identity, new values, new language, and new skills to support an alternative style of daily living.

8.4 *Engaging the Client through Cultural and Personal Identification*   Most clients entering a treatment environment/relationship do so with fear and ambivalence. The fear is the fear of an alien environment, the feeling of vulnerability and lack of control, and the suspicion that they are in a place where they will not be understood or accepted. The ambivalence embraces both their passionate desire to continue the drug relationship and the whimsical and desperate hope that something magical will occur and transform their lives.

The earliest moments in the initiation of the treatment relationship must communicate the following to the client:

- You are in the right place.
- You are with others like yourself.
- We understand you and the world from which you come.
- We accept who you are and who you can become.
- This is a place where magic (change) can happen.

This period of initial contact can be designed to enhance the conclusions above through a process of both cultural and personal identification.

Cultural identification is a process of shaping the treatment environment and staff-client communications in ways that reflect the client's addictive experience. This attention to the environment and to early communications will enhance the client's identification and engagement with the treatment milieu. A case study of a treatment program's failure to provide cultural identification can help illustrate this process.

A 30-year-old attorney and cocaine addict presented himself at a local alcohol and drug abuse treatment center requesting help. As he entered the treatment unit mentally questioning his decision to seek help, he visually scanned the environment and saw the following: a poster of the twelve steps of Alcoholics Anonymous was posted on the wall as were smaller posters of AA slogans, all the books and pamphlets in the waiting room dealt with alcoholism, the bulletin board had postings of the local AA meetings and two recent articles on alcoholism. During his intake interview, the counselor spent most of the interview asking about his drinking history and during the discussion of his cocaine addiction, the counselor had to ask for clarification of the terms "8-Ball" and "speedballing."

Following his admission, he was introduced to his two roommates who were older alcoholics that worked in local factories. He was also given program orientation literature which was replete with alcoholism references and did not mention cocaine once. In the next two days he attended lectures which contained no reference to cocaine, was assigned a counselor who knew little about cocaine but who explained that all drugs were basically the same anyway, attended groups with persons he felt little identification with, and practically got thrown out of an AA meeting when he reported that he never did like alcohol but that he was in love with cocaine. On the third day, he left the program.

The above vignette illustrates how a program can lose the opportunity to serve a client by failing to provide cultural identification. Imagine how the story above might have been different if the client had seen a poster about cocaine addiction, had seen an article on cocaine and a listing of Cocaine Anonymous meetings posted on the bulletin board, had seen books on cocaine in the waiting room, had been interviewed by a counselor who through his/her questioning revealed a detailed understanding of cocaine addiction, and had sat in groups and lectures that directly addressed the experience of cocaine addiction.

Cultural identification involves a fascinating paradox. To engage a culturally enmeshed client in treatment, we must acknowledge the client's specialness based on his or her drug of choice (since that is how cultural tribes are organized) and our understanding of the special experience of addiction to this drug. As soon as the client is engaged in the treatment process, we must begin to strip that same cultural identity and feeling of specialness that formed the basis of the client's initial identification with the treatment milieu. This paradox simply suggests that the methods we use to engage clients must be different from the methods we will later use to treat these same clients. This paradox will be explored in more detail in later discussions about developmental stages of recovery from addiction.

Personal identification involves communications of positive regard and acceptance to the client from the treatment milieu in ways that invite inclusion and relationship building. With cultural identification assured, each addict must still determine his or her personal feelings of comfort and safety in the treatment milieu. This determination, usually made in the first few hours of contact with the treatment milieu, often shapes the entire early style of approaching the treatment process. Where there is a failure to provide cultural and personal identification, the client develops a more resistive and elaborate defense structure and either prematurely exits treatment or reverts to cultural styles of "doing treatment."

Personal identification involves communicating our acceptance of what we see and what we don't see in the client's initial presentation of self. It involves acceptance of and sensitivity to the client's ethnicity, gender, sexual orientation, physical appearance, disabilities, and stage of life. By communicating such acceptance, we lower the client's defense system and encourage the revelation of hidden aspects of the self.

Residential substance abuse programs who lose a high number of clients during the first days of treatment often experience this problem due to the failure to enhance both cultural and personal identification. Cultural identification can be easily enhanced by structuring the treatment milieu to reflect the heterogeneity of the client population. The milieu should contain language, symbols, literature and role models that reflect the experience of the client population. Personal identification can be enhanced by increasing the frequency and duration of client contact during the fragile period of entry into treatment. Three conditions are essential for this personal identification process. The first is a high frequency of contact with the client by staff, by other clients who are further progressed in their treatment and by alumni and self-help volunteers. The second condition is that a significant portion of this time is spent *listening* to the client. The third condition is that these communications convey both an understanding of the client's past and hope for the client's future.

8.5 *Sustaining the Motivational Crisis* Clients often enter treatment as a result of a crisis that creates sudden pain and consequences related to drug use. This crisis is often induced through external factors such as arrest, threat of job loss, a financial crisis or fear of loss of family. While the crisis may precipitate sufficient motivation to enter treatment, the defense structure that has helped the addict sustain addiction is often quickly reorganized to accommodate the new crisis. In this situation, the crisis is of sufficient intensity to create motivation for entry into treatment but not of sufficient intensity to sustain motivation for the ongoing treatment process. Our job as treatment professionals in such cases is to help sustain the motivational crisis to keep the addict engaged in the treatment process.

This may be a difficult concept for some traditionally trained helping professionals to master. When we have been trained and see ourselves as persons who reduce a client's experience of pain, the notion that we must sustain a crisis and sustain a client's experience of pain may be particularly difficult to accept. To fully understand the need for such interventions, we must explore the concept of professional enabling.

Professional enabling is any action on the part of helping professionals that decreases the addicts' experience of consequences related to their alcohol/drug use. It is behavior which allows addicts to sustain their system of denial and minimization. It is behavior which rescues addicts from crises, thus allowing them to continue their addictive career unabated. It is behavior which allows addicts to escape the experience of treatment. It is mistaking compliance for enduring changes in attitudes and behavior. It is doing things for addicts that they should be doing for themselves. It is allowing addicts' attempted manipulation of the treatment structure to pass without confrontation. It is the failure to confront cultural styles of "doing treatment". It is being seduced into being a covert partner in addicts' natural inclination to sustain their addictive lifestyle.

The first task in sustaining the motivational crisis, and thereby sustaining the addict's engagement in the treatment process, is to avoid our natural inclination for enabling behaviors as well as the addict's efforts to manipulate us into an enabling role in the treatment relationship. Such mechanisms as rigorous clinical supervision, co-therapy, and team approaches to treatment of the addict are essential to keeping even the most experienced therapist out of the enabling role.

The second task in sustaining the motivational crisis is to bring to the addict's daily experience in treatment those events and consequences that precipitated admission into treatment. The goal is to anchor the memory of that pain and draw regularly upon that pain to create the impetus for change in the addict. This is not only done verbally by the therapist, but by actually bringing the source of such consequences in contact with the addict during critical points of the treatment process. By structuring timely input from family, friends, employers, lawyers, probation officers, and other influential individuals, staff can sustain the client's cognitive commitment to change and the client's emotional investment in the actual work that such change entails. If the client is allowed to escape the memory of the pain which triggered the motivational crisis, he or she will either physically or emotionally disengage from the treatment process.

The following is a common experience for treatment professionals. An addict is admitted to treatment pleading for help during a crisis produced by real or threatened consequences of his or her drug use, only to appear a few days later with the elaborate defense structure which sustained addiction once again intact. Such a scenario reveals the chameleon-like quality of the addict. The same addict who shed tears as a sign of motivation to change his or her life may within minutes or hours exhibit attitudes and behaviors that reveal a powerful and continuing commitment to the addictive lifestyle. Such vacillations reflect the variations in the strength of the defense structure which has allowed the addict to simulta-neously maintain addiction and self-esteem. To abort the continuing life cycle of addiction, one must first penetrate and weaken this defense structure and then reconstruct this defense structure to support the addict through the fragile period of early recovery.

While the penetration, weakening and restructuring of the addict's defense structure is achieved through empathy and love, pain may be an equally essential ingredient. The pain ingredient involves bringing the full consequences of the client's behavior within his or her consciousness and emotional experience. Staff become the vehicle through which reality can penetrate the addict's defense structure. It is then, through the pain and upheaval produced from such penetration, that understanding and nurturing can provide a pathway of hope and the restructuring of this defense structure.

Most readers are very familiar with the "intervention" techniques pioneered by Vern Johnson. The staged intervention captures the essence of the processes described above. Such interventions, however, tend to be seen only as something we do to get someone into treatment. The same intervention process used to precipitate a crisis in the life of the addict in order to stimulate admission to treatment can also be used for a much larger number of addicts who come to treatment not as a consequence of pain, but as an escape from pain. The intervention technique becomes not a vehicle to get these addicts physically through the doors of a treatment center, but to get them emotionally invested in treatment once they're already admitted for treatment.

A substance abuse counselor presented a case of a highly resistant client who had been recently admitted to inpatient treatment. After listening to a detailed description of the client's denial, minimization, projection, and emotional detachment from the treatment process, the counselor was somewhat confused at the recommendation that an intervention be staged with the client. Her skeptical response to this suggestion was: "But he's already in treatment." It took some time to elaborate for her the following proposition. The power of the intervention technique is not simply in the outcome: the ability of the technique to get an addict into treatment. The power is in the *process* of what the addict experiences during the intervention. By bringing key persons from the addict's life together with the addict under the leadership of a trained interventionist, three things are accomplished. Pain is generated by bringing to the addict's consciousness the full impact of addiction on himself and others. The addict's defense structure, which has served to buffer him from the exact pain precipitated by the intervention, weakens and begins to break down. An intense experience of love and support instills within the addict both the need for change and the possibility of change. These three elements collectively provide an experience of such intensity that the addict not only enters treatment but enters with an emotional openness to the change process.   Many addicts who enter treatment without such openness could greatly benefit from a post-admission intervention process.

A plethora of folk wisdom exists that suggests the rebirth of recovery is impossible without pain. The role of the treatment professional is not to prevent or diminish such pain but to support the channeling of such pain into the pathway of recovery.

8.6 *Addressing Secondary Drug Use* Once clients have been initially engaged in the treatment process, it is important that the therapist and client define the exact nature of the problem or disorder that is to be treated.   Such definition must inevitably address the question of secondary drugs.

Addiction treatment specialists have historically defined the risk of, and problems related to, addiction as substance specific. The risk of alcoholism was specific to the drug alcohol. It would be years before the problems related to the alcoholic's use of other substances, particularly other central nervous system depressants such as sedatives and tranquilizers, would be addressed. The risk of opiate addiction was defined as opiate specific. The early therapeutic communities would spend years teaching addicts to drink socially as part of their reintegration into responsible society before the malfeasance of this approach became clearly evident. It is hard to feel particularly critical of clients for their failure to comprehend risks associated with secondary drugs when both the culture at large and our treatment systems have been fragmented by notions of "good" and "bad" drugs and have promulgated both social policies and programs organized around specific substances.

So how does one approach the issue of secondary drugs? What does one say to the cocaine addict who in confusion asks the following. "I came here because of cocaine. Why are you so concerned about my drinking? I've never had a problem with alcohol." What does one do with the marijuana use of the alcoholic or the alcohol use of the opiate addict or the adolescent who presents multiple drug consumption with no single drug of choice?

A. *A Model of Risk* The substance abuse field is in desperate need of a model that helps both service providers and service recipients understand the exact nature of risks related to primary and secondary drugs. If there is genetic transmission of risks for addiction, is such risk specific to a substance or category of substances or to all psychoactive substances? There is no coherent model or models that help treatment professionals understand and talk about risks associated with secondary drug use. One can talk about the risks of alcoholics using sedatives via the mechanism of cross-tolerance. But how does one talk about the risks of the cocaine addict drinking or about marijuana as a secondary drug of abuse? Research has yet to provide a physiological/psychological model of understanding the risks of secondary drug use by addicts.

Lacking such a model, one is left with the collective folk wisdom of the field and our own clinical experience. The following propositions reflect the current state of such wisdom and experience.

- Physiological and psychological risks of addiction are probably rarely tied to a single substance but are more likely to involve risks to drugs which share similar characteristics and perform similar functions for the at-risk population. There is growing opinion, for example, that alcoholism does not simply involve risk related to alcohol consumption but to a whole category of central nervous system depressants, making perhaps the term "sedativism" a more apt diagnostic label.

- There is in all likelihood both a metabolic and psychological transformation which occurs through addiction to any drug that alters and increases risks associated with the use of other psychoactive drugs.

- Such risk is probably greatest for those drugs which share similar pharmacological properties and effects as the primary drug of abuse.

- The risks associated with use of secondary drugs is threefold: 1) continued contact with a cultural setting incongruent with recovery 2) development of an abusive/addictive relationship with the secondary drug, and/or 3) relapse back to the primary drug through impaired judgment produced by secondary drug intoxication.

- A client's desire to hang onto secondary drugs reflects bargaining and control behavior over his or her drug relationships and demonstrates a lack of "acceptance" that is likely to impede long term recovery.

The additional approaches below constitute avenues of addressing secondary drug use until such time as the above propositions can be validated, refined or altered by addiction researchers.

B. *Analysis of Substance Use History* The collection and analysis of substance use history data through client and collateral interviews is an essential element is addressing the issue of secondary drugs. A year by year developmental history of the evolution of the pattern of drug consumption is recommended with attention to drug choices, dosages, frequency of consumption, methods of ingestion, settings, and client-reported consequences of use. In examining this data for concerns related to secondary drug use, it is helpful to pay particular attention to the following.

- Is there an identifiable pattern of secondary drug abuse that predated the shift to the primary drug? Such a pattern could indicate a high likelihood of reverting back to this pattern with abstinence from the primary drug.

- Did the pattern of secondary drug use change with the onset of primary drug abuse? This often occurs such as in the case of the cocaine addict who episodically used alcohol and marijuana, but after the onset of cocaine use began to escalate dosage and frequency of these secondary drugs for purposes of self-medication. Any change in dosage, frequency and function of secondary drug use all indicate increased risks.

- Were there increases in secondary drug use during episodes of abstinence or decreased consumption of the primary drug? Such a pattern would predict the rapid movement of secondary drugs to the status of primary drugs of abuse.

- Are there consequences the client has experienced that may be more attributable to the secondary drugs than the primary drugs? Are there identifiable warning signs associated with the secondary drugs, *e.g.* preoccupation, hoarding behavior, inability to abstain, loss of control, gimmicks to control use, etc.? Such patterns would indicate the need to redefine secondary drugs as primary drugs of abuse.

- Were primary and secondary drugs always used concurrently? This pattern would indicate that use of secondary drugs is likely to serve as a trigger for use by stimulating hunger for the primary drug.

- Will continuation of secondary drug use sustain relationships and rituals from the culture of addiction? If so, such exposure will subject the client to multiple stimuli that will serve as triggers for relapse to their primary drug as well as slow their engagement in the culture of recovery.

The above constitute important patterns to identify and review with the client. They provide important data for defining with the client the exact nature of the problem being treated.

C. *Focusing on Secondary Drugs in the Intervention Process*   The intervention process can help address the issue of secondary drugs by focusing not only on the consequences of drug use, but the exact pattern of drug use which produced these consequences. Vague references to drinking and drug use without specifying the specific substances which have produced harmful consequences allows the addict to enter treatment with his or her own definition of the problem. Vagueness in the confrontation process enhances the ability of the addict to bargain—the agreement to address the primary drug with a passionate commitment to hang on to the those drugs "which aren't a problem for me." By having the family identify consequences related to specific drugs, a broadened definition of the problem to be treated is created at the very inception of the recovery process.

D. *Teaching Functions*   Teaching clients about issues and risks related to secondary drug use is an extremely important component of treatment and relapse prevention planning. The objectives of such teaching functions include the following:

- to assist clients in assessing their pattern of secondary drug use
- to assist clients in recognizing the risks associated with secondary drug use
- to broaden clients understanding of the concepts of "sobriety" and "abstinence"

The above objectives can be addressed through such media as lectures and films, literature, and one-to-one information sharing by staff. An equally potent methodology involves capitalizing on the experience of treatment peers, particularly those who are back in treatment at least partially due to their decision to resume use of secondary drugs following their earlier treatment experience. One program known to the author routinely utilizes a panel of such clients within their lecture schedule to specifically address the dangers of secondary drugs.

There are some clients in treatment who are so resistive to the issue of giving up a secondary drug that their resumed use of secondary drugs following treatment is very likely. With this client, the objectives of the intervention might change in focus. If one cannot prevent the use of secondary drugs, then it may be helpful to design interventions capable of altering the client's experience of these drugs.

A few years back, a client was encountered in treatment who, though openly acknowledging his cocaine addiction, remained resistive in spite of all efforts on the issue of stopping his use of alcohol and marijuana. Confronted with such impenetrable resistance, the strategy was reshaped in the form of the following objectives.

- to decrease the ability of the client to deny or minimize consequences related to his alcohol and marijuana use
- to "take the fun out" of the client's alcohol and marijuana use by heightening his consciousness about the effects of these drugs
- to decrease the duration of the client's alcohol and marijuana usage following treatment
- to increase the likelihood that the client would make contact with the treatment center if and when he

experienced serious consequences related to his alcohol
and/or marijuana use

To implement these objectives, a number of sessions were
conducted with the client. It was explained that the treatment
team fully expected him to return to his alcohol and marijuana use
and that we were no longer going to try to change his mind on this
issue. We went on to express our belief that he should know as
much as possible about the effects of these drugs so he would be
aware if these drugs were becoming a problem for him. We chose
selected aspects of drug research that related most directly to this
young man's own value system—he prided himself on both his
intelligence and his sexual prowess. We spent probably three to
four hours discussing alcohol and marijuana, with particular
detailed focus on such aspects as the drugs effect on memory,
attention span, concentration skills, testosterone production,
testicular atrophy, and sexual dysfunction. The latter topics were
discussed with excruciating detail and thoroughness. We were
resigned to the fact that we couldn't prevent his drug use, but we
were equally convinced that we could reframe and alter his
experience of these drugs. Three months after his discharge, he
came by to report that he had made a decision to remain abstinent
from all drugs, including his beloved alcohol and marijuana. What
had stimulated this decision? He reported that he began smoking
marijuana and drinking shortly after he got out of treatment
discounting, but not forgetting, those detailed discussions. During
his second and third months following treatment, he became
particularly preoccupied with what the drug might be doing to
him, noting one episode when high that he swears he felt his
testicles shrinking.   Following repeated self-observation of his
"spaciness" and one sexual encounter where he was unable to get
an erection, he made the decision to become fully abstinent. It is
unclear whether the effects he reported were related to his drug
use or the new cognitive framework that had been constructed

around his alcohol and marijuana use. Either way, the strategy was successful in achieving the objectives that had been outlined. Such strategies create mental anchors that prevent the user from experiencing intoxication without full consciousness of the potential consequences of use.

E. *Relapse Interventions Involving Secondary Drugs* The re-entry of a client back into treatment because of the abuse of secondary drugs is a fairly common experience. It is not particularly necessary or helpful for such clients to go through the same 28 days or same treatment regimen they initially experienced. What they do need is a framework to understand issues related to secondary drugs and a structure that will allow them to re-enter the recovery process totally abstinent. An intense, short term relapse treatment experience can accomplish this objective. At least part of this experience must help provide the client with an understanding of why such drug use resulted in such devastating consequences. Again we must provide models, or folk wisdom or clinical experience that provide for the client a way to understand and talk about the need for total abstinence.

8.7 *The Struggle for Control of the Treatment Milieu* No matter what variations in modalities culturally enmeshed addicts enter, there is an immediate struggle for control of the milieu in which treatment will occur. Whether in a one-to-one counseling relationship or in the large residential environment, addicts will attempt to reconstruct this environment in their own image—an image shaped within the culture of addiction.

Elements of the culture of addiction—language, values, music, symbols, styles of social interaction, etc.—have long ago been anchored as ingrained personal habits. Such attitudes and behaviors do not diminish or disappear just because of a crisis that has brought the addict into treatment. These attitudes and behaviors are brought into treatment with the addict and, left unchecked, will inevitably sabotage the treatment process. When addicts are brought together via outpatient groups or residential treatment, there will be a natural inclination for them to reconstruct the culture of addiction within the treatment environment. Although all addicts share some crisis that brought them to treatment, collectively they may forge a treatment culture that mirrors with equal intensity the culture of addiction of their natural environments. If we don't have control of the treatment milieu, clients may not only fail to respond to treatment, but may intensify drug use based on the cultural supports for addiction found in the treatment milieu.

The collective personality of groups of addicts involved in residential treatment varies greatly over time due to this process of transferring the culture of addiction into the treatment milieu. Each peer group of addicts in treatment will tend to reflect the tribal affiliation (from the culture of addiction) held by either the majority or by the most charismatic and influential of their members. One reason that groups of clients feel different to treatment staff when there is a shift from primary alcohol users to polydrug users or to cocaine users is the variation of tribal/cultural norms that influence or govern client behavior.

There can also be tribal wars for power and control over a treatment milieu. The author vividly remembers being asked to provide consultation to a treatment center that described its early efforts to shift from an alcoholism to substance abuse focus as a nightmare. When I entered the day room of this center, the self-identified pure alcoholics were gathered in one corner of the room sharing drunkalogs while the self-identified drug addicts were in the opposite corner sharing equally colorful tales of getting high. The clients had isolated themselves into tribal groups and were using the inter-tribal hostility and conflict as a major diversion from the experience of treatment. The reason this program was having difficulty with combined treatment of alcoholics and other drug addicts was that they had let the tribal cultures of each of these groups continue to exist within the treatment milieu. They had provided no alternative culture which would have created inclusion for all clients.

8.8 *Stripping the Culture of Addiction* If the addict is to benefit from the treatment experience, they must first disengage from the culture of addiction and then begin to reshape those attitudes and behaviors from the culture which reinforce excessive drug consumption. Those addicts showing intense patterns of cultural enmeshment will have already been isolated them from their primary culture by being placed in a structured residential setting and by having the frequency and intensity of their interactions with persons outside this environment controlled. The next step is to prevent the culture of addiction from being replicated in the treatment environment and then working with each individual addict to extinguish or reshape cultural behavior.

Stripping the culture of addiction begins immediately upon the addict's request for admission into treatment. Intake staff explain that there may be numerous aspects of the client's lifestyle that support drug use and that a willingness to examine all aspects of one's lifestyle is a condition for entering treatment. It is explained with great clarity that it is unlikely that we will be able to abort the cycle of addiction without helping the client reconstruct major aspects of his or her daily life. It is perhaps questionable how much of what is communicated in this initial contact is actually absorbed by the client, but there will be numerous repetitions to reinforce this message.

Teaching clients about the culture of addiction provides an important framework for stripping this culture. It is recommended that there be special lectures on the culture of addiction and culture of recovery within the treatment milieu and that teaching interactions in one-to-one counseling and in groups reinforce the principles set forth in these lectures. The "lecture" on culture of addiction is best conducted as an experiential learning process rather than didactic recitation. The following format is recommended.

1. With clients assembled for a regularly scheduled lecture/discussion, explain that the discussion today will focus on how addiction begins to touch and change every area of our lives and that we will explore whether both addiction and recovery involve total lifestyles or what will be called cultures.

2. Place three columns on a chalkboard which contain the headings "Culture," "Culture of Addiction," and "Culture of Recovery." See page 226 for a sample format.

3. Ask group members to brainstorm components of any culture and list them under the "culture" column as they are identified. If members get stuck, it will stimulate their thinking by asking such questions as: "What differences are there between what we often call White culture and Black culture?" "What things would we look at to describe the differences between the United States and Russia?" The sample format that lists those areas most often identified by clients during the brainstorming exercise. Feel free to add any key elements missed in the brainstorming process.

4. With column one completed move to column two and begin asking for each item of column one whether this element exists in the culture of addiction, noting participant responses under column two. Questions for each element can be asked in a variety of formats such as: "Is there a special language of the culture of addiction? What is unique about the diet-what and when people eat—in this culture? Are there particular songs or types of music you associate with your alcohol/drug use?

Were there any changes in religious beliefs or practices as a result of your addiction? How would you describe family life in the culture of addiction?"

5.   When the list is completed circle the whole column and provide a summary discussion on addiction as an all encompassing lifestyle and raise the following question: "Which of these areas do you feel must   change for you to achieve and maintain sobriety?"

6.   Move to the third column and explain that if we are to shed old habits that we must discover new habits to take there place. Repeat the same process as in step 4, but apply each element to the culture of recovery. Questions to group members again can take various formats. "Are there new values in this culture of recovery?   If so, what are they?   What is the role of diet/food in this culture? Are there changes in how we dress and how we take care of ourselves that are important in this culture? What are the important rituals within this culture of recovery? Are there physical places that we can associate with our sobriety?"

7.   Circle all of column three and conclude with a brief discussion of recovery as a way of life that will eventually touch all areas of life just as addiction did.

Outlining the above concepts in lectures, groups and in one-to-one interactions with   clients   serves   multiple   purposes.   Such communications:

- help break down denial and minimization by dramatizing the number of areas in the client's life that have been affected by alcohol/drug use
- provide a framework for the client to identify areas of needed change in lifestyle and to understand why issues such as language, diet, sleeping habits, etc. are indeed treatment issues, and

The Culture of
Addiction/Recovery Lecture

Culture	Addiction	Recovery
(Brainstorm) Language		
Food		
Music		
Religion		
Symbols		
Rituals		
Dress		
Sex		
Family		
Literature		
Values		
Leisure		

- provide a framework for self-confrontation and peer feedback related to elements of the culture of addiction that arise in the treatment milieu

The second major methodology for stripping the culture of addiction involves establishing boundaries for appropriate and inappropriate behavior in treatment and consistently confronting behavior which tests or violates these boundaries. Chapter Eleven outlines such boundaries of appropriateness in detail.

A third methodology involves shaping a peer culture within the treatment milieu so that an incoming client is socialized, and, when appropriate, confronted by other clients as well as staff on the need to let go of behaviors and attitudes from the culture of addiction. Shaping values and boundaries within this treatment culture and placing more treatment-mature clients in positions to orient and monitor newcomers not only prevents the introduction of street culture into treatment but serves as a vehicle to reinforce and strengthen new values for the older clients.

A fourth approach to stripping the culture of addiction involves building into the treatment structure periods for both individual and collective assessment. In residential treatment, such assessment should occur on at least a weekly basis. This process provides an opportunity for clients to identify specific areas of self-work that need to be done and an opportunity to monitor and tighten up the treatment milieu. The process of communicating to other clients areas of needed work and the sharing of commitments of changes to be made during the coming week has a significant impact on monitoring and shaping the treatment milieu to minimize cultural attitudes and behaviors that would undermine treatment.

8.9 *Changing Cultural Styles of "Doing Treatment"* A particularly difficult task is the process of altering styles of "doing treatment" for the culturally enmeshed client, particularly when such styles have been refined through multiple treatment episodes. The following steps are recommended to help disengage the addict from such styles.

A. *Isolation from the Culture* The first task in altering dysfunctional styles of doing treatment is to break the addict's contact with the culture of addiction through physical isolation. Residential modalities are recommended for addicts whose treatment styles have previously resulted in rapid relapse or for the treatment neophyte whose style is unalterable within an outpatient context. The purpose of isolation is to break the pattern of cultural contact that reinforces attitudes and behaviors congruent with the addictive lifestyle.

B. *Diagnosing the Treatment Style* It is crucial that the treatment team identify any emerging dysfunctional patterns of doing treatment as quickly as possible. To abort such a style, one must be able to identify and describe this style as specifically as possible and further delineate why such a style will undermine the treatment experience. The full identification of such issues through interdisciplinary team meetings is essential to the process of formulating treatment interventions.

The identification of dysfunctional treatment styles is particularly crucial for the client with a history of multiple treatment episodes. Any time delay in identifying such patterns often results in ineffective use of treatment time. Many of the clients with multiple treatment experiences follow highly predictable patterns of avoiding treatment. By examining the historical pattern exhibited by the client, such patterns can be confronted and altered. The essential elements in identifying these patterns include the following:

- Obtaining, at admission, confidentiality releases to communicate with all significant persons/agencies that have been previously involved in the client's treatment
- Telephone communication (Waiting for written records usually involves inordinate time delays) with professionals who have had prior treatment contact with the client
- Solicitation of input from the professionals mentioned above on the following issues:
  - Describe the client's relationships with treatment staff and treatment peers.
  - Are there predictable behaviors or attitudes that this client uses to minimize treatment involvement?
  - What unresolved issues do you see as crucial to the client's treatment?
  - Does this client have a predictable pattern of self-destructing during or following treatment?
  - If you were to treat this client again, what would be the focus of treatment and are there any things you would do differently?
  - What has this client failed to do that you view as crucial to his/her recovery?
- Observation and monitoring of client behavior to identify pattern of defenses used to escape the treatment experience

Our goal in treatment is to transcend the normal flow of predictable action and reaction between the helper and the client. Our goal is to move beyond role prescribed behavior. Our goal is to rewrite the script which drives failure within and outside treatment. We must eschew the prepared script and move into an area of improvisation which through its novelty enhances the potential for new and unexpected outcomes. Change is possible when we move beyond the institutionalized rituals of "doing treatment" exhibited by both clients and staff. If nothing else happens to such clients in treatment, they should experience themselves differently. In aborting compulsive patterns of behavior, we free up energy and create the opportunity for change.

C. *Focusing on Pain and Possibilities* A goal in early treatment is to weaken the defense structure that has helped sustain the client's addiction and create an openness for trying on new behaviors. The motivation for such openness springs from two sources—the experience of past pain and consequences and the experience of hope related to future possibilities. Our earliest treatment contacts should:

- Focus on exploring pain and consequences experienced by the client.
- Provide a cognitive framework that links such pain to the addictive lifestyle.
- Explore the lengths to which the client is willing to go to alter the toxic relationship with drugs and the culture which supports this relationship.
- Facilitate development of an idealized self—a vision of who and what they could become.
- Provide affirming communications and role models that instill hope that the idealized self is attainable.

The above steps create the conditions within which motivation for change can grow and they provide the impetus for altering self-defeating patterns of approaching addiction treatment.

D. *Teaching Interventions* Many clients entering treatment have severely impaired skills of self-perception. The denial, projection rationalization or grandiosity that has characterized their adaptation to addiction creates a highly distorted perception of self. If we are to alter cultural styles of doing treatment, we must enhance these abilities of self-perception through techniques that serve as a mirror for the client. The following approaches share two characteristics. First, they provide concrete information on self-defeating styles of treatment involvement. Second, they communicate this information through mediums that serve to decrease rather than increase client resistance and defensiveness. In short, they lower the addict's defenses to enhance self-perception.

The first teaching intervention recommended is the inclusion of regular lecture/discussion periods on the topic of self-defeating styles in treatment. As a lecture, the presenter describes those styles of "doing treatment" discussed earlier in Chapter Seven and then facilitates a discussion that allows clients to personalize the material. Two highly recommended audiovisual aids that can be incorporated into this process are the movies, *How To Sabotage Your Treatment*, and *Continued Acts of Sabotage*, distributed by Gerald T. Rogers Productions, Inc. These movies can also be shown as an individual assignment to a client and then personalized within the outpatient treatment interview. By teaching about self-defeating styles, we provide a cognitive framework through which the client can assess and modify his or her own style of approaching the treatment experience.

A second method involves the use of a panel of recovering addicts presenting to the treatment population. The focus of this panel is not on the traditional "this is the way it was; this is the way it is" review of addiction and sobriety. It is rather a focus on styles with which the panel members entered the treatment process and how those styles had to be changed for them to begin the recovery process. Panelists are chosen, not because they were the model patients, but because they presented highly dysfunctional styles in treatment which they were able to overcome. These first person accounts and the dialogue with clients which accompanies such presentations provides a powerful source of feedback on self-defeating styles as well as concrete examples by role models on how such styles can change. Such interactions can create hope in the possibility for change even in the most treatment resistant clients.

A third method to be used in conjunction with the above is direct feedback by the treatment team on the nature and intensity of each client's involvement in the treatment milieu. At the initial stage this is a process of information giving, not a process of confrontation. Such communications should be carefully designed so as to minimize rather than arouse the addict's defense structure. The timing should be well timed and should focus on concrete and specific behaviors over which the addict has immediate and full control. By monitoring the client's response to such information giving, we can test the client's receptiveness to feedback and openness to change. The initial response to such communications also allows us to gage whether more intense treatment interventions will be required to alter the self-defeating style.

E. *Interventions to Block Self-Defeating Styles* While the above approaches provide a beginning framework for altering self-defeating treatment styles, the more culturally enmeshed addicts will often require more powerful and sustained interventions to eliminate such styles. Four specific techniques are recommended to address these situations: self-assessment techniques, contracting techniques, confrontation techniques and paradoxical techniques.

Self-assessment techniques to alter self-defeating treatment styles consist of structured exercises in which the client is forced to consider the impact of historical and current behavior on his or her life following treatment. These exercises are often given to the client as assignments to be completed during treatment. The following are samples of treatment assignments given to clients who presented either chronic histories or acute episodes of self-defeating treatment styles.

- Examine each of your past treatment experiences and write a list of what you did and didn't do each time that diminished your treatment experience and contributed to your subsequent relapse.

- Let's explore your past cycles of treatment and relapse. Assuming this history repeated itself, write a story of what you will do in treatment and what you will do following treatment.

- Given what you know about yourself, describe those things you are most likely to do to screw up your treatment experience. (Used for clients who present extreme resistance but who have no prior history of treatment.)

- Write a story about your worst fears of what will happen if your alcohol/drug use continues to progress.

- Most of us have dreams about what we would like our life to be like. Write a story about your recovery with the best possible outcomes. After your story is done, consider what changes in your life are necessary for this story to come true. (Used to both create vision and hope and to focus on areas of needed change.)

- Interview three recovering persons (alumni/self-help members) about their early recovery and the changes they had to make. Based on their experience, describe areas of change you may need to consider while in treatment.

- Your pattern of addiction has brought you closer and closer to death. Let's assume this pattern continues and you die as a result of your alcohol/drug use. Choose two people who love you and two people who dislike you and describe what you feel would be their response to your death. (Used with clients who present high resistance, high risk-taking behavior, and frozen emotions.)

Assignments like the above enhance openness to change by forcing introspection into one's behavior. By focusing on such change through assignments to be completed alone, a situation is created in which clients assess themselves in a context where defenses are lower than in the client-therapist interview situation.

Contracting is a technique which creates specific behavioral agreements between the client and the counselor or treatment team. Contracting is a very effective technique in dealing with self-defeating treatment styles.   The contract specifically identifies behaviors/attitudes which the client has agreed not to exhibit in the treatment milieu or identifies new behaviors/attitudes which the client has agreed to try on as a more positive approach to treatment. Contracts may also seek to control rather than eliminate certain behaviors that in exaggerated form serve as diversions from the treatment experience.

An earlier discussion highlighted the ambivalence experienced by the addict entering treatment.   A part of the addict wants desperately to get well and hopes treatment will have some magical transforming effect. Another part of the addict is grieving the loss of both the drug and the culture. He or she clings tightly to behaviors and attitudes rooted in the addictive culture.

Contracting provides a concrete mechanism to tap and strengthen the more positive side of this ambivalence.

Confrontation techniques constitute the third ingredient in altering self-defeating styles of doing treatment. Confrontation techniques involve communications which point out discrepancies and incongruities in the client's presentation of self in the treatment milieu. Any feedback which presents clients a mirror or description of their own behavior constitutes. The intensity and methods used in this mirroring can vary greatly. Confrontation in its more intense forms is a higher risk intervention that usually follows the failure of other approaches to bring self-defeating behavior under control. Confrontation can be very effective in addressing self-defeating behaviors if the selective use of this technique follows the following principles:

- The use of confrontation techniques occurs only within the context of a relationship; empathy and trust, not anger, are the essential precursors to effective confrontation.
- The confrontation is aimed not at the person, but at specific, concrete behaviors which the client can change.
- Discrepancy confrontations are communicated clearly and succinctly, *e.g.*, "You say you will go to any lengths to achieve sobriety but you are resisting your family's involvement in treatment."
- Confrontations related to noncompliance with standards note the standard, specifically identify the area of noncompliance and identify the consequence of such noncompliance on the client and others.
- The timing and design of the confrontation communication should be selected so as to weaken rather than arouse the client's defense structure.

- The confrontation communication is followed by active listening and contracting.

Many substance abuse programs have become quite enamored of the use of confrontation techniques and frequently use them without a clear sense of the desired clinical outcomes or without an analysis of whether other techniques would be more clinically appropriate. Perhaps even more difficult for clients is the use of confrontation without clearly defined standards of desirable and inappropriate treatment behavior. Some counselors respond to clients in a style reminiscent of the boss who says to his employee: "This work isn't right. I can't tell you what I want, but I'll know it when I see it." If a client disagrees, they're confronted as resistant; if they agree; they're confronted as compliant. Clients experience such styles as if they were playing a winless game without rules—no matter what they do, they catch hell. The result is that they physically or emotionally disengage from the treatment process.

Effective confrontation presupposes a clear definition of both self-enhancing and self-defeating treatment behaviors and the clear and timely communication of such definitions to each client entering the treatment process. We have already discussed defining self-defeating behaviors for clients via teaching interventions. Most programs define some of these behaviors through "rules" for treatment—communicating to the client mostly what we don't want them to do. Self-enhancing behaviors are best defined as expectations established at admission to treatment and further defined through teaching interventions. Self-enhancing behaviors define for the client those actions which experience has shown us produce the most positive treatment outcomes.

Paradoxical techniques involve the use of therapeutic manipulations designed to get the client to try on new behaviors within the treatment milieu. These techniques, which capitalize on and redirect the client's resistance, can be particularly helpful when the client's defense structure is so aroused as to limit the effectiveness of other interventions.   Although paradoxical techniques must be used selectively, they are an additional tool that can be used to counter self-defeating styles of doing treatment.

Given the natural inclination of adolescents to test the limits of any boundaries or structure, paradox may be a particularly useful technique with this population. Consider the following vignette describing the use of paradox.

> An adolescent counselor in an inpatient substance abuse unit was becoming increasingly frustrated with one particular 16 year old. He was resisting exposure to literature which the counselor felt would be particularly helpful to the client. It was as if the more she tried to involve the client in these activities, the greater was his resistance. At the supervisor's suggestion, the counselor altered her approach to the following. She communicated to the young man that there was one particular book she thought he would like, but that she didn't think he should read it now because he wasn't far enough along in treatment, and perhaps he wasn't quite old enough yet for this particular book. The book in question disappeared from the staff library within two hours of the above interview.

8.10 *The Preferred Defense Structure and Cultural Conversion*
This chapter has focused on how we begin to disengage the addict from the culture of addiction via the treatment process.   The chapter would be incomplete if we did not address the support the addict needs to let go of the drug relationship and the culture in which this relationship is nested.

Stripped of the drug and its cultural trappings, the addict is psychologically naked and vulnerable. Under such conditions, the defense structure which has helped sustain addiction can be magnified and exaggerated as a form of psychological armor, or may crumble sparking feelings that serve to trigger drug hunger and drug seeking behavior. Both of these responses constitute barriers to entry into the recovery process. The interventions outlined in this chapter to strip the culture of addiction work only under conditions of consistent and sustained support which simultaneously lower the addict's defense structure while diminishing the experience of vulnerability. When this vulnerability is not supported, the addict relapses to primary or secondary drugs, develops alternative compulsive behaviors that may be equally destructive, or begins a process of psychological deterioration.

What we are seeking with the culturally involved addict is a conversion experience—the transfer of identity and affiliation from the culture of addiction to what will be described in the remainder of this book as the culture of recovery. Treatment provides both the maps and the vehicles to mark the journey from one culture to another. Just as the addict's entrance into the culture of addiction took place within the context of social relationships, their entry into the culture of recovery will occur within the context of treatment relationships. If successful, there will be many relationships to follow within this culture of recovery, but we are the beginning. As treatment professionals, we provide the human bridge from one culture to the other. For many of our clients, we are asking them to give up everything to make this journey into the unknown. Very few will continue this journey without guides whom they trust and through whom they experience safety and protection.

Safety comes from cultural replacement. For everything we take from the culture of addiction, we must give something from the culture of recovery. If we are to strip old values, we must provide new values. If we are to take language, we must give language. If we are to take an identity, we must give an identity. If we are to disengage the addict from destructive relationships, then we must have alternative relationships to fill this vacuum. If all leisure time has been tied to addiction, we must have alternatives to fill this time. If addiction has become an all-encompassing lifestyle, then recovery must be an equally encompassing lifestyle to fill the void. We must work to support the addict's defense structure through this replacement process. Our support and guidance sustains the fragile defense structure of newly recovering addicts as they rebuild their world within the culture of recovery.

8.11 *The Culture of Recovery: The Alternative Career Path* The culture of addiction and the culture of recovery are like twins who, while mirroring each other in many ways, pursue opposite paths—one nurturing life, the other ultimately embracing death. While so different in their goals, it is perhaps the fact that each still mirrors the other that smoothes the transition from the culture of addiction to the culture of recovery.

> *The culture of recovery is an informal social network in which group norms (prescribed patterns of thinking, feeling and behaving) reinforce sobriety and long-term recovery from addiction.*

Like the culture of addiction, the culture of recovery is a way of life, a means of organizing daily existence, and a means of viewing people and events in the outside world. It is a way of talking, dressing, gesturing, believing, working, playing, thinking, and seeing that separates those in recovery from those who are not. Like the culture of addiction, the culture of recovery encompasses values, artifacts, places, rituals, relationships, symbols, music, and art. The culture of recovery constitutes an alternative career path for those who have been enmeshed in the culture of addiction.

THE ORGANIZATION OF THE CULTURE OF RECOVERY

The culture of recovery is a loosely organized confederation of tribes or social networks which provide nurturing and support for recovering addicts. The organization of this culture in many ways mirrors the organization of the culture of addiction.

9.1 *Historical Evolution*   The earliest origins of the culture of recovery are open to speculation.   One could look deeply into human history and visualize a day when two of our earliest ancestors, hungover from drinking fermented honey found in the hollow of a tree, jointly concluded that the pleasure was no longer worth the resulting pain. Perhaps an event such as this was the very beginning. The history of the culture of recovery in the United States is much clearer.

The introduction of the distillation process resulted in exceptionally heavy drinking in colonial America. It forced most of the colonies to enact laws to address drunkenness and provided the roots for the first organized attempts to support abstinence from alcohol. Pledges of total abstinence from alcohol made between colonial citizens can be found dating back to 1637. Drinking in the late 1700s and early 1800s increased dramatically. Yearly per capita alcohol consumption rose from 2.5 gallons in 1792 to 7.5 gallons in

1823. (Conley, Sorenson, 1971) Increased alcohol consumption was accompanied by an increasingly visible culture of addiction. These twin events would sow the seeds for the temperance movement and spark developments in the formal organization of the culture of recovery in the United States.

The American temperance movement began roughly in 1825 and continued through the prohibition era. It was driven by thousands of local, state and national temperance organizations. While very few of these societies concerned themselves with reformation of the alcoholic, there is no question that many alcoholics used the affiliation with such societies as a self-help process. One such organization during the early temperance period is of particular note.

On April 12, 1840, a group of six men who had been drinking together for years met in a Baltimore tavern and pledged to each other to abstain from drinking alcohol from that day forward. This event, the beginning of the Washingtonian temperance movement, was the first fully organized effort in the United States in which alcoholics banded together for support in achieving and maintaining sobriety. This movement added a number of innovations. It was the first self-help movement that was focused on the individual alcoholic and whose leadership and members consisted of recovering alcoholics. Recovery was based on radical abstinence and attendance at regular meetings in which speakers and members reviewed in graphic and highly emotional detail the painful role alcohol had played in their lives. This movement spread rapidly, but lasted little more than five years, since its focus was diverted from the individual alcoholic to the broader political goals of the temperance movement. The Washingtonian movement did, however, mark the beginning of the first formal organizational effort of the culture of recovery in the United States, and its short history also triggered the beginning development of inebriate asylums in this country.

Washingtonian Hall was opened in 1845 in Boston, Massachusetts as a lodging house for inebriates, marking the first organized effort to bring addicts together in a residential setting for purposes of achieving sobriety. It was followed during the next 60 years by the opening of a large number of inebriate asylums in the United States. The inebriate asylum movement marked a number of significant milestones in the culture of recovery.

- The movement brought large numbers of addicts together for the first time under the care of physicians—adding significantly to the medical understanding of alcoholism and other addictions.
- The movement treated all addicts—regardless of drug choice—within the same setting and within the same treatment philosophies.
- The movement created the first formal organization in the addiction treatment field—The American Association for the Study and Cure of Inebriety (1870)—and the first journal devoted exclusively to the study of addiction—*The Journal of Inebriety* (1877).
- The movement would constitute the first organized advocacy of a disease concept of addiction. The Association's first three by-laws read as follows:

  1. Inebriety is a disease.
  2. It is curable as other diseases are.
  3. The constitutional tendency to this disease may be either inherited or acquired; but the disease is often induced by the habitual use of alcohol or other narcotic substances.

(Taken from the 1870 by-laws of the American
Association for the Study and Cure of Inebriety.)
(Crothers, 1893)

• The movement built on the Washingtonian experience by
organizing support groups in local communities run by
recovering addicts. The most elaborate of these would be
the nation-wide network of Keeley Leagues.

The next historical milestones in the development of the culture of
recovery involved two parallel movements—the Emmanuel
Movement and the Oxford Movement. The Emmanuel Movement
was founded in 1906 by two clergy, Elwood Worchester and
Samuel McComb. This movement combined psychological and
spiritual approaches for working with the alcoholic. Program
tenets focused on total abstinence, full self-revelation in group
therapy, individual analysis, relaxation and social services from
"friendly visitors." The Oxford Group was started in 1908 by Frank
Buchman as a non-denominational, evangelical religious group.
These groups would attract many alcoholics, particularly during
the movement's peak years of the late twenties and early thirties.
Key principles included self-survey, confession, restitution and
service to others. Not only did the Emmanuel and Oxford
movements provide an avenue of recovery for many alcoholics,
these same movements directly influenced later historical
developments within the culture of recovery.

Concurrent with the above movements, the Salvation Army had
been working with alcoholics since the organization's arrival in the
United States in 1880. In addition to clothing and feeding
thousands of destitute alcoholics, the Salvation Army had also
established inebriate homes and colonies with the goal of bringing
both sobriety and religious salvation to the alcoholic. In 1914,
many of the alcoholics who had achieved sobriety through the

Salvation Army programs organized themselves into the "United Order of Ex-Boozers" and dedicated themselves to reforming other alcoholics.

While the numbers may have been small by today's standards, there is no question that many alcoholics and addicts found a pathway to recovery through the movements and programs we have highlighted and through others which have escaped recorded history.   Such programs served to disengage addicts from the culture of addiction, provided a framework for recovery, provided social relationships that supported sobriety, and provided a role within recovery that allowed the addict to reclaim his/her self-esteem.   In short these programs provided the beginnings of the culture of recovery in the United States.

Radical changes in social policy occurred early in this century which would dramatically influence the continuation of our story. The temperance movement reached its zenith with the passage of National Prohibition in 1919.   The Harrison Act of 1914 and subsequent Supreme Court rulings on this act brought other drugs of abuse under strict legal control.   There was a growing movement to legally prohibit tobacco. It looked for a moment in time like the U.S. would develop a consistent policy of criminalizing and prohibiting the non-medical use of all major psychoactive drugs.   This period significantly shaped the continuing history of the culture of recovery. Most of the inebriate asylums closed during prohibition, shutting off the primary source of treatment for alcohol- and drug-addicted individuals. Those opiate addicts who had been maintained on opiates by their physicians were cut off from their drug supplies by the new laws. Forty-four communities set up morphine maintenance programs for these addicts between 1919 and 1924, but all of these programs were closed under threat of legal prosecution.   By the early twenties, nearly all access to treatment for the alcoholic and addict had disappeared. The emerging disease concept of addiction was buried by the prohibitionist belief that drugs and the persons who use them should be viewed in terms of morality rather than medicine.

By the early thirties, however, a split in national social policy occurred. Prohibition was repealed and alcohol became increasingly promoted and integrated into the very social fabric of our culture. Other psychoactive drugs of popular abuse—the opiates, cocaine, and later marijuana, hallucinogens, and a variety of other substances—came under increased criminalization. From such social policies emerged new conditions under which the prohibited drugs were used. An American illicit drug culture was born. As we shall see, these social policies greatly influenced both the nature of the culture of addiction and the future character of the culture of recovery.

Out of the abyss of the twenties and early thirties came two major events in 1935. The first and most significant was the founding of Alcoholics Anonymous in Akron, Ohio. The second was the opening of a federal "narcotics farm" in Lexington, Kentucky. Separate from the individual meanings of these two events, they collectively marked the rebirth of treatment efforts following a 15-20 year hiatus. They also marked the emergence of alcoholism treatment and drug treatment as separate fields. Up until this time, treatment efforts had been organized around the concept of "inebriety"—a concept that embraced the abuse of or addiction to any psychoactive drug. This split in treatment approaches, which emerged out of the split in social policies toward alcohol and other drugs, shaped both the nature of treatment and the culture of recovery for the next 50 years.

The founding of Alcoholics Anonymous (AA) crystallized and built upon the most successful components of all previous approaches to recovery from alcoholism. The twelve steps of AA were based on a brilliant and intuitive understanding of the dominant species of alcoholism in the United States, yet the wording of these steps was inclusive enough to encompass the broad spectrum of self-destructive patterns of alcohol use. The Twelve Steps were also based on an in-depth understanding of the developmental stages inherent to the recovery process.

AA brought forward the disease concept that had been the foundation of the inebriate asylum movement and modernized the concept by shifting the focus from cure to one of recovery as an on-going process sustained one day at a time. Recognizing that denial was the dominant defense structure that allowed the alcoholic to sustain his or her drinking, AA postulated admission and acceptance of powerlessness over alcohol as the initial step in recovery. Recognizing that narcissism, fear of insanity and loss of spirituality were integral to the experience of alcoholism, the second and third steps involved a reaching out beyond oneself and turning oneself over to the care of God. Recognizing that the alcoholic's guilt and shame served as fuel for continued self-destruction, AA incorporated the tenets of self-inventory and confession from earlier movements into steps four and five. Recognizing that the resolution of guilt and the restoration of self-esteem also required action, AA built in steps that allowed the alcoholic to make amends where possible for past wrongs against persons. Recognizing that service to others was an essential ingredient in self-healing, AA built in service to other alcoholics as an essential component of the recovery process. Recognizing that alcoholism was an all-encompassing lifestyle, AA provided a framework whereby recovery could be equally encompassing. AA would become the first fully developed culture of recovery available to addicts outside the walls of an institution.

The twelve traditions of AA, perhaps equally important for AA's survivability, also built in organizational safeguards to manage those conditions and influences that had often led to the destruction of earlier programs and self-help movements. While the twelve steps provided the program for individual recovery, the twelve traditions provided the principles upon which the group life of AA would be guided and governed. The Washingtonians had failed to sustain themselves in part because they got sidetracked into the politics of the temperance movement and lost sight of the individual alcoholic. AA tradition demanded loyalty to a single purpose—carrying the message to the still-suffering alcoholic—and prohibited taking any political or religious position which would divert attention from this cause. Early movements had splintered over issues of religious belief. AA separated the issue of spirituality from religious dogmas and denominations. Prior movements often relied on charismatic leadership. AA traditions demanded a decentralization and evolution of leadership. Many of the early inebriate asylums (and their contemporary counterparts) self-destructed when the ego needs of leaders blurred and diverted the institutional mission. The traditions of anonymity and "principles before personalities" were specifically designed to keep such ego problems under control.

From its beginnings in 1935, AA would grow to a fellowship of recovering alcoholics that numbers more than 1,500,00 members in more than 75,800 groups located in 137 countries. Its philosophy and principles would also come to dominate treatment approaches to alcoholism up to the present time. The halfway house movement evolved parallel to and as a result of AA, creating the historical links to many of the community-based residential substance abuse treatment programs which exist today.

The second, and less heralded, milestone in the evolution of the culture of recovery was the 1935 opening of the federal narcotics "farm" in Lexington, Kentucky. This program, and an additional facility opened in Ft. Worth. Texas in 1938, brought into treatment the largest population of opiate addicts since the closing of the inebriate asylums. The research conducted at these facilities made significant contributions to our understanding of the nature and treatment of opiate addiction. Of particular significance was the growing recognition of the exceptionally high relapse rate associated with opiate addiction.   No matter what medical/psychological interventions were utilized within the treatment units at Lexington and Ft. Worth, most addicts rapidly relapsed back to active opiate addiction when they were discharged back to the environments from which they came—environments described collectively in this book as the culture of addiction. For many addicts, Lexington and Ft. Worth were merely milestones in their addictive careers—a place to "do treatment" until their addictive lifestyles could be resumed. For a small number of addicts, however, these facilities were the point of entry into the culture of recovery.

Two additional milestones in the culture of recovery occurred in the 1950s. First was the founding of Narcotics Anonymous (NA). This was not so much an innovation as an adaptation of the AA program for persons abusing or addicted to drugs other than alcohol. The growth of NA was much slower than AA and did not emerge as a visible component of the culture of recovery in many areas until the late 1970s and 1980s. The founding of NA did mark the extension of AA's twelve step program beyond alcoholism—a trend that would continue to escalate over the next 30 years. The second milestone was the founding of Synanon by Charles Dederich in 1958. Like NA, Synanon was a self-help counterpart to AA for persons abusing drugs other than alcohol. Unlike NA, Synanon was based on a long term residential treatment model with a treatment philosophy that separated significantly from the

principles and traditions of AA. Synanon, and numerous early
variations of the Synanon program, became the model for
residential therapeutic communities that spread across the United
States in the 1960s and 1970s. These programs developed
extremely sophisticated techniques for disengaging the addict from
the culture of addiction and resocializing the addict for life outside
this culture. The major weakness of such early programs was their
isolation from the community and the inadequate technology to
transfer their treatment culture to a framework for long-term
recovery in the world outside the treatment facility. Many of the
techniques currently recommended for stripping the culture of
addiction, however, are techniques first introduced within these
therapeutic communities. The therapeutic community was the first
modality to emerge with sufficient intensity of treatment and
duration of treatment to address the needs of the chronic,
culturally enmeshed addict.

The 1960s and early 1970s posed a significant new challenge to the
existing culture of recovery. New drugs of abuse such as
hallucinogens seemed to spring quickly on the scene, and older
substances such as cannabis, barbiturates and amphetamines
gained new visibility. New populations of users were identified
and new addictive subcultures were emerging with unclear
pathways to recovery. The sixties saw the introduction of methadone detoxification and methadone maintenance which became the
major treatment approach to opiate addiction by the end of the
1970s. A whole new potpourri of psychological approaches to
counseling the polydrug user emerged from a wide variety of
service settings. Such new populations created focused attention
on the needs of special populations of addicts, *e.g.,* adolescents,
ethnic minorities, women, the elderly, the handicapped and the
Gay and Lesbian. Polydrug abusing clients and clients with special
needs increasingly presented themselves within treatment
programs and self-help groups. Although the demands for

adaptation produced by these new populations of users created growing pains for treatment programs and self-help groups, the outcome was a much more vibrant and heterogeneous culture of recovery.

Fueling the above changes was the dramatic infusion of federal and state dollars to build a network of comprehensive community based substance abuse treatment services. New service networks led to the increased identification of substance abusers and addicts who had previously been invisible within the communities in which they lived. For the first time in American history, a nationwide network of substance abuse services was accessible to the majority of citizens. This infusion of money dramatically expanded the organization of the culture of recovery within the U.S. and laid the foundation for further expansions of the culture in the 1980s. Along with the dollars came increased regulation and institutionalization of substance abuse treatment programs and increased professionalization of substance abuse treatment staff.

The 1970s and early 1980s marked a major attack on the stigma associated with addiction. Addiction and recovery took on heightened visibility within this time period. Beginning with "Operation Understanding" in 1976, an event sponsored by the National Council on Alcoholism at which prominent leaders from all walks of life stood up and publicly acknowledged their recovery from alcoholism, a remarkably large number of public figures acknowledged their history of addiction and subsequent recovery. A transformation in the society's definition of "alcoholic" and "addict" occurred that tore down much of the stigma associated with addiction. Such de-stigmatization would open the doors for many hidden addicts to explore entry into the culture of recovery.

By the mid-1980s, a number of additional changes occurred which altered the nature of the culture of recovery in the United States.

- New early intervention technologies, *e.g.*, employee assistance programs, student assistance programs, and the family intervention process become widespread enough so as to bring large numbers of early and middle stage addicts into treatment.
- New legislation accompanied a radical change in cultural tolerance toward drunk driving and brought large numbers of alcoholics to the attention of treatment professionals via mandatory assessment of DUI offenders.
- The infusion of money into the public sector to support substance abuse treatment was accompanied by changes in third party medical coverage which provided payment for substance abuse treatment. The era of the commercialization and industrialization of the substance abuse field began with the proliferation of hospital based and private for-profit substance abuse treatment programs.
- The combined treatment of alcoholism and other addictions, which was the norm in the 1800s and a radical treatment innovation in the 1960s and 1970s, once again came into prominence.
- New patterns of drug use, *i.e.*, freebasing of cocaine, and new populations of users continued to challenge the responsiveness and adaptability of the culture of recovery.
- Heightened concern and stigmatization of smoking spawned a plethora of new treatments and support groups for nicotine addicts.
- Newer self-help groups, *i.e.*, Women for Sobriety, Cocaine Anonymous, Pills Anonymous, Mentally Ill Recovering Alcoholics, gained increasing visibility in response to the more heterogeneous population of addicts.
- The growing codependency movement which focuses on the special needs of children of alcoholics, adult children

of alcoholics, spouses and significant others, and other family members whose lives have been affected by addiction achieved dramatically heightened visibility and attention. The culture of recovery began to fully embrace the family and social networks in which alcoholics and addicts are involved.

The above history reflects the progressive movement of the culture of recovery through three distinct phases: initiation, stabilization and specialization. From national and local perspectives, there have been efforts to build the basic structural components of the culture of recovery. Once in place, the struggle shifts to stabilizing and insuring the future existence of these structures. Once stabilized, these structures evolve to meet the needs of special populations of addicts and those whose lives have been touched by addiction.

9.2 *Tribal Networks*   The culture of recovery, mirroring the culture of addiction, is organized into a loose confederation of social networks, each of which is made up of numerous tribes. Each tribe consists of a voluntary social group of addicts who have banded together out of individual self-interest to support each other's recovery. Tribes and networks are tied together by shared beliefs about the recovery process and communicate through persons who hold membership in and have frequent interaction with more than one tribe.

There are at least two layers of organization within the culture of recovery, the first being the network of treatment centers and the second being the network of self-help groups. Each of these layers is organized differently.

9.3 *The Treatment Culture*   The treatment culture in the United States which has in this century been organized primarily around categories of abused drugs has more recently shifted to the selection of members based on social and financial status. The treatment culture has, in fact, begun to split into two parallel tracks. The public and private financing of substance abuse treatment has created one network of hospital-based and private treatment centers and another network of publicly funded treatment centers. Which addicts enter which network is dependent not on drug of choice or severity of addiction so much as one's social status and capacity to pay for the treatment. The treatment culture, which historically has been an extension of the self-help culture, has now become a business, and in many areas a highly competitive business.

The impact of these funding structures on the health and vitality of the culture of recovery merits examination. On the positive side, the proliferation of treatment programs and the aggressive marketing programs which often accompany them, have brought larger numbers of addicts into treatment at an earlier stage of addiction than have ever occurred before in the addiction field. Such programs, particularly those located in hospitals, have also brought whole new populations of clients into substance abuse treatment who would likely have never been seen in publicly supported programs. Research in the field is rapidly expanding. Physicians and other helping specialties have returned to the field in full force. The field has been legitimized as never before within the overall culture.

Some aspects of this proliferation of programs and the changing economic foundation of the treatment culture merit special concern.

- If there is a future trend toward shrinking public resources to support substance abuse treatment, is there a danger that access to substance abuse treatment will be limited to only the fully insured or financially secure?

- In our scramble to achieve procedural efficiency and regulatory compliance, are we in danger of shifting our organizational focus from people changing to people processing? Do we measure our success by what happens to our clients or by such factors as income, profit, utilization rates, etc.? How do we sustain our historical focus on the suffering of the individual addict and their significant others?

- To what extent are decisions such as admission or length of stay based on financial needs of the program versus the clinical needs of the client? Do we have sufficient safeguards to protect the clinical integrity of programs in the face of increasing financial pressure?

- Are there dangers involved in losing our focus through expansion and diversification , encompassing other disabilities within our organizations, *e.g.*, eating disorders, gambling, or pain control? Can a culture of recovery for addicts be adequately developed within such a diversified service setting?

- Are treatment programs producing new candidates for long term recovery faster than they can be effectively absorbed and integrated into the self-help culture? If so, do treatment programs bear a responsibility to nurture the expansion of this self-help network or at times create parallel long term support mechanisms?

The above issues address rapid growth in the substance abuse treatment field and the changing economic structure of treatment. Additional issues related to the organization of the treatment culture include both the organizational framework within which substance abuse treatment is provided and the nature of the people who make up the treatment culture.

Substance abuse treatment programs have a long history of vacillating back and forth from free standing entities with a specialized addictions focus to existing as a component of a larger health and human service organization. The sixties and seventies were marked by a trend toward isolation and specialization. At the current time the pendulum seems to be swinging back as many programs are being re-absorbed within larger organizations. Many such mergers or reorganizations are occurring due to financial necessity. The concern with this issue is a limited one that simply examines the extent to which a particular organizational structure enhances or inhibits the development of a culture of recovery. Consider the following illustration.

A free-standing adolescent substance abuse program was merged with a traditional outpatient mental health center. The youth program had developed an elaborate culture of recovery for their youth. An open door, drop-in policy created a high level of contact with the youth. Large numbers of older recovering adolescents and young adults served as volunteers, spending considerable time at the program.

The environment was loaded with posters and other symbols of recovery. Recovery songs written and recorded by the youth often played in the background at the youth facility. A strong peer culture had evolved within the program. Formal groups tended to be noisy either from shared laughter or verbal confrontations. The program had become a surrogate family and alternative lifestyle for clients. This electrified milieu contained the special magic that could both engage and sustain adolescent involvement in the recovery process. Following the merger, much of this culture was lost. The drop-in policy was changed to reduce traffic in and out of the center which was "bothering other center clients." Posters and other symbols were removed because they were "unprofessional." Staff were encouraged to develop more formal, professional relationships with their clients. Volunteers were discouraged because of their lack of education and formal training. By being in an organizational environment that understood very little about the needs of recovering adolescents, the heart of this program—its dynamic culture of recovery—was destroyed.

A treatment culture is to a great extent shaped by the characteristics of the personnel who fill the treatment environment. The nature of such personnel have changed dramatically over the past thirty years. Twenty to thirty years ago, the field was dominated by older, male, recovering alcoholics and addicts. With the infusion of money into the field, increasing numbers of professionally trained staff were integrated into this staff mix broadening the age and sex composition of the field. In the last decade, there has been a dramatic increase in the number of co-dependents working in the field. There are many factors which make up an ideal staff mix for a substance abuse treatment program.

- The composition of the treatment team should mirror the diversity of demographic characteristics of the client population, *i.e.*, age, race and ethnicity, sex, religion, and affectional preference.
- The treatment culture must contain recovering role models (staff or volunteers) whose prior drug choices and patterns of drug consumption mirror those of the client population.
- The treatment culture must expose clients/families to former clients/families who have made a successful transition from the culture of addiction to the culture of recovery.

9.4 *The Self-Help Culture* The self-help culture in the United States is growing rapidly and becoming increasingly specialized to meet the unique needs of its members. The processes of initiation, stabilization and specialization have been, and are being, replicated from city to city across the country.

In an early chapter, it was noted that cultural identification and personal identification were essential elements to engage the addict in the recovery process. Both of these elements are reflected in the current organization of the self-help culture.

Since tribes within the culture of addiction are primarily organized by drug choice, it is natural and perhaps desirable that the self-help networks be organized along similar lines. Cultural identification provide addicts entering recovery with the immediate recognition that they are with persons like themselves. Since the identities of the self-help neophytes are so enmeshed in their respective drug choices, they must feel this choice reflected in those with whom they enter the recovery process. The organization of the self-help culture into Alcoholics Anonymous, Narcotics Anonymous, and Cocaine Anonymous assures this instant cultural identification.

As addicts in the culture of addiction have shifted toward multiple drug use, however, such distinctions become less important. It is also apparent that the cultural identification by drug choice which may be important to the addict's entrance into the culture of recovery, is less important to the process of long-term recovery. Many members of Narcotics Anonymous, for example, who needed to be involved early in their recovery with others who shared their drug choice, eventually migrate to Alcoholics Anonymous as they age and mature in the twelve step recovery program.

Self-help cultures, like treatment cultures, must not only provide cultural identification with the addict's drug experiences, they must also provide personal identification that reflects an acceptance of each addict's unique characteristics and needs.   To facilitate personal identification, self-help cultures have become increasingly specialized.   There are young people's meetings, old timer's meetings, women's meetings, non-smoking meetings, Gay meetings, ethnic meetings, and occupational meetings, *i.e.*, physicians, pilots.   There have also been special adaptations of the self-help process that operate parallel to AA, NA, and CA. Women for Sobriety (WFS) and Mentally Ill Recovering Alcoholics (MIRA) are two examples of the latter.   This specialization allows recovering addicts to share common experience while addressing special needs and obstacles to the recovery process.

9.5 *The Family in the Culture of Recovery* It is only recently that the family has begun to move into equal status with the addict within the culture of recovery. In spite of the pioneering work of Al-Anon, the needs of spouses, children and parents touched by addiction of a loved one have historically taken secondary importance to the needs of the addict both within the treatment and self-help cultures. This condition is changing rapidly.

The foundation of this change was laid by the evolution of Al-Anon which would culminated in the publication of *The Al-Anon Family Groups* in 1955 and the inception of the Alateen program in 1957. Dedicated to providing support to those who feel their lives have been deeply affected by close contact with the alcoholic, these programs began to hammer out principles that guided the emotional healing of those wounded in the turbulence surrounding addiction.   There are currently over 25,000 Al-Anon Family Groups, including 3,000 Alateen groups, meeting in 81 countries.

Building on this foundation, early treatment programs began to actively engage family members, not just to aid the alcoholic's recovery, but to promote the recovery of family members, individually and collectively. From the early efforts addressing the needs of such families came the pioneering work of Sharon Wegscheider-Cruse, Claudia Black, Janet Woititz and others who fueled the beginning COA and codependency movement. New visions, new understandings and new models of intervention and healing are emerging which will legitimize and enhance the family's role in the culture of recovery.

9.6 *Strategies for Development of Treatment and Self-Help Cultures* This chapter has described the historical evolution and current organization of treatment and self-help cultures in the United States. Before closing this discussion, it may be helpful to outline some practical suggestions on how to enhance the development of this culture of recovery at a local program level. The following are strategies which have proven to be beneficial.

A. *Building the Treatment Culture* There are two aspects to building a treatment milieu that richly reflects the culture of recovery. There is a technology and a spirituality essential to this process.

The technical side of building the culture of recovery involves the design of the treatment milieu and the range of interventions which staff are trained to utilize within this milieu. It involves the development and refinement of a design capable of disengaging clients from the culture of addiction, then reinforcing entrance into the recovery process by immersing them in a milieu which creates new ways of thinking, feeling and behaving. Strategies and techniques for enhancing this cultural conversion are referenced throughout this text. Chapter Eleven, in particular, will describe approaches to integrating distinct components of the culture of recovery into the treatment milieu. The technical side of this process involves treatment structure and the skills of those persons brought together to implement that treatment structure.

Staff training is an essential component to the implementation of the most ideal treatment structure. It is not enough that staff understand the treatment structure. They must understand what that structure is intended to accomplish and when relaxation or tightening of that structure is warranted. They must be able to recognize behaviors and attitudes and values from the addictive culture which will pose barriers to recovery. They must recognize styles of "doing treatment". They must be armed with techniques that can disengage the addict from self-defeating treatment behaviors. They must understand how to work with the defense structure of the neophyte in recovery. They must understand the developmental stages of recovery and be capable of matching particular intervention techniques with each client's developmental level. They must understand the cultural nuances of recovery if they are to be the client's bridge to this new world. All of this implies a program of rigorous and ongoing training as well as rigorous and consistent clinical supervision.

Technology alone is insufficient to create a dynamic treatment milieu which reflects the culture of recovery. There are programs with excellent structural designs which lack the interpersonal chemistry to make this design come to life. Although spirituality is usually referred to as an individual issue in the recovery process, spirituality can also be seen as the ingredient that breathes life and passion into treatment technology. There is danger in the rapid growth and new business orientation of the substance abuse field. We may find as a field that we have mass-produced treatment structures but failed to imbue them with spiritual power. We may discover in retrospect that many of these structures had the power to make money, but lacked the power to change lives.

Spirituality humanizes our technology and creates a culture of recovery that is both dynamic and contagious. This spiritual dimension within the treatment milieu defies definition, but it can be described.

- It is the ingredient which generates the courage and emotional energy for us to get inside the client's skin and experience his or her world.
- It is the ingredient which allows us to stay focused on people rather than procedures and paper.
- It is the ingredient that allows us to generate involvement and hope in our relationship with "poor prognosis" clients.
- It is the ingredient which allows us to risk emotional involvement with clients who expect and court our rejection.
- It is the ingredient which allows us to confront when avoidance would be easier and less emotionally wearing.
- It is the ingredient which allows us to exemplify the very values from the culture of recovery which we are attempting to transmit to clients.
- It is the ingredient that allows us not to get overinvolved and to "let go," trusting in both the client's strength and that Power greater than ourselves who is also involved in the treatment process.
- It is the ingredient which allows us to set aside "ego" and pettiness and mirror, in our relationships with each other and with clients, the values of respect and support.
- It is the ingredient which creates a milieu in which personal growth is as encouraged for staff as it is for clients.
- It is the congruency between what we do and what we say.

Lacking spirituality, helping professionals individually and collectively become emotionally disengaged technicians. With spirituality, they individually and collectively become healers. By marrying technology and spirituality, treatment professionals have both the tools and the passion to create an environment in which the miracle of recovery can occur.

This spiritual component is initially nurtured through the selection of persons to work in the treatment milieu whose personal values and interpersonal styles reflect values inherent in the culture of recovery. There are, however, programmatic strategies that can continue to nurture the health of this spiritual component and to address problems and issues that tend to disrupt this spiritual health. Recommended strategies include the following.

- Explicitly define the values which will guide staff-staff and staff-client interactions within the treatment milieu, and make the daily application of those values highly visible through such media as team meetings and clinical supervision. The author has outlined a process to define such values in another work. (White, 1986)
- Build in regular times for staff to assess the process within the treatment milieu, to include problems in the process of team functioning.
- Monitor the prevalence of role stressors that tend to deplete staff emotionally and trigger interpersonal conflict. (See White, 1986, for a description of such stressors). Build in clear and workable mechanisms for problem-solving.
- Consider staff access to outside personal growth and spiritual renewal experiences on an equal par with technical skill training.
- Utilize the vehicle of staff retreats for collective self-assessment and reaffirmation of values. Use charismatic and motivational speakers from the field to help staff recharge their emotional/spiritual batteries.

B. *Building Linkages Between the Treatment & Self-Help Cultures*   If treatment is to be the bridge between the culture of addiction and the culture of recovery, then clear and smooth linkages must be established between the treatment culture and the self help cultures. It is not enough that treatment disengage the addict from the culture of addiction and initiate the earliest stages of recovery. The treatment experience must provide the pathway to long-term recovery either through linkage to the traditional self-help groups or to some alternative support structure. Failure to provide such linkage is measured in the incidence of client relapse.

A failure to provide such linkage is illustrated by the early therapeutic communities. These programs developed an extremely elaborate and complex treatment culture that was incongruent with the self-help cultures available to clients upon their re-entry into the community. The language was different. Rituals were different. Symbols were different. Philosophies were different. Confronting the alien self-help cultures upon their discharge, it was easier for clients to reach back to a culture they knew well—the culture of addiction. Since those early times, the therapeutic communities have integrated AA, NA, and CA into their treatment milieus to smooth this transition during re-entry.

There are a number of programmatic strategies that can help establish the linkages and transition between the treatment and self-help cultures. Some of the suggested strategies may seem simplistic or obvious to the traditional short term AA/NA/CA oriented residential program, but they are enumerated below for two reasons. First, many substance abuse treatment modalities such as outpatient programs and long term residential programs have frequently neglected these strategies. Secondly, there seems to be a propensity for linkages between treatment programs and self-help groups to deteriorate over time if they are not actively maintained. The recommended linkage strategies include the following:

- Provide access to self-help meetings held both at the treatment site and in the community from the inception of the client's treatment
- Make such exposure an integral part of the client's treatment plan
- Provide client education on the history, organization, steps and traditions of local self-help groups
- Integrate self-help literature, language, symbols, art, rituals and values into the treatment milieu
- Expose clients to self-help role models who can talk about the transition from treatment to self-help via alumni or self-help panels or one-to-one contact
- Learn the "personality" of various self-help meetings and try to assure the client's exposure to those meetings and people most likely to trigger the "chemistry" of engagement
- Develop a network of AA/NA/CA contacts within the program's geographical catchment area who can serve as the personal guide in the client's entry into the local self-help groups; Establish the client-guide contact prior to the client's discharge from treatment
- Process the client's response to self-help participation, affirming openness, exposing self-defeating attitudes, and encouraging sponsorship and other relationship-building within the self-help network
- Define the role of self-help groups in each clients relapse prevention and aftercare plans
- Meet regularly with Hospital & Institution Committees and other designated representatives of local self-help groups, constantly exploring ways to enhance this transition and resolving problems as they arise

C. *Nurturing Development of the Self-Help Culture*   The above
suggestions all presuppose the existence of a fully developed self-
help network.   But what about the community with no such
network or the community in which this network is in its infancy?
How does the treatment program enhance the transition from
treatment to self-help culture when:

- there are no NA or CA meetings available and difficulties
  are encountered integrating clients with drug choices
  other than alcohol into AA?
- newly developing NA and CA groups are very unstable,
  on again-off again, hampered by members with little
  sobriety time and frequent relapse?
- special client characteristics such as ethnicity, age, sex, or
  affectional preference pose obstacles to involvement in
  predominantly White, middle-aged, heterosexual, male
  support groups?

Approaches which have proven successful in responding to these
issue are detailed in the following discussions.

The openness of AA groups to the multiple drug user has
mellowed considerably during the past two decades. There are AA
groups all over the country now where an, "I'm Bill and I'm an
addict," hardly raises an eyebrow. It is first of all important that
treatment programs understand the difficulty AA groups have had
wrestling with this issue of appropriate inclusion/exclusion. This
is not a matter of casual intellectual debate, but a matter of intense
personal survival. For those who have addressed this issue, it has
been through consideration of the common welfare of AA and out
of concern whether broader interpretations would both threaten the
personal recovery of AA members and violate AA traditions. The
first task of the treatment program is to be sensitive to the personal
stakes involved in the inclusion/exclusion issue and avoid

approaches to self-help groups that smack of condescension or self-righteous advocacy. The fact is that AA eventually opens its doors to the multiple drug user in most communities, and, where such inclusion does not occur, alternative self-help structures evolve to compensate for such exclusion.

As treatment programs, we have a responsibility to engage the client within a culture of recovery. As such, we have a long-term interest in the health and vitality of the self-help components of this culture. It is desirable that treatment components and self-help components of this culture view each other as autonomous partners, each self-governed and independent, capable of mutual respect. While it is crucial the integrity of local self-help groups be respected by accepting their interpretations of AA traditions governing membership, there are a number of actions that can be taken by a treatment program to enhance the access of all clients to self-help membership.

- On-going meetings between the treatment program and the local self-help groups, particularly utilizing the vehicle of Hospitals and Institutions Committees, provide a mechanism to build relationships of mutual respect and to provide a forum through which the issue of inclusion/exclusion can be explored.
- Treatment programs must understand various elements within the culture of recovery and provide client exposure to those elements to which the client is most likely to identify and into which the client is most likely to be embraced. By knowing the "personality" of each AA group, we can coach clients toward those groups in which both cultural and personal identification will occur.
- We must prepare clients for entry into the self-help culture.   By teaching clients about the history,

organization, recovery principles, traditions, rituals, and
etiquette of AA, we decrease chances of person-group
mismatch and help the client understand how to use the
self-help meeting. Should a multiple-drug using client
know, for example, that a ten minute monologue
restricted to his/her travails with heroin would indicate
a poor understanding of custom and etiquette in most
AA groups?

- Some clients will enter the self-help process as a critic,
project blame for their failure to participate on the self-
help group, or try to exploit any existing tensions
between the self-help and treatment cultures. All such
behavior must be directly confronted for what it is—self-
defeating behavior that prevents the client's
disengagement from the culture of addiction and
entrance into the culture of recovery.

When on-going supports for recovery following treatment are
under-developed within the catchment area of a treatment
program, efforts must be taken to enhance the long term
development of the overall culture of recovery. This involves
providing support for self-help group development and providing
alternative support structures until these self help structures
emerge. This not only involves the emergence of new tribal groups
based on drug choice, e.g. NA or CA, but also involves the
emergence of new tribes based on personal identification, e.g.
groups organized by age, sex, race, affectional preference, etc.

There is a two stage process that treatment programs can utilize to
speed up this overall development in the self help culture. The
first stage is the development of group oriented support structures
where existing self-help supports are lacking in volume or
specialty. The second stage is to then shift the nature of these

groups from treatment to self-help. Let's examine how one program utilized this process of self-help development.

A residential and outpatient substance abuse treatment program was located in a midwestern community with a population of roughly 90,000. AA groups in this community had grown from 2 per week in 1965 to more than 25 per week in 1985. A follow-up study of clients discharged from the treatment program revealed that Black clients and women clients had substantially higher relapse rates than White male clients. A further analysis of the follow-up data revealed what treatment staff had periodically observed—women and Black clients were not successfully making the transition from treatment into long term self-help group involvement. Two strategies subsequently emerged in an attempt to alter this situation.

A meeting between the treatment program and the Hospital and Institutions Committee of AA led to a series of larger meetings which involved two female treatment staff and about 10 recovering women from the community. Two new resources would emerge from these meetings. First, the treatment program developed a formal women's volunteer program made up of recovering women who served as special guides in the introduction of women clients to AA. Secondly, out of the increased interest generated by the above meetings, a women's AA group was initiated. While there had long been talk of the need for a women's meeting, there were never enough women at one time sharing this idea who could bring it to fruition. The women's meeting, which is held in a room at the treatment facility, has served as a powerful resource for engaging women clients in the culture of recovery.

In looking at the special needs of Black clients, the treatment program was presented with a different situation. There were currently no Blacks involved in local AA groups. While the treatment program saw a number of Black clients, there were never enough at one time to constitute a core group that could have evolved into a special meeting for these clients. Blacks compliantly attended AA meetings during treatment but, even while attending aftercare meetings regularly, did not make the transition into the use of AA meetings as a support mechanism for long term recovery. The treatment program started an open-ended weekly aftercare group for Black clients. An invitation was sent out to all Black clients who had gone through treatment in the past three years. A Black counselor facilitated the group, whose structure and process was established and altered over time by the participants. In the first nine months, attendance vacillated back and forth from a low of 2 clients to a high of 15. By the ninth month, two things had occurred. First there was a core group of about 6 Black clients who had developed some sustained sobriety and who were regularly attending the Black aftercare group. Secondly, these six clients had started leaving their meeting which was held at 6:30, and going in mass to an 8:00 AA meeting. This would form the initial bridge between their aftercare group experience and their post-treatment involvement in AA. After 12 months, there was increased talk about setting up their own AA meeting. The counselor assisted them in getting in touch with representatives from two black AA groups in neighboring communities, who agreed to serve as outside resources if they were needed. By the 16th month following the establishment of a Black aftercare group, this group had formally evolved to become the first Black AA group in this community. Not only did this group provide Black alcoholics with a post-treatment support system with which they could identify, the increased numbers of Blacks also made it easier for these persons to utilize the whole spectrum of support group meetings.

The above illustrations show how a treatment program can play an important role in the development of the post-treatment culture of recovery. Similar strategies can be utilized to help stimulate the development of NA or CA groups or other special population self-help meetings. The keys to this development process include disengagement of the treatment program in this development role as early as possible, respect for the autonomy and independence of self-help groups, and patience that is nurtured by a vision of long-term development of the local culture of recovery.

The culture for recovering addicts is not restricted to only those currently existing groups which are publicly identified with recovery from addiction, *e.g.*, AA, NA and CA. There are other tribes in this culture of recovery which in the future will command greater attention from the substance abuse field. AA, NA and CA reflect dominant patterns, or species of addiction, and preferred styles of recovery for the majority of addicts. There are other addicts whose patterns of addiction are very different from those generally reflected in these self-help groups and whose pathway to recovery may be different than the map set forth in AA, NA or CA. In the future, as the field comes to understand these different species of addiction and different pathways to recovery, the treatment center may also have a role in enhancing the development of other tribal support systems within this culture of recovery.

There is no question, for example, that many addicts use religion and the social structure of the church as a vehicle for recovery and self-help. Do treatment professionals have a role, perhaps via clergy training, to enhance the ability of some clients to use this pathway to recovery? Could religious groups be encompassed within this culture of recovery and be sensitized to the special needs of recovering addicts? As new understandings about various species of addiction develop, what other tribal groups may need to be organized within this culture of recovery? The treatment professional's job extends beyond creating an openness for recovery in the individual addict. We must help construct a social world in which such recovery can be nurtured.

D. *Inclusion of the Family in the Culture of Recovery* Historically, the family has been excluded from the culture of recovery. From the days of the early inebriate asylums to the self-help groups which preceded AA, there is scant mention of the family. While Alanon provided the historical foundation upon which a holistic approach to family recovery could be based, the treatment field still reflects the historical exclusion of the family. A radical re-thinking of the role of family in the treatment and self-help culture is clearly indicated.

When a system is confronted with a demand for change, it is easier to add a new appendage to the system than to make fundamental systemic changes. This is precisely the stance the treatment field has taken relative to the needs of the family. Rather than rethinking and restructuring the very essence of what we do in the name of addiction treatment, we have added on small programmatic appendages in the name of family responsiveness. Addressing family needs means more than family interviews while the "client" is in treatment, or linking the family to Alanon or engaging the family in a formal "family program" operated by our newly hired "family counselors."

The addiction treatment field must eventually redefine its unit of service from the individual to the family and social network. Our "client" thus becomes not a single individual but a network of people who individually and collectively have experienced a deterioration in functioning as a result of the impact of addiction upon this network. With such redefinition, family recovery represents not a new treatment specialty, but the very essence of treatment itself. Assessment by definition encompasses assessment of the needs of the total family system. We admit not individuals, but families. Treatment plans encompass the individual and the collective recovery goals of the entire family. Whether a single member or an entire family network is engaged in treatment, a concept of family health and recovery drives the treatment process. Aftercare services by definition encompass aftercare for individual members of the family and the family as a whole. Within such a perspective, any family member has as much right and legitimacy in treatment as the addict. The goal becomes a continuum of family care from intake through aftercare through long term engagement in the culture of recovery.

The substance abuse treatment field has a long way to go before such redefinition of "client" is achieved, and there are major obstacles which will inhibit such redefinition. Service systems have been organized to serve individual clients, not family systems. Public and private funding of treatment is generally based on admission of a single person—the addicted client. Assessment models are based on an individual rather than a family system perspective. Confidentiality regulations and other regulatory codes governing treatment are all based on the needs of the addicted individual, rather than the needs of the addicted family. But the biggest obstacle will be how the field conceptualizes treatment. As long as it continues to address the needs of individuals in isolation from the family and social networks in which they are nested, then family members will continue to have only token legitimacy within the substance abuse treatment milieu and the culture of recovery.

The redefinition of "client" to embrace family will be a developmental process in the field. At the current time, it may be important that family appendages be added—family programs, family counselors, family aftercare groups, and family self-help groups. It is through increased exposure to the needs of family members and witnessing and participating in their healing and recovery process that more and more members of the field will be radicalized into the family perspective. Many treatment professionals have observed for years the tremendous strain placed on the family when the addict finally achieves sobriety. Perhaps one reason that strain has been so great is that the field has created a culture of recovery for the addict and pathways into this culture but forget to build a place in this culture, or provide pathways in, for family members.

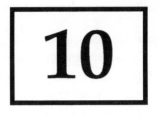

THE PSYCHOSOCIAL AND TECHNICAL FUNCTIONS OF THE CULTURE OF RECOVERY

Many addicts seeking to disengage from the culture of addiction find themselves alone, psychologically naked and vulnerable. There is a realization that every person and place they know is connected to their drug use. Every thought and action is related to their drug relationship. Their whole world is their drug relationship. As they seek to leave this world, there is an intense experience of culture shock. Old rules governing social interactions no longer apply. Old skills are inappropriate and maladaptive. Habitual ways of looking at the world are found to be inadequate. Sustained contact with non-addicts leaves them feeling like strangers in an alien world. Each of them also experiences decreasing ownership of and comfort with his or her own body. In short, newly disengaged addicts are homesick for their drug relationship and the social world where such relationships are highly valued. For recovery to occur, those physical, psychological and social needs which were met in the culture must be addressed in different ways within new environments and relationships. The movement from addiction to recovery is a transformation in worlds and world views.

Unfortunately, such transformations do not occur for most addicts, although the number is clearly increasing. Many addicts do not experience the combination of internal resources and external supports to allow such a transformation to occur. Like the chronically relapsing nicotine addict, they talk episodically and passionately about their need to quit while their continued drug use drives them into chronic and terminal phases of addiction. Short-term experiments with abstinence are so uncomfortable and so disorienting that relapse occurs quickly. Treatment professionals frequently view such relapse events as failure and imbue such events with great emotional significance. For the culturally enmeshed addict, relapse is often an act of impulse committed with little conscious thought. It is a return to that which seems natural, comfortable, desirable and inevitable. They are quickly reclaimed by the culture of addiction at the most vulnerable stage of their experimental disengagement.

If the addict is to make a sustained transition into recovery, then the culture of recovery must be capable of addressing the wide assortment of needs which acutely impinge on the newly abstinent addict. This chapter will catalogue the nature of these needs which must be addressed. The chapters which follow will discuss these needs in more depth and outline how such needs can be addressed in the treatment setting.

10.1   *Zones of Action and Experience*   The illustration on the following page offers a visual introduction to an holistic model of understanding the needs that span both addiction and recovery. This model proposes five overlapping zones or spheres of life activity which are constructed by all persons to create and sustain personal comfort and harmony in the relationships with the external world. These five zones include:

- The physical zone
- The psychological zone
- The spiritual zone
- The relationship zone
- The lifestyle zone

There is a natural drive to sustain a balance between needs, desires and comfort within each of these areas of life activity. There is an equally natural tendency for different spheres to take dominance in our individual lives. For some persons there exists a major motif around which all zones of action are organized. These can be:

- events (incest, rape, Vietnam)
- objects (money, home, cars)
- activities (work, sports, sex)
- people (symbiotic relationships)
- beliefs (political or religious dogma)
- status (power or powerlessness)
- conditions (age, sex, ethnicity, physical appearance, debilitating physical or psychiatric illness)

In the case of addiction, the progressive intensity of the drug relationship dominates and transforms all zones of action and experience. The following sections will detail how recovery must be equally consuming. Each zone of action and experience must be reconstructed as part of the long-term recovery process. Such reconstruction usually involves the following elements:

1. The assessment, identification and thawing of compulsive, self-defeating beliefs and behaviors that have served to sustain addiction.
2. The substitution of new recovery-enhancing patterns of thinking, feeling and acting.

3. The refinement and stabilization of new recovery-enhancing beliefs and behaviors through repetition and reinforcement.
4. The facilitation of the ongoing growth and development within each sphere of action and experience.
5. Support in establishing balance between the zones of action and experience.
6. The application of external technical resources, *e.g.*, professional problem solvers (physicians, psychiatrists, lawyers, clergy) as needed throughout the life cycle of recovery.
7. Mastery of the emotional stress involved in each step of the change process.

If the culture of recovery is to be successful in recruiting and retaining addicts from the culture of addiction, it must guide and support each of the above elements. The culture of recovery must be able to facilitate reconstruction of each of the five zones of action and experience that were transformed via the addiction process.

10.2 *The Physical Zone* The physiological transformations that occurred as a result of the person-drug relationship must be reversed and transcended in the recovery process. Developmental tasks in this zone revolve around three major areas: 1) the adjustment of the body to the absence of the drug; 2) the treatment of acute and chronic health problems; and 3) the construction of a health-enhancing lifestyle. Short- and long-term developmental

Zones of Action and Experience
in Addiction and Recovery

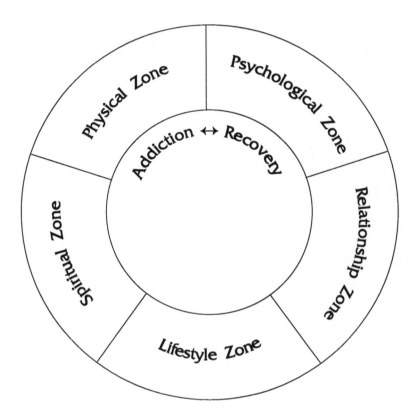

tasks in this area are listed below in a checklist format, as they may be used as an individual assessment exercise with clients:

_____   Breach of the person-drug relationship via detoxification; initiation of abstinence

_____   Resolution of acute life-threatening or sobriety-threatening medical problems

_____   Identification and treatment of concurrent primary or secondary physical or psychiatric illnesses

_____   Reduction/removal of risks to personal safety via violence

_____   Development of remediation plans for chronic health problems

_____   Assurance of recovery and comfort enhancing physical shelter

_____   Return of daily rituals of self-care, cleanliness, and dental hygiene

_____   Mastery of cellular hunger for drugs (exhibited by intense cravings, drug dreams)

_____   Improved nutritional health to speed healing of body tissue and stabilization of mood

_____   Reversal of drug-induced developmental retardation (particularly in adolescents and young adults)

_____   Readjustment of biological processes to absence of drugs, *e.g.*, digestion, menstruation

_____   Initiation of drug-free sleep patterns; resolution of sleep disturbances

_____   Alteration of physical image for congruence with one's new recovering identity

_____   Reversal of drug-related anhedonia; return of non-drug induced physical pleasure

_____   Initiation and stabilization of drug-free sexual functioning; treatment of sexual dysfunction of physical origin

_____ Elimination of other toxic habits, *e.g.*, toxic relationships with tobacco, caffeine, and sugar
_____ Acceptance of physical defects; emotional acceptance of one's own body
_____ Acceptance of irreversible or otherwise untreatable drug-related physical illnesses or injuries
_____ Management of physical changes of aging within framework of recovery

10.3 *The Psychological Zone* The psychological zone of action and experience in recovery encompasses an evolutionary reconstruction of the personality. Such reconstruction involves the elimination of the cognitive defense structure that evolved to support addiction and its replacement with a sobriety-based cognitive defense structure. Short- and long-term developmental tasks in this area include the following:

_____ Weakening/elimination of the addiction-sustaining defense structure, *e.g.*, denial, rationalization, projection
_____ Development of an alternative cognitive defense structure with sufficient rigidity to reduce likelihood of relapse
_____ Exploration of drug-free methods of managing early emotional thawing
_____ Emotional decompression from personal or cultural trauma, *e.g.*, sexual abuse, violence
_____ Achievement of initial emotional catharsis via self-disclosure of one's life-shaping secrets
_____ Resolution of cultural marginality and psychological ambivalence (indicated by relapse)
_____ Identification and removal of self-defeating patterns of "doing treatment"
_____ Resolution of shame-based patterns of self-destruction; purging of belief that one is unworthy of recovery
_____ Shedding of addiction-based nicknames

_____ Construction of a sobriety-supporting life story

_____ Identification and neutralization, or reframing, of sensory cues that trigger drug hunger and drug-seeking behavior

_____ Development of daily rituals that reinforce recovery identity and values

_____ Acquisition of sobriety-based stress management skills

_____ Mastery of self-command techniques to abort "stinkin' thinkin'"

_____ Mastery of assertion and refusal skills applied specifically to opportunities for drug consumption

_____ Initiation of drug-free work on age-appropriate developmental tasks

_____ Clarification of sexual identity and sexual role

_____ Emergence of the ritualistic telling of one's story as an exercise in identity construction

_____ Tempering of other excessive behaviors

_____ Initiation of conscious effort to reconstruct personality through daily work on character defects

10.4 *The Spiritual Zone* For many addicts, the spiritual zone of action and experience is the initiating and driving force within the recovery process. This zone broadly embraces empowerment from beyond the self, an openness to spiritual and/or religious experiences and the reconstruction of personal values. Short- and long-term developmental tasks within this zone include the following.

———— Emergence of motivational crisis from the experience of pain and a sense of ultimate isolation and abandonment

———— Experience of the potential loss of self is recognized through near-death and near-insanity episodes

———— Breakthrough of self-perception and intensification of the experience of self-hatred

———— Experience and recognition of complete defeat

———— Generation of hope through contact with some power beyond the self

———— Feelings of specialness, distinction and future purpose are instilled through an experience of empowerment

———— Sudden or slowly emerging experience of rebirth

———— Daily rituals of meditation/prayer established

———— Acceptance of mysteries and paradoxes of recovery

———— Purging of emotional toxins through the vehicle of confession

———— Conscious effort at, and growing experience of, self-forgiveness

———— Conscious pursuit of acts of restitution

———— Progressive replacement of narcissism and grandiosity with humility

———— Initiation and integration of acts of service into daily lifestyle

———— Listening to stories of others increases as an act of service and surrender

_____ Clarification of religious and spiritual beliefs; reconstruction of personal values

_____ Rigid control evolves to tolerance and acceptance of ambiguity

_____ Cultivation of sacred places where identity and spiritual values are reinforced and enriched

_____ Recovering identity embraced within broader spiritual identity

10.5 The Interpersonal Zone Addiction recovery entails a complete reconstruction of the self-world relationship. The relationship zone of action and experience in recovery involves the reconstruction of intimate, family and social relationships. Short- and long-term developmental tasks within this zone include the following.

_____ Management of fear and pain in intimate relationships

_____ Redefinition of the marital/intimate relationship; clarification of relationship values and rules

_____ Integration of drug-free sexual functioning into new relationship values

_____ Expiation of charged emotional energy surrounding experience of addiction within the family

_____ Sobriety-based reorganization of family roles and rules

_____ Reformulation of daily family rituals

_____ Reversal of anticipatory grief by family members

_____ Redefinition of family holiday rituals

_____ Return and enrichment of parental functioning

_____ Sobriety-based assessment of one's existing social network

_____ Disengagement from drug-related and other pathology-bonded relationships

_____ Replacement of pathology-bonded relationships with recovering role models and mentors

_____ Relationship-building and experience of acceptance and belonging within the culture of recovery

_____ Dependence upon culture of recovery for emotional and social support; some disengagement from the outside world

_____ Extension of social world beyond culture of recovery to encompass other interests and pursuits

_____ Extension of service activities beyond culture of recovery

10.6 *The Lifestyle Zone* The lifestyle zone of action and experience in recovery involves the systematic reconstruction of daily life. Short- and long-term developmental tasks within this zone include.

_____ Dissipation of addiction argot and profanity; acquisition of new language skills

_____ Replacement of symbols of cultural affiliation reflecting shift from addiction to recovery

_____ Cessation of criminal and non-criminal predatory behavior

_____ Identification of tabooed places and situations that pose a high risk of relapse

_____ Resolution of legal problems

_____ Complete restructuring of daily schedule and rituals

_____ Mastery of rituals of greeting and interaction within culture of recovery, *e.g.*, the rituals and etiquette of formal and informal AA relationships

_____ Initiation of action to resolve drug-related debt

_____ Redefinition of the meaning of work and money

_____ Reorientation of work relationships; return of consistent productivity

_____ Avoidance or working through of excessive relationships with work and money

_____ Development of sobriety-based leisure activities

_____ Development of new rituals of celebration
_____ Prioritization and simplification of lifestyle

10.7 *The Scope and Intensity of Change in Recovery*   Even a cursory review of the developmental tasks outlined above raises a crucial question: How could anyone initiate and sustain such massive reconstruction of his or her life? It is little wonder that phrases like, "One Day At A Time," "Easy Does It" and "First Things First" have become the marching slogans of recovery. Few would begin the recovery process if at the beginning they could fully perceive the entire scope of change which this process would entail. With such a vision, few would begin what in their broken state would have to appear as an impossible journey. Recovery is a complex, time-dependent process that must be made simple and immediate. If the pace and intensity of the metamorphosis of recovery is not controlled, the pilgrim will seek flight back to the toxic womb of the culture of addiction.

10.8 *Teachers, Healers and Travel Guides* Treatment professionals play many roles as they seek to respond to the needs of neophytes in the culture of recovery. They help newly recovering addicts interpret and label their past and current experience.   They intervene to heal physical and emotional wounds. They teach new skills. They help the client anticipate and prepare for new problems and opportunities. They identify and broker needed resources. They serve as advocates.   These and many other functions have been explored in other publications. There are two broad roles and functions which have received less attention and which have particular relevance to the model set forth in this book. The first of these is the role of actively linking the neophyte to the culture of recovery. The second is the role of integrating the client changes occurring within the various zones of action and experience.

Addicts tentatively exploring the universe of recovery need a tour guide. They need information, skills and support to move from one world to another. As they enter this culture of recovery, they need to know its rules and etiquette. They need to know its history, politics, religion, geography and pastimes. They need to know its language and its values. They need to know what is expected of them. And most importantly, they need to meet its members. As treatment professionals, it is possible to get so caught up in the client's emotional experience of early recovery that we forget to orient them to the social world which they have just joined. Treatment professionals should be the "welcome wagon" of the culture of recovery. Addiction and recovery are experiences around which two separate worlds have evolved. Treatment professionals can be the human bridge between the worlds of destruction and creation.

What stimulates and sustains addicts in making the passage from addiction to recovery is empowering relationships. Treatment professionals are the cement which initially bind addicts to this new recovery culture. From this experimental relationship, additional relationships are forged by the neophyte, each of which strengthens the link to the recovery culture. By stimulating such relationship-building, the client moves from the experience of being connected to the culture to the experience of being a member within the culture. It is the power of relationships in the culture of recovery that must offset the power of the drug in the culture of addiction. It is through recovery relationships that the plethora of needs experienced by the neophyte will be met.

One of the most important roles treatment professionals can play with the recovering addict is providing consultation on how to integrate the zones of action and experience into a sane daily existence. These zones of action and experience are pieces of a dynamic, living puzzle that keep changing in size and shape.

Zones ebb and flow in and out of daily life and ebb and flow through different developmental stages of recovery. They can move from dormancy to dominance quickly. The physical zone of action and experience is stabilized and then suddenly moves to dominance with the flare-up of a medical disorder or the intensification of drug cravings. The psychological zone takes center stage only to be replaced due to demands imposed from the relationship zone of action and experience. In early recovery, all of these zones are competing for center stage. Balancing and integrating these zones of action and experience is difficult. The ultimate destination of the recovery journey is not a place or an event, but the mastery of this integration process. The destination is a sustained experience of wholeness—the bringing of all zones of action and experience into balance and harmony. The process of bringing these zones of action and experience into harmony is never finally completed because each zone is constantly changing. It is the mastery and daily use of the process, not some static homeostasis, that makes up the essence of recovery. Teaching this integration process must be the organizing motif behind the delivery of the whole range of specialized substance abuse treatment services.

This chapter has outlined *what* addicts need as they disengage from the culture of addiction and proceed through the developmental stages of recovery. The coming chapters will seek to outline *how* the substance abuse treatment professional can respond to those needs within the culture of recovery.

11

CORE ELEMENTS
IN THE CULTURE OF RECOVERY

The metamorphosis that occurs to individuals through their affiliation with the culture of addiction has been extensively documented as have the broad range of needs experienced by addicts whose pain has created the need for escape from this culture. The next stage of the addict's journey involves passage through another culture and yet another metamorphosis. As the pilgrims flee their society of addicts and seek refuge in the culture of recovery, there is—in fact, must be—a clash of cultures and a struggle of wills. It is through this clash and struggle that the addict's experience of surrender and acceptance gives birth to the potential for recovery. It is in this clash that the addict's compulsive patterns of self-destruction are unfrozen and opened to change. This chapter explores the minute-by-minute details of this clash of cultures within the treatment milieu. It explores how each element of the culture of addiction imbedded in the addict's lifestyle must be stripped and replaced with its counterpart from the culture of recovery.

11.1 *From Culture of Addiction to Culture of Recovery: A Catalogue of Intervention Techniques* This chapter is replete with references to various techniques and strategies that can be used to assist addicts in their transition from the culture of addiction to the culture of recovery. Many of these have been adapted from diverse schools of psychological thought for specific use in the addiction treatment setting. Hopefully any purists among the readership will forgive the occasional bastardization of psychological theory and technique and the redefinition or refocusing of some psychological terms. Other strategies and techniques have been developed, adapted and refined in a wide variety of addiction treatment settings. A glossary (See Appendix B) has been provided that briefly defines and describes each technique referenced.

11.2 *Language* For addicts whose words and conversational themes have been shaped in the culture of addiction, treatment must be a language laboratory preparing the addict for life outside the deviant culture. This section will explore the role of language in the addict's movement from the culture of addiction to the culture of recovery.

A. *What's In a Name?*   There is perhaps nothing more central to personal identity than one's own name. It distinguishes us from others and connotes a history of places, people and experiences that have made us who we are. Just as a name reflects that identity, changes in one's name can reflect a transformation in that identity. The change in name reflects a separation from one's past, the choice of new values, the engagement in a new primary social network and, above all, a new definition of self. This phenomenon is evident in the propensity for nicknames in adolescent peer cultures, name changes commonly associated with entrance into various religious sects and movements, and, to a broader degree, the historical tradition of changing the names of women at the time of marriage. Our concern is with the role of nicknames, aliases and other name changes in the process of engagement in and disengagement from the cultures of addiction and recovery.

There are few persons in whose life these principles could be more graphically illustrated than the man the public would come to know as Malcolm X.   Malcolm was not one but four personalities—each emerging during a different period of his life, each constituting a different value system, and each symbolized by a different name.   There was Malcolm Little, born in Omaha and raised in Milwaukee and Lansing. From the persona of Malcolm Little would emerge "Detroit Red," the Harlem street hustler whose career in the culture of addiction would carry him into prison. Through the influence of his brother Reginald, the third persona would emerge as a follower of the Honorable Elijah Muhammad and eventually become the fiery and charismatic public figure of Malcolm X. Following his break with Elijah Muhammad and prior to his assassination in 1965, a fourth persona would emerge whose values were reflected in his Organization for Afro-American Unity. During this final period of his life, he had begun to sign his letters, El-Hajj Malik El-Shabazz. In the language of this book, Detroit Red was an enmeshed member of the culture of addiction who found, through Islam, a pathway into a culture of recovery. The changes in names during his life marked significant rites of entrance and exit from the cultures of addiction and recovery.

Like Malcolm X, many culturally enmeshed addicts experience name changes as part of their initiation into the culture of addiction.   They are known not by their Christian names or surnames but by such colorful nicknames as Frog, Sleepy, Speedy, Babe, Rabbit, Woody, or Spike; or by initials such as T.J. or L.B. that may or may not have any relationship to their real name; or by aliases or "professional" names such as Chastity Blue. These names, whether self-anointed or christened by others, symbolize the cultural experiences in which the identity was formed and tie one to the cultural values within which this identity continues to be based. For the client in treatment to hang on to his or her name from the addictive culture is one means of bringing the culture of addiction into treatment. If treatment involves a shedding of this culture, then one's name from this culture must be molted as a skin cast off through the process of growth.

The role of name changes in this process of identity transformation may be facilitated in a number of ways. Some programs simply address all clients by their legal names. Other programs, while prohibiting the use of any old nicknames, leave it to each client to select the name by which they would like to be addressed in treatment. The following exercise is recommended as an instructional and values clarification experience around the issue of one's name. It can be conducted with individual clients or with clients in group settings and is particularly helpful with clients who have been deeply enmeshed in the culture of addiction

Provide the client with three sheets of paper with the heading "Name/Nickname_____" at the top of each sheet. Ask the client to write their legal name and any nicknames they had up until the time they began using alcohol/drugs at the top of the first sheet. Then direct the client to list below on the sheet any words or descriptions that they would use or that others would use to describe them during this period. Repeat the process for the second sheet for the client's period of alcohol/drug use. On the third sheet ask the client to write in the bottom first noting how they would like to be described by others and by themselves in the future. Ask if there is a name that would best reflect the characteristics on the third sheet. This "Name Game" provides a forum for clients to be able to articulate changes they experienced through their addiction and to consciously project desired changes in their identity. Clients can be given the freedom to select a first name while in treatment as a symbol of their entrance into the culture of recovery.

B. *Profanity and Argot* It was noted earlier in the discussion of the culture of addiction that language plays a powerful role in either sustaining or transforming personal identity. Words and the manner and mannerisms which surround their expression can serve to open or close doorways to change. The words, the gestures, the conversational themes, and the everyday communication rituals of the enmeshed addict are all anchored to the social world of addiction. To leave this culture, one must let go of its language and learn or relearn the words which serve as tickets of admission to other social worlds.

One of the first tasks of stripping the culture of addiction is extinguishing the argot and profanity that constitute the bulk of spoken language in the culture. This task involves the following:

- Teaching clients how argot/profanity reinforces values, attitudes and behaviors from the culture of addiction
- Consistently discouraging the use of argot/profanity within the treatment milieu
- Providing relationships characterized by acceptance and safety within which clients can be supported to try on new behaviors
- Cultivating a language-rich environment within which clients can learn alternative communication skills

Must the substance abuse counselor understand and use the lexicon of the "street" to effectively communicate with the culturally enmeshed addict? The counselor serves the role of guide—leading the addict on a journey from one culture to another. While the guide must understand the lexicon of addiction as a means of early relationship building, the use of this language with the client is to fail to make the journey into the culture of recovery. Rather than providing the addict the language skills to leave the old culture, the argot-speaking counselor joins and remains with the addict in his/her world.

While strong controls in the treatment milieu may suppress addict lexicon early in the treatment process as a form of compliance, it is desirable that the addict become more personally involved in examining and rejecting this language and style of communication from his or her past life. To achieve this shedding of addictspeak, the client must be aided in actually seeing this style of communication. The use of simulation and role play in conjunction with videotape can be a very effective and powerful form of feedback in this area. Most people remember the first time they hear themselves on a tape recorder. Videotaping can be an even more powerful technique for mirroring to clients their presentation of self. The use of parody (exaggeration) and humor to lower client defenses can also be effective during these communication simulations. Such structured experiences in treatment serve to strain and diminish the client's relationship with the culture of addiction by holding this culture up for ridicule. They also enhance increased openness for self-examination and change.

C. *Reshaping Conversational Themes* The culturally enmeshed addict not only loses the words to communicate outside the culture, he or she also loses the content of communication. Addict speech becomes increasingly restricted to hustling tales, copping tales, getting off tales and tales involving hassles encountered in "the life." Addict communication reflects the narcissism of addiction—impaired listening, loss of empathy, grandiosity ("I," "I," "I") and projection of blame ("They," "They," "They"). Disengaging the addict from the culture of addiction involves both stripping the language from this culture as well as altering the themes that make up the content of interpersonal communication.

Clients must first be taught the following principles:

- Language—how one talks and what one talks about—is the mirror through which we know ourselves and are known by others.
- Change in language was part of the progression of addiction. Both words and the themes of language paid homage to the drug experience.
- Relapsing back to the language and conversational themes of the culture of addiction is high risk behavior that may trigger euphoric recall of drug intoxication, cellular craving, drug-seeking and drug-using behavior.

The above principles establish the need for change and provide a framework within the treatment milieu which allows for both confrontation and self-monitoring of communication during early recovery.

D. *The Language of Treatment and Recovery* The guiding theme of this chapter is that every component of the culture of addiction taken from the enmeshed addict in the process of treatment must be replaced with a component of the culture of recovery. If the treatment experience is going to take language, then it must also give language. If the old language supported addiction, then a new language must be provided that will support recovery. If the old language met specific needs of the addict, *i.e.*, social identity and inclusion, then a new recovery language must be provided that will meet these needs more positively.

Once the treatment milieu has begun to suppress and extinguish language from the culture of addiction, this same milieu must provide language and communication skills essential to the recovery process. If we expect the addict to change both how he/she talks and what he/she talks about, then the treatment milieu must take on, to some degree, the characteristics of a language laboratory. The menu of this language laboratory could provide diverse offerings.

The treatment milieu must provide addicts with a philosophy (language) of addiction that both fits and makes sense of their individual and collective experience and a philosophy (language) of treatment and recovery that instills hope. The words that make up these philosophies are essential tools in the construction of a cognitive framework for recovery. Addicts must not only understand this philosophy; they must refine this philosophy to fit their own experience through the construction of a personal story. All addicts must master selection of the words and phrases which will allow them to explain their past and current life to others. The language must provide a framework for the reconstruction of self-esteem. This mastery of language can be enhanced through:

- exposure to addiction literature
- lectures, movies, video and audiotapes, and self-help meetings which provide exposure to role models talking about their experiences of addiction and recovery, and
- treatment assignments that demand the personalization of key concepts related to addiction and recovery

For maximum utility following treatment, the language within the treatment culture should be transferable to both the culture of recovery outside of treatment, *i.e.*, self-help groups, and to the culture at large in which the client will be interacting.

The client must master the language skills involved in critical events that mark their transition from the culture of addiction to the culture of recovery. Identifying and preparing for such incidents is a crucial element of relapse prevention planning. The addict in treatment can be helped to formulate answers to the following self-imposed questions.

- What do I say to my family?
- What do I tell my friends and co-workers when they ask where I've been?   (The client leaving residential treatment)
- What do I say when co-workers want me to stop after work for a drink with them?
- What do I say to my friends, some of whom I now believe are alcoholic?
- How do I explain to people why I don't drink or use drugs anymore?
- What do I say when I run into ghosts from my old life, *i.e.*, persons owed money, persons hustled?

Creating situations where the client can identify his or her own anticipated critical incidents and rehearse such incidents through discussion and role play are essential treatment activities. Treatment centers must engender the skills of assertion if clients are to have the will and the words to resist re-engagement in the culture of addiction.

Some clients have been so enmeshed in the addictive subculture that they simply need to relearn how to talk to persons outside the life. Residential treatment and aftercare programs who care for such deeply enmeshed addicts may wish to explore treatment activities that can achieve the following:

- re-orient clients to world and community events outside the culture of addiction—not to just understand, but to be able to converse about such events
- increase client contact and interaction with persons and social situations outside the culture of addiction, and

- provide clients with basic language skills required for mastery of new roles in culture of recovery, *e.g.*, job interviewing and socializing

Many addicts do not possess skills of affective expression or have lost such skills through the progression of their addiction. Engagement in treatment inevitably begins to precipitate the emotional thawing of these clients. As feelings surface into consciousness, sometimes quite suddenly and painfully, the treatment milieu can provide both permission for affective expression and a language which can serve as the vehicle to release such emotion. Treatment activities must match the pace at which this emotional thawing occurs for each client. Treatment activities that prematurely demand emotional self-disclosure without providing the words for such disclosure and which assault the client's fragile defense structure are likely to stimulate escapist flight into the culture of addiction.

11.3 *Religion, Spirituality and Values* The moral career of the addict, which has been dictated by the drug relationship, reaches a point of reckoning when the addict is brought into contact with the culture of recovery. Addiction renders questions of religion irrelevant, dismisses matters of the spirit as inconsequential and demolishes values in favor of expediency. Recovery resurrects such issues and demands that they be consciously addressed. There is wide variability in how such concerns are addressed in the recovery process. There are, for example, specifically religious and non-religious pathways to addiction recovery. What is shared across recovery pathways is that the exploration of such questions is moved back into a position of importance within the person's life.

A. *God as I understand Him?* While non-religious pathways to recovery do exist—and there are fledgling organizations of recovering atheists and agnostics—the most dominant pathways to recovery in the culture of addiction share a focus on the transcendent. The transcendent is clearly evident in such pathways. It appears as the "Power greater than ourselves" or the "God as we understood Him" of 12 step programs. It appears in the common themes and experiences embedded within the great religions. It is also evident in that transcendent element of the human spirit that forms the collective "WEness" of the self-help process. Within the culture of recovery, religious questions and a clarification of one's personal religious beliefs is often part of the recovery process. As addiction treatment professionals, it is particularly important to understand those aspects of religious experience that can serve to crystallize and sustain the recovery process.

It is important that therapists remain open to the power of religious experiences as a source of life change. All of the great religions provide a framework for personal transformation. The calling of the religious experience is a calling of change. It is a calling that demands a reconstruction of personal identity and a reconstruction of one's relationships in the world. Religious experience is a viable, legitimate and, for some individuals, the most personally accessible pathway of addiction recovery.

In working with clients having such religious experiences, it is helpful if the therapist can help focus the energy freed up in such experiences on specific areas of behavioral change. In the case of addiction, it is important that such experiences not be a diversion from recovery, but in fact get focused on the resolution of addiction-related problems and the construction of a sobriety-based lifestyle. Any emotional force which intensifies and sustains the sobriety decision should be capitalized upon during early recovery. Any emotional force which diverts attention from the issue of alcohol-drug abstinence constitutes a major threat to early recovery.

B.   *Finding the Spirit Path*   There are many dimensions of spirituality that have been explored through the addiction/recovery literature. For the purpose of this book, it is most important to explore (1) those dimensions which play a role in the transformation of the addict, and (2) those dimensions which have been institutionalized within the culture of recovery, such that they are experiences that can be accessed through social learning. Such experiences are so universal within the recovery process that the culture has provided cues and rituals to recognize and label them in ways that push one further along the recovery path. This section will briefly explore six such dimensions and return to them later in the discussion of developmental milestones in the recovery process.

1. And the Blind Shall See: The Experience of Rebirth The first spiritual experiences of recovery occur during brief episodes when the addict's armor of self-obsession and self-delusion is pierced, creating brief perceptions of self in relationship to the world. These brief episodes of self-perception are marked by almost overwhelming clarity. This view of the self and the self-world relationship can be both painful and terrifying. Embedded in such moments are opportunities for change that can be embraced or rejected.   It is the ability to create such self-perception that lies much of the magic and power of therapy.

Many addicts describe a "conversion experience" that marked their transition from addiction to recovery. Such an episode can be simply defined as a powerful emotional experience that both crystallized a decision for change and imbued hope in the possibility of such change. A common element in such conversion experiences—both religious and non-religious varieties—is a sudden breakthrough of self-perception. It is as if addicts were thrust outside of their own bodies and clearly perceived themselves through the eyes of others. In the revulsion that comes from this vision can be found the seeds for change. The episodic intrusion of sight and self-perception amidst drug-induced blindness may be the first inklings of their discovery of the spirit path.

This ability to see and experience oneself through the eyes and experience of others is a motif that surrounds stories of radical transformations that have been captured in story and myth in all generations and in all cultures. It is in such dark moments of self-perception that the light appears. It is in the most intense experiences of self-hatred that the pathway to self-love becomes visible.

There are many therapeutic techniques designed to facilitate and sharpen the clarity of self-perception. Techniques may be as simple as regular feedback to a client from therapists and treatment peers to the more rigorous self-inventory assignment of step-oriented treatment programs. Some clients require very powerful techniques to enhance self-perception. Such techniques include aggressive confrontation tactics, the mirroring or doubling techniques of psychodrama and a variety of techniques drawn from transactional analysis and gestalt therapy. While such techniques may be clinically indicated, one must guard against the tendency with such tactics to drift to remote areas of the client's emotional life that have no immediate significance to initiating or sustaining recovery. Early recovery techniques must direct the client's available emotional energy to the alcohol/drug axis of his or her life.

Passive confrontation techniques can be helpful aids in enhancing self-perception. Passive confrontation provides the client information about themselves at a time when their defenses are not actively engaged. Passive confrontation can encompass journaling techniques or other written assignments, reading assignments of material to which the client is likely to have strong emotional responses, assignments to listen or watch audio/videotapes of oneself to identify patterns of self-defeating behavior, or mirror assignments in which one must spend a designated time daily looking at oneself and speaking to oneself in a mirror. Passive confrontation can also encompass a variety of projecting devices, *e.g.*, "write or tell a brief story that reflects your life and include a moral to the story."

Addicts have profoundly impaired abilities to accurately perceive themselves and the outside world. Breakthroughs in self-perception in treatment most often occur in a treatment milieu rich with the constant flow of feedback.

2. The Courtship with Death All along the addiction path, the addict may encounter strange experiences that provide vehicles of escape from "the life." For many, these experiences will intensify in middle and late stages of addiction as the courtship with death intensifies. Such courtship inevitably brings one face to face with one's own death, either through one's own near-death (or near-insanity) experiences or through the death of others in the life. Such confrontations escalate the intensity of the addict's emptiness, intensifying the feeling of spiritual void and spiritual longings. This may not be a profoundly mystical experience—it may be simply an alcoholic alone and drunk, pondering as they have so often lately and with more pain than usual, the meaning of life. As death draws closer, the questions of life and its meaning loom larger.

3. Victory in Surrender: Sisyphus Revisited The addict is like the Sisyphus of myth, who having angered the gods was condemned to eternity to, again and again, push a huge rock up a hill only to have it roll down as he approached the top. This modern Sisyphus tries thousands of gimmicks and approaches to sustain mastery over the drug relationship only, like his predecessor, to experience failure just when success seems in sight. To sustain addiction, Sisyphus continues his obsessive manipulation of the drug relationship. He does not give up the struggle for power and control. It is he, not the drug, who shall triumph. If Sisyphus asked a drinking alcoholic for advice, he would get a thousand new and grandiose ideas on how to win the battle and get the rock to the top of the hill. If Sisyphus asked a recovering alcoholic for advice, he might be told:

> *You are locked in a game that cannot be won. You will never get the rock to the top of the hill. But your fate is not bound by this task, only by your acceptance of the game and your compulsion to play it. If you want to win, admit your defeat. Surrender to the impossibility of the game so you may get free of the game. Your option is to simply walk away from the stone and climb the mountain yourself. By surrendering, you will be free.*

Within the spiritual dimensions of recovery are a deep appreciation and understanding of paradox. Perhaps the most powerful of such paradoxes is that victory comes through surrender. The addict's life is a struggle for power, control and dominance over the drug relationship. As long as the addict fights to win in this relationship, addiction continues. Recovery begins with surrender. It is within those moments of complete submission that one can be touched by people and powers outside the self.

The opportunity for transformation is imbedded within the moment addicts stand naked in the light of self-perception and simply give up. The illusions are finally stripped away. Having sought pleasure, they found pain. Having sought peace, they found only discord. Seeking love, they loved only the drug and abandoned those who loved them. Seeking an escape from the world, they found confrontation instead. Seeking self-confidence, they found self-hatred. Losing control of the drug that made them feel normal, they experienced insanity. Having exerted enormous effort to maintain power over the drug relationship, they failed consistently and completely. The game was unwinnable. It was time to surrender.

The spirit journey begins with defeat, as the illusion of personal control and power is forsaken. It begins when the resources of the self are exhausted and one is forced to seek power and strength from outside the self. That moment of surrender (and in the daily moments of surrendering which follow) opens the spirit path. In opening this discussion on the role of spirituality in recovery, it is important to outline the context of this discussion. Spirituality is not a peripheral issue in recovery. It is not simply some poorly understood and secondary benefit that accompanies the recovery process. It is the driving force that initiates and sustains recovery. Understanding the nature of the spiritual metamorphosis which accompanies this surrendering is not an area of obscure interest for those interested in the religion or mysticism. It is at the very heart of the addiction recovery process.

The task of the therapist is to create opportunities for such surrender. Such opportunities are created when the addict is cornered and must see and fully experience themselves and the consequences of his or her drug use. Embedded within near death or near insanity experiences is the potential for change. The first task is to not disregard or minimize the potential within such experiences. The second is to not prematurely rescue the client in the midst of such experiences. Such premature intervention results in superficial compliance, not surrender. What is desirable is to fully explore such experiences with the client, maximizing their effect, while channeling and focusing such experiences into an experience of surrender. The job of the treatment specialist is to intensify the client's perception and experience of the Sisyphian nature of the addiction game to a point of such clarity, that he or she experience a surrender—a disengagement from the game.

4. Empowerment There is within the spiritual dimensions of recovery a process of empowerment. Through a relationship with something beyond the self, one draws strength to initiate and sustain the recovery process. These relationships bear the fruit of hope, self-forgiveness and self-acceptance. Without this dimension, those windows of opportunity described above would quickly close, allowing the process of self-destruction to continue.

Empowerment takes place in the context of relationships in which clients experiences themselves differently. Clients experiences hope and self-forgiveness and self-acceptance because the therapist has a contagious hope in them, forgives them and accepts them. Within such chemistry is the very essence of the helping relationship. By transcending the stereotyped role-playing of addicts "doing" treatment, clients are forced to perceive and experience themselves in a new way. Through such changes, clients experience not the greatness of their therapists, but the greatness of themselves. Change is possible because they have already experienced change within this helping relationship.

There are a number of empowering therapeutic interventions that can buttress the fragile nature of hope, self-forgiveness and self-acceptance during early recovery.

- The most crucial intervention is providing clients a cognitive framework to make sense out of how they became addicted, the consequences of such addiction, and what specific actions need to be taken to rebuild themselves and their world.

- Alterations in the physical appearance or image of clients can be a constant reminder of the change process.
- Guided visualization as directed by the therapist and taught as a ritual of affirmation and problem-solving is particularly effective in sustaining hope and confidence. Through this technique, clients sculpt themselves—projecting an image of themselves shaping both the qualities they would desire and visualizing these qualities in action—and use visualization as both a centering ritual and as rehearsal for real life situations to be faced.
- The sustained experience of self-disclosure to the counselor, to their treatment and self-help peers and to outsiders is an essential element of self-forgiveness, which is intensified and formalized through completion of the 4th and 5th steps of AA/NA/CA or alternative rituals of self-inventory and confession.
- For many addicts it will only be through sustained interaction with persons like themselves—in a self-help framework—that they will sustain hope and achieve self-forgiveness and self-acceptance.

5. Transforming the Self-World Relationship   All human development from infancy forward is a transcendence of the narcissistic self.   Addiction reverses this process through a developmental regression back to the narcissism of infancy.   This regression must be reversed in recovery.   The self-world relationship must be reconstructed.

Addiction is a form of chemical autism, numbing one to experiences beyond the drug and rendering one unresponsive and unconnected to other living beings. It is like a malignant tumor that consumes the self and then the physical and social world beyond the self. Addicts are users. They see themselves, and have lived, in isolation from the world. The world and others exist only in relationship to themselves. Their relationships are exploitive rather than reciprocal. Addiction has relegated other people to the status of things to be manipulated in the service of the drug relationship.

An essential element of the spiritual transformation experienced by recovering addicts is the radical redefinition of the self-world relationship. The essence of spirituality in recovery is the reversal of narcissism. The narcissistic armor is penetrated and addicts experience, through their connectedness to others, the sensation of being vibrantly alive. Rather than seeing themselves in an antagonistic relationship with the world, they experience themselves as part of the world. The narcissistic isolation is broken and they experience themselves as part of a larger whole. They experience "WEness". Bateson (1971) labeled this process "complementarity" and noted that this shift was the very essence of the metamorphosis from addiction to recovery. Recovering addicts can not only tell their story, but actually hear and be moved by the stories of others. They acquire or regain the ability to listen and experience empathy and compassion. They experience connectedness to the world.

Addicts have been very out of balance in their relationship with the world. In recovery, the principles of reciprocity and respect are restored and guide their relationships with the outside world. The harshness and discord that marked the self-world relationship are replaced by gentleness and harmony. For those who will faithfully follow the spirit path, recovery will be transforming. For them, addiction will cease being a curse and will be understood later as a gift that led them to the spirit path. Recovery for them is much more than managing a disease. It is a way of thinking, feeling and acting that makes living without drugs not only tolerable but desirable. It is a philosophy of living and learning and loving. It is the possibility of rebirth.

There is in this spiritual transformation a final and irrevocable affirmation of life and living. Seeing the best and worst of our human legacy and experiencing themselves as part of this continuum of history, recovering persons say yes to life. Having seen the best and worst in themselves, they decide to move forward. Stripped of sentimentalities and illusions, they can look at themselves and the world and decide to fully participate. Having resisted the regressive pull of the chemical womb, they choose the world. Having escaped death and addiction, they continue their leap of faith into life and recovery.

6. The Search for Wholeness The spiritual path is among other things a search for wholeness. The consuming quality of addiction isolates one from many areas of human experience. Addiction narrows the range of experience and pushes this narrow band of experience to the extreme. Life becomes both limited and excessive. The long-term task of the addict is to crawl out of the far extremes of his or her own character and experience balance.

Spiritual wholeness requires a courtship with that which is foreign to one's nature. Man must experience the woman within. White man must seek to experience the world as Black, Brown, Red and Yellow. Middle-aged man must discover the small boy and old man within. The gifted of mind must struggle to empower the heart. The gifted of speech must cultivate and find meaning in silence. The thinkers must learn to cry. People of peace must discover that which is warlike within their own soul. The "strong" must discover the strength in gentleness. Those who have thrilled to the role of helper must let themselves be helped. Spiritual wholeness comes from bringing into harmony those elements of character which have been magnified into excess with those which have been suppressed and denied.

C. *The Reconstruction of Personal Values* The culturally enmeshed addict entering the recovery process must begin the construction of a sobriety-based value system. The intensity and duration of this value reconstruction is illustrated by comparing values from the culture of addiction and the culture of recovery. The culture of addiction is driven by survival of the fittest; the culture of recovery is driven by mutuality and compassion. Addiction is exploitation of others; recovery is service to others. Addiction demands retribution; recovery demands restitution. Addiction is narcissistic, arrogant and grandiose; recovery is quiet self-acceptance and humility. Addiction is deceit and manipulation; recovery is honesty. Addiction values emotional aloofness; recovery values emotional self-disclosure. Addiction promotes excess; recovery promotes restraint.

For some, the return to pre-addiction values occurs fairly early in the recovery process. This is particularly true of persons whose values were congruent with recovery values prior to their addiction and who interrupted their addiction at early or middle stages. But what of persons who may never have experienced such values or for whom such values are only a dim memory? What of persons born and raised in the culture of addiction who have known no other values? Value reconstruction in the latter group may be a particularly difficult task, most effectively completed within the framework of long-term residential treatment. In such cases, a highly controlled environment is needed to strip the deviant values and slowly construct and internalize a new set of personal values.

There are a number of essential elements within the therapeutic milieu which speed up the reconstruction of personal values early in recovery. These include:

- Teaching interventions related to values in the culture of addiction and the culture of recovery
- Experiential exercises that speed emotional thawing and create a re-sensitization and recreation of empathy and compassion (where such faculties are not completely dead)
- Experiential exercises that allow opportunities for values from the culture of addiction to be consciously examined
- A clearly articulated set of treatment values and a willingness to confront values (and behavior reflecting these values) from the culture of addiction when presented within the treatment milieu
- The presence within the treatment milieu of role models who demonstrate how recovery values are operationalized
- The capitalization upon every serendipitous event within the treatment milieu as an opportunity to explore and teach values

11.4 *Symbols* An earlier chapter noted how culturally enmeshed addicts possess symbols (objects) which reflect their drug-related identity and their tribal affiliation within the culture of addiction. This section will explore how such symbols can be confronted and replaced during the treatment process.

A. *Stripping Symbols of the Life* It was noted earlier that culturally enmeshed addicts inevitably take on the trappings of the culture—surrounding themselves with physical objects from the drug culture that reflect their personal identity and values. These symbols may include the drug itself, injection paraphernalia, beepers, jewelry, dress or tattoos that reflect drug identification or related values. Our goals in treatment related to these symbols is threefold:

- To prevent the unstructured presentation of these symbols in the treatment milieu
- To enhance the client's disengagement from the culture of addiction by promoting the voluntary shedding of cultural trappings, and
- To replace symbols from the culture of addiction with symbols from the culture of recovery

The stage must be set for addressing cultural symbols through two facets of the treatment milieu. The first is a clearly stated value and behavioral expectation that symbols of the culture of addiction are not appropriate for the treatment milieu except under special circumstances involving treatment activities. The second is a teaching facet which provides a foundation for each client's understanding of the role symbols play in reinforcing addiction and the addict identity. The goal is not to simply suppress the presentation of such symbols in the treatment milieu, but to engage clients in an active dialogue and investigational process on the role of such symbols in their life.

B. *Symbols and Identity Transformation*   There is a unique synergism between people and symbols. Those objects of dress and decoration one chooses reflect values and identity while, at the same time, the presence of these objects exerts its own influence on one's sense of personal identity. It's as if once chosen, these symbols possess an independent power to reinforce and shape one's values and behaviors. The enmeshed addict has embraced both a drug and the culture in which the drug is housed. To sever the drug relationship permanently, one must peel away the cultural trappings—the symbols—of this marriage.

C. *Symbol Replacement*   The very essence of treatment for the culturally enmeshed addict can be found in the process of symbol replacement. Consider the following three stories.

Reggie showed up for lecture his second day in residential treatment wearing a T-shirt emblazoned with the label for Jack Daniels whiskey and a marijuana leaf prominently displayed on his brass belt buckle. The Director of this adolescent program called Reggie in following the lecture to explore what it meant that Reggie, while seeking treatment for addiction, seemed to be proudly displaying symbols of his drug use. In concluding this conversation, the Director made it very clear that such symbols could not be worn while Reggie was in treatment. He went on to tell Reggie that if at anytime in treatment Reggie felt these items no longer fit him, the Director would trade Reggie for his old T-shirt and belt buckle.   After almost four weeks of increasing involvement in this treatment culture, Reggie entered the Director's office, T-shirt and belt buckle in hand, asking to make the promised trade. Within minutes, and following some personal congratulations, Reggie walked from the Director's office with a "Stoned Sober" T-shirt and an "Easy Does It" brass belt buckle. Symbols from the two cultures had been exchanged. A client had reached a critical point in the transformation of his identity.

Members of an outpatient cocaine treatment group, while going through a number of grieving rituals to expiate the emotions surrounding their love-hate relationship with cocaine, began to confront the amount of cocaine paraphernalia they continued to possess. While all members agreed that hanging on to such items was unwise, there was a lack of consensus on the best means of disposal.   After a couple of group discussions, members had developed individual plans for eliminating these symbols from their lives. Two actions were taken in consort by group members. First, each brought some items with them to group and participated in psychodramatic funeral for these objects and the experiences of their past which the objects represented. This was concluded by a quite animated physical destruction of these symbols by group members. A second action was taken at the

suggestion of one member who had worked as a jeweler. Group
members turned over an assortment of gold spoons, gold razor
blades, and gold straws to a jeweler, who at their instructions,
melted all of the items and created nuggets that could be worn on
a chain by each group member. The group was particularly
captivated by the metaphorical nature of the ritual. The melting of
the paraphernalia represented all that they had shared in their
addictive experience. The actual destruction of the paraphernalia
symbolized the severing of their cocaine relationship. The mixing
of the gold together and the nuggets symbolized the sharing and
support members had received from each other through their
treatment group. Symbols of addiction had been transformed into
symbols of recovery.

Two recovering addicts confronted unique symbols from their
sojourn in the culture of addiction. Each wore a tattoo that served
as a grotesque contradiction to their new recovery values. The first
wore the slogan "Born to Die" across his left arm. This motto had
been particularly apt for a man born into four generations of
alcoholism in which nearly all males died in their 30s or 40s as
victims of violence, suicide or accidents. His decision to have the
tattoo surgically removed marked a milestone in his early recovery.
He had shed the brand which condemned him to his heritage. A
second addict wore an artistically drawn marijuana leaf on his arm
that, while once a source of pride, now stirred feelings of anger
and embarrassment. Unable to afford surgical removal, he
explored options of altering the tattoo. His final choice was a red
cross enclosed within a circle that was superimposed over the
marijuana leaf. A new symbol had achieved dominance over the
past.

All three stories above reveal different aspects of the importance of
symbol replacement in the recovery process. The treatment
community must develop the technology to help clients identify

and shed symbols from the culture of addiction and replace these with symbols from the culture of recovery. We need treatment milieus rich with such recovery symbols. To strip the addict of symbols from the culture of addiction is to provoke nakedness and nothingness. To trade symbols through the above described replacement process is to assure psychological safety and enhance identity and self-esteem.

D. *Symbols and Relapse Prevention* Symbols can reinforce recovery and serve as a tool for relapse prevention just as symbols can tie one to the culture of addiction. Consider the following story about the potential role of symbols in recovery.

John had been out of treatment for about six months when the following events occurred. He had two back to back "Murphy's Law" days in which everything that could go wrong did go wrong. By the end of the second day, John's craving for alcohol was overpowering. Saying "the hell with everything," John left work and went to his old bar. Upon entering, he sat on a bar stool and, just as he had a thousand times before, emptied his right pocket on the bar providing a wad of money and change to begin feeding his appetite for alcohol. This time he found himself staring down on the bar looking at the ceremonial coin he had received upon his graduation from treatment. Picking up the coin from the bar, he read the Serenity Prayer imprinted on the coin and thought about his life before and after treatment. His reverie was interrupted by a cheery, "What can I get for you?" Looking up at the bartender, John said, "I'm sorry, I just remembered a meeting I have to be at." Picking up his money from the bar, John proceeded to the meeting (AA) he had just decided he had to attend. In this case, a potential relapse situation was averted when John confronted a very powerful symbol of his recovery.

The heroes and heroines of classic mythology, when sent on a pilgrimage, were often given an object of power such as a magic sword or charm to protect them on their journey. While the dragons have all but disappeared, the new pilgrims who must fight the beasts within the self are in no less need of magic. To conquer these beasts Treatment professionals must first empower the treatment milieu with rituals which celebrate transformation and rebirth. We need to provide the new pilgrims with amulets or talismans to protect them on their continuing journey. The ceremonial coin, worry stone, or marble given each client as they leave treatment is a modern version of a very old ritual. These objects link the client symbolically to the birthplace of their recovery. The power of such rituals and the magic with which such objects can be empowered should never be underestimated. As a symbol of a client's commitment to sobriety, perhaps such objects really do ward off evil.

E. *Intervention Summary*   The role of the treatment center in encouraging and facilitating this symbol replacement process can involve such functions as the following:

- identifying objects currently in the possession of the client that reflect identification with the culture of addiction
- assisting the client in deciding what to do with such objects from the culture of addiction, *e.g.*, values clarification exercises, symbol destruction, grieving rituals
- extinguishing, via satiation, the power of these symbols to trigger drug hunger and drug seeking behavior (a technique some feel is ineffective and potentially harmful)
- reframing the meaning of symbols so they reinforce recovery values rather than active addiction

- providing a treatment milieu rich with symbols from the culture of recovery
- providing role models within the treatment milieu who exemplify appropriate use of symbols

11.5 *Rituals*   It was noted earlier that most addicts develop elaborate rituals that govern when, where, and under what conditions drug use will occur and that such rituals over time become independent triggers for use. One goal of the treatment professional is to identify such rituals for each client and to assist the client in developing replacement rituals that reinforce recovery.

A. *Ritual Identification*   The first task is to assist the client in identifying patterns of ritualistic drug use that have become compulsively ingrained into his or her lifestyle. Such patterns can be identified by discussing questions like the following with each client.

- If drinking is episodic, are there identifiable events or times associated with onset, *i.e.*, paydays, a particular day of the week, or emotional crises?
- Are there daily time rituals associated with use, *i.e.*, lunch, before the children get home from school, or immediately after work?
- Are there other activities that are almost always associated with alcohol or drug use?
- Are rituals different for weekends than for weekdays? If so, define these differences.
- Are there differences in pattern, frequency or quantity of use depending on time of menstrual cycle?
- Are there different rituals of use associated with the major holidays? If so, describe.
- What times/events do you most strongly associate with alcohol/drug use?

Identifying each client's rituals of use pinpoints the times the client will need to develop and utilize replacement rituals. If, for example, the counselor studies a client's drinking pattern and discovers that the most powerful and consistent drinking ritual is associated with getting paid on Fridays, cashing the check and drinking oneself into oblivion, then this client's treatment experience must address what this client will be doing on Fridays from 5:00 to 11:00 P.M.

It is quite helpful to conduct this assessment of rituals of use in a setting which includes the intimate partner or family members of the client. These individuals, for their own emotional survival, have often needed to identify and anticipate patterns in the alcoholic's drinking of which the alcoholic may be completely unaware. The family can also play a helpful role in discussing alternative family rituals, particularly those that have involved drinking.

B.   *Ritual Replacement*   Culturally enmeshed addicts entering recovery must do two things related to the role of rituals in their lives. First, they must develop alternative activities to fill the void during times that were occupied with drinking. Second, they must in a much broader sense develop a new range of rituals that specifically serve to support the recovery process. These two areas may go hand in hand. Persons who have a history of explosive drinking on Friday nights can, for example, choose a Friday night AA meeting for their "home" group. Rituals of recovery can thus be used to fill the high-risk time periods.

Recovery rituals are activities which reinforce abstinence, promote physical, emotional and spiritual health and which enhance personal identity and self-esteem. The counselor can, through the vehicle of treatment, expose clients to a wide variety of activities that can be incorporated as rituals of recovery. A recovering person was interviewed regarding the rituals he regularly performs that support his sobriety. The following is an excerpt from that discussion.

Bill: Gene, you went through treatment almost five years ago. What daily or weekly rituals have you developed over that time to sustain your recovery?

Gene: I've continued a lot of rituals which I began in treatment and have added some others. To start with, I always make at least 2 AA meetings a week, usually on Wednesday and Sunday. I attended a lot more meetings when I first got out of treatment but a lot of that was just a need to fill up the hours I had spent in bars.

Bill: Have there been any other changes in your need or desire for meetings?

Gene: Meetings are still important to me but I view them differently now. When I first got on the program, I thought the program was the meetings. There's a lot of things outside of meetings that are important to recovery that are invisible early on.

Bill: Could you give specific examples of some of these things?

Gene: Sure. I read and meditate for about 15 minutes every morning. I read *A Day at a Time* and then spend time thinking about my day—not what I want to do, but what I want to be! I build in regular times to meet with people I feel good about and who support me. I have two weekly breakfast meetings—one with my sponsor and another with a new member I'm sponsoring. I sometimes stop by a coffeeshop I know folks will be at even if I didn't make the meeting. I run regularly and have found this to be both relaxing and a wonderful time to think about things. I make frequent visits to persons I neglected and hurt during my drinking—particularly my mother and my own children. I have also learned some special tricks that help me get to sleep without alcohol. All these kinds of things are little pieces of the puzzle that each person has to put together for themselves.

Bill: The things you listed sound like they are maintenance activities or rituals that you have built into your daily lifestyle. Are there special rituals you have developed to handle crises or situations that in the past would have triggered a drinking episode?

Gene: Most of my crises occur when I feel bombarded from a variety of directions and need to slow down. I use a lot of program slogans and the Serenity Prayer to try and slow myself down. When it gets real bad, I have an escape. I discovered a wonderful little ice cream shop. It is decorated with antiques and reminds me of a little shop I went to as a kid. It's a great place to get away and think. If things are particularly bad, I call my sponsor and have us meet there. I run to my ice cream shop the way I used to run to a bar. The difference is I can always remember leaving the ice cream shop.

The dialogue above illustrates how replacement rituals evolve over time to support the recovery process. It is important that clients develop rituals during treatment that can help sustain them through the early stages of recovery.

11.6 *History and Mythology* All cultures possess both a body of history and mythology which is used to enhance member identity and to transmit cultural values. This section will explore the roles history and mythology play in binding new members to the culture of recovery.

A. *A New Oral History* Storytelling, as a transmitter of history and myth, within the culture of addiction glorifies drugs as objects of worship, ridicules and scorns non-users and their society, and promotes a value system that sanctions indulgence of self and exploitation of others.   The world view imparted within this culture must be reshaped through the experience of treatment and recovery. History must be rewritten. Essential elements that can be effectively utilized by treatment programs in this process include the following.

- The past objects of worship (drugs) are demonized within a new fully articulated history. Tales help clients look back and see the ogres and witches and trolls who sought to take their life.
- The pain and stigma of one's past are affirmed and blessed as part of the admission requirements for this new society of recovery. The milieu communicates that self-acceptance and self-love can be created out of the ashes of self-hatred.
- The glorification and celebration of the possibility of change permeates the entire treatment environment. The treatment culture exudes the symbolism of rebirth. Addiction is portrayed as death from which treatment can offer the hope of resurrection and a return to living. Folk stories abound with transformations, conversions, metamorphoses, shedding old skins, the breaking of chains, and flights to freedom.

- There is a well-defined history in which the exploits and journeys of cultural heroes and heroines illustrate the pathways and pitfalls involved in the recovery process.
- Personal recovery is characterized as a spiritual journey aided by magical and unseen forces from within and outside the self.

B. *The Traditions and Folklore of Recovery*   Many culturally enmeshed addicts enter treatment in crisis under external duress and are still psychologically and socially bound to the culture of addiction. If treatment is to alter this cultural affiliation, then the treatment milieu must have both power and intensity. An essential ingredient of such power and intensity is tradition. The ideal is to create an energized environment that engages and propels addicts, often in spite of themselves, into the recovery process. An effective program milieu has momentum and excitement derived from its own history and the collective history of the culture of recovery. Addicts experience themselves as being swept up by, and at the same time choosing to become part of, a long tradition of recovery. They discover that pioneers have gone before them, opening the trails and discovering the way around and through obstacles and dangers. The milieu embodies an excitement that makes recovery contagious.   What is particularly profound to addicts is the discovery that this culture was designed specifically for THEM.

Creating and sustaining powerful treatment milieus is handicapped today by the pace and intensity of change within the substance abuse field. The high turnover of staff and the constantly changing organizational configurations within the field contribute to a lack of cohesion and continuity.   These conditions produce a fragmentation of values and create a loss of history and tradition. They diminish the power necessary to achieve the cultural conversion from addiction to recovery. The issue of staff turnover is particularly problematic. How can change-resistant clients be expected to bond to a treatment milieu to which paid staff do not bond? In the midst of constantly changing personnel and program configurations, both staff and clients mechanically perform their respective roles unaware of their place in history and the import of their actions upon the future. Passionless philosophies and treatment structures stripped of their souls allow both clients and staff to "do treatment" in a way that requires commitment and change from neither.

If, in contrast to the above, one builds a powerfully energizing and contagious culture of recovery, what roles will history and mythology play in this culture? The following characterizations and descriptions depict those programs that have achieved a state of excellence in this area of cultural development. These are the programs which have been culturally empowered.

- **Historical "WEness"** Culturally empowered programs provide, through the richness of generations of treatment history, an experience of membership in a recovering community and an experience of brotherhood and sisterhood that transcends the present. One is encouraged to seek strength from the experience of those who came before and challenged to share strength with those who will follow.

- **The Big and Little Pictures** Culturally empowered programs provide both a panoramic and microcosmic view of the culture of recovery. From portrayal of the historical evolution of treatment and recovery movements spanning both national and local milestones, the programs construct a world of pride and hope within which the client can feel a part. Through lectures and literature and visual images, the program constantly affirms that both the individual client and the staff are part of a broader movement with its own self-fueling momentum. The hub of this worldwide movement is constantly portrayed as the individual recovering addict staying sober one day at a time.

- **Heroes and Heroines** Culturally empowered programs cultivate, collect, and constantly display and acknowledge heroes and heroines who embody values from the culture of recovery. Such heroes include founders of self help movements, famous recovering individuals and local heroes. The culture has history and that history has flesh and blood. The milieus of the most empowering programs are filled with images of and direct contact with role models that instill hope and self-esteem (via identification and affiliation) for the newly recovering addict. The addict fresh from the culture of addiction rarely can identify with abstract concepts of recovery, but may be powerfully drawn to persons who exemplify such concepts in action. Heroes and heroines are extensively displayed and modeled within the milieu through story-telling, visual media, guest lectures, biographies, newsletters, alumni meetings, and recovering volunteers.

- **Demons and Dragons** Culturally empowered programs have a well-developed ideology which radically reframes key values and beliefs from the culture of addiction. Prior objects of worship—drugs and their cultural context—are demonized. The power to intoxicate is reframed as the power to demean and destroy. The drug is imbued with a demonic persona and ascribed awesome powers of seduction, cunning and manipulation. Battle with the demons is characterized as a war which can only be won through the help of higher

powers and magic rituals. One must be constantly
vigilant and uncompromising, winning the battle moment
by moment always alert for the demon's exploitation of
one's vulnerability. Framing the movement from
addiction to recovery in such images as the above
generates the commitment and passion capable of
empowering the treatment milieu.

- **The Folk Wisdom of Recovery** Culturally empowered
programs have both oral and written traditions that
provide guideposts for the reconstruction of the addict's
life. Collective wisdom is revealed through oft-repeated
folk tales, allegories, aphorisms and slogans drawn from
the national and local recovery culture. Such communications exhibit a richness of language and images which
convey hope, transmit values, offer simple guidelines for
sober living and provide a medium for shared humor.
Some stories so richly convey essential learning within
the culture that they have been retold by generations of
recovering persons within a program. Such oft-repeated
stories get institutionalized within the life of a program
so that members who share the culture can transmit
complex concepts through a simple phrase or punchline.
In the most vibrant programs, this collective oral history
takes on a coherence and continuity that becomes a
powerful socializing agent for the newly recovering
addict.

- **Of Myths, Metaphors and Motifs** Mythology is a way
to come to grips with individual and collective
experience. Myths are stories within which are imbedded
basic truths and lessons drawn from human experience.
They entertain. They teach. They are a vehicle of
emotional catharsis. They inspire. They admonish. They

provide an organizing framework through which one sees and interacts with the world. Within the mythological stories are metaphors and motifs (consistent themes) that reflect the shared experience of persons within a particular culture. The substance abuse field needs to continue to evolve myths and metaphors and motifs that serve to emotionally guide an extremely diverse population of persons through the recovery process. The treatment field must continue its search for myths and metaphors that are recovery enhancing. It is desirable but not necessary that these myths reflect scientific truth. Millions of persons have based their recovery from alcoholism around the metaphor of "disease." The concept of "alcoholism as a disease" is metaphorically true regardless of its eventual scientific status. The concept of "allergy" is emotionally true for millions of alcoholics. Something different really does happen when they drink, a fact reflected in the aphorism: "I'm allergic to alcohol; every time I drink, I break out in a drunk." The metaphorical and emotional value of the concept of allergy is important regardless of whether this concept has scientific utility. As a treatment field, we need to continue our development of myths and metaphors that can anchor and enrich the recovery process.

Having reviewed the history and mythology of the culture of recovery, it is time to proceed to an exploration of its geography.

11.7 *Institutions (Places)* The pursuit of addiction or recovery occurs in a physical world of land and landmarks. There is, in fact, a habitat unique to each pursuit. This section will explore the process through which clients disengage from the habitat of addiction and begin their affiliation with the habitat of recovery.

A. *Places and Persona* There is a special synergism between personal identity and the places and institutions within which one passes time. One's identity influences daily choices of places and yet, once chosen, these places exert their own influence in defining or redefining one's conception of self.   The progressive involvement in the culture of addiction illustrates this process well.

Every day alcoholic newcomers arrive on the fringe of Skid Row. The road that brought them to Skid Row involved a progressive disengagement from relationships with persons and institutions within the culture at large.   Their changing sense of self has brought them to this new environment, but as neophytes on the Row, they are about to participate in institutions which will dramatically escalate this transformation in self-identity.   The coming months will demand mastery of the institutional rituals of cheap hotels, lodging houses, temporary employment agencies, blood banks, missions, soup kitchens, shelters, drunk tanks, detox centers, pawnshops, bus/train stations, and, above all, the Skid Row bars. Socialization within these institutions completes this transformation of persona and ties the neophytes inextricably to Skid Row. Original identities must be erased and replaced with the new. Every step in the mastery of the Row erases part of one's past and burns a bridge back into the culture at large. Treatment centers responding to such culturally enmeshed addicts can be of two distinct types.   They can constitute one of the institutions within the culture of addiction—one more physical place that reflects and sustains the addict's identity—or they can constitute a bridge out of the culture of addiction into a culture of recovery. To achieve the latter, they must disengage the addict from the institutions which reflect and sustain the addiction lifestyle

While the places and institutions that sustain addiction for most addicts are very different than those described for the Skid Row alcoholic, there still remains a geographical dimension. For culturally enmeshed addicts of numerous varieties, most of the physical places they frequent in their life are tied to the addictive lifestyle.

While treatment has aimed primarily at altering the addict's psyche, very little attention has been paid to altering the nature of the addict's environment. Increased attention needs to be focused on the physical reconstruction of the addict's world. Treatment centers can facilitate this reconstruction by:

- isolating the addict from the physical world of the culture of addiction during the treatment process
- teaching that enhances the addict's understanding of the geographical dimensions of addiction and relapse
- facilitating the personal identification of high-risk locations within which relapse would most likely occur, and
- constructing an alternative physical world within which recovery can be nurtured

B. *Saying Goodbye to Slippery Places*   Alcoholics Anonymous and other self-help groups have long understood this geographical dimension of addiction. Aphorisms such as, "If you don't want to slip, stay out of slippery places," have always been part of the verbal folklore of such groups. In spite of this folk wisdom, substance abuse treatment programs have only rarely addressed the physical environment of their clients as a significant treatment issue.

Clients must first understand the nature of the conditioning that accompanied their drug use. In lecture and one-on-one sessions, the following three points must be internalized by the client.

1. Over the years, I have conditioned myself to connect drinking and/or drug use with certain places and people and situations.
2. Sensory cues—sights, sounds, smells, tastes—can trigger both physical craving for drugs and drug-seeking behavior.
3. I must isolate myself from the most powerful of these cues, develop new ways to manage myself when I am inadvertently exposed to such cues, and decrease the ability of such cues to arouse my appetite for intoxication.

When clients have achieved the above understandings, it is then possible to begin to personalize these concepts by identifying high risk people and places. Such identification is a crucial element of relapse prevention planning. Group review and discussion of high risk cues is particularly helpful. Clients will often correctly identify powerful cues to drinking or drug use, but report that these cues will no longer bother them because of their new insights and commitment. Feedback from treatment peers can often break down such grandiosity and continued efforts at control. The final step during this phase of relapse prevention planning is to help clients decide which places they must avoid and discuss how they will stick to such resolutions.

For clients who are deeply enmeshed in the culture of addiction, placement in residential aftercare or halfway house environments may be quite appropriate to break the power of the old physical/social environment over the client and to assure adequate time for reconstruction of an alternative world for the client.

C. *Finding Drug-Free Havens* Entrance into the culture of recovery must have physical dimensions. The newly recovering addict must replace the map of addiction with a map of recovery. Places tied to addiction must be replaced with places tied to recovery. As the addict sheds affiliation with places tied to hustling, drug procurement, and using, new physical environments must be discovered that nurture sobriety and psychological safety. Traditional recovery pathways involving AA/NA may involve elaborate networks of treatment centers, churches and meeting places, coffee shops, AA/NA affiliated clubhouses, and homes of AA/NA members.   Treatment centers can enhance the development of this recovery habitat through such activities as the following:

- Allowing the treatment center itself to serve as one informal haven (drop-in center), if not the physical centerpiece, of the local culture of recovery
- Encouraging involvement in outside self-help meetings during residential or inpatient treatment
- Promoting client exposure to diverse self-help meetings spanning multiple locations
- Providing clients broad exposure to those aspects of the local self-help culture that transcend formal meetings, *i.e.*, post-meeting social activities, club-house activities, retreats, special holiday events, and recreational activities
- Assisting clients to identify alternative sites for performing activities previously tied to the habitat of addiction, *e.g.*, check-cashing, eating, business meetings
- Planning pathways of flight to drug-free havens as part of relapse prevention planning
- Providing newly-recovering clients an appreciation of the national/international network of recovering persons that can provide almost immediate access to drug-free havens and supports

Clients recently released from treatment centers may be having a difficult day in their early recovery. Alone and fidgety, they leave their homes for a walk or drive. Where will they go? Will the pathway of their journey lead back to the habitat of addiction or to a new habitat of recovery? Have new pathways been created that will lead them to drug-free havens?

Physical places in late stage recovery take on different meanings. As recovery evolves, one must begin to define one's own sacred places. Such places, which Joseph Campbell (1949) refers to as "Bliss Stations," represent physical locations where one can escape into peacefulness from the thunderous demands of the outside world. In such places, one can cultivate activities which bring joy and deepen the experience of being free and alive.

11.8 *Dress/Appearance*   Chapter Four noted the deterioration in care of self that often marks the progression of addiction. As the addict disengages from the culture of addiction, new standards of self-care and a new self-image must evolve to reflect one's identity transformation.

A.   *The Return of Self-Care*   "Pops," a self-proclaimed charter member of the culture of addiction, arrived at the detoxification center wearing the trappings of his tribe. Smears of dirt on face and hands. An obviously untreated abrasion on the forehead. Hair uncut, unkempt and unclean.   Glasses of unknown prescription taped together. Blanched complexion set off by a reddened nose and yellowing teeth.   Multi-layered, hand-me-down clothes of mixed style whose uncleanliness is confirmed by both sight and smell. Mismatched socks. Worn black shoes with brown shoestrings, revealing multiple knots of repair. Pops is a caricature. Give him a bottle in a brown paper bag and prop him in the doorway of a rundown building and we would have the prototype of the American "wino." Just as the creation of "Pops" over a number of years was marked by a physical transformation, his long-term recovery will also be measured in step-by-step physical transformations that reflect the return of self-respect and self-care.

Pops represents a small, and increasingly hidden tribe within the American culture of addiction. The physical transformation his story illustrates is, however, common in less extreme forms to the majority of American addicts. The value from the culture of addiction has been that the drug experience takes precedence over all other physical needs. Money, time, and emotional energy must be devoted to the drug relationship; all other concerns of self are secondary. One element of disengaging addicts from this culture is the provision of a treatment milieu with extremely strong values of self-care.

A treatment milieu can initiate or re-establish these values of self-care through such media as the following:

- Conducting comprehensive health care assessments and developing comprehensive health care plans with each client that encompass, at a minimum, the treatment of acute medical problems, action to address dental needs and immediate action to resolve problems of motion or sensorium, *e.g.*, glasses, hearing aids, walking aids
- Explicitly defining standards of hygiene and self-care within the treatment milieu and confronting deviations from such standards
- Providing both role models (staff, volunteers, alumni) of positive self-care and positive reinforcement to clients for self-care behaviors

B. *I'm Too Beautiful to be Addicted*   Mary floated into the treatment unit followed by an entourage of family doctor and family members, looking as if she had just stepped off the cover of a fashion magazine. Her physical persona was a work of art constantly touched up and presented. During her early days, enormous time was spent preparing for her entrance into the treatment milieu. Time between groups was spent changing clothes, redoing hair, or touching up makeup. What this image of impeccability was masking was revealed when Mary's liver profiles returned from the lab. Mary's alcoholism had produced an extremely late stage of what would prove to be a near-terminal liver disease. Mary's image had been refined as a way of hiding her escalating loss of control over alcohol. Her physical appearance so defied the stereotype of the disheveled drunk that it allowed her to hide her alcoholism. Her image had become an integral part of her denial system. It would also become a principle cornerpiece in the enabling behavior of the family. Family members were known to have remarked more than once, "How can she be an alcoholic? Look at her!"

Images that are integrally bound to the addictive lifestyle must be shed. In the case of Mary, she was both challenged and supported to give up the "Barbie Doll" veneer and discover who she really was. The process began with teaching interventions that examined the role of image in her denial system. Both staff and peer support were provided to enhance Mary's openness to change. Specific behavioral contracts were made with Mary that forced her to step out of role end experience herself without the veneer. (Mary's first entrance into the activity room with non-designer jeans and a simple blouse brought a standing ovation, cheers and hugs from her treatment peers and staff.) As Mary moved forward in the recovery process, her image of beauty and impeccability became a choice rather than a compulsion. Her spiritual transformation was paralleled by changes in her physical presentation. Inner self-acceptance brought a decreased need for external perfection.

C. *Experimenting with New Images* A superficial look at Mary and Pops would disclose few areas of commonality and yet both presented physical images that had become integrally linked to their addiction and their identity as an addict (denied in one case, advertised in the other). Any image which reinforces characteristics and values from the culture of addiction must also be altered in treatment.

Physical and psychosocial presentations of self are intricately bound together. Physical appearance is sculpted and presented through postures, gestures and verbalized attitudes and values which are intended to paint a portrait or make a statement about who we are to the outside world. Consider the following three clients' presentations of self as they enter the treatment milieu.

- Everything about Will is a statement of intimidation. Will's physical size and muscles are accentuated by his tight clothes and his propensity to violate other' physical space by standing very close to them, feet spread and arms either crossed or held out from his body. His collarless and tank top shirts reveal both his muscles and knife scars on his neck and arms. Will's face is noteworthy for its set facial expression (described by some as a permanent scowl) and by his eyes which are most often described as menacing or piercing. Word spreads rapidly through the treatment milieu that Will once made a living as a "hitman." Will's "aura" guarantees emotional distance. The image, in essence, says, "I dare you to approach me, talk to me, question me, confront me." This is understood by others as, "if I make him mad, he could kill me." The statement Will is making about himself, if left unchanged, will almost guarantee treatment failure.

- "Dr. Richards," as he prefers to be called, has the cultivated look of the "distinguished." His well manicured look is enhanced by an exceptionally expensive wardrobe. In spite of the norm of informal dress on the treatment unit, he presents himself regularly

in tie and jacket. He constantly carries medical journals
with him throughout the treatment milieu, lest anyone
forget that he is a doctor. His overall demeanor is a
paradoxical combination of detached boredom
interrupted regularly by technical questions or challenges
to the staff. He alternates between social aloofness and
holding court with other clients, providing them advice
on their medical problems. His constant
intellectualization has already giving him the nickname
of "Dr. Spock" by some of his fellow clients. His pedantic
arrogance both angers and threatens staff. Our good
doctor, like Will, has created a physical and psychosocial
presentation of self that can buffer him from the
experience of treatment and allow him to sustain denial
of his addiction.

- If Tanya were a sculpture, it would be considered erotic
art. Everything about her physical and psychosocial
presentation of self exudes sensuality and eroticism. A
lifetime of exploitive relationships beginning early in
childhood and spanning her recent history as an addicted
prostitute have shaped her image as a sexual object. Her
hair, makeup, nails, jewelry and clothes along with every
nuance of verbal and non-verbal communication reinforce
this image. Tanya's presentation of self in the early days
in treatment differs little from such presentation on the
streets. Seductive towards men and competitive with
women, she presented well-rehearsed postures and
masquerades in the treatment milieu. After a lifetime of
refinement, she had become the image in the mirror.
Changing the image would mark the first step in
redefining who she was.

All of these clients had constructed a physical image that was integrally tied to their addictive lifestyle. Any image that can buffer the experience of treatment is part of the amour that allows one to sustain the addictive career. How should helping professionals respond to such images when presented within the treatment milieu? The following vignette from a counseling session with the above-described Dr. Richards captures a number of the essential approaches to image transformation. Included in parentheses are interpretations of both what the client is experiencing and labeling of the techniques and interventions utilized by the counselor.

Counselor: Jerry, I'd like to review with you your first few days on the unit and begin to identify some of the problem areas that we will focus on during the next several weeks. How would you describe your first few days? (Refusal to use "Dr. Richards" or any other name which either reflects culture of addiction, *i.e.*, nickname, or formalizes or creates emotional distance in the counselor-client relationship; focusing and goal-setting for the interview)

Jerry: I think things have been quite interesting so far. I've only worked at one hospital that had a unit like this; I'm learning quite a bit. It's still a bit disturbing to me that I'm here. All I can think about is what's going on with my practice right now; you know, it's going to be very difficult for my partners to fill in for me for as long as you want me to stay here. They aren't trained in all my specialty areas and don't have nearly the years of experience I have. It still seems like it should have been possible for me to go through outpatient treatment. It's not like I was killing patients or something.   (Reinforcement of doctor [God] role; grandiosity; minimization and denial)

Counselor: Jerry, you have serious medical problems related to your drinking, you have had two DUIs in the last year and you have lost your admitting privileges at one hospital for repeatedly showing up to make evening rounds in a state of extreme intoxication. You need to be here, but I'm sure it's very difficult for you. Are you getting to know the other patients and staff? (Confrontation presented in concise concrete terms as information rather than arguments following by supportive reflection of feeling)

Jerry: Yes. You know, you've got some pretty good nurses here. I wish I could take a couple of them back to work for me. (Denial of role as patient; continued reference to doctor role)

Counselor: Jerry, you've had a few days to settle in and we have had a few sessions to begin to get to know one another. I think it's time to focus on how you are approaching your entrance into treatment here. (More explicit focusing of topic)

Jerry: What do you mean?

Counselor: It is my experience that doctors are very special people and that they often present very special problems in alcoholism treatment. Isn't there some general notion about doctors and nurses making horrible patients? (Manipulation of narcissism; confrontation of professional group rather than person to keep resistance low)

Jerry: Yeah. We can be pretty horrible at times. [laughing] I've only been in the hospital twice and I suppose I was pretty intolerable both times. I also don't like to have other doctors as patients.

Counselor: In your experience, what makes doctors so hard to treat? (respect for and therapeutic use of client's professional experience)

Jerry: We tend to question and challenge everything and we are also not particularly good at practicing what we preach. I could tell you some real horror stories about trying to treat doctors. I can remember once...[recites story of obstreperous physician-patient].

Counselor: We often have similar problems with physicians in treatment. It's hard to get the doctor hat off and the patient hat on. Are you finding that to be difficult for you here in treatment? (Movement from abstract to personal; creation of principle that client can use for self-analysis)

Jerry: The patient role is pretty foreign to me. And you surely can't expect me to sit through all those lectures and films pretending that I'm not a doctor. After all, I'm still going to be a doctor when I get out of here. Besides I disagree with some of the information you present. (Fear and resistance experienced at thought of letting go of identity)

Counselor: It must be difficult for someone with your extensive medical training to sit in lectures presented by nonmedical personnel. Many of our other physicians who went through treatment here had similar feelings.

To overcome this difficulty, you can meet anytime you wish with Dr. Chadwick, our Medical Director, and discuss any technical questions you have. We also can put you in touch with a special AA group that is all recovering physicians. I'm sure these people could answer your questions much better than I could. Would you like me to arrange for either of these? (Counselor refuses to compete at cognitive level; recognition and affirmation of client specialness)

Jerry: Yes, perhaps after I get settled in a little more.

Counselor: The issue we are focusing on is how images can get in the way of treatment. [General discussion of images and treatment continues going from abstract, to other clients, and finally to Jerry] (teaching interventions)

Jerry: Are you saying that my being a doctor is somehow bad?

Counselor: No. It is not being a doctor. It is your use of that image to separate yourself from patients and staff and your use of that image to place yourself as a *critic of* treatment rather than a *participant in* treatment. It's the most frequent way doctors sabotage their own treatment. Can you identify things you are doing like that?

Jerry: You mean things like my dress?

Counselor: Yes. Your dress would be appropriate if you were a staff member, but it sets you apart from the other patients. Is it time you acknowledged that you are a patient here and not a visiting physician?

Jerry: I suppose so. You know, even though I'm out of town,
              I've been terrified of running into someone I know. I
              thought if I stayed dressed up, they would assume I'm
              here on a consultation rather than as a patient.

Counselor: [Interview continues focusing in on other image related
              behaviors; negotiations occur that look at alternative
              behaviors for each area]

Counselor: O.K. Review your list and see if you can summarize
              what we've agreed to. (Contracting technique)

Jerry: For the next week, I will shed the coat and tie, refrain
              from giving medical advice to other patients on the
              unit, will focus on personalizing rather than critiquing
              lecture information, will minimize references to my
              occupation and will attempt to construct an honest
              history of my alcohol and drug use. Did I leave
              anything out?   [client voice tone indicates some
              scariness over the proposed agreements]

Counselor: No. That covers all we've talked about. Do you feel
              there are any other important things to add at this
              point?

Jerry: No.

Counselor: Nearly all of the physicians who have gone through
              treatment here have had a difficult struggle with this
              image issue. They all had to break through this barrier
              at their own speed and for some of them this occurred
              very late in their treatment. If you feel you're not up
              to tackling all of those areas, perhaps we should
              postpone some of the agreements till later. (Paradoxical

injunction; engagement of client's competitiveness in
the experience of treatment)

Jerry: No. If I can't be a doctor, I'm at least going to be a
            good patient. [said with some sarcasm] (resistance is
            engaged positively)

Counselor: Something tells me you could be one of the best.
            You've made a good start today. I think we'll get
            together every day for a while to review how you are
            doing. (Verbal strokes for positive work; increasing
            frequency of contact serves as reward for constructive
            decisions; increased contact also will help offset
            increased stress that will be experienced by client due
            to role change)

Changes in physical image can be a powerful stimulus to sustain
or change personal identity and values. There is perhaps an
inherent drive for congruity between one's internal and external
reality. If one sustains patterns of self-care and physical images
from the culture of addiction while trying to initiate recovery, there
is an inevitable war within the self. The external image must
eventually become congruent with recovery values or the internal
values must be brought back into congruity (via activation of
addiction) with the external image. Perhaps there is some deep
psychological insight to be rediscovered through the seemingly
moronic adage: "If it looks like a duck, walks like a duck and talks
like a duck; it probably is a duck."

While the shaved heads marking entrance of addicts into the early
therapeutic communities seem perhaps barbaric by today's
standards, this practice was based on the same principles discussed
in this chapter. These programs shaved head and facial hair and
altered numerous aspects of physical appearance with the

understanding that transformation in internal identity and values could best be initiated by, and in some cases were impossible without, a transformation of the exterior self. Contracting for changes in physical appearance of culturally enmeshed addicts may not only be clinically appropriate, it may be essential.

11.9 *Diet/Food* The transformation in frequency and quality of food consumption that occurs through increasing involvement in the culture of addiction was noted in an earlier discussion. This transformation takes on particular significance in light of emerging research revealing the contributing role of diet and malnutrition in the etiology, progression and consequences of alcoholism. And yet one could ask, "Isn't making a big deal out of food in treatment counterproductive when there are so many more important issues to address? If adolescents want to sustain themselves through treatment on junk food, isn't that just normal adolescent behavior?" This section will explore the role of food in the culture of recovery.

A. *The Physiology of Sobriety* Few clients will take concerns about diet seriously unless a solid foundation is laid which clearly links food to physical and emotional recovery. Treatment staff speak daily of the "disease" nature of addiction but often fail to fully explore the implications of this concept to the physiology of recovery. The following sequential points form the basis of this foundation and should constitute a repetitive and well-elaborated message in treatment.

Sequence One

1. The acute and chronic effects of your alcohol/drug use have resulted in cellular damage that has impaired how you think, feel and behave.
2. The body can repair and replenish some of this tissue, but this repair can only be completed if the body is given the needed

ingredients—vitamins, minerals, trace elements—which can be provided only through proper diet.

3. The speed at which your body can physically recover will to the greatest extent depend on what you put in it. There is a direct relationship between what and when you eat and how you feel, think and act.

Sequence Two

1. Nearly all of your body functions, *e.g.*, digestion, sleep, and menstrual cycles have adapted to the presence of alcohol/drugs. Over time, the presence of such drugs has become "normal."

2. Your body must now adapt to the performance of these functions without the presence of the drug. Both physiologically and psychologically, sobriety must move from a new and abnormal to a normal state.

3. You must help your body through this adjustment process. Proper nutrition will both smooth and speed this adjustment period.

Sequence Three

1. Through the progression of your addiction, the drug took dominance over all other physical needs often leading to deteriorating patterns of self-care. Habits of eating, sleeping, grooming were often established that reflected this disregard for self.

2. Disregard and disrespect for your body are incongruent with recovery. To continue habits that were integrally tied to the addictive lifestyle is to court relapse.

3. Establishing programs of proper diet and exercise and eliminating toxic habits such as smoking are acts of self-respect that speed the recovery process.

The application of these principles in the acute treatment setting is explored below.

B. *Food and Mood* There is an important hour-by-hour relationship between one's level of physiological and psychological arousal and the material ingested in the body. This principle can guide our clinical monitoring of clients in early recovery and can constitute an essential area of client education. How many reported symptoms of alcohol detoxification and sleep disturbance over the years have actually been signs of acute caffeine intoxication? How many mood swings experienced in early recovery were interpreted in psychological terms rather than within a physiological framework of hypoglycemia and high-dose sugar ingestion? Four areas of programming to address the food-mood connection are essential.

1. **Caffeine Control** Caffeine must be eliminated or strictly limited within the treatment milieu. An essential task in early recovery is re-establishing the body's physical and emotional homeostasis in the absence of artificial stimulants and depressants. The common abuse of stimulants early in recovery postpones the achievement of homeostasis and in fact may produce conditions (i.e., sleep deprivation) that the body may link with (and thus stimulate craving for) drug intoxication. The elimination of artificial stimulants in coffee, tea, and soft drinks enhances the return of the body's own natural means of mood regulation.

2. **Sugar Control** Alternatives must be found to the use of fast-acting sugars such as candy, soft drinks, and ice cream during early recovery. The movement away from addiction is a move from short-acting to long-acting mood modifiers. There has been much discussion of the emotional roller coaster often produced by seesawing blood sugar levels in early recovery. Folk wisdom attributed this to the rapid and preferential manner through which

the body could get sugar from alcohol. This link established over time thus resulted in cravings for alcohol anytime blood sugar levels would plummet. Folk remedies based on this understanding used to prescribe regular consumption of candy and ingestion of candy at any time cravings for alcohol were experienced. While it may be heresy to challenge such folk wisdom, it is clear that the acute ingestion of sugar sustains rather than eliminates this chemical roller coaster. It also continues a preference established within the culture of addiction for drug experiences with rapid onset and short duration of action. One, in effect, gets a rush from the rapid metabolism of sugar, only to experience a plummeting of psychic arousal as this metabolism is completed. The alternative and recommended approach is to help clients sustain predictable blood sugar levels avoiding both the peaks and valleys characteristic of active addiction. This can be done by replacing sugar with a high-protein diet supplemented with complex carbohydrates. Creating 5-6 smaller daily meals or interspersing high-protein, low-carbohydrate snacks between meals can serve as special mood stabilization aids during the earliest period of recovery.

3.   **Eating Schedules**   Recovery is enhanced through the establishment of predictable eating schedules that serve to stabilize and manage blood sugar levels. The recovering addict must learn to see the consumption of regular and appropriate meals as a form of medical treatment similar to the way one might look at a medication schedule. The goal is not simply to provide symptom relief for the widely vacillating moods, a practice which enhances the reinforcing (and some would say addictive) properties of sugar. The goal is to establish a nutritional regimen that actually prevents the onset of symptoms. The disregard for nutritional health in the culture of addiction must be replaced by a conscious understanding of the importance of regular, well-timed, and well-chosen meals.

4. Nutrition Assessment and Planning   Nutrition is horribly boring unless it can be somehow linked to highly personal and immediate concerns. Nutritional assessments and plans for each client must be constructed around these principles of relevance and immediacy. Whether the client's concern is fatigue, hyperactivity, insomnia, or depression, treatment staff must be able to personalize the link between nutrition and the alleviation and prevention of symptoms. Such nutritional assessment and treatment planning requires a level of technical knowledge and sophistication that has only recently begun to appear in most substance abuse programs.

C. Managing Drug Hunger Through Diet and Exercise   An increasing number of clinicians are discovering the role of combining food and exercise to manage episodes of drug hunger experienced during the early months of recovery. Fruit and high-protein snacks/meals and at least a 20-30 minute period of sustained aerobic exercise are excellent rituals to include to address the physiological dimensions of cellular craving for drugs.

D. Self Healing   Perhaps the most essential message about food in the culture of recovery relates to the crucial role of nutrition in speeding healing of body tissue damaged from acute and chronic drug ingestion. Activating this dimension with a treatment milieu involves identifying areas of physiological impairment for each client and constructing a nutritional remediation plan that relates specifically to the client's areas of impairment.

As noted earlier, the process of integrating nutritional issues within treatment plans must be extremely concrete. Good nutrition, as an abstract value or issue, has almost no appeal to individuals early in recovery. The issue of nutrition must be linked to immediate problems and concerns of the client. Trained nutritionists with a technical understanding of the physiology of addiction may provide invaluable assistance in dealing with such client-reported concerns as fatigue, headaches, sleep disturbance, skin and complexion imperfections, concentration and memory impairment, skeletal-muscular pain, abnormal bowel movements, abnormal bleeding and bruising, retardation in sexual development, sexual dysfunction, as well as concerns over recovery from diagnosed alcohol/drug-related medical disorders. By taking reported concerns and explaining both the physiology of their origin as well as outlining particular diets that may speed their resolution, nutrition is moved from an abstract to a highly personal concern of the client.

E. *Self Healing Versus Self Pollution* (Toxic Relationships with Nicotine, Caffeine, and Sugar/Food) Can addiction treatment professionals promote health and wellness in the culture of recovery while promoting or enabling the continuation of other toxic, potentially life-threatening behaviors? Historically, we have!

While preaching the gospel of abstinence, addiction professionals have historically promoted the replacement of alcohol intoxication with excessive and toxic relationships with nicotine, caffeine and sugar. While the need for replacement rituals as one moves from the culture of addiction to the culture of recovery is very clear, the continued celebration of tobacco in the culture of recovery stands as a grotesque contradiction that must be confronted. It is only the massive and deceptive promotion of this drug in our culture that could, until recently, allow recovering persons to sit in smoke-filled rooms sharing the joys of drug-free life, oblivious to any incongruity between the preachings and the practice.

Our self-confrontation as a field has begun and must continue. Toxic elements inadvertently integrated within the culture of recovery must be excised and replaced with non-toxic, health-promoting alternatives. Desirable directions include the following.

- If recovery involves a program of rigorous honesty, then the addiction treatment field must acknowledge the historical mistakes of failing to conceptualize nicotine and caffeine as secondary drugs of abuse and of blatantly and excessively promoting these substances.

- Treatment professionals must boldly recognize nicotine as a secondary and highly lethal drug of abuse. It is time the field stopped burying founders, leaders and members, who achieving abstinence from alcohol and traditionally defined drugs of abuse, have their lives cut short as a result of drug-related (nicotine) disease. Day-by-day, month-by-month, the field must stigmatize and sever its continued relationship with this drug.

- The field must expand its expectations for professional role models to include abstinence from tobacco and the maintenance of non-toxic relationships with caffeine and sugar/food. Persons currently failing to meet such expectations should be supported and given access to formal treatment related to such problems.

- The treatment of nicotine addiction must be increasingly integrated within the substance abuse treatment umbrella. It must be discovered through research whether such treatment is best achieved concurrently with other addictions or sequentially at some period after abstinence from other drugs is achieved.

- Treatment professionals must begin to signal warning signs to newcomers in recovery that relationships with caffeine and food are potential danger areas, particularly during early recovery. We must help clients avoid the shift to other excessive and toxic behaviors during early recovery.

- If smoking and caffeine consumption serve as replacement rituals as one moves from culture of addiction to culture of recovery, and if these rituals are determined to be no longer desirable, then new rituals need to be developed that serve the same functions as smoking and coffee consumption.

Self-love and self-poisoning cannot consciously coexist.   They represent incongruities that create a war within the self. The forces in this war must eventually be reconciled tipping the scales toward health or toward personal destruction. As the substance abuse field looks to the future, the role of nutrition and exercise must be elevated in the consciousness of the recovering community. Toxic relationships with nicotine, caffeine and sugar need to become increasingly stigmatized and eliminated.

Given the usual excessiveness that tends to mark both the providers and recipients of substance abuse services, the field must be cautious in how it achieves the above-stated goals. We must guard against scapegoating members in the culture of recovery who continue toxic relationships with nicotine, caffeine and food. It is ironic, for example, that persons who make a living from their knowledge of addiction can so quickly turn on their co-workers and demand that they quit smoking as an act of will. Such persons need to be supported rather than punished or enabled. The field must guard against exclusionary practices, which out of elitism and arrogance, bar persons from membership in the culture of recovery due to their failure to achieve some new standard of personal "purity." Our approach must be inclusive, rather than exclusive.

11.10 *Music* The drug experience captured in words and music serves to both normalize and celebrate drug-using behavior. Established links between certain types of music or certain songs and euphoric recall of drug intoxication are particularly prevalent among culturally enmeshed addicts. Reinforced through thousands of repetitions, these musical cues serve as powerful links to the culture of addiction. They are stimuli capable of instantly eliciting drug hunger and triggering drug-seeking behavior. One aspect of the treatment of the culturally enmeshed addict is the identification and neutralization of such musical triggers.

A. *Identifying High Risk Cues*   The assessment of the existence and intensity of musical cues from the culture of addiction can be completed through a fairly simple interview process.   Key questions might include the following.

- Do you enjoy listening to music?
- What types of music do you most enjoy?
- Was music commonly a part of the environment within which you were drinking or using drugs?
- Are there particular types of music you associate with your drug use?
- Are there particular songs or musical groups you associate with your drug use?

When musical cues are present, the counselor can explore with the client the link between such music and his or her drug-using social world and drug-using identity.   The risks involved in continued exposure to such cues must also be explored. As the client sorts through issues related to his or her musical tastes, the following questions are appropriate to raise as a means of self-appraisal:

- Are the values reflected in the lyrics of these songs congruent with addiction or recovery?
- What physical and emotional sensations do I experience when I hear this music? Are such sensations positive, neutral, or negative in relationship to my recovery?
- Are the places I listened to this music so bound up with my addiction, that continuing to frequent such places would place me at a high risk of relapse?

B. *Neutralizing Musical Triggers for Intoxication* When musical cues have been identified that constitute an inhibiting force in recovery, a number of interventions are possible to diminish the power of such stimuli.

Isolation techniques which involve protecting the client from exposure to drug-enhancing stimuli are quite appropriate for the most powerful of such stimuli. This approach is usually reserved for that music which is so integrally bound (through thousands of repetitions of exposure followed by primary reinforcement) to the client's drug use as to make it nearly impossible to diminish its power as a conditioned stimulus. The client, after looking at this issue, is in essence confessing, "I cannot experience exposure to this music without experiencing intense cravings for intoxication." Helping a client sort through such high risk stimuli can be an essential part of relapse prevention. The client is brought to a point of recognition that he or she is not only powerless over alcohol, but also powerless over certain sensory cues that are associated with the drug experience.

Another category of techniques seeks to alter the power or meaning of sensory cues that have previously been tied to the experience of intoxication. All of these techniques seek to alter the power of the cue to trigger euphoric recall and hunger for the drug experience. The techniques described below can be applied to a broad range of sensory cues, *i.e.*, the sight of drug paraphernalia or of others using, the smell of ether for the freebase addict.

It would seem that the ability of a sensory cue, such as a particular song, to stimulate drug craving could be extinguished by constant repetition of the sensory cue without the reinforcement of drug intoxication. One could provide such massive exposure of the stimuli without the historical reinforcing antecedent that the stimuli would lose its power. Rather than isolating the client from high risk stimuli, this approach seeks to so saturate the client with these cues that they lose their power and significance. One could, for example, assign a client to listen repetitively to high-risk musical cues in the hopes of satiating the client's response to such cues. The approach could even be improved if the high-risk cues are paired with selected rituals such as relaxation techniques that are incompatible with physiological arousal. Theoretically, the client is being retrained not to respond to previously conditioned stimuli. The most current variation of this technique in substance abuse treatment today is found in some cocaine treatment programs which repeatedly expose their clients to cocaine paraphernalia in an effort to extinguish the ability of such cues to trigger drug hunger. While this technique may have utility in extinguishing low level sensory cues from the culture of addiction, its effectiveness with the most powerful of these cues is limited by the following.

- Cues established through primary reinforcers involving intracranial stimulation of the pleasure centers are quite resistant to extinction.
- The euphoric recall—the re-experience of intoxication through a state of mental imagery—triggered by the sensory cue may stimulate a placebo effect, producing concomitant physiological changes (i.e., endorphin production) that continue to reinforce the cue's pleasurable link to intoxication.
- While short-term extinction of drug-related sensory cues may be possible during acute treatment, the reinforcers (drug effects) are so powerful as to make spontaneous recovery (the reappearance of a conditioned response, thought to have been extinguished) quite likely following treatment.

Aversive conditioning techniques seek to alter the power of drug-enhancing sensory cues by consistently and repeatedly pairing such cues with unpleasant stimuli. One could, for example, work with a client by consistently pairing a drug-enhancing musical cue with unpleasant visual images graphically portraying consequences of addiction. Aversive techniques have not been widely utilized as an adjunct to traditional substance abuse counseling techniques.

Another approach to drug-enhancing musical cues is to create intense learning experiences for clients that alter the very meaning of these cues. Rather than neutralizing the drug-enhancing cue, the cue is transformed into a recovery cue. The technique metaphorically reverses the Biblical miracle by turning wine into water. This approach, more complex than the above-described techniques involving principles of conditioning, constructs a cognitive framework which transforms addiction cues to recovery cues. The following example is illustrative.

An 18 year-old crack cocaine addict, recently admitted to treatment, was found sitting in his room listening to a cocaine song on a cassette which he had brought into the treatment milieu. When confronted about the inappropriateness of listening to a song which glamorized cocaine, he readily admitted that it was his favorite song to get high to and that he had been listening to the song fantasizing about splitting treatment. It would have been easy to have let this confrontation drop via a "read the Big Book and hang in there" speech. Instead, this incident began a process that would extend over the next several days. The process involved the following steps.

1. The client was given a treatment assignment to listen to the song again, write out the lyrics of the song and assess whether the lyrics reflected *his* experience with cocaine. He was to share the results of this assignment in group two days later.

2. His presentation to group was quite insightful. After reading the lyrics to the song, he shared some of the problems and hassles in his life produced by cocaine which the song failed to mention. The song produced a lively conversation among group members both about consequences of cocaine use and drug-promoting music. The group leader suggested that the client, with the help of any interested group members, might try rewriting the song's lyrics or writing an alternative song to reflect the group members' experience with cocaine. Several younger group members enthusiastically volunteered to assist the client with this project.

3. After two days of drafts and revisions, the client and his cohorts presented their composition to the enthusiastic cheers of other group members. Their composition spoke eloquently of cocaine's promises and cocaine's pains.

4. The group response was so positive that the client and his co-composers were asked to sing their song before the treatment community at morning meeting, a performance that would bring thunderous applause and congratulations from their fellow clients and staff.

What do you think this client will think of after treatment when he hears the cocaine song? A musical cue from the culture of addiction was reframed and transformed into a cue that reinforced recovery principles and values.

C. *Songs to Get Well By* Consistent with the principle discussed repeatedly in this chapter, there is a replacement process with music as with other elements of the cultures of addiction and recovery. If music is to be taken, then music must be given. Treatment professionals can encourage the musically-involved client to reach out and find new forms of music which reflect experiences and express values congruent with the recovery process. An increasing number of programs are exploring the integration of music into the treatment milieu which celebrates recovery. There are increasing numbers of resources to provide assistance with this process. The work of Peter Alsop whose song writing talents and promotion of song as a tool in recovery deserve greater recognition from the field. The following verse and chorus from Peter's "When One Is Too Many" is indicative of his work.

"WHEN ONE IS TOO MANY"
by Peter Alsop

Verse One

One drink, one smoke, one snort of coke
A sugar slip, hey, a mainline trip.
Are you sick and tired of feeling sick and tired?
My friend, I know what's required!

Chorus

When one is too many, and a thousand ain't enough,
You cannot do any, hey, you got to get tough!
When one is too many. and a thousand ain't enough,
You cannot do any, hey, you got to get tough!

Information regarding Peter Alsop's songs can be obtained by writing Peter Alsop, Moose School Music, Box 960, Topango, California, 90290. Wyatt Webb and Aurel Lewis have each assembled audiotapes that carry the message of recovery through song. These tapes are available from Hazelden Educational Materials.

The White Oaks Treatment Program in Peoria, Illinois has also begun the integration of music and song to facilitate this cultural replacement process, with a special focus on alcoholic women.

They are currently completing a song book entitled "WE ARE SINGING FOR OUR LIVES: A Songbook of Recovery." Information on this resource can be obtained by writing Human Service Center, 600 Fayette Street, Peoria, Illinois, 61603.

While there are a number of practical advantages to the conscious integration of music within the treatment milieu, such integration also brings with it certain magical, non-measurable dimensions. Men and women have been circling to chant, laugh, sing and dance since recorded history. Such rituals must touch deep human needs for social bonding, social identity and safety. Musical sounds and the lyrical stories provide rituals that create and sustain hope. They provide opportunities to celebrate deep historical strains within the human spirit—from death can come life, from adversity can come courage and strength, from sin can come salvation, from hate can come love, from conflict can come harmony and from loneliness can come intimacy and fellowship. Such themes abound in the lyrics of the songs of recovery.

11.11 *Art* While the role of art has diminished within the culture of addiction since the decline of the hallucinogenic art of the late sixties and early seventies, art objects continue to play a role in some tribal groups of promoting excessive alcohol/drug use. In fact, the discussion of art and art objects is inseparable from the earlier discussion of symbols. The following discussion   will explore special dimensions of art and art objects in the culture of recovery.

A. *Art as a Tool of Disengagement* The crisis that places the addict on the brink of entry into recovery or re-entry into active addiction quite literally has the individual torn between two worlds, each foot planted in a culture that is the antithesis of the other. To say that such marginality is marked by emotional pain and confusion, competing loyalties and conflicting values is an understatement.

Most of this text has addressed the role of the treatment professional in tipping this balance so that the client can divorce themselves from the drug relationship and the culture which nurtures this relationship. Art can be a helpful tool in this disengagement process.

Art and artistic expression are highly underutilized therapeutic tools in the field of substance abuse treatment. Art can be extremely useful as both a projective assessment technique and as an expressive technique. Such techniques do not require sophisticated materials and equipment or extensive training. At their most basic level, they simply involve indirect and pre-verbal means of expressing emotion that can then be verbally processed with the client. Materials as simple as crayons or colored markers and newsprint can be utilized for the following individual/group assignments.

- Sketch a scene that captures the essence of your drug-using life.
- Sketch a scene that reflects your view of your lifestyle in recovery.
- Draw a self-portrait that reflects how you currently see yourself in treatment.
- Draw a picture of how your family (intimate network) looked in the past and how you hope it will look in the future.
- Draw an object or scene that conveys some of the feelings you are having difficulty expressing right now.
- Sketch the places, people or situations you think pose the greatest risks to your continued sobriety.

Such assignments utilize projective art as a means of self-exploration and self-confrontation. They use visual images created by the client as a magnifying mirror to see themselves and the culture which has surrounded their alcohol/drug use. They become mediums for exploring and shaping values. They become rituals that help clients accurately see, and emotionally disengage from, "the life."

B.   *The Folk Art of Recovery*   Posters, medallions, key chains, bookmarks, bracelets, pins, stationery, and bumper stickers all constitute artforms. These objects which portray the symbols, slogans and phrases of recovery from chemical dependency constitute the folk art of the culture of recovery. By procuring and portraying such folk art, recovering persons signal to themselves and the outside world their transformation in identity.

The explosion in availability of folk art from the culture of recovery provides great opportunities for treatment programs to incorporate such art as a support in client recovery. Concrete steps that can be taken by programs to enhance such supports include the following:

- Providing a treatment milieu rich in the presentation of folk art from the culture of recovery.
- Teaching clients how art objects can be used as visual cues to support and enrich recovery.
- Providing clients with access to folk art items which can be taken into the client's living environment outside of treatment.

An overall goal for both art and symbols is the integration of a large number of visual cues within the day-to-day physical environment of the client that serve to reinforce and anchor the recovery experience.

It is somewhat surprising given the population explosion within the culture of recovery that more traditional artforms, *e.g.*, painting, sculpture, have not emerged to depict and celebrate the experience of recovery. Such artforms will inevitably emerge and will in all likelihood reflect the death-transcending, life-promoting themes that are evolving within the history and mythology of the culture of recovery.

11.12 *Literature* Literature, like other cultural media, can be an influencing agent supporting values congruent with either addiction or recovery. The essence of the culture of recovery, which has historically been transmitted in face-to-face oral communication, is now being captured in a rapidly growing body of literature. This proliferation of writing about addiction and recovery offers new opportunities and a new technology available to substance abuse treatment programs.

A. *We Are What We Read* The literature one selects to read and own reinforces essential aspects of identity both to oneself and others. The written materials one chooses to have or not have communicates a great deal about a person and the things he or she values. Changes in identity and values should then be accompanied by changes in the literature found in one's environment. These observations can be capitalized upon as a tool to support the addict's transition from the culture of addiction to the culture of recovery.

An earlier chapter described how many culturally enmeshed addicts surrounded themselves with literature, *i.e.*, first person accounts of drug use, technical books on drug effects, recipe books such as bartender's guides, which promoted excessive alcohol and drug use. The procurement, ownership and constant perusal of such literature marks increasing devotion to the drug experience. For many users this is one of many actions that marks their transition in drug-using status from amateur to professional. Literature from the culture of addiction sustains and supports both the person-drug relationship and the world view and values of the culture of addiction. The mere physical presence of such literature and the reading of such literature constitute visual and experiential cues that trigger drug-hunger and drug-seeking behavior. All of these functions are incongruent with recovery, making a look at the role of literature in the client's life an important element of relapse prevention planning. The treatment center's role in this process involves:

- Assisting clients in identifying the presence of any literature in their possession that was linked to and supported their addictive lifestyles.
- Helping clients make decisions about the disposition of such possessions.
- Providing literature from the culture of recovery as a replacement process.

The psychological symbolism and emotional impact involved in such replacement rituals can be quite profound. From the client who destroys or discards a bartender's guide to the client who discards books promoting hallucinogens and satanism, the process is the same. One emotionally disengages from the drug and drug-enhancing values as one lets go of artifacts from the past life. The ritualistic destruction of books from the culture of addiction is a means of emotionally burning bridges leading back to that culture. Every ritual of disengaging from the culture of addiction, *i.e.*, letting go of books, paraphernalia, music, relationships, repeats and reinforces the emotional disengagement from the person-drug relationship. They are rituals of divorce. For maximum therapeutic effect, such rituals constitute decisions by the client, not dictates of the treatment program. The role of the professional helper is in processing and supporting client decision-making, not dictating the content of those decisions. It is the *decision* of the client in relation to such rituals that has power in terms of sustained changes in behavior and values, not the program's power to create temporary compliance by the client.

B. *New Ways to Carry the Message* The culture of recovery is an increasingly literate culture. Twenty-five years ago, there were few publications designed as aids in the recovery process. Today there are literally thousands, addressing nearly every imaginable issue related to addiction and recovery. Thanks to the role of such organizations as Hazelden Educational Materials and CompCare Publishers, these materials are being increasingly integrated into substance abuse treatment programs throughout the United States and beyond. Local treatment programs today have the opportunity, through the new availability of recovery literature, to enrich the treatment experience of recovering clients, to play a significant role in enriching knowledge in the local culture of recovery and in spreading such knowledge to the broader community. The following activities related to literature replacement and promotion are recommended.

1. **Define the "Bibles"** Given the plethora of recovery literature available, treatment programs must take care not to overwhelm the neophyte in the culture of recovery with an indiscriminate quantity of such material. Each program, given its own philosophy and traditions, must define its "Bibles"—those pieces of literature that capture the essence of beliefs about addiction and recovery espoused by the program. While the thousands of supportive books and pamphlets can deal with specialty issues in recovery, the "Bibles" create the foundation of recovery to which one must regularly return. The effective and discriminate use of literature as a treatment tool requires delineation between essential and supportive literature for the client.

2. **Assure Personal Ownership of Recovery Literature** One way to delineate essential from supportive literature is to provide to

each client the essential literature—the "Bibles"—at intake. Promoting personal ownership of recovery literature by the client is highly recommended. The client should have recovery literature that he or she owns. This can be assured through the inclusion of literature within treatment costs and the provision of literature (in written or audiocassette form) to all clients. Personal ownership of literature is established when the client writes his or her name in each book and pamphlet—a not insignificant act considering the denial that often characterizes addiction. The client gets to mark and underline and write in it. In short, the book becomes part of them. Literature, when taken into the client's home environment, constitutes powerful visual and experiential cues reinforcing abstinence and the client's new identity within the culture of recovery. The book has value as a symbol and recovery artifact within the client's environment, even if the book is never read.

3. **Provide a Literature-Rich Treatment Milieu**   How many treatment programs have libraries filled with recovery literature available to clients? Such access serves multiple purposes.

- It communicates to the client the existence of an extensive culture of recovery outside the treatment program and local community.
- It conveys to the client the wide diversity of literature within the culture of recovery, *e.g.*, books, magazines, pamphlets, newsletters.
- It provides a medium through which information provided within the program via lecture or one-on-one counseling may be validated and reinforced by and for the client.
- It provides a vehicle through which a client can seek information that may be too threatening to seek interpersonally, *e.g.*, perusing a pamphlet from the library shelf on addiction and sexuality.

4. Create Local Literature   Local literature can take many forms. It can be books about addiction and recovery written by local authors. It can be short pamphlets on a local treatment program or local self-help groups. It can be short informational articles written by treatment staff.   It can be a local newsletter.   A newsletter can play an important role in enriching a local culture of recovery. It can serve as an important vehicle in linking people together and transmitting cultural information. It becomes the culture's newspaper—sharing news of people and events and, most importantly, sharing both the trials and joys of recovery.   An increasing number of treatment programs or alumni associations of treatment programs are taking over this important communication role within their local culture of recovery.

5. Promote Literature in Recovering Community and Beyond
Treatment programs must begin to position themselves as one of the centerpieces in the local culture of recovery. One such role that can be served from this position is promoting and providing easy access to recovery literature.   Substance abuse programs, in addition to their treatment responsibilities, can serve their local communities by both lending (via library services) and selling literature on addiction and recovery.   Such services not only provide direct access to such literature for recovering persons, but also serve an important role of information dissemination within the larger community.

C. *Recovery, Literacy and Illiteracy*   While it is important to utilize the expanded literature of recovery, it is equally important that treatment programs not forget those clients who due to illiteracy or disability may not be able to utilize these treatment and recovery aids. Accommodations must be made so that such clients have full access to information that will support and enrich their recovery experience.   Such accommodations could include at a minimum the following actions.

- Maintain an extensive library of audiocassettes which capture all of the basic readings provided to clients in treatment.
- Maintain copies of the treatment "Bibles" in Braille.
- Utilize volunteers to read and discuss key literature with clients who are reading-impaired.

11.13 *Visual Media*   Popular visual media such as television, movies, and videos contain promotional cues that reflect the culture's preferences and tastes in psychoactive drug consumption. To the extent that such cues promote or normalize drug consumption, they reinforce addiction rather than recovery. It was noted earlier that addicts are particularly drawn to visual media that either celebrate the drug experience (as in *Arthur* or *Up in Smoke*), mock society's values about drug consumption (as in *Reefer Madness*) or enhance drug effect (as in *Fantasia*). This section will explore the role of visual media in treatment and recovery.

A. *Extinguishing and Reframing Old Cues*   Anecdotes like the following are often reported by persons in early recovery.

"Kathy and I were watching *Casablanca* the other night on one of those old movie stations. About halfway through the movie, I realized that I wasn't focusing on the movie; I was watching Bogart smoke. He smoked through that whole movie and every time he lit up or took a drag, I could feel the smoke going into my lungs. It was almost hypnotic. I couldn't figure it out. I mean, I hate the idea of smoking now. But watching Bogart smoke was almost more than I could handle."

Whether the focus is on nicotine, alcohol, cannabis or cocaine, stories like the above illustrate the power of visual media to trigger physical and psychological hunger for a drug. The following steps can be incorporated into treatment to prepare clients to anticipate and respond to such experiences.

1. **Anticipating the Experience** Clients must be taught to expect otherwise unanticipated impulses of drug hunger and to understand that such impulses are responses which spring from years of conditioning. When such experiences occur, the first step is to identify the stimuli or cues that are triggering the response. Such cues may involve varied sensory as well as emotional stimuli. If clients aren't prepared for such experiences, they often experience feelings of guilt or a belief that they have somehow failed in working their recovery program. It is important to mention the presence of drug-promoting cues in the visual media of television and movies, as most clients will be unaware of the source of the stimuli to which they are responding. The experience of drug cravings following acute withdrawal often simply signify that client's have been exposed to powerful stimuli that have historically been linked to the drug experience. By identifying such stimuli and recognizing the normalcy of such experiences in recovery, clients can be empowered to start the reconditioning process.

2. **Verbalizing the Experience** Generations of recovering persons have discovered a special magic that occurs when the experience of drug hunger is verbalized within recovery-supporting relationships. Verbal disclosure of such experiences almost immediately diminishes the intensity of drug craving. The recovering person who shares such experiences in therapy, in aftercare or self-help groups, or to a sponsor can use this communication to weaken and eventually destroy the conditioned stimulus—drug craving connection.

3. **Cue Replacement** Historically, the conditioned response of drug hunger became strengthened every time the experience of

drug hunger was followed by drug consumption. Such responses will be weakened simply through continued abstinence, but the process may be accelerated by replacing the historical reward (drug consumption) with a noxious stimuli. Such conditioning can be done quite simply by having clients develop key negative images associated with their drug use, and to pull such images into consciousness every time they experience drug hunger. I used this technique extensively during the first year I quit smoking. As a seriously addicted nicotine addict (2 packs a day), there were hundreds of cues that had become inextricably bound to my smoking behavior. As one would expect, these cues continued to trigger drug craving during my early months of nicotine abstinence. When I experienced cravings, I projected and held two images within my mind. The first was the image of an ugly ashtray mounded with ash and broken cigarette butts. This image helped bring forth the notions of disgust and filth associated with smoking. The other image replayed an actual scene from my life in which a participant in a workshop I was conducting noted with uncharacteristic candor that he was shocked that I smoked—that such behavior seemed so contradictory to my apparent values and knowledge about addiction. The latter scene reinforced the feelings of humiliation and stupidity that I had come to increasingly associate with my smoking behavior.

4. **Utilizing Diversion**   Addicts who subject themselves to sustained exposure to drug promoting cues dramatically increase their risks of relapse. While anticipation, verbalization, and elicitation of drug inhibiting images are all helpful relapse prevention techniques, there are times when the conditioned stimuli are so powerful that one must extricate oneself from such exposure. Are there movies that should be avoided in recovery? Probably so, even though the particular movies may differ from person to person. Are there television programs that may trigger drug hunger in the recovering addict? Probably so. What does the

newly arrived cocaine addict in treatment experience through the visual cues present in *Miami Vice*? Clients must be taught to gauge the strength of conditioned responses, as well as to identify their source, and, when necessary, to use diversion and/or escape as a preferred method of response to drug-enhancing cues.

B.   *Television in the Treatment Milieu*   Television plays such a dominant role in the culture at large as a source of information, value transmission and leisure, one must inevitably explore the role of this medium in the treatment and recovery culture. Thoughts about this role differ greatly from treatment center to treatment center. One school posits that television should be banned from the treatment environment. In defense of this position, proponents note the propensity of clients to use television as an escape from dealing with the emotional intensity of the treatment process. Another school notes the link between television and drinking behavior and suggests that clients need exposure to television in treatment to experience leisure activity without the drug. Other programs haven't even thought about the issue and simply have television available during unscheduled time in the treatment milieu because they simply never conceived a living milieu without television.

As they approach this issue, treatment staff must separate their own feelings and habits related to television from their judgments about the role of this medium in the treatment milieu. The role of television may also differ depending on the nature and intensity of the treatment modality. A good working principle on this issue might be the following: the earlier the stage of sobriety of clients, the greater the degree of control that must be exerted over television in the treatment milieu. The essential tasks in this area are:

- To assist clients in identifying media cues such as the repetitive onslaught of beer commercials during sports events that may trigger intense cravings for intoxication
- To assist clients, for whom television has been integrally associated with their drug use, to separate the act of watching television from the act of drinking, *e.g.*, helping clients learn to be comfortable watching television sober
- To provide a milieu which prevents clients from escaping the treatment experience through excessive involvement in passive leisure, *e.g.*, television
- To monitor during aftercare whether television is being overused to avoid or postpone activities essential to sustained sobriety

To achieve the above goals, particularly in the acute residential treatment setting, requires that television be present but highly controlled. Most programs are achieving this by having television available but limiting its access to a few hours a day or to weekend hours only.

C. *We've Come a Long Way Since "Chalk Talk"* Today's programs have access to an increasingly sophisticated arsenal of visual aids to enhance the intensity and effectiveness of substance abuse treatment. From the early days in which video aids consisted of nothing more than "talking heads," the addiction treatment field has progressed to a state in which visual media constitute a powerful tool for behavioral and attitudinal change. Today's media tools can target such multiple dimensions as:

- Penetrating the addict's defense structure to reduce denial, minimization and other self-constructed obstacles to recovery

- Transmitting information about addiction and recovery
in a manner that enhances both personal application and
retention
- Facilitating emotional thawing of clients through the
portrayal of intense emotional experiences on the screen
that mirror episodes in the addictive career of the client
- Demonstrating skills and positive responses to critical
incidents in recovery
- Providing motivational aids through the presentation of
charismatic recovering heroes and heroines, and
- Clarifying and reinforcing values congruent with
recovery

The above discussion notes how video technology in the acute
treatment milieu has advanced. A new and expanded role of video
can be seen in its use as a teaching and motivational tool
throughout the recovery process. With the growing number of
persons who own videocassette recorders, the television set can be
transformed from "boob tube" to a powerful support for recovery.
By expanding the message of recovery into this medium and by
developing new video formats designed for the home rather than
the treatment center, a new vehicle for inspiration and relapse
prevention is possible.

The availability of high quality visual media designed as tools for
changing behaviors, attitudes and values of addicted clients is
increasing every day. Such aids, along with an increasing number
of television specials and popular movies (*My Name is Bill W.*,
Clean and Sober) that address addiction and recovery, constitute
powerful new resources that can be utilized in addiction treatment.

D. *The Concept of "Passive Confrontation"*   Addiction treatment
professionals frequently encountered clients whose cognitive

defense structures are almost impenetrable. The intensity of their denial or intellectualization or projection makes it almost impossible for any data from outside to penetrate this defense structure. In some cases, it seems the harder staff confront, the more intense becomes the client's resistance. One tool that can be extremely helpful in such cases involves the concept of "passive confrontation."

In active confrontation—situations in which the contradictions and incongruities in a client's values, statements, and behaviors are pointed out—client defenses often escalate so rapidly that the client experiences little new information in the confrontation process. While others are talking to the client, he or she is actively preparing positions of defense rather than weighing the accuracy or applicability of new information about themselves. "Passive confrontation" bypasses this defense system by presenting new information to a client while defenses are minimally engaged. The use of reading assignments or assignments for clients to watch certain movies or videos (while alone) takes the client out of the defense-activating interactional role and enhances receptivity to new information. It forces the information from an oppositional to an introspective arena. Visual media, when used in a treatment assignment context, can be a powerful vehicle for such passive confrontation.

11.14 *Work and Leisure* The meaning of work and play must both be redefined in the culture of recovery. The treatment experience can facilitate the beginning of this redefinition process.

A. *Redefining the Meaning of Work* The addict's experience of work has often become integrally linked to addiction. Whether through the job equals money equals drug supply equation or through the energy expended to avoid drug-related job performance problems, the addict's world of work has been defined around the primacy of the addiction experience. In sustained sobriety one must rediscover the non-drug related meaning and purpose of work. The following interventions can be utilized by the treatment center to assist the addict in this process.

1. **Exploring Non-drug Values** Work, for the culturally enmeshed addict, can be a bit disorienting in early recovery. In the past, alcohol and/or drugs have been the direct product and reward for one's labors. In recovery, new reasons and rewards must be discovered to justify these labors. By exploring values during treatment, an appropriate reallocation of income can be made that was previously directed to sustain drug supply. If this clarification of values has not taken place, the presence of money can constitute a major trigger for relapse. Adolescents as well as adults can benefit from this process of values clarification. The fifteen year old in treatment needs to redefine the meaning of school and money.

2. **Restructuring Work-related Rituals** There are many characteristics, decisions or rituals related to work life that were shaped by the addiction experience. Particular job choices or shift choices may have been influenced by addiction where, for example, such choices resulted in decreased supervisory scrutiny and increased opportunity for on-the-job drug use or undetected on-the-job recovery from episodes of drug use. Other rituals and characteristics can include conflicts in the supervisory relationships, strain in one's peer relationships, lunch hour and break rituals, daily post-work rituals, and check-cashing rituals. It is helpful to identify with adolescents similar rituals in the school that have been shaped by drug use. By exploring such areas, the counselor can examine the extent of drug-influenced work behaviors with the client, and assist in the construction of a recovery based style of relating to the school or workplace.

3. **Conducting Employer Conferences**   Many alcoholics and addicts in the legitimate workforce have suffered a progressively deteriorating relationship with their work environment. By the time of entry into treatment many of these relationships are strained to their limit.   By providing opportunities for and encouraging the hosting of employer conferences during the treatment experience, a vehicle is provided through which this relationship can be repaired. The purposes of such conferences are to educate the supervisor about addiction and recovery, to identify past addiction-related performance problems experienced by the particular client, and to clearly define performance expectations in measurable behavioral terms that will be expected of the client upon his or her re-entry into the work setting. Such meetings often result in turning the supervisor from a potential source of sabotage into a source of support for client recovery.

The parallel of the above for adolescents is a conference which brings together the adolescent client and his or her family, staff from the treatment center and officials from the school to which the adolescent will be returning or entering. Representative agenda items and goals for such a meeting would include the following:

- providing a clear, concise synopsis of the events precipitating treatment admission and reviewing the course of treatment;
- reviewing the prior history of school related problems, setting new performance objectives, and clarifying role responsibilities;
- identifying and discussing those situations or events the adolescent fears most related to his or her return to school;
- identifying both technical and social supports available to the adolescent inside the school, *e.g.*, tutors, special classes, counseling, support groups;

- identifying the single person through which school-based problems will be addressed; and
- clarifying any issues related to confidentiality boundaries that will guide ongoing communications between the treatment center and the school.

Our historical failure to prepare clients for this re-entry into the school or the workplace has had a contributing influence on post-treatment relapse.

4. Extending Support into the School/Workplace Many substance abuse programs are seeking to extend the influence of the culture of recovery beyond the bounds of the treatment center into the school and the workplace. Activities that seek the spread of the culture of recovery into these institutions include:

- working with employee assistance program and student assistance program personnel to promote the development of aftercare and self-help groups inside the school/workplace;
- providing outreach services from the treatment center to include potential for continued contact with clients in the school/workplace;
- linking returning clients to other recovering persons in the school/workplace;
- hosting educational programs for students/employees to decrease stigma of addiction recovery; and
- training and utilization of recovering clients as peer counselors in the school/workplace.

5. Providing Warnings on Workaholism A significant number of recovering persons become obsessed workaholics in early recovery. It's as if the performance problems and addiction-related financial problems that have occurred over years must be made up for during the early weeks and months of recovery. In cognizance of the propensity for persons in early recovery to bring their characteristic excessiveness to most efforts, particular warnings should be provided on the hazards of workaholism. There may be many past sins in the workplace for which the addict may overcompensate. Work can also help fill the time vacuum of early recovery. But the danger of over-extending oneself to the point of exhaustion and letting work become a substantial diversion from basic recovery activities poses significant risks in early recovery. By providing client education on workaholism and monitoring the work relationship of clients during aftercare, this danger can be minimized.

6. **Clarifying Vocational Choices** There are occasions in which a client's job is so intertwined with the addictive career that the question of the client's ability to concurrently sustain sobriety and the job must be raised. Under such circumstances, it is appropriate for the treatment professional to help the client determine when and under what conditions the job must be sacrificed. For the client who has had no legitimate career and whose vocation or lack of vocation has been synonymous with his or her addiction, a pathway must be found to a legitimate role that can provide both sustenance and esteem. Vocational services provided as an adjunct in treatment must both guide the selection and preparation for this pathway and fill the time void that precedes one's achievement of role legitimacy. Guidelines on assisting clients with this role transformation from the culture of addiction to the culture of recovery will be discussed in more detail later.

B. *Finding Drug-Free Pleasure* Where the work of the addict had to accommodate addiction, play for the culturally enmeshed addict became synonymous with addiction. Interventions designed to remove the drug orientation of the client's leisure time include the following.

1.   **Assessing the Leisure/Addiction Link**   Part of the comprehensive assessment of each client entering a substance abuse treatment program includes an assessment of the degree to which leisure activities were shaped by the addiction experience. Such an assessment involves the following three basic elements or dimensions. What are the primary leisure time activities of the client and how have these activities changed through the progression of addiction? What are the physical places where such activities are conducted and to what extent do such places reinforce excessive alcohol/drug use? Who are the people with whom these activities are conducted and will such persons serve as a source of sabotage or support for the client's recovery? The greater the degree to which activities, places and people have been shaped by addiction, the more aggressive must be the approach to relapse prevention planning in this area.

2. **Integrating Play into the Treatment Milieu** The idea of drug-free play and laughter is often quite alien to the culturally enmeshed addict. While newly arrived addicts may have been increasingly forced to commit themselves to the prospect of continued sobriety, they often approach such a resolution as if it were a death sentence. Through the eyes of the addicted, sobriety looks like such a serious and somber business. The first thing a treatment milieu can do is destroy this conception by creating a highly energized environment. In the best of such milieus, sobriety is presented through living examples, not as a disease-necessitated curse, but as a gift. Laughter is used as an instrument for healing and celebration. There is a playfulness that in its contagion pushes one toward the perception and enjoyment of simple pleasures. A major influencing agent in this milieu is the inclusion of recovering role models.   Through their actions and story-telling, they can illustrate the range and richness of drug-free play and pleasure. By integrating play into the daily treatment design and by capitalizing

on spontaneous opportunities for laughter and play, clients begin to discover the experience of drug free joy and pleasure.

3. **Providing a Forum for Leisure Planning** The major interventions involved in leisure planning for the culturally enmeshed addict include the following elements:

- To identify any healthy leisure activities which were phased out of the client's life due to the progression of addiction;
- To identify types of leisure activity of potential interest to the client which have not been fully explored;
- To identify activities, places and people which would pose high risk for relapse;
- To expose clients to drug free activities, places and people within the culture of recovery;
- To prepare a plan (schedule) of drug free activities, places and people that will be explored by the client during leisure time; and
- To monitor the frequency and richness of leisure activity during aftercare contacts with the client.

Drug-free leisure has come a long way in the past fifty years. As the size of the recovering community has exploded and alcohol/drug abstinence has become increasingly acceptable for a variety of reasons, the recovering person has an increasing number of drug-free environments through which to explore new leisure pursuits. Neophytes in the culture of recovery may be surprised at the extent to which such environments are available. Major institutions within the culture of recovery, *e.g.*, self-help groups, churches, are becoming increasingly involved in creating drug-free leisure activities. Alcohol and drug-free "clubs" are opening in a number of cities. "Alternative" holiday parties are proliferating. Sporting activities such as amateur sports leagues are increasingly including drug-free teams made up of recovering persons. Alcohol-free seating is becoming increasingly available at major sports stadiums. While attractive to recovering persons, such sections also are attractive to others who would prefer some isolation from heavily drinking fans. There are even special vacations available to be planned through the assistance of such groups as Sober Vacations International of Los Angeles. A recent review of such assistance found a "dry" African Safari sponsored by Agency International of Atlanta, and New England ski trips and Caribbean cruises sponsored by Recovery Adventures of Brookline, Massachusetts. All such activities mix recreation and social support for sobriety.

Our role in treatment is that of a guide—linking new arrivals in the culture of recovery to the ever-expanding resources that provide fun and leisure in physical and social environments that support recovery.

11.15 *Sexuality* Neophytes in the culture of recovery bring with them not only sexuality issues that predated the onset of their drug use, but also any transformations in sexual values and experiences that occurred through the addiction process. The collective reports of the addicted note that both of these areas often involve trauma and emotional pain and that sexuality constitutes a minefield that can explode into relapse. In geographical areas where the culture of recovery is most fully matured, the culture provides a milieu for the neophyte to enter that is both non-exploitive and a source of sexual healing. This section will discuss how this process of sexual healing can be enhanced within the culture of recovery.

A. *Intimacy, Sexuality and the Culture of Recovery* Members of the culture of recovery bring with them a history of great turbulence in their sexual lives—a turbulence that fused the issue of sexuality within the broader pathology of addiction. If the threads of this pathology are to be unraveled, then the culture must provide a context that explicitly addresses the issue of sexuality. Such context setting for substance abuse treatment programs involves four distinct elements: reversing patterns of sexual exploitation, shaping sexual norms in the treatment milieu, redefining the purpose of sexuality, and clarifying and/or redefining personal sexual values.

Culturally enmeshed clients emerge from a milieu within which the purpose of intimacy is manipulation. Sexuality is replaced by or subjugated to serve the more primary passion of addiction. It is an environment of predators and victims. It is an environment where persons with substances are valued more than persons of substance. It is above all an environment of exploitation. Fleeing from this environment into the culture of recovery, the latter must provide a decompression chamber free of exploitation. Everything one does with sexuality in the name of treatment first hinges upon a milieu free from staff-client and client-client exploitation. Continued reports of sexual exploitation of clients by "professional helpers" and continued reports of predatory sexual behavior encountered by persons in the self-help setting suggest that efforts in this area need to intensify. Sexual healing requires above all an environment of sexual safety.

A second requirement to effectively address issues of sexuality with clients is that professional staff consciously shape the sexual culture of the treatment organization. This means that the milieu contains strong permissions to address issues of sexuality, an organized body of knowledge and information about sexuality, an explicitly defined vocabulary that assists communication about sexuality, attitudes that reflect an understanding of and tolerance toward the great variety in forms of non-exploitive sexual expression, and values verbalized and modeled that set new expectations and relationship standards. In short, the milieu provides both permissions and vehicles through which sexual pain can be explored and sexual healing facilitated.

The third and fourth elements include the provision of built-in opportunities for clients to redefine the meaning and purpose of sexual activity and to formulate personal values to govern their sexual activity. Again, this raises the need for the treatment milieu to serve as a decompression chamber in which clients can engage in both introspection and dialogue on the issue of sexuality. In a broader sense, it affords the opportunity to define the role of sexuality in the more expansive reconstruction of personal identity and values.

The above issues shape elements of the milieu within which sexual healing can occur. The discussion below will explore more direct interventions to promote sexual healing within the culture of recovery.

B. *Addressing Sexual Trauma* An alarming number of addicted women and an increasing number of addicted men report histories of incest or other forms of sexual exploitation in childhood. Reports on the incidence of such abuse reported by alcoholic women in treatment can be as high as 95% (White & Godley, 1988). Numerous reports (Neilson (1984), Covington (1986)) note that alcoholic women, when compared to abused non-alcoholic women, have experienced a wider variety of sexual abuse perpetrators, more episodes of abuse, and more physical abuse/violence associated with sexual abuse. While the role of such abuse in the etiology of addiction remains unclear, there is little doubt about the need to address issues of sexual trauma within the context of addiction treatment. The best timing for this type of intervention must be carefully assessed and is likely to differ from client to client.

C. *Clarifying Sexual Identity* Many addicts experience confusion, conflict or pain related to their sexual identity. Data on sexual orientation of addicted clients suggests that the incidence of self-reported homosexuality increases in sobriety, a fact that has led Covington (1986) to suggest that alcohol may help some persons in denying their physical attraction to persons of the same sex. If such confusion or pain can serve as an initiating or sustaining factor in the drug relationship, then the culture of recovery must provide a context to clarify sexual orientation and to provide on-going support for sobriety regardless of one's affectional preference. Guidelines and suggestions in this area might include the following.

- As with the issue of sexual trauma, some clinical assessment needs to be made to ascertain at what point in the client's treatment/recovery the issue of sexual identity can best be addressed. While it may be important to identify this as an issue in early recovery, we must take great care that the issue not become a diversion from the treatment of addiction.
- Staff who lack skill or comfort addressing issues of sexual identity can respond best to this issue by addressing the addiction, identifying other resources through which the client can explore issues of affectional preference and providing general emotional support for the client's work on this issue.
- Specially designated Gay and Lesbian AA or NA groups can be a particularly helpful resource for clients who identify themselves as homosexual. Within such groups can be found not only the traditional 12 step framework for addiction recovery, but also a social support system that addresses some of the special needs experienced by Gay and Lesbian clients.

D. *Exploring Sexual Roles*   Nearly everything written during the past two decades on alcoholism in women suggests emotional pain and discomfort with sexual role can be an initiating and sustaining factor in addiction and constitute a major obstacle to recovery for women. The development of gender sensitive treatment and self-help approaches will greatly enhance the recovery of addicted women, and eventually the recovery of addicted men, who are less likely to see how sexual role proscriptions have affected them. Approaches that warrant further development include:

- the development of aggressive outreach and intervention programs for addicted women,
- the development of day care, homemaker, and transportation services as adjunctive services for women in treatment,
- the development of family oriented and mother-child oriented treatment approaches,
- the development of separate therapy and support groups available to men and women,
- the provision of strong women role models, *e.g.*, staff, volunteers, sponsors, within the treatment milieu, and
- the use of an extended treatment design that provides a sustained period of aftercare services to stabilize and internalize treatment gains.

The list above provides the structure through which sex role conflict and pain can be addressed. The process involves a continuing focus on such issues as passivity, dependency, learned helplessness and hopelessness, and self-esteem. It requires a commitment to address the evolving needs of recovering women without preconceived models or modalities designed exclusively or primarily from experience with addicted men.

E. *Managing Shame and Guilt*   Pilgrims often enter the culture of addiction with a great deal of sexual shame and guilt. Some comes from sexual activity, and the earlier noted incidence of sexual exploitation, that predates the onset of excessive alcohol and drug consumption. Additional, and for many the most intense, areas of sexual guilt stem from sexual behavior that occurred during the progression of addiction. The loss of control, impaired judgment, disinhibition, radical personality change and drug-sustaining financial needs may have all meshed together to create a loathsome breach between personal sexual values and sexual behavior. The culture of recovery must provide a framework through which one can make sense out of such painful incongruity. How can self-acceptance and self-love spring from the roots of guilt-driven self-hatred? Left unresolved, guilt courts continued self-destruction. The reality of it makes one feel unworthy of recovery. The scope of it breeds hopelessness. The intensity of it demands self-punishment. The emotional pain of it fuels self-medication.

The culture of recovery has evolved a number of straightforward and effective mechanisms for diffusing the destructiveness of guilt to the recovery process. Nearly all pathways of recovery, the traditional and the non-traditional, provide mechanisms to:

- share normative data on sexual behavior and sexuality and addiction in particular as a means of breaching the isolation of guilt and shame;
- explore areas of unresolved shame and guilt through both clinical assessment and self-inventory processes;
- identify the manner in which such issues sustain current patterns of self-defeating behavior;
- achieve emotional release through the expiation of shame and guilt via a self-disclosure or confession process;
- cognitively organize past behaviors in ways that provide a foundation for current and future esteem;

- make selective amends and restitution to those persons harmed by past action or inaction;
- share the experience of healing with other "sinners;"
- collectively achieve the experience of acceptance and forgiveness; and
- emotionally disengage from the past and build identity and esteem in the present.

The culture of recovery is a healing culture. It provides the opportunity for a cleansing rebirth and reconstruction of the self. From the burial of guilt rises the birth of self-esteem and self-acceptance.   From the ashes of harm to others flickers the beginning of service to others.

F. *Treating Sexual Dysfunction*   Addiction may play a role in masking, alleviating, creating or compounding sexual dysfunction in men and women. Sexual dysfunction may precede the onset of addiction or be a consequence of addiction. In either case, there is a fairly high rate of self-reported problems and fears related to sexual functioning reported by clients in treatment. If the culture of recovery is the context for the restoration of personal and interpersonal health, then it must provide some medium through which members can either initiate or restore sexual functioning or accept and compensate for this loss. There are three distinct functions—teaching, assessment and treatment, and support—that treatment components of the culture of recovery can initiate to address client concerns related to sexual dysfunction.

1.   **Teaching Functions**   Through lectures, media aids, and discussion groups, the treatment program can deal openly and honestly with the issues of sexual dysfunction. The essential elements of such education would include:

- a catalogue of types of sexual dysfunction commonly associated with addiction;
- the overall causes of sexual dysfunction in women and men;
- the physical mechanisms of addiction-related sexual impairment, to include:
  - drug consumption that retards onset of sexual development
  - drug-related suppression of sexual interest and arousal
  - disruption of sensory pathways of sexual arousal due to drug-induced neuropathy
  - disruption of sex hormone metabolism due to drug-induced liver damage
  - a catalogue of other drug-related medical problems that effect sexual functioning;
- psychological and emotional dimensions of sexual dysfunction;
- the overall prognosis for treatment of addiction related sexual disorders;
- how problems of sexual dysfunction in men and women are assessed and treated; and
- the role of abstinence, overall physical healing, and specialized treatment in the restoration of sexual functioning.

2. **Assessment and Treatment Functions** Each program can enhance the assessment and treatment of addiction-related sexual dysfunction by:

- including a review of clients' sexual history and an identification of problems related to sexual functioning in both the medical and psychosocial components of the comprehensive assessment at intake,

- providing a forum through which clients can explore concerns related to sexual dysfunction and discuss the appropriate timing for more intensive work on this area of their lives, and
- providing clients access to referral sources who specialize in the assessment and treatment of sexual dysfunction.

3. **Support Functions** Support functions for clients experiencing sexual dysfunction include:

- creating an environment of emotional safety and acceptance to enhance client self-disclosure on issues of sexuality,
- raising issues of sexuality and sexual functioning in aftercare groups to identify problems that may be surfacing for the first time post-treatment, and
- providing on-going emotional support to clients experiencing problems with sexual functioning.

G. *Including Sexuality in Relapse Prevention Planning* A final note on the issue of sexuality in the culture of recovery involves the recognition of relapse risks inherent in sexual situations. An essential element of relapse prevention planning involves exploring and creating alternatives to the historical link between alcohol/drug use and sexual activity. This is particularly needed for clients who have never functioned sexually while drug-free.

11.16 *Family Relationships* Familial dimensions of addiction and recovery are being increasingly explored in both the professional and popular literature. This section is not intended as a summary or new examination of the psychodynamics of family life through addiction and recovery. It will not address the impact of addiction and recovery on the intrapsychic health of family members, but rather the changes in the family's internal and external relationships that occur via the recovery process. This section will build on previous discussions of family by focusing specifically on the relationship between the family and the culture of recovery.

A. *Family: An Expanded Definition* It is important for the reader to view and extend the meaning of "family" in this discussion considerably beyond its traditional connotation. The term encompasses the traditional concepts of family of origin and nuclear family, but the term as used here will also encompass blended and extended family members, intimate social networks not linked by blood ties, households, paramour relationships and other sustained intimate partnerships of heterosexual or homosexual variety. In short, "family" will be defined as those kinship relationships of both blood and choice which are characterized to be of self-ascribed, sustained emotional importance to the addict.

This definition is not just an abstract exploration of semantics. One's definition and understanding of family creates access to or exclusion from recovery resources. A man has been admitted to inpatient addiction treatment. Although married, he has a sustained intimate relationship with another woman over the past five years. He has considered divorce-remarriage, but right now is unclear about his future intentions. Should the "other woman" be involved in his treatment? Should she be offered services through the "family program"?

B. *The Future of Family in the Culture of Recovery* An earlier chapter explored the role of the family in the culture of recovery, noting the history of Al-Anon, NarAnon, Co-Anon, the Adult Children of Alcoholics movement and the evolution of family centered programming within substance abuse treatment agencies. Key questions and challenges related to future role of the family in the culture of recovery are outlined below.

1. **Family as Unit of Service** Will more holistic and family centered treatment approaches emerge which will shift the definition of "client" or "unit of service" from the individual to the family unit? Will the programs of tomorrow admit families into a continuum of services aimed at a broadened concept of family health and family recovery?

2. **The "Disease" of Codependency** Will the movement to define codependency as a disease process—and therefore eligible for service reimbursement continue? What future perspective will be given to those voices inside and outside the substance abuse field who argue that this application of "disease" is inappropriate and of potential long-term harm to the culture of recovery? To what extent will the "codependency" movement lead to a broaden application of addiction and disease concepts to the whole range of human ailments and will such a move be to the benefit or detriment of substance abuse treatment?

3. **Specialty Services** To what extent will specialized family components that focus on healing and enhanced effectiveness in marital/adult-adult relationships, parent-child relationships and child-child sibling relationships become integrated into all treatment and self-help components of the culture of recovery?

4. **Continuum of Care** What will eventually emerge as the ideal continuum of family-oriented substance abuse services? Based on a developmental model of family recovery, will treatment programs offer family oriented treatment interventions and support processes strategically timed over the span of long-term recovery? Will this continuum of services maintain or lose its substance abuse specificity?

C. *Balancing the Four Levels of Family Healing* As the culture of recovery becomes an increasingly family shaped and family serving culture, there will be a continued evolution of treatment and self-help services. Such services will begin to isolate four distinct dimensions of family recovery.

1. Each individual family member—addicted and non-addicted—has his or her own personal recovery process which involves a restructuring of addiction shaped patterns of thinking, feeling and behaving.

2. There are adult relationships—the marital or intimate relationship dyad—which also require a recovery process, separate and distinct from each member's individual recovery process. This dimension would also embrace healing the breach in the broader extended family relationships that frequently accompany the addiction process.

3. Parent-child relationships must also be reviewed and reconstructed within the broad scheme of family recovery. The establishment or restoration of parental functioning is paramount.

4. The family adaptation to addiction may also be accompanied by a deterioration in child-child, sibling relationships within the family, the reconstruction of which may constitute a fourth dimension of family healing.

Family recovery thus proceeds along four tracks. Treatment and self-help resources which focus on the individual recovery process are rapidly expanding for all family members. Areas of needed development within the culture of recovery involve specialized knowledge and resources that address healing and enhanced skills in adult-adult relationships, healing and enhanced parental effectiveness in parent-child relationships and healing in child-child relationships.

Perhaps what is most needed is a model that helps explain how these four tracks are integrated into a process of family recovery. What is the relationship between individual recovery and the healing of adult-adult and parent-child relationships? Are there developmental stages and predictable time frames within which the restoration of these relationships occurs? What are the consequences of individual recoveries progressing independently from and at the expense of adult-adult and parent-child relationships? Are there risks that therapeutic and educational work with families in early recovery could, through unrealistic expectations or inappropriate and ill-timed interventions, rupture rather than restore family relationships? What is needed is a developmental model of family recovery—a model that reveals the developmental sequence of family recovery and defines types of treatment and support activities that are appropriate for each stage of recovery.

D. *Developmental Stages of Family Recovery* From the early work of Dr. E.M. Jellinek (1960) to the more recent work of Stephanie Brown (1985), the substance abuse field has slowly begun to construct a developmental model of addiction recovery. Such a model provides a research based understanding of the stages or steps of addiction recovery and the sequence and timeliness most frequently associated with each step. Models such as these are immensely important as they facilitate the construction of treatment models through which staff expectations and intervention technologies can be tailored to developmental tasks appropriate to a particular stage of recovery. These models are focused on the individual recovery process and are based on data collected from recovering addicts. The role of family in the recovery process is being explored primarily through the eyes and experience of the recovering person. This section, which is more a plea for knowledge than a summary of knowledge, will further explore the need for a developmental model of family recovery.

What is known about the family-transforming power of addictive disorders? Both research and folk wisdom on this topic suggests that addiction results in:

- a radical transformation of family roles that can include a reversal in parent-child roles; a disordered division of family labor created by the overfunctioning of some members and the underfunctioning of others; and the construction of roles which protect the addict and the family from the consequences of addiction.
- a reformulation of family rules designed to protect the family and sustain addiction, *e.g.*, silence, denial, isolation.
- decreased boundary transactions with the outside world resulting from increased isolation and internal enmeshment,
- pervasive feelings of shame and guilt driving problems of low self-esteem for all family members.
- an addiction-shaping influence on, and eventual dissolution of rituals of, family leisure.
- a repression of all feelings, particularly anger and fear.
- an increase in stress-related medical problems within the family.
- the development of rigid and judgmental attitudes.
- an increase in compulsive behaviors of all types.

Treatment professionals know a great deal about what addiction has done to the family system and to individual family members. It is also known by implication that many of these same dimensions (roles, rules, and rituals) must be changed through the recovery process. But what is known about the developmental sequence through which such changes can and should occur? The answer is that treatment professionals *know* very little. We may have personal experience or instincts that can guide our expectations and our interventions, but the fact is there is no research-based models to guide the understanding of the developmental stages of healing in the addiction impaired family and how professional helpers can provide developmentally appropriate assistance.

Until such time as research allows us to create developmental models of family recovery, great care must be taken in our work with recovering families. Treatment professionals are developing increasing abilities to articulate and diagnose addiction-driven family pathology. Families, through our guidance, can easily self-identify all the areas of family life that need to change. The danger lies in our less than ideal capacity to understand and assist families with the long term reversal of such problems.   One may overdiagnose and escalate expectations for family functioning that are unrealistic and developmentally inappropriate for the early months of recovery. In the effort to reverse family pathology, there is a risk of setting up failure and emotional or physical disengagement. There is a risk of creating impotence in one's desire to empower. In the efforts to establish a new sobriety-based equilibrium in the family, there is the risk of violating the fragile defenses that provide stability and safety through early recovery.

Until there are research-driven models of long-term family recovery, the motto for family intervention should be, "Easy Does It." As professionals in the culture, we know the frequently reported transformation of family life that accompanies addiction and we know what families look like in the earliest weeks of recovery. Most of us have no idea of the sequelae of family recovery beyond this point. We don't know what "normal" recovering families look like at one year, five years or ten years into the recovery process. We don't have norms that tell us realistic expectations for the evolution of family roles and rules.

Until there is a foundation of knowledge based on long term family recovery, the field would do well to rely heavily on family centered self-help components within the culture of recovery, *e.g.,* Al-Anon, NarAnon, Co-Anon, and Families Anonymous. The oral history and collective experience within such groups may be the closest thing that exists to a developmental model of family recovery. Given the current state of knowledge, it would be to our credit as addiction professionals to approach such groups as students rather than teachers.

The above discussion does not suggest the abdication of aggressive family-oriented, professional addiction service models. It does suggest the need for a high degree of humility and gentleness as one enters the life of the recovering family. The substance abuse field (and co-dependency movement) would do well to heed the oath of a sister profession: "First do no harm!"

E. *The Intimacy Crisis: The Culture as Buffer* There is great danger if the emotions accompanying early sobriety must be absorbed totally within a marriage or other intimate relationship. Such relationships, which have weathered active addiction, can be tested to the breaking point in early recovery. How many addicts have reactivated their addictions to alcohol, nicotine, or other drugs when this breaking point was nearing? What is the nature of this crisis and what role can the culture of recovery play in easing family passage through this period?

A crisis in intimate relationships is fairly predictable early in recovery. That should be the first and oft repeated message to couples in early recovery. This message can be elaborated and underscored by the following.

- Addicts are quite uncomfortable in their struggle to re-establish some form of physiological and psychological balance without the drug. In short, they may be a lot more obnoxious and intolerable during early recovery than they were when they were drinking/drugging.

- Don't feel guilty if you find yourself thinking that you liked him/her much better when they were using. Such feelings don't mean you're a bad person; they are normal.
- The drug was the most powerful relationship in the addict's life. It was the lover you could never compete with. With that relationship gone, all other relationships must now be redefined.
- Don't be surprised at increased fears your partner or spouse won't like you now that he or she is sober. These feelings are normal. They are part of what happened to you and your esteem in the addiction process. They are part of what must be addressed in *your* recovery.
- The most significant threat to your relationship will be if your partner proceeds with his or her recovery without you being involved in a parallel recovery process.
- Both of you need persons outside the relationship to assist and support you through this readjustment process.

- Don't be surprised when you find yourself sometimes resenting the other person's personal recovery activities. Such feelings spring from the myth that we should be able to meet all of the needs of our partner and from our fears of abandonment. Separate recovery paths must proceed and accompany the recovery and rebuilding of the relationship.

Without some form of buffer between individuals involved in early recovery, the relationship is at high risk for termination. The stress and pain and joy of restructuring intimate relationships in early recovery needs to be spread over a broad network of people. By providing human buffers, the culture of recovery decreases the pressure on the marital or intimate relationship, provides parallel pathways of recovery, and provides folk wisdom on the trials of relationship recovery. Cultural supports diffuse the intensity of emotional needs that must be met inside the relationship. Cultural supports decrease relationship mythmaking—those unrealistic fantasies of what he/she should be in recovery and what the relationship should be. Cultural supports also provide a forum for reality-testing about relationship issues in early recovery.

There are also conditions under which a relationship seen in the bright light of early recovery is so toxic in its effects on both partners that the relationship must be terminated. In this situation, the culture can play an important role in supporting the individuals through the process of dissolution of the relationship. The culture can also act to keep under control the neophyte's propensity to rush into new, equally toxic relationships.

F.   *Parenting in the Culture of Recovery*   Parenting is a highly neglected issue in the culture of recovery. Addiction-related turbulence in adult intimacy relationships and addiction-related emotional conflict in parent-child relationships are often a focus of treatment.   The identification and remediation of sustained deficiencies in knowledge and skills of how to parent rarely occurs. Such neglect emerges out of a number of assumptions about the nature of parenting during addiction and recovery.

Assumption One:	Knowledge and skills of parenting once existed in the addict and the addict's spouse but deteriorated through the progression of addiction.

This assumption is quite suspect, particularly when applied to all addicts. Given that a significant number of addicts report family histories of multiple generations of addiction and histories of emotional, physical and sexual abuse, where would such skills have been acquired? It is quite clear that for many addicts, there existed no role models or environments through which such knowledge and skills could be transmitted. Even where such abuse was lacking, it may be questionable to assume the existence of effective parenting skills.

Assumption Two: If the addict is able through treatment to achieve sustained sobriety, the problems of parental functioning will be automatically reversed.

Assumption Three: The abuse of children by an addicted parent resulted from the loss of control and radical personality change inherent in the addiction process; abuse will stop automatically with sustained sobriety.

Assumptions two and three suggest that recovery from addiction is accompanied by a reversal of pathology in, and a spontaneous regeneration of health and effectiveness in, the parent-child relationship. It is the author's experience that such spontaneous reversal rarely exists and that the regeneration of love, respect and mutuality in the parent-child relationship does not always occur as a result of parental sobriety. Where such regeneration occurs, it is more a function of extraordinary effort and perseverance than of spontaneity. Assumption three, while true for many addicted parents, is a dangerous assumption when applied to the total universe of addicted parents. For some parents, the etiological roots of abusive behavior are separate and distinct from addiction and will require treatment and interventions that far transcend the traditional mediums of addiction recovery.

Assumption Four: Parent effectiveness can be expected
                                to return (or develop) during early
                                recovery.

Research advances are just beginning to unravel the sequential
stages that mark recovery from addiction. While the speed and
sequential steps in recovery clearly reflect differences from
individual to individual, it can be stated with some assurance that
the emergence or re-emergence of quality parenting for many
recovering addicts and their spouses occurs during middle or late
stages of recovery. This suggests that our expectations related to
the full return or development of parental functioning in
recovering addicts and spouses should perhaps be measured in
years rather than weeks or months. This also suggests that whole
new vehicles of child support may need to evolve to nurture
children during the period that precedes the emergence of parental
effectiveness.

Assumption Five: Parental functioning is primarily a
                                concern for women addicts.

Few would explicitly verbalize or admit support for the above
proposition, but much of the clinical practice in today's substance
abuse treatment programs hinge on this view. Parental
functioning, for example, is a major issue as therapists explore
"powerlessness and unmanageability" with women and yet it
constitutes an omitted or minor issue in these same discussions
with men. Consequences of addiction for women are defined
through impairment of roles inside the family. Consequences for
men tend to be defined through impairment of roles outside the
family. Focus on internal family functioning for men addresses
marital, but rarely, parental relationships.

Assumption Six: Children of addicts will welcome the
                                           sobriety   and   re-assumption   of
                                           authority of the addicted parent.

Parental sobriety, while desired, constitutes a sudden and dramatic
change thrust upon children who have adapted to both the subtle
and blatant transformations of the addicted parent. Jerry, having
adapted to his father's physical and emotional absence, resents his
father's sudden intrusiveness in early recovery. Ruth, having
floundered through adolescence with no parentally imposed limits,
suddenly rebels at the overcontrolling and overprotective behavior
of her recently sober mother. Eric, a frequent victim of his father's
drunken rage, finds himself both angry and mistrustful in response
to the overindulgence of his newly recovering father. Having
adapted to the pathology of addiction, the children of addicted
parents must go through renewed adaptations to parental sobriety.
Both the pace and intensity of changes precipitated by
treatment/recovery of a parent are likely, in the absence of
specialized supports, to trigger heightened defenses, increased
resistance and sabotage behaviors from his or her children.

The above discussion highlights the need to elevate the issue of
parental effectiveness within the culture of recovery. Options to
enhance the effectiveness of parenting in the culture of recovery
which can be initiated through the leadership of local treatment
programs include the following:

- Exploration of parenting skills acquired in families of
  origin of addict and spouse.
- Heightened focus on impairment of parental functioning
  as an assessment/treatment issue for men.
- Forums through which recovering addicts can explore
  parenting, motherhood, and fatherhood as a long-term
  recovery issue.

- Articles or parenting advice columns included within newsletters sent to recovering alumni and their spouses.
- Sponsorship of parenting training workshops and seminars.
- Support of local parenting/family health focused support groups such as Tough Love or Families Anonymous.
- On-going "family nights" where children and parents meet to ventilate and resolve pain, problems and issues in parent-child relationships.

G. *Breaking the Transgenerational Cycle of Addiction* There is overwhelming evidence that suggests that addiction presents itself not through the randomness of the roulette wheel but through more predictable patterns of genetically influenced family transmission. Our concern with family is thus not just the adaptation of a single nuclear family to an addicted member, but rather on a much broader perspective of the transmission of physical and family pathology across multiple generations.

Children who spring from family trees which contain addicted members are much more likely to become addicted than are persons without such histories. Children of addicts have measurably altered physiology that presents itself through biological markers such as EEG-measured alpha activity and developmental markers such as increased incidence of hyperactivity and attention deficit disorders. Children raised in alcoholic families are more likely as adults to marry alcoholics or other persons with some chronic disability. Persons abused as children are themselves at risk to abuse their own children. Examined over lifetimes, issues of biology, psychology and social environment come together in 'some families with devastatingly predictable consequences. As a clearer image emerges of the transgenerational nature of addiction, perhaps the substance abuse field will find beginning answers to such questions as the following.

- How can one diagnose children at high risk for addiction and related pathologies and intervene to alter this risk prior to onset of the person-drug relationship?
- How and when does one break this cycle of transgenerational transmission of addiction and related pathologies? Must people continue to be lost and must people from the same families be treated generation after generation?
- How can persons whose involvement in the culture of addiction began at conception be resocialized? They were born in this culture, learned values in this culture and shaped their identities within this culture. They know no other world. Without intervention, their children will enter the same life. How and when do we break the cycle?
- Are current interventions of sufficient power and duration not only to treat the individual addict but also to break the continued transmission of addiction and related pathologies to the addict's progeny?

It is with great sadness that treatment professionals witness recovering adults, finally achieving sobriety and emotional healing in their own lives, who are suddenly confronted with the painful reality of addiction in a son or daughter. Perhaps it has been enough in the past fifty years to have discovered pathways of recovery from addiction. The challenge for the next fifty years will be to evolve technology within the culture of recovery that stops the transmission of addiction to one's descendants. Looking back at chemical slavery spanning generations, we must eventually find the means to say, "Here it stops!"

H. *The Culture as Surrogate Family* For many culturally enmeshed addicts, the culture of recovery must become their family. Whether through death or physical/emotional disengagement, many culturally enmeshed addicts have been cut off from family. The culture of recovery from its earliest historical inception has served to fill the void of loss of family. Treatment programs and self-help appendages such as treatment alumni associations, drop-in centers, and Alano clubs can greatly benefit by understanding their need to take over certain family functions for the culturally enmeshed addict. The ability of the culture of recovery to provide this role of surrogate family can be enriched through such activities as follows.

1. **Create an open door.** Family life at its best connotes places of "asylum," places of shelter and safety where one is always welcome. This openness ("you're part of the family; stop by anytime") can be consciously cultivated in key institutions within the culture of recovery. Treatment programs that lose their vitality and specialness often do so when this open door becomes closed through some misguided notion of "professionalism."

2. **Create belonging.** Once through the open door of institutions within the culture of recovery, both oldtimers and newly arrived members must feel a sense of belonging. They are welcomed. They are part of a broader network. Others are glad to see them. They are missed when they are not there. People here share common histories that are reflected in oft-told stories and new stories are always welcome. People feel a sense of "home" when in cultural environments. Residence West, an extended residential aftercare program in Elgin, Illinois, enhances this identification by keeping personalized coffee cups hanging on a wall for its current residents and returning alumni. One is emotionally linked to the treatment center in the same manner one is linked to a birthplace.

3. **Provide physical nurturing.** One is physically touched in this culture. Hands are shaken and patted. Pats on the back and arms around shoulders are commonplace. Hugs are exchanged. There is concern about one's physical self—how one looks and how one is taking care of oneself. There is bantering and affectionate concern expressed around self-care issues.

4. **Provide rituals of gathering.** The culture provides an alternative locus for normal family gathering times such as holidays. There is a deep recognition of the lonely vacuum persons disengaged from families feel during such times (and the risk of relapse posed by such occasions). The culture takes an active role in filling the vacuum of such high risk periods. The sharing of time during such occasions intensifies the bonds to the culture and between cultural members.

5. **Provide assistance with daily living.** The culture of recovery, like the healthy family, provides a forum for sharing and assisting with problems of daily living. The culture is an informal resource bank that, like the family, can be tapped for special information or special help.

11.17 *Social Relationships*   The social worlds in the cultures of addiction and recovery are radically different. This section will explore how to facilitate the client's journey from one world to the other.

A. *Managing Visitors in the Treatment Milieu*   The first tasks in the treatment of the culturally enmeshed addict is to extricate the addict from the culture of addiction, assure continued isolation from this culture and to provide an environment of safety within which the client can begin a process of cultural disengagement and decompression. These tasks cannot be achieved without control over the client's boundary transactions with the world outside the treatment setting. Quite specifically, this involves varying degrees of regulation of visitors as well as telephone contact with the outside world until such time as the client demonstrates an ability to manage such contact responsibly. The degree of regulation will vary greatly depending upon the characteristics of the client population. As a general rule, the greater the degree of cultural enmeshment of clients, the greater the degree of restriction in contact with the outside world.

Left unchecked, the culturally enmeshed addict will attempt to sustain drug supply and the drug relationship within the treatment milieu as well as sustain contact with the culture which supports this relationship. It is a clinical absurdity to blame and punish the enmeshed addict for bringing drugs into the treatment milieu. Such behavior is the very essence of addiction. If by definition the client chronically experiences inability to abstain from drug use and loss of control in the drug relationship, can such power and control be expected as a precondition for entry into treatment? It is a program's power and control, not the client's, that must assure the existence of a drug-free milieu.

Continued contact with the culture of addiction while in treatment precipitates a continuing state of regression by the client. Any client progress achieved during treatment activities is immediately sabotaged through face-to-face or telephone contact with representatives from the culture of addiction. How many counselors have left work at the end of a day pleased with a particular client's progress, only to return the next morning to find the client again regressed in attitude or behavior? Some counselors often instinctively feel as if they are competing with some unknown ghosts for the life of the client. Such ghosts are often quite real members of the culture of addiction who reinforce the client's affiliation with this culture through their visits or telephone contacts.   Clients have a right to a drug free environment unencumbered by contamination from the culture of addiction.

Once the culturally enmeshed client has been disengaged from the culture of addiction, the formal assessment of the client's social world and the reconstruction of this world can begin.

B. *Assessing and Transforming Social Relationships* In an earlier discussion of assessing the nature and intensity of cultural involvement at client admission to treatment, a technique was described which involved the construction of a diagram of the client's social network.   Persons in this diagram could then be assessed as to whether they would inhibit or support the client's involvement in treatment and long-term recovery.   Through such assessment processes, each client wrestles with the question, "Who are my 'real' friends?"   As a result of such examinations, most clients quickly recognize the superficiality and mutual exploitation involved in relationships within the culture of addiction.   This process speeds and strengthens the client's social disengagement from the culture of addiction.

Assessment and treatment planning issues related to the reconstruction of the client's social world include the following.

- Are there existing family, extended family and social network relationships which are supportive of the client's recovery?
- Are there extended family relationships and activities which the client would like to re-establish?
- Are there constructive social relationships that were lost due to the client's addictive behavior? Are there some of these relationships which the client would like to renew?

- Are there historical deficits or deterioration in the client's relationship-building skills? What particular skill areas are most needed for the early stages of recovery?

One of the significant powers of self-help groups is that they offer not only a program of recovery but also a social world in which that recovery can be nurtured. It is important that clients be oriented and afforded opportunities to experience this social world. They must see AA or NA as an elaborate network of relationships and activities, with formal meetings constituting only one element of this world. Within this world, clients can begin the construction of a sobriety based network of friends and associates.

C. *From Suicide Pacts to Sponsorship* The culture of addiction and the culture of recovery mirror each other in many respects. There exists in both a few key relationships that wield extraordinary power and influence to sustain either addiction or recovery. One of the major tasks in treatment is to sever the former and create the latter.

Most addicts have a small number of relationships whose glue is a pact of mutual self-destruction. Constant and excessive alcohol and drug use is so bound into the relationship that the mere presence of the person is a powerful stimulus for use. Each of the partners in such a pact is bound to sustain both their own addiction, as well as the addiction of their partner. Efforts at self-imposed sobriety by one partner in such a pact will trigger aggressive efforts of sabotage from the other partner. Relationships such as this contain an implicit suicide pact that serve as a powerful obstacle to recovery and a major stimulus for relapse. The tasks of the treatment professional are to:

- Identify the existence of pathology-bonded relationships,

- Explore and make explicit with the client the exact nature and import of these relationships,
- Introduce and reinforce the concept of "toxic" or "poisonous" relationships as a potentially life-threatening obstacle to recovery,
- Stimulate and strengthen the client's recognition of the need to terminate pathology-bonded relationships, and
- Provide skill training and emotional support to assist the client in terminating such relationships.

Clients can be helped to identify pathology-bonded relationships by using the following relationship checklist.

_____ I frequently break promises and resolutions I have made to myself or others when I am with this person.

_____ I like this person but I have often thought that we probably weren't good for each other.

_____ It is very difficult for me to imagine being with this person sober.

_____ I often feel guilty about what I did when I was with this person.

_____ I don't think I have any willpower when I am with this person.

_____ I think this person brings out the worst in me; I might also bring out the worst in him/her.

_____ I do crazy things with this person that I don't do with other people.

_____ This person can really get to me; I tend to do very explosive or impulsive things when I see him/her.

Those special and powerful pathology-bonded relationships in the client's life must be replaced by equally special and powerful recovery-bonded relationships. While the newly recovering persons may develop many new and supportive acquaintances and associates, it is those few very powerful relationships of friend and mentor that bind one most closely to the culture of recovery. Most contexts, within which addicted people have discovered and sustained sobriety, provided this medium of "sponsor," "big brother/sister," "elder" or "strength." These roles are characterized not by professional detachment but by the desire and openness to be with the client in the recovery process. These roles serve to protect, teach, guide, support and share. By creating treatment milieus rich with heroes and heroines, one enhances the development of these very special relationships that historically have been so important in recovery from addiction.

D. *From Anti-Drug to Non-Drug Relationships*   Many recovering addicts go through fairly predictable stages in the reconstruction of their social world. The earliest stages, as noted above, are marked by the severing of relationship ties within the culture of addiction. When completed, this obviously produces a huge social vacuum in the life of the addict. The next stage of development involves the establishment of anti-drug relationships. The reconstruction of the social world begins with a social network of persons who share the new anti-drug, pro-abstinence values. At this stage, the recovering person's complete social world may consist of the world of AA or NA or the church.

The social world of the self-help or religious group constitutes a decompression chamber within which addicts build physical and emotional distance between themselves and the culture of addiction. Within the safety of this new world, recovering addicts can solidify the foundation of their sobriety through the construction of a new recovery- based defense structure. Once this new defense structure has been constructed and tested, addicts can then begin to extend themselves into a broader social world in which relationships are based on shared interests and experiences that transcend the issues of addiction and recovery. In this latter phase, the social world is expanded beyond the self-help or religious support group. Having painfully confronted the identity of addiction and nurtured the identity of recovery, one can now take on new identities which, while not denying addiction-/recovery, add new dimensions to one's activities and relationships.

11.18 *Time Orientation* The transformation in one's orientation to time that accompanies the addiction process must be examined and restructured during treatment. From the learned use of the past and future as justification and fuel for one's drug use to the organization of one's daily schedule, addiction-shaped orientation to time must be confronted and changed.

A. *From Addiction Time to Recovery Time* It was noted earlier that time in the culture of addiction is organized around the immediacy needs of its members. All life is condensed to immediate need to maintain drug supply, sustain drug use, postpone or medicate sickness, and avoid consequences of use. Whereas most other elements of the culture of addiction must be transformed within the culture of addiction, the issue of "immediacy" is an exception. Twelve step programs simply take the time orientation to which addicts were already acclimated (immediacy) and made it the basic time unit (24 hours) of recovery. Immediacy which in the past served addiction, now serves sobriety.

Whereas the "now" orientation can transfer from one culture to another, the addict's construction of past and future requires radical transformation within the culture of recovery. The addict's learned use of past and future to sustain and justify his or her addiction constitutes a major source of sabotage in early recovery if left intact.

Addicts have long been known to dwell on the past and use the past to fuel and justify their drug use. Phrases like "let it go" and "turn it over" are often heard sprinkled through conversations in the culture of recovery when the past is raised in the old way. The old formula of self-pity (painful preoccupation with the past) equals self-destruction (activation of addiction through relapse) must be broken. This shift from projection of blame to personal accountability will be explored in greater detail in the discussion of the "construction and telling of one's story" as a major milestone and activity in the culture of recovery.

Continuing the addict's conception of the future can be equally risky to recovery. To the addict, the future is haunted by alternating delusions of grandiose success and impending doom—both of which serve to fuel and justify current intoxication. Like the past, one's mental movement into the future must be approached with great care, if not eliminated completely in recovery. Some tribal groups within the culture of recovery reinforce this new time orientation in fairly extreme terms. The following remark from one such tribal member typifies this stance: "Worry? What for? Once you've turned your will and your life over to God, what happens to you after that is none of your business."

Immediacy (hour-by-hour; day-by-day) must be reinforced as the time unit of recovery. All recovery pathways must structure past and future in ways that emasculate their historical ability to fuel intoxication.

B. *Daily Schedules* If past and future are to be banished, one is then left with organizing existence into a style of daily living. In the absence of addiction related activities, the addict's daily schedule is suddenly filled with open space. If the people, places and activities in the addict's life are all related to addiction and treatment strips them from the daily life of the addict, then what is to fill this void? This question strikes the heart of the relapse prevention issue.

There are two treatment tasks related to this current discussion. The client must first be helped to assess the extent to which his or her daily schedule has become dominated with addiction related activities. This exercise is intended to determine the nature and magnitude of changes in the client's daily lifestyle necessary for continued sobriety. Once completed, the client can be helped to begin the reconstruction of a sobriety-based daily lifestyle. Both of these elements can be achieved by actually working out daily activities. The construction of one week schedules, in which the client first constructs a typical pre-treatment weekly schedule is quite helpful. The schedule is an hour by hour, seven day schedule, allowing a detailed analysis of both weekday and weekend time and activity rituals. When completed, the client can circle those daily activities which will be deleted in the post-treatment schedule. The circles are then used as the basis for creating and selecting alternative post-treatment activities. No culturally enmeshed addict should leave treatment without extensive work on the construction of this daily schedule. The rigorous monitoring of such schedules should constitute a significant portion of aftercare counseling.

C. *Sleep and the Body's Biological Clock*   A frequent issue that surfaces with culturally enmeshed addicts relates to their daily pattern of sleep. The issue, in fact, encompasses two distinct problems.

1. The addictive lifestyle may create a daily pattern of living in which the schedule of sleeping is dramatically out of synch with the rest of the world.

2. The physiology of sleep for many addicts has been altered such that natural sleep has been lost and replaced by drug-induced sleep.

When addicts enter treatment, they inevitably bring with them patterns of sleep and wakeful activity from the culture of addiction. Many want to stay up all night and sleep all day. Some even defensively report that they were up half the night in a bull session talking about things important to their recovery—even claiming that the bull session was better than group. While the content of the bull session may have focused on recovery, it was quite likely being conducted on addiction time. Patterns of staying up half the night, sleeping through morning activities and daytime napping must be confronted as a continuation of the addiction time cycle. The treatment milieu must establish a framework of time within which the addict's daily cycle of sleep and wakefulness can be acclimated to recovery time.

While the structure of a residential milieu can set the structure for appropriate sleeping schedules, it does not necessarily guarantee that sleep will easily occur. A large number of addicts experience disturbances in sleeping during early recovery. Such disturbances may include inability to get to sleep, early awakening with inability to regain sleep, sleeping without restfulness (failure to achieve REM sleep), disturbing dream and nightmare activity (particularly those involving drug use or drug-related events), and excessive sleeping. Clients must come to understand the physiology of sleep and how their normal biological cycles have been disrupted by drug use. Such education helps clients understand the nature of the adjustment process their bodies experience in early recovery. While any enduring problem of sleep disturbance needs to be medically evaluated, the following can prove quite helpful in speeding the return of natural, non-drug-induced sleep.

- Eliminate consumption of all daily caffeine and closely regulate (if not eliminate) nicotine consumption at end of day.
- Prohibit daytime napping by any clients experiencing delayed onset of sleep.
- Provide some form of aerobic stimulation, *e.g.*, walking, approximately 90-120 minutes prior to bedtime.
- Provide a snack, preferably a complex carbohydrate such as milk, before bedtime.
- Teach clients techniques which lower level of physiological arousal such as progressive relaxation, breathwork, and visualization.
- Utilize neutral relaxation tapes (rain, ocean) to block out sleep-disrupting auditory stimuli.

Through a combination of structure, technique and encouragement, clients can be helped to regain non-drug induced sleep and to do so on a schedule that reinforces recovery rather than addiction.

11.19 *Violence* The dramatic escalation of violence in the culture of addiction is requiring new adaptations in the culture of recovery. The culture of recovery must provide emotional decompression for neophytes who have been traumatized by violence, must stigmatize and prohibit violence in the culture of recovery and must evolve new assessment and treatment approaches for clients who are perpetrators and victims of violence.

A. *Decompression* An increasing number of clients are entering substance abuse treatment programs reporting both remote and recent episodes of physical and/or sexual assault. They often present with sleep disturbances, emotional numbing, guarded and mechanical relationships with others, hypervigilance, impaired memory and concentration and impulsive and aggressive behavior. Such symptoms are usually seen by treatment staff as simply a result of the substance abuse disorder. A growing number of programs are recognizing these symptoms as a form of post traumatic stress disorder (PTSD) triggered by the experience of violence. The emerging view is that this disorder can be both a factor initiating substance abuse and a factor fueling patterns of self-defeating behavior that serve to sabotage recovery efforts. Given changes in the culture of addiction in the United States, treatment efforts must increasingly address violence induced PTSD as a component of substance abuse treatment. The author has found the following understandings crucial to effective responses to violence-related PTSD.

- The emotional decompression of the client with PTSD must occur in an environment that, above all, assures physical and psychological safety.
- The recollection and reporting of violent trauma must be repeated until there is both the experience and release of suppressed emotion.
- Emotional thawing and catharsis for the PTSD client occurs through multiple episodes of recollection and disclosure. The traumatic events, which often play a central role in the client's presentation of his or her recovery story, dissipate in intensity and importance in late recovery.
- The client must be helped to identify the link between trauma and self-defeating patterns of behavior.
- The client must learn to recognize those situations or stimuli that trigger self-defeating behavior.
- The emotional thawing and replacement of self-defeating behaviors with more adaptive defense structures is a developmental process spanning months and years.
- Psychotherapy and specialized self-help groups can be helpful adjuncts to substance abuse treatment for clients with PTSD.

- Both emotional encouragement and skill training are needed to support the client's construction of a more health-enhancing personal and interpersonal style.

It would be helpful if existing and emerging concepts and techniques related to PTSD treatment could be integrated into the substance abuse treatment process.

B. *Stigmatizing Violence* The efforts of the substance abuse field to transmit values that stigmatize and prohibit violence must intensify in light of the dramatic escalation of violence in the culture of addiction. Potential interventions to achieve this goal could include the following.

- the use of values clarification exercises that expose client values related to aggression and violence;
- more active values indoctrination around the issues of violence;
- integration of anti-violence values within the peer culture of treatment;
- repeated stigmatization of violence and threats of violence as the antithesis of recovery values, as stupid, as predatory, as impulsive, and as immoral.

C. *Assessing Risk of Violence* A third component of the substance abuse treatment field's response to increased violence is the development of new assessment technology that helps the treatment professional assess a client's potential threat to the life and safety of others. Clients with histories of violent assault are entering substance abuse treatment in greater numbers than ever before in history. These violent acts may or may not be related to acute or chronic drug impairment. The question, "to what extent did the client's alcohol and drug use influence or cause the violent act" is becoming an increasingly difficult question as clients appear with new characteristics and new values from the culture of addiction. The field's assessment technology needs to catch up with these changes. A technology is desperately needed that allows treatment professionals to answer the question, "does this client, right now, pose significant risks to the life and health of others?"

11.20 *Death* All cultures must develop mechanisms to deal with the inevitability, untimeliness and finality of death. It was noted earlier that beliefs and rituals within the culture of addiction are designed so that even drug-related deaths can be structured to sustain the affirmation and promotion of drug use by tribal members. How is death handled differently in the culture of recovery? How can death be handled within the social fabric of the recovering community to enhance bonds between tribal members and to reaffirm recovery values?

A. *The Fear of Death in Early Recovery* It is somewhat surprising that persons who have engaged in all manner of extreme and exotic forms of risk-taking behavior during active addiction should become so afraid of death in early recovery. During the first sustained entrance into recovery, one looks back with great horror at what are seen for the first time as near death experiences—from thousands of drug-impaired journeys in automobiles, to drug-influenced risks of daring to the sustained chemical assault upon body organs to close brushes with violence in the addictive culture. The fear is an irrational belief that, having cheated the Angels of Death so many times, they will now come and make their claim in some freak accident of sobriety. This fear is intensified as one thinks of others whom he or she has known well from this past culture whose deaths could have been one's own. This transient preoccupation with death and survivor guilt is a normal rite of passage between the cultures of addiction and recovery.

These experiences must be recognized as normal, and opportunities must be provided within the culture of recovery for their full expression and exploration. The intensity of this emotion must be explored rather than pacified or medicated. Treatment staff must be the client's support and guide through (not around) such confusion and pain. It is through the contemplation of such issues that many clients forge their first non-non-non-non-superficial commitment to the search for sobriety. The sober confrontation of such concerns precipitates a form of existential/spiritual crisis that temporarily aborts one's self-destructive inertia and provides a unique opportunity for dramatic change. An inner voice hushed for years by intoxication is both haunting and unnerving in its urgent command, "There is a plan; there is a purpose for which you were saved." It is a metaphor that suggests one has been given life but that this gift carries a burden of duty and responsibility. Acceptance of one's fate to pursue the sometimes circuitous journey in search of this purpose is often the beginning of recovery.

The spiritual crisis inherent in contemplation of near death survival cannot be planned or programmed via treatment interventions. Treatment staff can, however, set the stage for such events by exploring death as an historical theme in the client's life. Treatment professionals can, through acute observation, recognize the presence of such crises and capitalize on the opportunity for change provided by such crises. The intensity of such crises can be sustained and the energy and emotion of such episodes channeled toward life transforming decisions. While fear of death, or its precursors (AIDS) may have been unable to deter use during periods of active addiction, it may be revived during early recovery as an important element within the overall support structure of sobriety.

B. *Tribal Deaths and Reaffirmations* Rituals of grief and mourning exist within the self-help community to mark the passing of members, but such rituals are not fully defined in most treatment programs within the culture of recovery. Treatment programs need to learn from the self-help community how rituals marking the death of a tribal member can serve to celebrate and reaffirm values from the culture of recovery. The following discussion outlines a broad approach, which can be adapted by treatment programs to respond to deaths of clients. The task of the treatment program experiencing the death of a client is to provide rituals of grief and mourning for both staff and clients and to develop rituals in response to the death that can stimulate other clients' recommitment to the recovery process.

There are two very different types of death related rituals depending on the circumstances of how the person died. When a person in the culture of recovery dies sober, it is experienced as a loss, but a very triumphant loss. Triumph for the addicted person is to get sober, struggle within that sobriety to live a meaningful existence and to die of something other than alcoholism. When a person achieves these goals, it is appropriate that his or her passing be marked by celebrating this victory over the disease. This personal victory is also a tribal victory. It reaffirms belief and commitment.

The rituals that surround such a death help each surviving member extract the maximum benefit from the loss. At the visitation, funeral, special memorial services, and at meetings and coffeeshops, members retell the stories of the lost member. Words and actions are recalled and extolled that serve as guidance for those left behind. It is as if each person must get for themselves the most important personal lesson from the passing member's life.

The stories of some deaths so exemplify cultural values that they get institutionalized in mythical proportions and are retold for years and years during tribal gatherings. The story of Sharon was one such heroic tale. Sharon was a frail woman who came into alcoholism treatment at a young age but very late in the progression of her disease. She was told early in treatment that she had late stage liver disease and that her prospects for living beyond another year were very slim. In spite of the absence of pressure to continue her alcoholism treatment, Sharon threw herself deeply into the treatment experience seeking to rebuild and draw from her remaining time all that she had destroyed and missed in her life. She remained sober and deeply enriched her relationships with her family in the coming months. The progression of her illness was marked by extreme pain and discomfort. The day before she died, her pain was so intense that her husband, feeling desperate and powerless, offered to get her a bottle if she thought it would help. He would later report that she simply smiled at his thoughtfulness and responded, "I've come this far; I'm going out sober!" This story became an often told heroic tale within Sharon's local culture of recovery. While the length of Sharon's sobriety would only be measured in months; the quality of her sobriety, her courage, and the strength of her commitment would afford her a certain immortality. Tales such as Sharon's serve as a reaffirmation of faith for the recovering community.

If sober deaths offer a celebration of cultural values, then what of member deaths related to relapse? How do we make sense out of relapse deaths in ways that can increase bonds within and enhance values of the recovering community? The relapse related death holds a mirror up to the recovering community, allowing each member to vicariously experience his or her own relapse and death. "There but for the grace of God go I" is a frequent remark heard marking the relapse death of a tribal member. Relapse deaths reaffirm the stakes involved in the recovery process.

Through rituals involving relapse deaths, individuals can acknowledge the disease's lethality, reaffirm the struggle and battle against the disease and draw lessons from the life of the passing member that will better prepare them to sustain continued recovery. To some degree, relapse deaths serve as a type of martyrdom—the life of the deceased member is given meaning by using his or her experience to sustain life for those left behind. In this manner, the death of one member can enhance the adaptability and survivability of remaining members.

C. *AIDS and the Culture of Recovery* The broad impact of AIDS on the culture of recovery is beyond the scope of this book, but the following issues are critical in understanding how AIDS is placing new demands on the culture's efforts to help its members respond to terminal disease and death.

- There are growing numbers of persons in the culture of recovery who are HIV positive, have ARC (AIDS Related Complex) or who have AIDS. The growing specialization in the culture of recovery must include both counseling and self-help groups to meet the unique needs of these individuals.
- Some of the darkest stories of the AIDS epidemic are being shared in counselor offices—stories of predatory and unsafe sex practices by HIV positive individuals who know (but in their rage disregard) that such actions will bring death to others. Addressing the rage and guilt of HIV positive addicts entering treatment must be brought into standard clinical practice.
- The growing presence of terminally ill persons in the culture of recovery opens up a whole new area and dimension of 12 step work.
- The presence of the above individuals in the culture of recovery demands the creation of new heroes and

heroines whose lives—captured in myth and story—extol and emphasize the quality rather than the quantity of sobriety?

- The role of substance abuse counselors in (or their response to) planned and assisted suicides will emerge as a major ethical question in the next decade.

D. *The Problem of Anticipatory Grief* Anticipatory grief is a process through which one begins to emotionally rehearse the experience of an expected loss. One actually begins the process of grief and mourning before the actual loss occurs. Anticipatory grief poses special dilemmas for the various members of the culture of recovery.

1. **The Addict** Many late stage addicts experience their own death as imminent and begin to grieve for the multiple losses implicit in this death. They may have so fully experienced their imminent demise that there has, in fact, been a death of the self. Life has been reviewed repeatedly, including its final end, almost as if a pact with death has already been sealed. They have, in short, already grieved their own death. These addicts may never be seen in treatment or they may be repeatedly admitted for detoxification until the task of drugging themselves to death is complete. These clients are trapped in limbo. They have experienced psychological death but their bodies linger on.

Within the culture of recovery today walk living examples of men and women who were brought back to life from a state of psychological death. Treatment professionals can learn lessons from these individuals about methods for promoting such modern resurrections.

- Psychological rebirth is built upon sustained sobriety and the restoration of physical health, even when externally imposed, *e.g.*, halfway house, jail, nursing home.
- The spark of rebirth originates most frequently from outside the self, *i.e.*, sustained involvement and faith of others.
- There must be a leap of faith back into life—a prolonged period of "acting as if"—to initiate and sustain renewing behaviors.
- Life review techniques commonly used with the terminally ill or the aged can be adapted to help rewrite the addict's life script. The consistent messages from treatment staff must be: "Rewrite the last chapter! You are not dead and you don't have to die that way! Start over! An addiction-related death is *not* inevitable! Only you can rewrite the last chapter, but we will be here to help you."
- Rebirth comes from action. Action primes the spiritual pump to regain the experience of living and the experience of connectedness to other living things. If the body acts out self-renewing behaviors long enough, an emotional thawing and psychological rebirth will eventually follow.
- If this premature mourning of the loss of self cannot be reversed, the addict will die. Physical death will be sought as the logical fulfillment of the psychological death which preceded it.

2. The Family The addict's spouse, lover, children, parents, siblings and friends also experience anticipatory grief. They see the addict's progressive impairment, and projecting that impairment to its eventual outcome, begin the process of grieving and emotional disengagement. The death event and the experience of grief are rehearsed so many times that the emotional bonds of the

relationship begin to dissipate.   The relationship becomes
mechanical because, to the family member, the addict is already
dead and buried.   Such anticipatory grief has helped prepare
legions of family members for the day their addicted loved one
dies. The dilemma for the culture of recovery is how to respond
when, rather than dying, this addict suddenly begins a recovery
process. How can family members rebuild a relationship with
someone they have already emotionally grieved and buried? Such
relationship reconstruction must be facilitated with great care and
gentleness.   Treatment efforts which prematurely violate the
family's fragile defense structure (of which anticipatory grief is a
part) will serve to sever rather than rebuild these relationships.
Family intervention and reconstruction models based on earlier
stage addiction may be very inappropriate in this situation. The
self-help communities have evolved separate addict and family
member recovery tracks that may precede by months and years the
emotional reconstruction of intimate/family relationships. Where
anticipatory grief is present, the rebuilding of these relationships
is a middle to late, rather than early stage recovery task.

3. The Professional Helpers Professional helpers, like family
members, can begin to emotionally disengage from a client through
the process of anticipatory grief. Consider the following vignette
from the author's clinical career.

My sage and skilled clinical consultant had been gently probing a
pathway through my defensiveness to explore the source of my
emotional detachment from a client who was involved in extreme,
risk-taking behavior.   Having noted—not to indict, but to
teach—the signs of my detachment, he simply said, "could it be
that you are shrinking from the smell of death?" I had rarely felt
more vulnerable, as this gentle mentor peered into my soul and
talked to me about anticipatory grief. Of course, he was right.
This client's drug use and risk-taking behavior was so out of

control that I always felt the presence of death when I was with the client. I feared the retrospection and sense of failure that would come when the client died. I instinctively understood the enormous emotional energy that would be required to work with this client—a level of intensity that was bound to make the experience of loss more profound. I had visualized the client's death many times. I had picked up the morning paper every day expecting to read of his death. And in anticipation of this loss, I had disconnected. I had depersonalized the client (he was my "garbage can"—a reference to his propensity to consume enormous quantities and varieties of drugs). I had minimized contact through shortened appointments. I was *laissez faire* and nondirective with a client screaming for structure. In short, I had prematurely mourned and buried this client.

How is the problem of anticipatory grief managed within the culture of recovery? If professional helpers are to stay emotionally engaged with our high risk-taking, death-courting clients, there must be special supports for such professionals built into the treatment process. Co-therapy with high risk clients, increased levels of clinical supervision, specialized training and full staff debriefings on all client deaths are examples of such supports.

CORE ACTIVITIES

All cultures have core activities that integrate and define the essence of the culture. In the earlier discussion of the culture of addiction, the work of Agar (1973) was utilized to define four core activities (hustling, copping, getting off, and avoiding busts, burns, ripoffs and hassles) that dominated the daily lifestyle of members within this culture. This section will explore those core activities that define daily lifestyles in the culture of recovery. The essential daily sobriety-sustaining activities in the culture of recovery include:

- Centering Rituals
- Mirroring Rituals
- Self-Constructing Behaviors
- Acts of Service

One of the most essential elements in the treatment of the culturally enmeshed addict is the replacement of core activities from the culture of addiction with these core activities from the culture of recovery. Substance abuse treatment programs throughout the country are beginning to tend to this task within their treatment activities. By instilling such activities from the very initiation of treatment, such programs are facilitating the sobriety-based reconstruction of the daily life of the addict.

12.1 *Centering Rituals*   Centering rituals are highly routinized behaviors which keep one recovery-focused during one's day-to-day activities. They constitute the means through which abstract principles of recovery get personalized and actualized in the play of daily experience. Some centering rituals promoted across tribes within the culture of recovery include the following.

A. *Identity Rituals*   Identity rituals prevent the resurgence of the cognitive defense structures of active addiction, reaffirm one's identity as a recovering addict and reinforce values integral to that recovery process. Common identity rituals include the reading of recovery literature or listening to recovery tapes, carrying symbols from the culture of recovery on one's person, keeping such symbols in one's daily environment (auto, office, home), mixing in brief references to one's recovering status in conversations, or performing the ritual of introduction at self-help meetings ("I'm John and I'm an Alcoholic.").

B. *Focusing and Evaluating Each Day*   Many recovering persons, struggling to master one day at a time living, find it helpful to perform the following ritual. Each morning during a short period of alone time, the person tries to completely clear their mind of past and future and focus on nothing but the forthcoming day. Reviewing both opportunities and challenges, the person tries to focus on the day and actually visualize the experience of going through the day in a manner congruent with the new recovery values. This visual imprint then becomes the pattern to guide actions through the day. At the end of the day, a similar period is taken to go back over the actual performance during the day. The person replays scenes which mirrored the ideal, experiencing strength from the mastery of these areas. Scenes which fell short of this ideal are replayed visually as the person will strive to perform them in the future. Such focusing and evaluating often take place within the broader context of prayer or meditation.

C. *Seeking Strength*   Another centering ritual involves the use of prayer and/or meditation to seek spiritual strength to live the day within one's new recovery values. Many recovering persons begin and end each day with their own special ritual. For many this will mix reading, focusing and evaluating, with prayer and meditation. These rituals strengthen the new values of the recovering addict. Also, the search for strength outside oneself via prayer or meditation steadily weakens drug-shaped narcissism.

D.   *Self-Commands*   Under the best of circumstances, recovering addicts sometimes find themselves slipping rapidly back into old, self-defeating patterns of thinking, feeling or behaving. Occurring often when they have lost touch with the use of the above daily maintenance rituals, these persons now need some ritual to break the spiral of negativism and get themselves centered within the recovery   pathway.   Self-commands,   or   thought-stopping techniques, are examples of such intervention rituals.

Anne brought to her recovery a self-defeating pattern of behavior not uncommon among addicts. She didn't apply for jobs because she was sure she wouldn't be hired. She hadn't considered school because she was sure she was not smart enough. She broke up with a boyfriend because she was sure he was about to break up with her. She hadn't tried treatment before because she was sure she would be unable to live without drugs for the rest of her life. While she was able, in treatment, to identify this pattern of thinking as self-defeating behavior, it continued daily during her early treatment. Anne needed a way to stop the sequence of such thinking once it started and to then consciously and positively reframe her approach to the particular issue. She was taught a self-command technique by her counselor in treatment that allowed her to achieve power and control over this failure promoting style of thinking.   The steps involved in the self-command (and visualization) technique she was taught are as follows.

1. Identify patterns of self-defeating thinking, fully exploring their origin, frequency, triggers, and consequences.
2. Pick a self-command to be used at any time to interrupt the self-defeating thought sequence. (Anne simply yelled "STOP!!!" within her own mind.)
3. Immediately following the command, free your mind of all thoughts, simply relaxing for a few moments.
4. Return to the issue to which the negative sequencing was directed, and visualize various responses that are personally affirming and congruent with recovery values.
5. Select the response about which you feel best and repeat it visually several times.
6. Let your visual rehearsal provide the pattern for your future response.

Self-command techniques are excellent ways to interrupt and shorten episodes of "stinkin' thinkin'," "dry Drunks" and other aberrations of thinking, feeling or behaving that serve to sabotage the recovery process.

E. *Decompression Rituals*   There are times in the daily life of recovery that one needs to retreat into the self and lower one's level of physiological or emotional arousal. Whether this is in response to recurring episodes of drug hunger or other types of physical discomfort or to situational stressors that trigger emotional arousal, it is important that the recovering person learn tools of mastery over such physical and emotional states. Stress management training is increasingly being viewed as an invaluable aid to relapse prevention. The development of a sobriety-based style of managing stress and change and the mastery of specific physical techniques of stress management are being increasingly integrated as client goals into substance abuse treatment milieus. Techniques that may be particularly helpful in lowering physical and emotional arousal include techniques of muscular relaxation, breathing techniques, visualization techniques, self-hypnotic techniques and specialized meditation techniques.

12.2 *Mirroring Rituals* Mirroring rituals have much the same purposes as centering rituals, but they involve interaction with other recovering persons or non-recovering persons who share a recovery-based value system. Mirroring rituals prevent the re-emergence of the addiction based defense structure, support radical abstinence and strengthen the recovery based identity and value system. Mirroring rituals allow persons to define themselves through the characteristics of those with whom they most closely interact. Mirroring rituals can be seen within the self-help meeting structure or in the communications between a cultural member and his or her sponsor.

A. *Mentor Contacts*   Maintaining contact with one's elders, mentors, or sponsors is an important core activity within the culture of recovery. Such persons guide one's initiation into the tribe and provide the oral history which will help guide one through the recovery process. It is through such persons that the collective wisdom of the tribe is transmitted to succeeding generations. Through mentor contact, one can begin to identify characteristics or qualities one would like to develop in oneself. By watching and listening to such mentors one can begin to convert abstract principles and values into action. The values become understandable when presented in the form of behavior. Mentor relationships are quite complex—integrating dimensions of the priest's confessional, the psychotherapist's couch, the teacher's classroom, and the evangelist's pulpit. The relationship is that of brother or sister, and yet there is the hint of parental authority and concern. There is love, but it is the tough love of one who can see inside your soul because they have journeyed the same pathways. They know all the colors of the chameleon because they have been the chameleon.

The phenomenon of mirroring is complex in this relationship. One sees through the mentor the self one has been and hates. The mentor gives one words to name and understand and bury this self. One sees much of what one hopes to become in the mentor. The mentor points out the pathways that lead forward and backwards, but refuses to take away one's freedom to choose either destination or specific pathway. Through the mentor's consistent presence, one can experience in the mirror of this relationship the possibility of hope.

B. *Daily Contact with Other Tribal Members* The propensity for addicts to surround themselves with persons for whom the intensity of drug involvement paralleled their own was noted earlier. In a similar vein, many persons in recovery seek out other recovering persons with whom they can have frequent contact. They look for other recovering persons in their profession, in their workplace, and in their neighborhood. Different in nature and intensity from the mentor or sponsorship relationship, these relationships make up the brotherhood and sisterhood of the recovering community.

Informal contact between tribal members of the culture of recovery serves many functions. Such contact:

- fills the void created when one breaks contact with the culture of addiction,
- provides daily support for sustained sobriety,

- • provides a forum through which new attitudes and values of the neophyte and old timer alike can be affirmed and strengthened,
- • provides an escape valve or safety net when members are confronted with situations that pose a high risk of relapse,
- • provides a safe forum for testing approaches to daily problem-solving, and
- • provides a vehicle for drug-free leisure and laughter.

The active cultivation and maintenance of a sobriety-based social network can be an invaluable source of enrichment to the recovery process. Recovery is not a spectator sport. It is a team sport requiring active and sustained involvement from each member. For the individual to win, the team must win. The daily lifestyle of recovery cannot be sustained from the sidelines. It requires action, involvement, participation. It requires relationship building. It requires relating. The neophyte must learn that recovery requires action in equal intensity to that required to sustain addiction. Recovery requires activism. It requires social activism—social involvement with other recovering people.

C. *Tribal Meetings* Tribal meetings bring members of the culture of recovery together to affirm and cement the "Weness" of their shared identity. Through the act of attending such meetings, pilgrims affirm the reality of their addiction and their commitment to the recovery process. Tribal meetings provide a menu of recovery enhancing activities available to members. The act of attending meetings is actually a series of actions within this core activity, and can include:

- • the decision to attend a meeting on a particular day,
- • the decision of which meeting to attend,
- • the physical act of getting to the meeting,

- the option of meeting with one's mentor before or after the meeting,
- the act of phoning someone to get a ride or offer a ride,
- the act of listening and personalizing what is shared at the meeting,
- the act of speaking and self-disclosing in the meeting,
- the act of reaching out to support another at the meeting,
- the act of contributing financial support to the group,
- the act of socializing and relationship building,
- participation in post-meeting rituals, *e.g.*, informal socializing at restaurants or coffeeshops.

As can be seen from the above list, "making meetings" requires multiple acts that individually and collectively reinforce the recovery process.

The tribal meeting plays a dominant role within almost all of the recovery pathways. What characteristics do tribal meetings share in common that make them such an integral part of the recovery process?

- They provide an intense experience of acceptance and belonging.
- They build esteem through identification with a world-wide and history-making movement.
- They provide a belief system through which shame and defeat can be transformed into victory. They provide a vehicle for psychological and spiritual rebirth.
- They provide a vehicle for the safe discharge of powerful emotions.
- They provide a consistent set of rituals that facilitate emotional decompression and value focusing.
- They provide a forum for consultation on daily problem-solving.

- They provide rituals that allow the tribe to celebrate individual and collective achievements.

12.3 *Self-Constructing Behaviors* Self-constructing behaviors are activities that consciously alter the nature of personal and interpersonal identity. They are actions which shape a new sobriety-based conception of self.

A. *Acts of Self-care* Acts of self-care encompass a broad spectrum of decisions and actions that are integral elements within the daily lifestyle of recovery. In total, they are actions that reflect the return or beginning of self-respect. Acts of self-care include daily rituals that assure proper nutrition, exercise, hygiene and sleep. They include actions to rehabilitate the self, *e.g.* doctor/dentist appointments. They include the sculpting of a sobriety-based image, *e.g.*, dress, removal or altering of tattoos. Acts of self-care include experimenting to discover new sources of non-drug related pleasure. They include creating special self-rewards, *i.e.*, drug-free experiences that enhance pleasure and comfort.

The sudden entry into a recovery process can be extremely disorienting. The central organizing force of the addict's existence, the alcohol/drug axis around which everything has revolved, has been lost. The newly recovering addict is acutely conscious, nearly every waking moment, of this missing ingredient. Acts of self-care are important activities that can fill this unnatural void. Acts of self-care in the early days of sobriety enlist and engage the addict's narcissism in the service of the recovery process.

B. *Telling One's Story* Another self-constructing activity of the recovering addict is the telling of one's story. A later chapter on career milestones in the culture of recovery will explore in some depth the reconstruction of the addict's personal story in the transition from active addiction to recovery. For now, suffice it to say that the old addiction justifying and sustaining story must be shed and a new recovery enhancing life story must be developed in its place. The telling of one's recovery story plays an important role in the daily lives of many recovering addicts.

During the early years of recovery, sharing one's recovery story may be particularly important. First, it is the antithesis of denial. Having resisted and fought off the label of alcoholic or addict for years, the newly recovering may present his or her new story with a frequency and intensity that borders on exhibitionism. Second, such storytelling explains and salvages one's past while generating esteem in the present. After all, the ultimate hero is one for whom personal success is achieved by overcoming great handicaps and adversity. Third, the repetitive, almost compulsive sharing of one's story serves to strengthen the neophyte's fragile hold on recovery.

The power within the ritual of storytelling should never be underestimated. It's as if the repeated presentation of one's story is a magical ritual which keeps the beast within under control. The well constructed story is like an incantation or chant that affords protection from evil. The story is a guilt-purging confession of sin and commitment-instilling profession of faith. The story can reveal the inner world of only half-comprehended thoughts and experiences in ways that allow one to escape self-indictment. Fear can be quieted with the story. Hope can be re-generated. Anger can be quelled. Regret can be released. Resentment can be cast out. Storytelling is a ritual of power within the culture of recovery. It is a ritual that can be simultaneously an act of self-healing and an act of service to others.

Storytelling in early recovery matures into story sharing in later recovery. As recovery unfolds, one's story evolves and the act of story listening is added to the act of storytelling. As the self-consciousness and self-centeredness of early recovery gives way to increased capacity for relationship-building and empathy, the recovering person expands his or. her capacity for reciprocity in relationships.   He or she can be the listener as well as the storyteller. Treatment professionals should patiently look upon the neophyte in recovery, who often exhibits dominance and competitiveness and ineptness in storytelling, as one would look upon the ungraceful, almost spastic steps of the infant.

While the story evolves and the storytelling and story sharing skills increase, the presentation of one's story will remain a core activity throughout recovery.

C. *On Vocations and Vacations* The removal of the drug from the center of the culturally enmeshed addict's life leaves a huge vacuum to be filled. A major element of the recovery initiated construction of self must be the hour-by-hour, day-to-day filling of this vacuum. New daily goals must be formulated. New activities must be developed to achieve these goals. The neophyte in the culture of recovery needs a new way to keep score. In the past, they kept score based on core activities in the life—hustling, copping, getting off, and avoiding busts, burns, rip-offs and hassles. If one achieved the first three and avoided the latter, the game was won that day. The new game requires a new way to keep score.

The recovering addict's daily life—in work and in play—needs to be reshaped to fit the new definition of self. Activities must be found that at a minimum, fill time, and at best, add some sobriety-based meaning and pleasure to one's existence. The ability to sustain this focus on sobriety, meaning and simple pleasures requires both conscious planning and vigilance. In the earliest days of recovery, when one's hold on sobriety is fragile and tenuous, the lack of a daily plan or daily structure almost assuredly means relapse. It is in these earliest days that a new purpose to daily living and the beginning reconstruction of one's daily activities must commence. While the definition of this purpose of daily living inevitably expands and the nature of daily activities evolves throughout recovery, the presence of a daily plan, sobriety-based activities and a new system of keeping score continues throughout recovery.

12.4 *Acts of Service* The fourth core activity within the culture of recovery is service. Addiction, by definition, elevates the drug-relationship to a position of primacy in the addict's life, transcending all other concerns, and shrinks the addict's capacity to perceive and respond to the needs of others. Addiction is isolating, implosive, desensitizing, self-feeding, myopic, masturbatory, insolent, and arrogant. Addiction is superficial, cunning, deceitful, manipulative, and exploitive. It is in service to others that the addict finds the key to unlock the chains of such addiction driven narcissism. Service is the means through which addicts begin to experience the world outside their own egos.

Indoctrination about service begins for most in the earliest days of recovery. Neophytes are asked to help make coffee at a meeting. They are thanked by an old timer for thoughts they shared during a meeting. They learn the rituals of mutual encouragement. They volunteer to make literature drops. They help a member who is moving. They offer someone a ride to meetings. Slowly, through service, they begin to feel a part of a community. In time, formal "Twelfth Step" work, will be added to their menu of daily acts of service.

Addicts are users. Their first experiences in recovery, when others thank them for *giving* something, are quite profound. Their first significant experiences responding to others in need may be reported as a "high" or "intoxicating." The first time they are in a position to "carry the message" to another, and have that other person respond to that message, can be particularly powerful. It is in that experience that they fully understand such previously incomprehensible jargon as: "To get this program, you gotta give it away." Service provides the breakthrough that allows connectedness to others, and through such connectedness, the reconstruction of the self. This latter point is particularly important. There must be the element of anonymity within the service act. Its purpose is internal reconstruction of one's character, not the ego-gratifying recognition from others that could come from such acts. The purpose and reward is internal, not external.

One of the most difficult elements of service to be mastered by the recovering addict is the act of listening. Carrying the message through the telling of one's story is much easier than the act of listening. Dr. Earle M. (1989) in his eloquent description of the recovery process points out that listening—truly hearing another with one's own ego disengaged—is an act of service and surrender. Listening, not to judge or respond or defend, but to truly hear and experience another is a true flight from the narcissism of addiction. As the roar of one's own ego diminishes with each passing day of recovery, this service of listening becomes easier and more fulfilling.

Acts of service in early recovery usually are defined in interactions with others in the recovering community. "Carrying the message" is understood to mean carrying the message of recovery to alcoholics and addicts in need. As recovery progresses over time, acts of service are fully integrated into daily life both in interactions within and outside the recovering community. "Carrying the message" comes to encompass a broader transmission of a philosophy of life to addicted and non-addicted alike. It is through such transformations that predators can one day become protectors, that the takers can one day become the givers.

All of the core activities in the culture of recovery—centering rituals, mirroring rituals, self-constructing behaviors, and acts of service—seek first to instill internal harmony within the recovering person and then instill harmony in one's relationship with the outside physical and social world. Simplicity. Serenity. Service.

KEY CULTURAL ROLES

Chapter Six explored the primary roles within the culture of addiction and noted the function of such roles in transmitting cultural values and performing activities crucial to the culture's continued existence. This chapter will explore the cast of characters and roles that make up the culture of recovery. Each role will be briefly described, noting the specific functions the role performs within the culture. Particular note will be made, where applicable, regarding special issues that arise when treatment professionals interact with these roles.

13.1 *The High Priest and High Priestess* High priests and priestesses are recovering men and women, who through their seniority, intelligence and/or personal charisma, hold informal positions of leadership within the culture of recovery. Such leadership is one of influence rather than title or office. It is sustained by the leader's passionate and skillful articulation of recovery principles. The high priest/priestess plays multiple roles within the culture of recovery. He or she is often called upon to represent the culture to the outside world. He or she is involved in the indoctrination of new members and in reinstituting passion in those who are becoming lazy about their recovery. He or she plays key roles in addressing members during tribal ceremonies.

Many high priests and priestesses from the culture of recovery performed similar roles in their earlier sojourn within the culture of addiction. Although the faiths were polar opposites, the skills required for such roles in both cultures were quite similar and therefore easily transferable. The danger for high priests/priestesses is that they may move into such positions before they have fully integrated recovery principles into their personality and lifestyle. When this occurs, the immature ego needs of high - priests/priestesses may prove destructive to both themselves and other members of the recovering community. While the culture of recovery can greatly benefit from the skills of high priests/priestesses, it is the elders of the recovering community who must assure that the ego needs of high priests/priestesses are kept under control. When such ego needs get out of control, high priests/priestesses wound themselves and the community through relapse, the creation of a personality cult, and/or the exploitation of tribal members.

The self-help tribes within the culture of recovery have evolved unique organizational structures that limit the power and sphere of influence of any single high priest. Such is not the case with the formal substance abuse treatment agencies within the culture. White (1986) discussed the high casualty rate associated with high priests/priestesses in this field.

While high priests and priestesses will continue to make immeasurable contributions within and on behalf of the culture of recovery, the culture of recovery must continue to evolve mechanisms of feedback and support that reduce the casualty rate for these roles. While the high priests/priestesses can bring great passion to the culture, it is the elders who will assure cultural stability and survival.

13.2 *The Elders* Elders are men and women, who through the quantity and quality of their sobriety, constitute the senior role models within the recovering community. Not necessarily possessed with the charisma or silver tongue of high priests, they teach using their own life as the palette upon which to illustrate the pathway to sobriety and serenity. Like the Shamans before them, the elders don't impose belief; they only answer questions. Their province is the personal consultation, not the pulpit. The elders use their own spiritual journey to help interpret the experiences of others. Grandiosity having long ago dissipated into a quiet humility, they have no need for the ego rewards of visible leadership. Theirs is often the last rather than the first voice heard on an issue, the final voice that summarizes the best of group will and conscience. They have seen people come and go and through the intensity of their searching have abstracted the essence of that collective wisdom that guides individual sobriety and group survival.

Substance abuse treatment programs are drawn to the power of elders in the culture of recovery. They wish to bring such power within their umbrella by engaging the elder as volunteer or by recruiting the elder to become a staff person. While both actions are understandable and on occasion desirable, history has proven that the latter can be fraught with difficulty. Seeking the esteem and wisdom and magic of the elder, programs try to force these special qualities into a framework of caseloads, form completion, restrictive admission criteria, meetings and more meetings, inter-agency competition and politics, and marketing strategies. Elders become so suffocated by the mechanics of service delivery that the agency fails to allow their special magic to flourish within the treatment milieu.   Rather than learn from the elders, some programs use elders to sustain their fragile credibility within the recovering community.

13.3 *The Storytellers*   Storytellers are the oral historians and lay preachers in the culture of recovery. They transmit the history, traditions, values, etiquette and folk wisdom of the culture of recovery through anecdote, allegory and metaphor. These individuals have unique abilities to entertain and educate through the medium of storytelling.

Storytellers from the culture of addiction often need assistance in making the transition into the culture of recovery. They discover that their old addiction-enhancing stories are both inappropriate and at times offensive in this new cultural setting. The transition can be facilitated if treatment personnel saturate the newcomer with stories embedded in the recovery literature and expose them to the champion storytellers in the culture of recovery. These persons can not only learn the principles of recovery best through the vehicle of story, but they can at the same time learn the nuances of storytelling in the culture of recovery. Treatment professionals can simultaneously address these persons' addictions and help them channel their unique talents in the service of their recovery and the recovery of others.

13.4 *The Comedians*   Humor, as a tool of healing, has an exalted role within the culture of recovery as do those members who have mastered the use of this tool. Where the high priest teaches through passion and the storyteller teaches through allegory, the comedian teaches through laughter. The comedians are sought after as speakers at meetings and for informal companionship. Members of the culture of recovery who bring the gift of laughter may need special support from mentors or treatment professionals with whom they are involved. The natural ability to heal and support others through their humor may make it difficult to disengage from this role to address their own emotional pain.

13.5 *The Medicine Man/Midwife* Medicine men and midwives are the folk healers within the culture of recovery. With or without traditional medical training, such persons are regularly consulted on a wide variety of health issues. When a member arrives at a meeting with a new prescription, the medicine man or midwife is asked to pronounce judgment on the appropriateness or inappropriateness of the medicine in question. Such persons often have a remarkable understanding of the pharmacopoeia of both licit and illicit drugs. Through accumulated time in the cultures of addiction/recovery, they may have a quite astute understanding of a broad number of addiction-related medical and health problems. They often practice a type of folk medicine that blends diet, exercise and psychological/ spiritual rituals to speed healing in the recovery process.

Many medicine men and midwives within the culture of recovery often performed similar roles within the culture of addiction. They found it possible to transfer and enhance the skills to their recovery process that once sustained addiction. If substance abuse treatment professionals can avoid being threatened by these folk healers, the latter can he utilized as a powerful informal educational force within the culture of recovery. These recovering folk healers can also be drawn into various staff positions within substance abuse prevention and treatment programs.

13.6 *The Organizers* Cultures could not exist without organizers. They make things happen. They are the doers. Organizers may not be in highly visible positions of leadership, but they have unique skills in orchestrating the detailed tasks involved in any project, whether it be a meeting, a picnic, or the preparation of a newsletter. They serve on committees, organize new meetings and plan and orchestrate social functions. Organizers are highly valued in the culture of recovery. Organizers, whose skills had been utilized in hustling activities in the culture of addiction, can be guided through a transfer of such skills to highly legitimate and valued activities.

13.7 *The Ambassadors*   Ambassadors are human telephone lines that link tribes within the culture of recovery. Holding membership in multiple groups, they provide the rapid transmission of information throughout the culture. The ambassadors allow information and innovation to be exchanged between groups in an apparently unorganized but quite efficient manner. The ambassador also serves as a type of clearinghouse for cultural members. They are the yellow pages of the culture of recovery. Need to find a particular resource? Ask the ambassador. Heard a rumor about an upcoming retreat in a neighboring city? Ask the ambassador. You just heard a member was in the hospital but don't know which one? Ask the ambassador. When in doubt, ask the ambassador.

Holding no formal power within the culture of recovery, the ambassadors may have significant informal status and power based on the reliability of their information and the service they perform on behalf of the culture. The role of ambassador is another role that often transfers directly from the culture of addiction to the culture of recovery.

13.8 *The Mentors*   Mentors or sponsors play a particularly important role in the culture of recovery by serving as a guide to other pilgrims in their journey through recovery. The mentor is a friend, a comrade, a brother or sister, an ally, and yet is much more than these. The mentor is imbued by the community with the privilege and responsibility of service to one or more community members. The mentor is a role model, a teacher, a lay therapist, and a personal consultant. All of these roles come together to bond individuals to the culture of recovery, support them in achieving and sustaining sobriety, and guide them through the reconstruction of self and the reconstruction of their social worlds.

As treatment programs extend their continuum of services to span the entire developmental process of recovery, new models will emerge which bring together service teams which include both treatment professionals and mentors/sponsors from the culture of recovery.

13.9 *The Pigeons* Pigeons, or "babies" as they are sometimes called, are the new arrivals in the culture of recovery. They arrive with one foot firmly planted in the culture of addiction and the other gingerly testing the waters of this thing called recovery. Their pain is fresh. Their ambivalence is intense. Their need is great. They are the lifeblood that daily transfuses and enriches the culture of recovery. They offer cultural members daily opportunities for service.

Pigeons play a number of extremely important roles in the culture of recovery. The pigeon's painful story reinforces anew all members continued powerlessness over alcohol and drugs. The hearing of each pigeon's story allows the vicarious experience of relapse and pain, thus strengthening the sobriety-based defense structure. Pigeons force confirmed members to articulate the guiding principles of sobriety and serenity, therefore strengthening these principles and beliefs. The pigeon's responsiveness provides fresh evidence of the power of the recovery principles. The opportunity for service to the newcomer brings oldtimers together in a unified "weness." The culture of recovery expands by adding pigeons to its list of permanent members. Through such expansion the culture is strengthened and diversified, creating the possibility to extend its sphere of influence to new generations of pigeons.

Anyone in the role of pigeon receives a great deal of attention in the culture of recovery. While this level of attention and support may create initial bonding with the culture, eventually the pigeon has to find another role he or she can perform within the culture. This is an early stage transition that, if not mastered, may lead to flight back into the culture of addiction.

13.10 *The Pilgrims* The pilgrims are the majority of the members of the culture of recovery. They play no specialized roles nor hold any special status within the culture, but make up its basic citizenry. Their affiliation with each other and the culture is tied to a shared history and a shared destiny. Their shared values and rituals have provided a way to sustain sobriety, serenity and sanity.

13.11 *Pseudo-Addiction; Real Recovery* In an earlier discussion of roles within the culture of addiction, pseudo-junkies were defined as persons who were deeply enmeshed in the culture of addiction and who had taken on the trappings of the culture of addiction but were, in fact, not addicted. Such persons could often find a niche only within the culture of addiction. Such persons as part of their pseudo-career in addiction may end up in substance abuse treatment or in self-help groups. They can utilize 12-step recovery programs and psychological counseling to initiate a real transformation in their lives even though there was no real addiction. Their transformation within the culture of recovery confirms what many have known for a long time—the elements within the culture of recovery provide a framework for spiritual rebirth that transcends the condition of addiction.

13.12 *The Martyrs*   The Martyrs in the culture of recovery are persons who made enough contact with the culture to be known by members, but who lost their lives as a result of continued addiction. The stories of such martyrs get embellished and retold within the culture as a testament to the belief that addiction is not just a disease, but a chronic, progressive, and (if untreated) fatal disease. The repeated sharing of such stories is inevitably met with "There but for the Grace of God go I" responses. The creation of such stories is also a way the culture of recovery provides some level of immortality even to those who failed in their quest for sobriety. By creating martyrdom through storytelling, the culture attempts even in death to turn defeat into triumph, to use the loss of one member to sustain the life of another.

13.13 *The Professors*   The professors are persons of great intellectual gifts within the culture of recovery who attempt, often with great difficulty, to rationally plot their way through the recovery process. What has been the greatest source of their pride and achievement—the mind, becomes a major obstacle in early recovery. Put off initially by what appear to them to be simplistic platitudes and cliches, it will be some time before their need for complex analysis, proof, logic, congruency, and consistency will give way to acceptance and simple faith.

The professors in the culture play an important role for all members. Nearly everyone in the culture of recovery is plagued with transient notions that they should have been smart enough to avoid problems with alcohol/drugs. The professors, with all their intellectual armament, provide visible testimony that raw intelligence provides no immunity from addiction.

13.14 *The Bleeding Deacons*   The term "bleeding deacons" has been around for a long time within 12 step programs to refer to members or leaders who, obsessed with their own self-importance, believe that a group cannot survive without their leadership. Wounded by the group's failure to recognize their importance, bleeding deacons are overcome with self-pity. Bleeding deacons can become so diverted from the principles of recovery that they relapse or they can mature into greatly respected elders within the culture of recovery.

13.15 *The Chronically Falling Sinner* Chronically falling sinners are members of the culture of recovery who seek active involvement in this culture, but are plagued by continuing episodes of relapse. These persons often involve other cultural members in helping or rescue roles during active periods of relapse. They involve themselves with (and may "burn out") multiple mentors before achieving stable sobriety or fleeing the culture. These persons may have accepted the identity of "addict" or "alcoholic" but have failed to make the final identity transition to "recovering addict." Chronically falling sinners perform a unique role for the culture. They provide unlimited opportunities for service activity by other members. Even if they fail to achieve sustained sobriety, their presence in the culture has strengthened the sobriety of many members, who through their service activities, have tried to impact the life of the chronically falling sinner.

13.16 *The Professionals*   The professionals in the culture of recovery are those men and women who make a living working within institutions that are part of the culture. Historically, this has been limited primarily to persons working as counselors within substance abuse treatment agencies. As the culture has exploded in its size and diversity, these roles are expanding to include prevention personnel, recreational specialists, physicians, administrators and managers, marketing and public relations specialists, employee assistance program specialists, DUI assessment and remedial education specialists, teachers, trainers, consultants, researchers, and publishers.

The potential contribution of professionals within the culture of recovery has not been fully realized in spite of the proliferation of treatment and specialty programs in the last quarter century. This is partially because many professionals come and leave these programs and, while seeing themselves as performing a valuable job, never perceive themselves as a member or part of a recovering community or culture. They may also work in organizations that regard themselves as businesses rather than institutions within the culture of recovery with responsibilities which transcend profit. A future day of political and financial reckoning may arrive when members of the culture of recovery demand, in exchange for the millions of dollars they feed into professional organizations, a broader level of understanding of and participation in the recovering community. As anger escalates in some quarters over the perceived financial exploitation of the addicted, there are revived visions of the moneychangers being thrown out of the temple. There is an increasing sense that professionals and the service institutions supported by the culture of recovery must assume a full and responsible role within this culture.

13.17 *The "Two-Hatters"*   "Two-hatters" hold dual roles as both a recovering person and a professional working in the culture of recovery. Historically, this role referred to recovering alcoholics who were working as counselors. Today, it has not only been expanded to encompass many other professional roles, but also has been expanded to cover persons who may be in a 12-step recovery program for codependency. Two-hatters provide a human bridge between the professional and self-help institutions within the culture of recovery.

Two-hatters have made invaluable contributions to the field and yet this dual status often poses unique obstacles in their own transition from the culture of addiction to the culture of recovery. The lack of understanding of such difficulties leaves this pathway to recovery strewn with the bodies of recovering alcoholics and addicts who relapsed while working as counselors in substance abuse treatment programs.   Today, there is much greater knowledge about which recovering persons would be appropriate and inappropriate for such dual roles, the training and preparation required for recovering persons to assume these roles, the best time in sobriety such positions should be initiated, and special supports that two-hatters may need to sustain this role over time.

13.18 *The Self-Cured*   On the fringes of the culture of recovery, one can always find self proclaimed, self-cured alcoholics or addicts who present their formula for sobriety. While there may be many recovering persons drawn to the culture from non-traditional pathways—without treatment and self-help involvement—the self-cured make up a special subpopulation. They are drawn close to the culture not for support, but for a stage upon which to exhibit their grandiosity.   Demonstrating the narcissism of the actively addicted, the self-cured boast of their ability to stop drinking without going to any of those treatment programs or meetings.   Their sole claim to fame, reflected in the singular theme of their storytelling, is the achievement of sobriety through an act of personal will.   These worshipers of willpower may temporarily detour or divert many addicts in their search for the recovery pathway.

13.19   *The Fundamentalists*   There are a wide variety of fundamentalists within the culture of recovery. What they share in common is an extremely narrow belief or view of how one can best achieve and sustain sobriety. For the fundamentalist, others must get sober by following their pathway. If they didn't go through treatment, then no one needs to go through treatment. If they went to a particular treatment program, then everyone needs to go to that program.   Fundamentalists can also include professionals who share an equally restricted view of both the treatment and the recovery process. Such fundamentalism within the culture is not surprising. One's view of the nature of addiction and recovery in this culture is not a matter of idle intellectual debate, it is a matter of personal survival. Recovering people may need to cling to a narrow understanding of recovery because that narrow understanding is, for them, the foundation of their current sobriety. Such passion should be expected. There is, in fact, wide tolerance within the culture for such passion. At the same time, there are forces within the culture which eventually tend to soften the rigidity of the fundamentalists and enhance their understanding and tolerance of various styles of recovery.

13.20 *The Confused Protectors* On the periphery of the culture of recovery are a group of confused bystanders. These persons—referred to here as the confused protectors-are involved with many active addicts, and yet find themselves shunned by these persons when they get sober. Confused, resentful and angry, these persons cannot understand why the addicts they helped so often during the bad times, once sober, seem to lack appreciation for them and their past efforts. These are the super enablers. What they do best is rescue. They personally intervene on behalf of the addict. They lend money to the addict. They cover for the addict. They help the addict extricate themselves from crises. They help the addict sustain both their denial and their addiction. Once sober, the recovering addict instinctively understands that to sustain such relationships is to court relapse. This sudden disengagement obviously leaves such protectors angry and confused.

13.21 *The Saboteurs* Saboteurs are persons both inside and outside the culture of recovery who actively sabotage the efforts of recovering addicts. Saboteurs may be neophytes in the culture whose continued relapse and predatory behavior undermine the recovery of others. Saboteurs may be persons outside the culture—both addicts and non-addicts—who for varied reasons actively seek to sabotage the recovery of persons with whom they are involved.

13.22 *Summary: Cultural Roles and the Treatment Process*   If addicts seeking entrance into the culture of recovery are to make this culture a home rather than a vacation spot, they must be able to carve out a role or niche for themselves within this culture. The ability of treatment staff to disengage addicts from their historical roles within the culture of addiction may to a great extent hinge on the ability to offer addicts new esteem-salvaging roles within the culture of recovery. This movement between cultures requires both the acquisition of new skills and, in many cases, the redirection of old skills from the culture of addiction. It is important for treatment professionals to understand the nature of this role transformation and the part they can play in facilitating such transformations.

Addicts in the culture of addiction take on roles, identities and daily activities that create knowledge and skills and set the context within which all needs must be met. These roles and activities and the needs met through them may, separate and distinct from the drug relationship, help bind persons to the culture of addiction. One task of the treatment professional is to guide clients out of addiction-sustaining roles into recovery-enhancing roles and activities. If addicts are to master this role transformation, they must be guided into niches through which they can experience safety, esteem and comfort and through which they can grow and contribute.

CAREER MILESTONES IN THE CULTURE OF RECOVERY

The movement from addiction to recovery has been portrayed throughout this book as a form of pilgrimage or odyssey through which one reconstructs both internal experience and one's relationship with the external social world.   There are clearly kaleidoscopic variations in the paths, steps and detours through which men, women and near children have found their way through the recovery process. Yet, within these cumulative stories of recovery, there appear many common threads that become clear only through the frequency with which they are reported. This chapter will explore those points or milestones at which recovery paths often cross. It will focus on those events or experiences that mark this career conversion from addiction to recovery. In the parlance of this book, this chapter will attempt to identify the developmental stages or milestones mark this career of recovery. Particular attention will be given to the social context within which the progression of recovery occurs.   How the treatment professional may intervene to support the initiation of developmentally appropriate behaviors which allow the progressive metamorphosis of recovery to continue to unfold in its richness and complexity will also be explored.

14.1 *The Motivational Crisis*   Much has been written over the years about the nature of the motivational process which stimulates the addict's decision to enter treatment or otherwise begin the recovery process.   Most of this writing has focused on internal psychological processes.   This section will explore the ways in which the external social world strongly influences both the presence and outcome of this motivational crisis.

It was briefly noted earlier that the assessment of motivation of the addict is to a great extent an assessment of pain. Most addicts will continue their drug relationship until the pain of continuing exceeds the pain of breaking off the relationship. There appear to be two major social influences that often come together to precipitate the motivational crisis of the addict.

The first occurs when the social world outside the culture of addiction unequivocally applies or threatens to apply consequences for the addict's drug-related behavior and addicts find themselves unable to manipulate their way out of this threatening situation. Such external threats often include threats of dissolution of a relationship, threats of loss of employment or income, or arrest and incarceration.   Such threats, in order to produce a motivational crisis, must be clear and unequivocal, *e.g.*, "If you..., I will..."   In short the addict is cornered.

A second social influence occurs when the addicts' progressive deterioration results in increasing isolation within the culture of addiction.   Other addicts avoid them because of volatility or violence.   They can't even find havens within the culture of addiction.   They have lost status and are increasingly isolated within the culture. They experience more frequent arrest because of incompetence and drug-induced stupidity in the commission of criminal acts. Their impairment produces increased risks to their own personal safety, *e.g.*, overall risk-taking behavior, ripping others off in dope deals, failure to repay money, or selling information to the police. In short, many addicts find themselves so impaired that they have been ejected from both the straight culture and the culture of addiction. Within the experience of such isolation is the possibility for change.

Addicts often have long histories of such socially influenced crises, none of which have resulted in any sustained sobriety. The historical pathway for addicts is from crisis to manipulation to escape to resumption of the drug relationship. Crisis alone does not result in sobriety; it simply represents a brief opportunity for change. The task of professional helpers is to convert crisis into commitment. The job is not to prevent the experience of pain but to use the experience of pain as a tool for creating consciousness and conversion, *i.e.*, commitment to change. By preventing manipulation and escape, addicts are forced to experience the full consequences of alcohol and drug use. By weakening or breaking through the addict's defense structure during a period of crisis, professional helpers create the possibility of change.

14.2 *The Conversion Experience* Many recovering addicts when they recount the history of their addiction and their recovery report a powerful emotional/spiritual experience that marked the turning point in their shift from addiction to recovery. For such addicts, entrance into recovery included what could be described as a conversion experience. If a better understanding of the nature of this conversion experience could be achieved, it might provide important clues on how to set the stage for and capitalize on such experiences. The author has listened to stories of such experiences for twenty years. There are common elements reported within these conversion experiences. The greater the number of these elements that can be brought together during the crisis of early recovery, the greater the probability that the addict will experience a life-transforming, conversion experience. Whether described as a cataclysmic spiritual experience or a slow pervasive revelation of awareness, the conversion experience often includes one or more of the following elements (described in as close to their reported sequence as synthesis would allow).

1. There is a period of emotional and/or physical isolation from the cultural supports for addiction. The experience of aloneness is a precursor to conversion.
2. There is a breakdown in the normal ability to manipulate or escape from addiction-related consequences, sparking a sudden weakening of the normal addiction-sustaining defense structure. The addict is truly cornered.
3. There is a breakdown of the denial system that allows the addict to suddenly see and experience themselves through the eyes of others. Denial—that blind spot in the center of the addict's existence—collapses, creating a painful and overwhelming vision of the truth.
4. There is an overwhelming experience of self-loathing; drug hunger is temporarily replaced by revulsion.
5. There is an acute sense of one's own impending insanity or death, that may have an almost hallucinatory quality, with terror-evoking images of disintegrating, drowning, suffocating, or being sucked down a dark tunnel.
6. There is a breakdown in the addict's grandiosity and narcissism. The addict cries deeply for those he or she has hurt and is repulsed by the vision of his or her self-centeredness. The angry, rebellious, destructive spirit of self is broken. There is an experience of surrender.
7. A belief system, perhaps rejected hundreds of times previously, is suddenly seen in its totality. Order and cohesion appear out of scattered fragments of pain and insanity. Words that once were repelled as empty rhetoric suddenly come to life and are embraced. The cognitive reconstruction of the addict's view of self and the world provide justification for radical abstinence.

8. There is an emotional breakthrough—a letting go of the old self, a purging of internal poison, a cleansing of the self, an emotional release.

9. There is a new awareness of spirit and hope—a sense of forgiveness, darkness becomes light, some power pulls one from the abyss, there is the sense of rebirth.

10. The horrible isolation collapses and one is overwhelmed by the sense of belonging with those who share vision and understanding. There is the full experience that one is loved and loves. The self is merged in a community. There is a powerful experience of brotherhood and sisterhood.

Clients have often approached the author troubled by their experience of some of the above elements. They would inevitably conclude their report with the query of whether they were going crazy. In the early days, I wasn't quite sure. Today, I might quite confidently respond: "You aren't going crazy, you're trying to get well. Don't run from those experiences; they could save your life. Hang on to and embrace these experiences. Don't ask why, just use them as springboards for change." I can't rationally explain all these phenomena, but I do now recognize them as powerful forces that can be channeled to support the recovery process.

The above elements are common across ideological belief systems. Addicts for whom Islam was the transforming power, addicts for whom Christian conversion was the transforming power, addicts who report a conversion experience within the framework of Alcoholics Anonymous and addicts who describe the experience of "spontaneous remission" all note elements from the list above.

14.3 *The Initiation Rites* A motivational crisis and a conversion experience provide not the assurance of recovery, but the opportunity for recovery. The crisis can temporarily disengage one from the culture of addiction and create an openness for sustained change, but it could also be just one more crisis that is proceeded by relapse and reactivation of addiction. For many addicts, a critical milestone at this juncture is participation in formal initiation rites into the culture of recovery.

Initiation rites differ significantly from the motivational crisis and the conversion experience. In the latter, the addict is a respondent to internal experience and external events. Things are happening to the addict. In initiation rituals, the addict must take positive action. Decisions are required. Commitments are expected. The addict must speak. The addict must act.

There are numerous initiation rites that have marked entrance into the culture of recovery. In the days of the inebriate asylums of the late 1800s and early 1900s, when anonymity was not yet in vogue, alcoholics returning to their communities were often expected to proclaim their alcoholism and recovery as a means of spreading the word to other alcoholics. One's "coming out of the closet" was a highly public initiation rite. In the early years of AA, one initiation involved what was called "the surrender." The surrender was an early ritual of initiation into AA in which the new recruits in the presence of other AA members got on their knees in prayer to admit their powerlessness over alcohol and the unmanageability in their life and to profess their belief in a higher power that could return them to sanity. Anecdotal reports from AA oldtimers testify to the power of this early ritual. Another initiation ritual involves the first self-proclamation of addiction. The words, "Hi. I'm Joe and I'm an alcoholic" are the ticket for initiation and continued participation. They constitute a refutation of denial and a resolve for personal action.

Other addicts describe other initiation rites that accompanied their own recovery. Some cite a simple and singular commitment made to a person of great significance in their life. Some describe an unequivocal and spoken commitment to themselves. Others describe their initiation into Islam—perhaps the change of their name. Others who went through the therapeutic communities of yesterday describe both the confrontation and humiliation and the shaved head as powerful initiation rites. Others describe their baptism in the Christian faith—the experience of being born again. Others describe the graduation ritual on the day they left treatment.

All of the above rituals extend the period of crisis and conversion into a period of more sustained action and commitment. Rituals of initiation into the culture of recovery serve such multiple functions as the following.

- They help reinforce the physical and emotional disengagement from the culture of addiction.
- They reinforce and sustain the emotional experience of conversion.
- They create an experiential footnote and an anniversary that marks the separation between the old life and new life.
- They intensify the experience of membership and belonging in the culture of recovery.
- They provide an opportunity for the addict to witness—proclamation and affirmation of faith.
- They provide a powerful call to service.

Those who design and operate addiction treatment programs need to enrich their understanding of the power of rituals. Treatment professionals need to formalize and expand their use of initiation rituals that burn emotional bridges to the culture of addiction and seal one's courtship with, and commitment to, the culture of recovery.

14.4 *Joining and Rejoining: The Experience of Relapse* Early recovery is like an ambivalent courtship. One is quite drawn to the new relationship, but there remains power in the bonds to the former lover. Addicts in early recovery have disparate parts of themselves that are congruent both with active addiction and recovery. At times these elements co-exist in tandem, but most of the time there is a war within the self. Neither the motivational experience, the conversion experience nor the initiation experience fully excises these addiction-seeking elements from the self. When these elements surface in times of vulnerability, relapse can occur.

Relapse can be a transient footnote on the road to recovery or it can mark a complete disengagement from the recovery process. The task of professional helpers is to capitalize on the relapse experience to solidify bonding to the culture of recovery. The relapse experience can be used to further purge elements of the old self in ways that decrease the risk of future relapse.

The overall response to the issue of relapse involves three dimensions. The first, which has been discussed earlier, is the development of an active plan of relapse prevention for each client. The second involves teaching addicts so much about addiction that there is a weakening in the cognitive defense structure that supports active drug use. They may be able to continue to use, but they will never be able to use without awareness and consciousness of the addictive process and the reality of their addiction. This second dimension often gets referred to as "taking the fun out of the drinking." This intervention is designed to shorten and intensify the relapse experience in ways that may return one to the recovery pathway. The third dimension involves the treatment professional's response to relapse incidents. This third dimension will be explored in more detail as it has not been touched on in earlier chapters.

If there is to be even a single relapse incident, the goal is to turn that incident into a milestone in the progression of recovery. If such meaning cannot be created, the incident is likely to indicate a milestone and an acceleration in the progression of addiction. Before exploring ways to respond to such incidents, the wide variation in dynamics surrounding the relapse incident should be noted. A sampling of such variations is catalogued below.

A. *Relapse as Response to Drug Hunger* This type of relapse, usually occurring very early in recovery, occurs when one simply succumbs to the power of the cellular craving for the drug. This is the—"my cells were screaming" or "I felt like I was going to crawl out of my skin"—stage and usually occurs during initial detoxification or the period of post-acute withdrawal. It may also occur when individuals put themselves in the presence of powerful cues previously conditioned to elicit drug hunger.

B. *Relapse as Impulse* This relapse occurs without plan or warning when individuals find themselves in a drug consuming situation and simply offer no resistance to the opportunity to use. Their lack of preparation for the situation and lack of assertiveness results in drug consumption. They present as quite befuddled in the post-relapse interview, trying to figure out how the drinking/drug use incident occurred.

C. *Relapse as a Cognitive Test* This relapse is highly planned and constitutes a calculated decision to use. The addiction-sustaining cognitive defense structure has been reactivated and has tried to rewrite the person's past experience within the familiar framework of denial, *e.g.*, "You're problem back then really wasn't alcohol, it was...." The mind has constructed a theory that can only be tested—in the relapse-preparing thought sequence—by drinking or drug use. Use is an experiment. "How else will I really know?"

This relapse is so rationally defended and well planned, it deserves to be christened a "scheme" rather than a "slip."

D. *Relapse as Flight* When the emotional experiences of conversion and initiation wear off, they are sometimes replaced by panic. Addicts, suddenly and fully experiencing the heightened expectations from others, are overwhelmed with the prospects of failure. Paralyzed by the fear of imminent failure, they seek flight through relapse. When the expectations are gone, the pressure is off.

E. *Relapse or Go Crazy* Some addicts experience very painful and terrifying thoughts and feelings as they detoxify. Their fear of insanity, rather than subsiding, intensifies in early recovery. As symptoms and fears escalate, these addicts reach back for the transient, self-medicating tranquility of intoxication. Many addicts in this category suffer from primary or secondary psychiatric illnesses that must be addressed both in their primary treatment and in the relapse prevention process.

F. *Relapse and Loss* There is a risk of relapse during emotional crisis. Addicts in this category, even those who have had some stable period of sobriety, find their sobriety-based defense structure collapsing in the face of painful loss, *e.g.*, divorce, death, or job loss. The anxiety and depression are so overwhelming that the person regresses back to more primitive modes of escape—the reactivation of addiction.

G. *Relapse as Rage* Rage at others constitutes risk for relapse. The insatiable desire to do harm fuels one's destructiveness. Body and psyche are sacrificed as an act of violence toward others. Relapse is a way to show "them." Relapse can be a way to inflict hurt and to make others feel responsible. Relapse can be a poorly chosen weapon.

H. *Relapse as Self-loathing* Relapse can creep up as a form of punishment for persons who feel they are unworthy of recovery. Relapse can, separate from the primary addiction, constitute part of a pattern of self-defeating behavior that seeks eventual self-destruction. Addiction can be just one element in a broader pattern of self-destructive behavior. Relapse can constitute not simply a reactivation of addiction, but the resurgence of the broader pattern of self-destruction. In this profile, it is the broader pattern that must be the target of relapse prevention efforts.

I. *Relapse as Vacation* Some recovering addicts go through periods of aberrant thinking where they plan timeout periods in the recovery process. These are periods of drinking and drug use planned as one would plan a vacation—with a projected starting time, itinerary, and finishing time. Some recovering persons even make light of such periodic sojourns. The driving force behind this pattern can be quite puzzling.

J. *The Professional Relapse* What of the chronically relapsing client who never seems to achieve any sustained periods of uninterrupted sobriety? A history of chronic relapse may best be viewed, not as an interruption of recovery, but as a pattern of active addiction. What must be sought in such circumstances is not the usual relapse prevention technology, but the creation of a motivational crisis from which can come conversion and the initiation in recovery.

K. *The Relapse Response* If relapse or a series of relapse experiences constitutes a developmental milestone of recovery for many addicts, then how can treatment professionals intervene to capitalize and use this experience both to prevent subsequent relapse and to strengthen the recovery process? For most of the patterns of relapse described above, the relapse intervention process involves three stages: confession and confrontation, recommitment to the recovery process, and the formulation and implementation of a relapse prevention plan.

1. Confession and Confrontation One initial response is to confront the reality of the relapse and elicit details surrounding the relapse experience. The purpose is both to collect data to assist in diagnosing those causative and contributing factors and also to provide clients with an emotional catharsis of feelings regarding the relapse. While the pain of the relapse experience is not dwelt on in a shaming manner during this stage, the full range of real and potential consequences of the relapse episode should be explored by the therapist. The professional helper is in some ways going back through the initial sequence of motivational crisis, conversion and initiation described earlier. To achieve this, it is desirable for the client to feel the full emotional intensity of the relapse experience. The professional helper is also seeking in this stage an understanding of the dynamics of the relapse and the client's identification of such dynamics as part of a self-defeating pattern of behavior. At the end of this initial stage, the client should be able to specifically define the behaviors, attitudes, thoughts, feelings and situations that constitute obstacles to continued recovery.

2. Re-Commitment Once the precipitating cues are identified, the professional helper can then call for a renewed commitment by the client to continue the recovery process. It is of great benefit if this step can be imbued with emotional intensity. Variations of public (within the group) confession and a repledging of faith are common routes to such emotional intensity and rebonding within the culture of recovery.

3. Relapse Prevention The final stage in the relapse response is working with the client to formulate a concrete plan for relapse prevention. The plan takes the problem statements identified in step one and develops a program of action to address each obstacle. The emphasis is on the client *doing* something. It is not a program of vagueness, *e.g.*, "I will work harder to understand...", it is a program of action. It is not a program of insight, contemplation or indecision; it is a program of strategic action, such as:

- "I will have my check direct-deposited until I demonstrate an ability to safely carry cash."
- "I will exercise daily as a positive way to minimize drug craving."
- "I will seek counseling to help manage grief over the death of my wife."
- "I will get a sponsor and maintain regular contact with them."
- "I will stop playing silent critic and begin participating and speaking in groups and meetings.
- "I cannot be with Jerry and remain sober; I will terminate this relationship."
- "When I feel...; I will...."

14.5 *The Apprenticeship* Like any pilgrim embarking on a new career, the neophyte in the culture of recovery serves an apprenticeship period to master the knowledge and skills required to pursue the recovery process. Through mentor relationships with elders in the culture, the neophyte must first learn the ropes of cultural participation.

Such learning includes:

- Remembering both rituals of greeting and names.
- Understanding and comfort with insider "jargon."

- Mastery of the rules governing appropriate and inappropriate behavior, *e.g.*, etiquette, (what is expected; what is taboo?)
- Expectations for neophyte participation.
- Mastery of sequence and content of meeting rituals.
- Mastery over fear of the unknown—trying on new behaviors and opening up exposure to new experiences, *e.g.*, trying different meetings/rituals within the culture.

Through immersion in the culture of recovery, neophytes learn how this culture works and begin to define themselves as an insider. The perception of the tribal group shifts from a "they" to a "we."

During the post-initiation apprenticeship period the neophyte learns the most important early lesson of recovery—how to not drink or use drugs. There are numerous elements in this early milestone, many of which have been touched on in early chapters. There is a rupture in the prior affiliation with the culture of addiction and a fragile reconstruction of a sobriety-based lifestyle. There are already early changes in thinking and responding to emotional stimuli. There are earlier noted transformations in the person's family and social relationships, capacity to work and play, and other elements of daily lifestyle. Above all, the novice has mastered the tentative ability to sustain sobriety through a variety of new rituals.

During the apprenticeship, neophytes are as preoccupied with not using as they were preoccupied with using during their days in the culture of addiction. During the apprenticeship, recovering addicts begin to stabilize their hold on sobriety. Having achieved some sustained period of abstinence, the neophytes frequently develop a number of compulsive rituals which they feel are keys to sobriety. This early period is marked by superstitious and magical thinking which drives compulsiveness. Newly sober persons often have a fragile hold on sobriety and fear that only through some magical rituals will they escape the inevitable experience of relapse. In short, the cognitive defense structure of the neophytes get reorganized in early recovery and may exhibit a number of the same characteristics that typify active addiction, *e.g.*, rigidity, black-white thinking, rationalization and projection.

Some recovering persons never transcend the apprenticeship period. They master only enough skills to refrain from relapsing. Their recovery does not extend beyond the earliest defenses that allowed them to achieve the initial period of sobriety. Some of this fixation on the early style of recovery is understandable. There is tremendous fear that tampering with what has worked may somehow jeopardize continued recovery. The fear is a healthy one. In general, such compulsivity is a healthy mechanism that assures the return of stability and predictability in the life of the newly sober. As both strength and maturity in recovery develops over the early months and years of recovery, the stage is set for a metamorphosis in the early recovery style—a metamorphosis that holds the seeds for a more fundamental transformation in the personality of the recovering person.

During the apprenticeship period, there is an inevitable emotional thawing. This forces the recovering person to look back on his or her life and try to achieve some understanding of what happened. During this period, a major developmental task of recovery is the construction of a life story that explains the pilgrimage through addiction to recovery in a way that can lead to a restoration of self-acceptance and self-respect.

14.6 *Constructing One's Story* Earlier reference has been made to stories and storytellers and the role each plays in transmitting knowledge and values within the cultures of addiction and recovery. This section will explore a different kind of story and a different function of storytelling.

Each person's life is a series of events and experiences. Those events to which one attributes special meaning get selected, abstracted and massaged into stories which communicate to others the nature of one's identity. Identity—that sculpted perception of self and the outside world at any given moment—both springs from and is in turn shaped by storytelling. Life is a continuing process through which one adds new elements to this personal story, eliminates old elements from the story that no longer fit and revises the old story to achieve new meaning. Story construction forms the bridge between self-perception and one's self-presentation to others. The most superficial to the most intimate of relationships involves the reciprocal exchange of stories. Stories and particularly "Our Story"—a dramatic summary of one's self-shaping experiences—provide both a justification of one's history and a means of scripting present and future. Each story is a personal allegory with its own internal mythology and moral. One's story is a synthesis of self-selected tales, the stories within the story. The experience of intimacy is a process of peeling through the superficial and fabricated stories of one's life and opening the possibility of constructing crucial emotional elements into stories which have rarely been exposed to the outside world. Story construction and storytelling, far from being insignificant pastimes, embody the essential medium through which the self is shared with or hidden from the outside world.

The importance of this "story" is not in factual accuracy. This is not biography or objective history. What matters is the psychological and social whole shaped by the selection, deletion and meanings attached to experiences within the story. One's story places oneself in a particular relationship with the world. The construction of personal history shapes both present and future.

It is a justification and defense of one's existential position. It can dictate one's part and one's lines in a play which unfolds with terrifying predictability. Each of us plays out scenes and chapters in our life in line with the motifs imbedded within our own story. The construction of the past shapes the future. By telling you who I am, I tell you my fate. To change my fate, I must redefine who I am. I must reconstruct my story.

In addiction, the drug relationship becomes the essential story-shaping agent in one's life. In early stages of addiction other elements of experience dissipate, parts of the past are erased, and story-telling centers around denial of the intensity of the drug relationship. As control over this relationship diminishes, stories become increasingly filled with themes of grandiosity and power. Confabulation begins not due to neurological damage, as in the case of the Korsakoff patient, but in response to the destruction of self-esteem that escalates during middle stages of addiction. As addiction progresses, story-telling becomes increasingly dominated by core activities within the culture of addiction—hustling, copping, getting off and avoiding hassles. In late stages of addiction a more elaborate web is woven into the fabric of storytelling that provides a justification for use. The addict's stories become filled with elaborate denials or justifications of addiction. This story may, through the use of repression, minimization, confabulation or projection allow one to concurrently deny and sustain addiction. A story can also embrace the status of addiction but provide an esteem-salvaging justification of one's condition.

Many addict's have a carefully constructed life story which portrays them as being victimized by people and forces and conditions over which they had no control. The "victim" status and role serves as a righteous justification for continued self-destruction through addiction. It is as if revenge against the world can be achieved through obliteration of oneself. Through treatment and recovery, the addict's history must be reconstructed, portraying the individual not as victim but as an active player who contributed to the past through personal choices. Addicts present their history through stories of what the world did to them; recovering addicts speak of who they were, what they did, what they valued and how they thought. Projection of blame is replaced by taking personal responsibility for one's past. Within this transformation is found an incredible paradox involving the major philosophy of alcoholism in the U.S. Out of the "disease concept"—attacked since the 1700s as an escape from personal responsibility—comes a plan of personal recovery that emphasizes self-examination, self-responsibility, humility, confession, restitution, self-acceptance and service to others. The responsibility abdicated in addiction is embraced in recovery.

When the addict begins to disengage from the world of addiction, his or her personal story must be reconstructed. The old story will not enhance recovery; it provides permission for relapse. For recovery, the addict must be helped to reconstruct the story of his or her life—a story that will reflect a different conception of self, a different view of the world, and a new value system. An essential milestone of recovery is the sobriety-based construction of one's story. The story which will get the addict through the early months of sobriety will continue to evolve throughout the life of the recovering person.

It is not particularly necessary that the first story constructed by the addict in treatment or early recovery be factually correct. Factual omissions and distortions are to be expected. It is necessary that the addict's life be reframed within the story in a manner that supports recovery. The self-story in recovery must be different than the self-story in addiction. Whether factually true or not, the self-story in recovery must be metaphorically true. The story must be constructed in ways that give meaning to one's own suffering. The story must be constructed to explain the suffering one has caused others. Factual truth—which the addict may be incapable of in the earliest days of recovery—is secondary to emotional truth. The freedom achieved through the purging of the emotional content of the story and the power of the injunction for change that emerges from the story should take precedent over factual accuracy. As recovery proceeds the story will evolve over the years in ways that bring factual and emotional truth closer and closer together.

What roles can professional helpers perform in facilitating this reconstruction of personal identity? Recommended guidelines for facilitating story reconstruction involve assisting addicted clients to structure their life experience within a cognitive framework that responds to the following questions.

- Who was I before I began using alcohol/drugs?
- Who and what did I become as a result of my use?
- Why me? How do I explain what happened?
- What happened to break this pattern?
- Who and what am I now?
- Where am I going and what do I need to do to get there?

The cognitive dimensions of treatment revolve around discovering answers to these six questions. Written and visual media, lectures and group discussions, and, in particular, individual counseling directed to the neophyte in the culture of recovery must be designed to collectively address these questions. By replacing each "I" with "we" in the above questions, it is possible to isolate the parallel issues that must also be addressed by the addiction-impaired family.

The key clinical question related to this discussion is how to help the client transform this addiction-shaped and addiction-sustaining story into a story that, while continuing to support self-esteem, provides a foundation for recovery. The task of treatment is to expose the flaws in the addiction-sustaining story and assist in the construction of a recovery-based personal history. The culture of recovery, particularly its self-help components, nurtures such story transformations through these mechanisms.

- Where the culture of addiction promoted stories which denied, minimized or diverted attention from addiction, the culture of recovery promotes stories which proclaim an open and unequivocal acceptance of addiction. On the theory that the greater the sin the greater the miracle of salvation, there may even be a tendency by some to exaggerate the intensity or duration of addiction.

- Where the culture of addiction promoted story construction around the values of grandiosity, secrecy, cunning and deceit, the culture of recovery promotes stories which value humility, openness and honesty.

- Where the culture of addiction teaches one to project blame, the culture of recovery teaches one to assume total responsibility by focusing on self-inventory.

- Where humor in the culture of addiction is at the expense of others, humor in the culture of recovery is highly valued as a vehicle of healing and humility—humor is directed at oneself.

The story reconstruction of the recovering addict requires new knowledge, new language, and new values. The new story is the anti-script, the new sobriety-based model of the old self. The most dynamic treatment milieus are filled with stories and storytellers. They are language laboratories through which addicts learn to change their future via the semantic reconstruction of the past and present.

14.7 *Through Excess in Search of Harmony* Newly sober addicts are painfully out of balance. The object—the drug-around which their life has revolved is gone and they find themselves in a world without meaning or order. "Getting sober" does not produce harmony, it simply creates the condition that allows the search for harmony to begin. The pathway to achieving this harmony can be long and tortuous and can include detours through many types of excessive behaviors, many of which may be righteously justified in the name of sobriety. Consider the following scenarios.

- John is six months sober. During this time he has, through recently acquired workaholism, attempted to overcome the past ten-year alcohol-related deterioration in his business. He works 12-14 hours per day, compulsively attends 5 AA meetings a week, volunteers at a local treatment center, and has begun to reinvolve himself in a number of civic organizations. His family is complaining that they saw more of him when he was drinking.

- Eric and Cynthia share, in addition to their recent recovery, an altered relationship with food. Both have gained an excessive amount of weight in their early months of sobriety. Both are becoming increasingly conscious about their weight, but early efforts to control their diet have been unsuccessful. Several aspects of their eating behavior have a striking familiar: failed efforts at control, failed promises and resolutions, and guilt and remorse.

- Bart, sober all of 2 months, arrives for an aftercare group at a treatment center announcing with self-righteous pride that he has finally gotten up the courage to take control of his life. Upon questioning, he reports that he has left his wife and family, quit his job and is going to enroll in college to become an alcoholism counselor. He admits after some encouragement that he is also involved in an affair with a woman also early in recovery whom he had met at a self-help meeting. He feels that his courage to make a completely fresh start with his life and the support from his new relationship will enrich his recovery. He is, needless to say, quite surprised by the group's less than enthusiastic response to his declarations.

- Mary is calling the treatment center to express concern about her husband. She doesn't believe he's drinking but she's very concerned about his recent interest in gambling. She wants to know if it is normal for people in early recovery to go to extremes in other areas.

- Jeremy, whose long history of addiction has been a source of unending pain for his family, calls his parents to announce that God has called him to service and that he has joined a charismatic Christian sect and will shortly be leaving for missionary work. He proudly boasts that he has not had alcohol or drugs for six months and asks for the family's blessing on his new venture. Jeremy's prior bouts of sobriety were equally unpredictable—in fact, much more unpredictable than his pattern of addiction—but this one is particularly exasperating, in light of the family's Jewish faith.

There is great variation in this drive toward excessiveness in early recovery, but it commonly appears as a theme and a source of danger for the recovering addict. It is not enough that one must survive the experience of active addiction. One may also have to survive a broad spectrum of other crazy behaviors which surface in early recovery and are often justified in the name of sobriety.

The addiction process subjugates all other human appetites. The cellular relationship with the drug renders as insignificant other physical, psychological and social appetites. With sobriety, there is a resurrection of these appetites. For so long suppressed, these appetites forcefully and competitively reassert themselves in the life of the addict. The appetite for food, sex, risk/excitement, recognition, achievement, money, power, emotional intensity or acceptance may surface with surprising intensity in the newly sober. The tendency to respond excessively to any such appetite is at least one reason the slogan, "Easy Does It" has earned such a central place in the culture of recovery. The suppression, satiation or active management of excessiveness constitutes a major rite of passage during early recovery. Excessive responses to revived appetites constitute a major danger in early recovery, a danger that can reactivate the drug relationship or initiate an alternative but equally compulsive pathway to self-destruction.

While there is much folk wisdom within the self-help community about this concept of excessiveness, there has been little recognition of it in the substance abuse treatment community. Treatment interventions that can assist recovering persons through this critical developmental stage include the following.

1. Create consciousness of excessive behavior in the treatment environment: nicotine/caffeine consumption, using food/sugar for self-medication, and rapid swings from elation to self-pity.

2. Actively teach about "excessiveness" as a developmental stage of recovery.
3. Encourage daily rituals for self-assessment and centering.
4. Teach sobriety-based coping skills that include at a minimum techniques for physical and emotional decompression.
5. Facilitate the establishment of a sobriety-based social network that can provide external sources of moderation and balance.

6. Periodically assess clients in aftercare for patterns of excessive behavior.

It is doubtful that treatment professionals can fully prevent this stage of excessiveness for most clients. Treatment professionals can, however, play an instrumental role in mellowing the intensity of this pattern. One can watch for such behavior and provide mechanisms of early intervention that will support clients through this stage without enduring scars or sustained secondary disorders.

Not all excess is bad in early recovery. Most members of the culture of recovery would agree that getting sober and sustaining early sobriety requires an excess of passion, vigilance and commitment. Survivors in the culture of recovery achieve such status to a great extent by being radicals and extremists on the issue of alcohol and drug use. The vacillators, the ambivalent, the program critics, the second-guessers, and the hesitaters get lost early in the journey. Extremism on the issue of abstinence became not an issue of intellectual debate, but a tenant of personal survival. It is when excessive zeal spills into other areas that problems arise. Perhaps the essential message for this early period could be summarized as follows:

Extremism in the pursuit of sobriety;
Moderation in the pursuit of everything else.

14.8 *Dependence on the Culture of Recovery* Many addicts, particularly the culturally enmeshed addicts, will experience an extreme stage of dependence upon the culture of recovery during the earliest stages of their transformation. The culture of recovery becomes a decompression chamber in which one can socially and emotionally disengage from the culture of addiction. The culture of recovery becomes a womb in which the addict is nurtured in safety during the process of rebirth. The culture of recovery becomes a preparatory school refining knowledge and skills in preparation for one's entry or re-entry into the culture at large.

It is not abnormal for the life of the person in early recovery to be dominated by recovery relationships and activities. The world once dominated by addicts is now dominated by recovering addicts. The social world which supported self-destruction has been exchanged for a social world which supports self-renewal. Some recovering addicts will live inside the social world of recovery for the rest of their lives, having discovered that it is the only world in which they feel safe and comfortable. Others will experience such symbiosis during early recovery but will become increasingly more comfortable and self-assured in the broader social world as their recovery evolves and matures over time. For some, the culture of recovery is a cocoon which never opens. For others, it is a cocoon within which they withdraw and experience a transformation of the self, and are then released to continue the sojourn in the world. There is an openness within the culture of recovery for both those who seek monastic isolation from a substance polluted world and for those who seek to draw strength from the culture to live fully in the world.

14.9 *The Reconstruction of Self* The reconstruction of the addict's identity is an overlapping process of death and rebirth. Major aspects of the old self must be killed as elements of the new self are being born. This reconstruction begins in the earliest days of recovery and spans periods of great ambivalence in which two identities co-exist, fighting for dominance. It is through such co-existence that one can witness such paradoxical and incongruent behaviors as attending AA meetings and drinking afterwards, reading the "Big Book" while drinking, and stealing recovery literature.

Six overlapping steps appear to be involved in the reconstruction of personal identity in the recovery process. These steps seem to be present regardless of the nature of the recovery pathway. The passage through these steps constitutes not unique or discrete events, but a continuing cycle throughout the recovery process. Like an onion, the self of the addict is peeled away and reconstructed one layer at a time. Each of the steps within this continuing cycle will be briefly summarized.

A. *Self-Loathing* The first stage in reconstructing a new self is the rejection of the old self. A crisis-precipitated breakthrough in the addict's ability to clearly see him or herself often results in the experience of self-loathing. During such an episode, the addict sees himself or herself stripped of all the denial and projections and grandiose confabulations. They retrospectively experience things they've done and what they have become, and at this existential moment, experience intense self-hatred. It is by experiencing the worst of themselves as addicts that new energy and desire is generated to support change. The exploration of the worst makes possible the emergence of the best. With support, this step opens opportunities for change. In isolation, this step often drives relapse and continued self-destruction.

B. *Self-Examination* The initial and subsequent periodic breakthroughs of self-perception in recovery call for rigorous self-examination. The culture of recovery provides frameworks to assist the addict with this self-examination. Whether it is the "searching and fearless moral inventory" of twelve step programs, the explorations of personal history in psychotherapy or the spiritual self-scrutiny in the major religions, nearly all pathways of recovery involve a self-inventory process. Most frameworks for this examination require an inventory of both personal liabilities and assets. The former are to be confessed and purged; the latter make up the shell upon which new elements of the self will be constructed.

C. *Confession and Forgiveness* The aphorism, "we are only as sick as our secrets," has been deeply imbedded within the culture of recovery to convey how repressed shame and guilt serve to fuel the progression of addiction. All successful efforts with addicts share the ability to alleviate rather than intensify shame and guilt. Having helped the addict to catalogue one's sins of omission and commission and flaws of character, the culture of recovery provides a forum for expiation of guilt. Nearly all tribal groups within the culture of recovery provide a ritual of confession, although the description of this ritual may be couched in widely varying jargon. Whether through the experience of disclosure in the psychotherapy relationship, the Fifth Step ritual of Alcoholics Anonymous, or the religious confessional; the addict begins to both confess and purge that which is reprehensible in the old self. The experience of acceptance and forgiveness inherent in such rituals is quite powerful.

The initial and episodic involvement in the ritual of confession serves to discharge and render impotent emotions which have historically fueled self-destructive behavior, *e.g.*, relapse. Through exposure, secrets lose their ability to haunt and control. By thrusting secrets outside the self, there is the opportunity to recapture lost innocence.

The fact that the ritual of confession must be periodically revisited by the recovering addict is a subject of much discussion in recovery circles. Like the earlier noted onion analogy, the recovering person peels off one layer of shame and guilt at a time. Following the exploration of each layer is the experience of relief and elation, the discovery and acceptance of new parts of the self and the inevitable surprise at the discovery of a new layer of experience which long suppressed now emerges into consciousness. For most persons, the psyche will only move to the top layer of consciousness that which one is prepared for and that which is the next milestone of one's journey.

D. *Restructuring of Identity* The above steps all involve an evolution in identity. During most of the active stages of addiction, the addict sustains denial of this status. Addiction can touch every area of the addict's life while the very existence of addiction is kept from consciousness. When denial is penetrated during the motivational crisis, the full realization of one's identity of "alcoholic" or "addict" is realized. The third step of identity transformation in early recovery is the shift to see oneself as "recovering alcoholic", "ex-addict", or "non-smoker." An important clinical role, in addition to the oft described role of breaking down denial, is to help the client make the full shift in identity from alcoholic to recovering alcoholic. The acceptance of alcoholism does not in and of itself assure recovery. Clients stuck in this second stage—acceptance of addiction—may continue addiction in increasingly self-destructive cycles. One job of the treatment professional is to facilitate this transition from a stage of self-loathing and self-destruction to a stage of hope, *e.g.*, conversion experience and initiation into the culture of recovery.

By embracing the new identity, the client is given a framework to sustain radical abstinence and, perhaps equally important, is given a new esteem-enhancing identity. The identity of addict which can intensify self-hatred is shifted to the identity of recovering addict which provides a foundation for self-respect.

E. *Restitution* The reconstruction of self in the culture of recovery emphasizes action. It is a processing of doing—"walking the walk". Nearly all pathways of recovery provide a way of walking backwards through one's experiences in an effort to emotionally re-write and correct elements from one's past. Whether the language is one of "making amends", "atonement", or "penance", the culture of recovery provides a framework and support for going back to express sorrow and to compensate others for past deeds. Restitution is a medium through which the recovering person can bury old sins which, if left unexpiated, could gnaw away at the foundation of his or her recovery. Unexpiated guilt says, "you are not worthy of recovery". Restitution says, "go forward, the sins of the past have been paid for."

Addiction transformed persons inevitably suffer humiliations and degradations. Having wounded others, their own selves have been severely wounded. They have lost face. The whole recovery process—and acts of restitution in particular—provide a way to restore personal honor. Honor and faith are restored not by words—which for the addict became tools of manipulation and deceit—but by sustained action. Honor is restored not through promises, but through preparation and performance.

F. *The Purging of Hate and Resentment* The addict collects and cherishes hate and resentment as if they were precious jewels. These powerful emotions serve as currency through which the addict purchases guilt-free drug use. Both real and imagined injustices are woven into the emotional fabric that supports and fuels continued drug use. In recovery, hate and resentment boil up like regurgitated poisons begging for their intoxicating antidotes. Unless put to rest, hate and resentment will abort the recovery process. The recovering addict must reach back through his or her experience and grant forgiveness. Having forgiven oneself and having sought forgiveness from others, one must now reach out and grant forgiveness *to* others. Without forgiveness, one is forever chained to an emotion that robs one of peace and joy. Without forgiveness, one is forever chained to the object of one's hate. Freedom is achieved through acts of forgiveness.

G. *Mastery of Self-Defeating Behavior* The final and ever-continuing step in the reconstruction of self in recovery involves mastering the character flaws that continue to emerge in the struggle between the ideal self and the real self. Using new values from the culture of recovery, the recovering person attempts to integrate these values into his or her daily life.

There are two stages in this mastery of self-defeating behavior. The first, which constitutes an early stage recovery task, involves identifying and changing those patterns of thinking, feeling and behaving that pose risks for relapse. This early stage reconstruction of self has but one purpose—the stabilization of sobriety. As this stabilization is achieved, a second and enduring stage emerges in which the recovering person begins a more wide-sweeping reconstruction of the self. This latter stage involves more intense and less alcohol/drug focused self-examination. These stages are well illustrated if one observes the changes in how recovering persons utilize 12 step programs over the duration of their recovery. During early recovery, the steps serve a singular purpose of achieving and sustaining initial sobriety. In later recovery, these same steps will take on much broader meaning as a philosophy of life and a framework for daily living and problem-solving.

14.10 *Reaching Out to Others* The narcissism of addiction has been a theme throughout this book. Through the progressive intensification of the drug relationship, the addict loses the ability to perceive or respond to the needs of others. Other persons and events pale in significance to the addict's preoccupation with self. Addiction is a world of "I" and "me"—my needs, my pleasure, my discomfort. Addiction places the addict and the drug relationship at the center of the universe around which all other persons and concerns must revolve. In recovery, there is a progressive reversal of this narcissism. In recovery, the self-centered addict child slowly develops into maturity, finally able to perceive and respond to a world beyond themselves.

In early recovery, as in addiction, one is engulfed in a bubble of self-centeredness that restricts one's sensitivity and response to others. The ability to listen and experience empathy and compassion which will emerge in later recovery are quite impaired in the neophyte. As a result, the neophyte's first efforts to reach out to others may be quite awkward and misdirected. As recovery time accumulates, acts of service and the activity of "carrying the message" will take on increased meaning and importance.

14.11 *"I'm Sober, Now What Do I Do?"* In the midlife of sobriety lies an existential crisis few long-term recovering persons escape. This crisis, which may last for some period of time, marks the major milestone of maturation within the recovery process. The crisis emerges after a program of daily sobriety has been established and sustained over a number of years. Its characteristics often resemble the following.

There is a growing sense of discomfort and dissatisfaction, the source of which is both undefined and troublesome. There is an intense experience of one's own mortality—the acute sense of eventual death—and the need to define the meaning of one's life. Old values, activities and relationships may be questioned. Vocations, marriages, political and religious beliefs, and recovery programs may all be closely scrutinized and re-evaluated. The achievement and maintenance of sobriety which held great meaning in early recovery now does not seem to be enough to fill this new existential void. The intense struggle to maintain daily sobriety is past. Sobriety has been achieved and the rituals to sustain it on a daily basis have been mastered. The new question is: "I'm sober, but for what?"

Responses to this crisis vary greatly. Some suppress the crisis entirely and retreat into even greater rigidity of both personality and rituals of daily living. They cling even tighter to the fragile personal defense structure and activities that marked their early recovery. Some may be so disturbed by the emotional intensity of this crisis that they regress via relapse. By reactivating addiction, they force themselves back to earlier stages of the recovery process with which they are more comfortable. Both of the above represent a flight response from the midlife crisis of recovery. Other persons may take a more aggressive response to this crisis—fleeing long-term relationships, changing vocations, experimenting with different belief systems, exploring new personal images. The problem with "excessive behavior" noted earlier, may reappear or even intensify during this period. For many, this existential crisis in the midlife of recovery marks a spiritual turning point in their life. Working their way through this developmental stage, many recovering persons begin the final stage of their metamorphosis. Having struggled to rid themselves of active disease, they now get better than well. The disease of addiction which had cursed their lives becomes a springboard for personal and spiritual growth.

14.12 *Getting Better than Well* Recovery can mean the absence of addiction and it can also mean a life-transforming process. The metamorphosis implicit in the latter is a common occurrence in later stages of recovery. Often beginning after the early stabilization of sobriety (3-5 years), this process or force enters and transforms the life of the recovering person. Although the process itself defies easy description, the results of the transformation can be catalogued.

A. *Joy* The recovery-transformed person experiences a deep joy of living. The fear which dominated the years of addiction and dissipated during early recovery is now only a whisper. Knowing themselves and having shared themselves, they are now ready to participate in life without fear or pretense. Freed of both the cynicism and pessimism of addiction and the superficial euphoria of early recovery, they embrace both the pleasures and pain of life without illusion or resentment. Looking back on their history, most feel that they should be dead—that their survival is a special gift that must be cherished. Is it possible that the escape from hundreds of death courting experiences in active addiction makes possible a deep and unique appreciation of life?

B. *Keeping It Simple* If there is one word that describes the lifestyle of the recovery-transformed person, it is the word, simplify. They have left the chaos of addiction and the fear and franticness of early recovery behind them. Out of the midlife crisis of recovery has come an appreciation for simplicity. Grandiosity and pretense are shed. Preoccupation with acquisition of power, fame or wealth have faded. Having seen and escaped death, there is a sharpened perception and personalization of life's meaning.

C. *The Mastery of Paradox* A paradox is a truth captured within an apparent incongruity. Paradox is a common element within nearly all of the tribes within the culture of recovery. Samples of such paradoxes include:

• Addicts are not responsible for their addiction but once educated are responsible for their recoveries.

- Empowerment comes through the admission of powerlessness.
- Victory is achieved through surrender.
- Change can't occur until you accept yourself exactly as you are.
- When you think you're lookin' good; you're lookin' bad.
- Freedom comes through restraint.
- Serenity is often found when the obsessive search for it is given up in failure.

One would not think the recovering addict could afford such subtlety, and yet the recovery process is rich with paradox. The recovery transformed person, who in early recovery accepted the paradoxes of recovery with simple faith and little understanding, in later days comes to appreciate the multiple layers of complexity and meaning buried within this "simple" program. The mastery of paradox, as noted earlier, is an essential element within the spiritual dimension of recovery.

D. *Softening the Sharp Edges* Between the midlife and twilight of recovery, there is a softening of those personality characteristics most often used to describe both those actively addicted and those in the earliest stages of recovery. The lies that shrouded addiction give way to honesty. Grandiosity gives way to humility, a transition that is often reflected in mildly self-deprecating humor. Rigidity and hyper-criticalness give way to tolerance and acceptance of others. Aggressiveness gives way eventually to gentleness. From the extreme self-centeredness of addiction comes the growth of empathy and compassion for others. Self-pity gives way to quiet self-acceptance.

The above transformation is not intended to exaggerate or glorify the state of late-stage recovery. Not all persons achieve such final transformations, but those who do become the conduit for spiritual strength within the culture of recovery. The above description does give testament to the special qualities of survivors, who having confronted and escaped premature death, approach life with new vision and new values.

This mellowing and softening of personality is not a spontaneous intrapsychic process, but a transformation that is actively initiated and nurtured within the culture of recovery. It is the continued application of principles of 12 step and parallel programs, and the social chemistry within the culture surrounding these applications, that initiate and sustain this reconstruction of self. It is a process in which treatment agencies can play active and supportive roles.

E. *Personal Identity in Late Recovery* The addictions field, in its focus on the earliest stage of recovery, conveys the illusion that the collapse of denial and acceptance of addiction is the final identity transformation in recovery. In late stages of recovery, the identities of addict and recovering addict—so long denied and finally embraced—now get integrated into a broader definition of self. The existential crisis in the midlife of recovery forced one to query, "I'm a recovering alcoholic, but is that all I am?" In this need to extend one's self-definition, persons at this stage can be heard saying, "Alcoholism is my disease, not my total identity!" The disease and recovery process that shaped identity in early recovery is extended to cover a broader identity in late recovery. For most, it is a spiritual identity, not merely mastery of a disease, that provides that sense of specialness and distinction that humans seem to cherish. The addiction recovery process is viewed as a vehicle for spiritual awareness, not the crowning achievement of one's life. Sobriety, which in early recovery was the goal, is understood in later recovery to be merely one of numerous pathways through which men and women have explored powers beyond the self.

F. *The Social World* The recovery transformed person's social world has gone through a number of transitions. The social world has gone from the disengagement from the culture at large to the enmeshment in the culture of addiction to dependence upon the culture of recovery. The social world is again changed and extended in late recovery. The culture of recovery becomes a place of renewal, not a locked asylum hiding the recovering addict from threats in the outside world. The recovery transformed person can enter the world now because safety comes from within. He or she seeks out others based on shared values and interests. The culture of recovery becomes part, rather than the whole of one's social world. This re-entry into the world also provides a broader arena for service. Where service in early recovery meant carrying the message to other addicts, the recovery transformed person carries a message—as a philosophy and way of life—to addicts and non-addicts alike.

G. *The Spiritual World* Earlier note has been made of the importance of spirituality in the individual recovery process and the role of spirituality in the culture of recovery. The spirit path, lost in addiction and approached with great resistance and apprehension in early recovery, is embraced fully by the recovery transformed person. There is a spiritual dimension to all stages of recovery, but there is a special deepening of this spiritual dimension in late recovery. Other elements of life have been brought under control as best they can through early stage recovery—physical and mental health, family restabilization, vocational/financial stability, and legal disengagement. Having brought such chaos under control and having mastered a daily lifestyle of sobriety, the spiritual journey inevitably deepens and intensifies. Such spirituality may present itself in both religious and non-religious frameworks.

14.13 *The Therapist's Role in Milestone Management* The understanding of recovery as a developmental process is still in its infancy. In spite of such tentativeness, there are a number of clear implications of this knowledge to the current state of clinical practice in substance abuse treatment. Such implications include the following.

- There is a need for further research building on the work of Brown (1985) and others to elucidate the precise stages involved in the recovery process, the developmental tasks inherent within each stage, the degree of variation in such stages and tasks from client to client, and any unique developmental stages and tasks shared by persons with special characteristics, *e.g.*, women and adolescents.

- The developmental model of recovery, as currently elucidated, provides a helpful model to guide both therapists and clients to define, select and address developmental tasks that are appropriate to the client's stage of recovery.

- Teaching developmental models of recovery will allow clients and family members to both anticipate and achieve greater control over key developmental milestones or crises.

- The concept of developmental milestones can be an extremely helpful concept in the design and implementation of relapse prevention/intervention programs.

- The developmental model of recovery can help guide therapists in the choice of intervention techniques, reinforcing the notion that techniques appropriate for one developmental stage may be extremely inappropriate for other developmental stages.

- The concept of developmental milestones and the wide variation in how clients can achieve mastery over key developmental tasks can help minimize problems of counter-transference, *e.g.*, the therapist's need to project his or her current developmental needs into the treatment process or the need for a therapist to have his or her own recovery pathway validated through the choices of the client.

14.14 *Recovery Milestones and The Service Continuum* When one speaks of a continuum of care in the chemical dependency field, the concept generally encompasses intervention through detoxification through active treatment through a time-limited period of aftercare. Even with the growing interest in relapse prevention/intervention services, the primary focus remains on the earliest months of the recovery process. With the advent of a developmental model of recovery that views recovery as an evolutionary process spanning years, the field has the opportunity to extend the continuum of care to reflect this understanding.

In the future, clients and families in substance abuse treatment agencies could be offered a menu of services that could result in continuing or episodic involvement over a period of years. Programs could offer support services for clients and families that focus on support through, and mastery of, key developmental tasks within all the stages of recovery. The program of tomorrow might offer a comprehensive menu of learning materials, workshops, retreats, discussion groups, and varied forms of psychotherapy in such areas as the following.

- Family reconstruction
- Marital/intimate relationship enrichment
- Parenting training
- Addressing family of origin pain
- Spirituality retreats
- Discovering the child within (leisure/play workshops)

- Grief work
- Special concern groups, *e.g.*, seniors, women, incest survivors.
- Old-timers therapy groups
- Mastering those other excessive behaviors (food, sex, workaholism).
- Support services for recovering addicts who are terminally ill.

An excellent example of the applicability of this developmental model of recovery is the opening of the Hazelden Renewal Center by the Hazelden Foundation in Center City, Minnesota. This center was designed to provide spiritual renewal and personal growth for persons in twelve-step recovery programs. It is an excellent illustration of the kind of services that could be offered to persons in later stages of recovery.

The substance abuse agency of tomorrow, may reach back to its earliest roots, and shift its identity from a business-oriented provider of health services to the hub of a recovering "community" or "congregation". Persons in search of recovery tomorrow may choose a community or tribe in the culture of recovery the way one joins a particular church today. The agency at the center of this tribe, rather than an impersonal provider of contractual services, will take a leadership role in responding to the collective psychological and spiritual needs of its members. One may choose a treatment agency in the same way that one might choose a home group within AA today. The choice connotes long-term support from and services to the tribe or particular treatment community. As the pool of long-term recovering persons grows, there will be continued evolution in the overall structure of the culture of recovery. Member needs may push treatment agencies into this leadership role within the recovering community at the same time there are external financial and regulatory forces pushing these same agencies into a business profile. The former force shapes an agency that sustains an elaborate service milieu driven by the needs of its members. The latter force pushes the creation of structures that serve organizational survivability and profitability. The challenge of the future will be to integrate and balance these dichotomous forces. The challenge will be to shape organizations that respond to the needs of recovering persons, not simply in the initiation of recovery, but throughout the years that span the developmental stages of recovery.

STYLES OF RECOVERY

This book has explored numerous dimensions within the culture of recovery, from its tribal organization, its major elements, its core activities, its dominant roles to the developmental milestones of its members. This closing chapter examines different styles of how persons relate to this culture in their recovery process.

15.1 *Profiles of the Pilgrims* In 1984, Dennis Wholey authored a book entitled *The Courage to Change* in which he presented excerpts from his recorded conversations with famous persons who were recovering from alcoholism. The inclusion of well-known figures from business, sports, politics, music and entertainment made the book a rapid best seller and added this work to others which had served to destigmatize alcoholism within the United States. Lost or omitted from the accolades for this book was the fact that the collective stories within this book document the tremendous variation in how people achieve and sustain sobriety—a fact rarely acknowledged in the professional literature.

Before proceeding into a formal discussion of the great divergence in recovery pathways, it would perhaps be helpful to introduce the topic with brief profiles of some of the pilgrims who have sought and found such a pathway. This book has sketched broad generalizations about the initiation and developmental stages of the recovery process. These generalizations were consciously framed to embrace commonalities within a number of divergent recovery pathways. And yet there are still exceptions. The vignettes below will put some flesh and blood on the discussion of such variability before the different styles in how recovering persons affiliate or refuse to affiliate with the culture of recovery are fully described.

A. *The Traditional Pathway* Robert's personal pilgrimage brought him to Alcoholics Anonymous long before alcoholism treatment programs became either available or popular and profitable. Having resisted any help until nearly his whole world crumbled around him, Robert found a pathway for both sobriety and serenity within AA. While the availability of this pathway should have been known to him—his alcoholic father spent the last years of his life sober in AA—Robert experienced a troublesome and relapse-plagued courtship with AA until he finally accepted the program. Robert has now achieved more than nineteen years of uninterrupted sobriety and has evolved into a role of elder statesman within his AA community.

B. *The Professionally Supported Traditional Pathway* Lee's drinking closely paralleled Robert's drinking in both pattern and intensity but would be of shorter duration in his life. Thanks to an aggressive employee assistance program at Lee's worksite, he was confronted in the middle stages of his alcoholism and forced to seek treatment to avoid loss of his job. His anger, resentment and denial were forcefully confronted by the treatment professionals and Lee found himself getting caught up in the treatment and recovery process. He still swears he got sober in spite of himself. Through treatment, Lee was able to look at not only his alcoholism but a whole other array of emotional pain he had been hauling through life. Introduced to AA during his treatment, Lee found himself inevitably and inextricably drawn to the fellowship. With a combination of professional counseling and his step work within AA, Lee was able to get sober and initiate what would become a radical transformation of his personality and values. Like Robert, AA is the foundation of his continued sobriety. He is actively involved in the formal and informal rituals of AA participation and service even after a decade of sobriety.

Comment: Robert and Lee both sustained their alcoholism until in a motivational crisis, one with and one without professional help, they entered a 12-step recovery program. Their recovery is based on radical abstinence and continued, lifelong participation in AA. Robert and Lee's pathways to recovery represent the dominant, most visible and most professionally legitimized pathways to recovery in the United States. There are, however, alternate pathways that others have used to achieve and sustain sobriety.

C. *Sobriety by Mail* Marylou approached the author gingerly after a speaking engagement on alcoholism at a church conference and related the following story. Springing from a family tree riddled with alcoholism for as far back as anyone had kept track, Marylou discovered her own drinking becoming increasingly out of control by her late 20s. Afraid and ashamed to speak to anyone regarding her fears, Marylou looked in her church library and there stumbled onto a copy of *Alcoholics Anonymous*, and, in the *Big Book*, found irrefutable revelations about herself. She stopped drinking, began ordering recovery literature by mail, and made a daily ritual of praying and reading recovery literature. She had not spoken to anyone about her history before, had never talked with another alcoholic or attempted any direct contact with AA. She felt guilty that her shame had kept her from service to other alcoholics, but with more well-known women acknowledging their addiction and recovery, she reported she was considering being more open about her own history. She had not had a drink in eleven years at the time of the conversation with the author.

Comment: A remarkable story. It could lead one to wonder how many other silent, invisible addicts have gotten sober by mail and developed their own daily recovery rituals.

D. *Shifting Program Affiliation* Donna owed her early sobriety to the support she found within Cocaine Anonymous. As her sobriety continued, however, she found herself stuck, unable to move forward in her recovery. It seemed to her that she and her CA cohorts were still too drug-focused—that too much of the meetings still focused on getting straight. She was already straight, she just couldn't figure out what to do next. Invited by a friend to attend an AA meeting, she was amazed at the maturity and depth of feelings expressed during and after the meeting. After overcoming her initial awkwardness in AA—she had an almost non-existent relationship with alcohol in her life—she quickly shifted to AA as her primary framework for continued sobriety and growth.

Comment: Donna's story is not unusual. Many persons in the earliest days of their recovery, require a program that recognizes the distinctiveness or specialness of their drug choice (Cocaine Anonymous) or experience (Adult Children of Alcoholics). In late stages of recovery, the need for such specialness dissipates and one tends to be drawn to those settings which contain the greatest maturity in the 12-step recovery process. The newness and short collective sobriety time of CA and NA in most communities, combined with the historical longevity of AA, make AA the logical choice for migration in later recovery. The shift in affiliation from NA or CA to AA is a common scenario when what one needs from others shifts from identification with one's drug experiences to identification with one's emotional and spiritual growth.

E. *From Dry Drunk to Sobriety* Ralph found himself sitting in on a supervisory orientation session being conducted several years ago during the initial implementation of an employee assistance program at his company. Somewhere in the give and take of questions and answers, the speaker defined and discussed the concept of dry drunk. Ralph approached the speaker later and reported the following story. The child of an alcoholic father, Ralph, in spite of his promises and admonitions to the contrary, quickly followed in his father footsteps, developing serious problems in his relationship with alcohol by his mid-twenties. Following a series of alcohol-related humiliations, Ralph stopped drinking and had not had a drink in the past 16 years. The problem, as Ralph reported it, was that he had been on what was being called a "dry drunk" the entire time. After he summarized his discomfort and unhappiness over those years, it was suggested that he seek out an active recovery program and, if necessary, seek some outpatient substance abuse counseling. He was given a number of an AA member to whom the speaker thought he would relate well, although the speaker had doubts that Ralph would follow through with the contact. Several months later the speaker received a call from Ralph thanking him for "pushing" Ralph into contacting AA. It seems that Ralph had found his home and after 16 years of not drinking was beginning his recovery process.

Comment: How many miserable, non-drinking Ralphs are there in desperate need of a recovery program? If the collective goal of the culture of recovery is carrying the message to the alcoholic and addict still in need, it is important that professionals within this culture not forget the non-using who are still in need.

F. *AA as a Developmental Stage* Jerome went through alcoholism treatment nine years ago and has maintained uninterrupted sobriety since that time. He maintained active involvement in AA for the first five years, but disengaged from active AA involvement following his move to a new city. He is deeply indebted to AA and openly acknowledges his alcoholism and his need for continued sobriety, but reports less need for active involvement in AA meetings to sustain his recovery process. He is deeply involved with his family, his job, his church and a number of volunteer activities.

Comment: Is it possible that for some people active involvement in self-help groups is something which, while crucial to their early recovery, may become optional or at least not a required precondition for their sustained sobriety? Is it possible that self-help involvement for some marks an important developmental stage, but not an involvement that needs to be sustained throughout the recovery process? How many people are there who got sober in AA and continue this sobriety, but do so without active involvement in AA?

G. *Women for Sobriety* "The Nun" developed alcoholism as a slow insidious process—self-medicating back pain, self-medicating guilt, and resentment and boredom—that elicited shameful self-realization and external denial. In crisis, she entered treatment and initiated her sobriety within AA. She continued to have problems in AA shaking shame and self-indictment. She would later be exposed to Women for Sobriety meetings (and subsequently disengage from AA) and in this new framework find a sustained pathway to sobriety and self-acceptance. She, like the other women in WFS, will participate in this program as long as necessary. In the WFS program, there is no expectation for lifelong participation. ("The Nun" story is briefly abstracted from *Goodbye Hangovers, Hello Life* by Jean Kirkpatrick, founder of Women for Sobriety.)

Comment: Given the growing research suggesting that the genetic predisposition, incidence, progression and morbidity/mortality of alcoholism in women is different than for men, the possibility exists that the recovery pathway for many women may reflect distinct variations in response to sex-specific needs.

H. *Mentally Ill Recovering Alcoholics* Alice's pathway to addiction recovery was long and tortuous, meandering into dead end after dead end. For years, both her emotional and chemical health were out of control, during which time she was being told by alcohol programs that she needed mental health services and was being told by mental health workers that she needed alcoholism counseling. Being bounced back and forth between service programs and often excluded from both, the beginnings of her recovery were marred by conflicting directives. The beginning of stability occurred when a psychiatrist diagnosed her as manic-depressive, started her on lithium, and explained that her future happiness hinged on her meticulous compliance with this medication. At the same time, she was being told by some AA members she should get off the stuff because it was addictive or harmful to alcoholics. Into this confusion entered a woman who spoke to Alice of a special group called MIRA (Mentally Ill Recovering Alcoholics), a 12-step program for men and women who have experienced both alcoholism and psychiatric illness. Sober today and stabilized on medication, Alice would find in her psychiatric treatment and MIRA affiliation a pathway which would open up the twin gifts of sanity and sobriety.

Comment: MIRA is an example of how increased specialization in the culture of recovery is opening up new pathways of health to alcoholics and addicts with special needs—addicts and alcoholics who have been historically blamed for their inability to sustain sobriety via traditional pathways.

I. *Adolescent Maturing Out with Controlled Drinking* Jeffrey began his alcohol and drug-abusing career quite explosively at the age of 14, amid the disintegration of his parent's marriage and a number of his own developmental crises. His usage of both alcohol and drugs was extensive and the consequences of such use quite profound, *e.g.*, expulsion from school and trauma from alcohol-related traffic accidents. Jeffrey's parents, pulling together to intervene in this crisis, admitted Jeffrey to a substance abuse treatment program. Jeffrey responded well to the structure and nurturing of the program. This structure would help the parents disengage from each other more appropriately, redefine their individual relationships with Jeffrey and help Jeffrey grieve the loss of the parental relationship. In the vacuum created by the disintegration of the parental relationship, the program would take on the role of a surrogate or secondary family, supporting Jeffrey through a number of developmental milestones of late adolescence. Jeffrey was actively involved with self-help groups during and following his treatment. He maintained uninterrupted sobriety through the remainder of his high school years. Late in his freshman year in college, Jeffrey drank in a social situation, experiencing neither intoxication nor loss of control. In spite of his initial guilt, he found subsequently that he could drink without loss of control or the past consequences that had accompanied his drinking behavior. During the past nine years, Jeffrey has maintained an episodic, non-problematic relationship with alcohol, spanning his marriage, fatherhood and several career transitions.

Comment: Did Jeffrey outgrow his risk of substance abuse and addiction/alcoholism? Is this risk still lurking in the background now? Jeffrey's story reinforces the need for a model that can distinguish transient abuse of intoxicants from addictive use of such substances. Purists would say—and the author would agree—that Jeffrey was not alcoholic in any traditional sense of that term and that his ability to sustain controlled drinking as an adult is proof of this position. In short, Jeffrey's history adds no illumination to the issue of controlled drinking. Jeffrey's history provides ample evidence of our difficulty in understanding and intervening in drug *abuse* with a drug *addiction* model. Does one simply say Jeffrey needed no treatment services because he didn't meet the traditional definition of alcoholism? Does failure to apply the term alcoholism or addiction make Jeffrey's explosive alcohol and drug consumption any less life-threatening? There is a need for substance abuse models of treatment and recovery as well as addiction models of treatment and recovery. There may be pathways out of various patterns of abuse that markedly differ from pathways of recovery from addiction. The development of such abuse models and the discovery of biological and developmental markers that would delineate for each client the choice of an abuse or an addiction model would be an invaluable contribution to the addictions field.

J. *Drug Recovery with Controlled Drinking* Woody spent three years in treatment in a therapeutic community (TC) for drug addicts in the late 1960s. As a confirmed heroin addict from a very young age, Woody had had little exposure to alcohol. He went through treatment at a time addicts in treatment were exposed to "normal" drinking as part of their re-entry into society. Woody moved into a staff position within the TC and has continued to work in the substance abuse field since that time. He has not used any drugs other than alcohol since his discharge from treatment, although he has not been involved with any on-going self-help groups. The latter was not an expectation when he went through treatment nor has he experienced any particular need for such support. While many of his peers in treatment, including some of his staff peers, encountered serious trouble with alcohol following treatment, Woody has maintained episodic, social, non-problematic drinking since he left treatment. He reports that alcohol has no particular attraction to him, and that although he drinks on occasion, he rarely ever drinks to intoxication.

Comment: Collective wisdom in the substance abuse field holds forth that drug addicts have significant risks of alcohol abuse and alcoholism and that alcoholics carry significant risks in their use of other psychoactive drugs. Most treatment professionals in the field have hundreds of horror stories to buttress this folk wisdom. Yet, the story of Woody and others like him bear testament that there are exceptions to this rule. The Woodys raise a number of important questions. Can one be considered a recovering addict while continuing a socially defined, non-consequential relationship with alcohol? If one posits that such a person should not be considered recovering, does not then philosophical consistency demand questioning the use of the term recovering for alcoholics who continue their relationship with physically addictive drugs that inflict profound life-threatening consequences, *e.g.*, nicotine. On a more technical level, what characteristics separate the Woodys from those persons who encounter disastrous consequences related to secondary drug use in recovery? Are some patterns or types of addiction drug specific, while others are inclusive of particular categories or all categories of psychoactive drugs? While danger signs should continue to be posted beside secondary drugs in the pathways to recovery, the existence of some persons who seem to have immunity from such hazards is unexplained.

K. *The Christian Path* Dean, by his late 40s, had developed a serious drinking problem. He had lost his business, he was experiencing alcohol-related health problems and his marriage had deteriorated due to his drunken infidelities. The precipitating event in Dean's transformation would be the death of his son. In the midst of the grief, pain, guilt and self-hatred experienced following this event, Dean reached out to a local clergyman. Today, many sober years later, Dean talks openly about being born again and the importance of Jesus Christ in his life. He also talks openly about his past alcoholism, using his sobriety as a living testament to the powers of salvation. His life is now organized around his church involvement and he never misses the opportunity to "carry the message"—an equally sober, and yet different message than that carried by his AA counterparts.

L. *The Path of Islam* Khalid discovered his pathway to freedom in a jail cell. Addicted to heroin for most of his 32 years, he had again come to prison for his drug-related hustling. He was initially put off to discover that his cell mate was a recently converted Moslem. And yet day after day he became quite transfixed with the man's quiet dignity, his detachment from the usual con pastimes, his cleanliness, his industriousness and the reverence with which the man approached his daily religious rituals. Khalid began to question and to learn. By the time Khalid left prison, he was a believer. Upon his return to the outside, he discovered a community of Islam that opened up whole new possibilities for his life. Today, sober and productive, Khalid leads a life that would have been unthinkable to him before. Among his many service activities, Khalid draws particular irony and pleasure from his participation in a street patrol organized out of the local mosque to drive drug dealers out of the neighborhood.

Comment: The stories of Dean and Khalid illustrate religious pathways to recovery and a major theme of this book—that in crisis is the opportunity for a life-transforming reconstruction of personal identity and values. In spite of the increased openness of the substance abuse field to the role of spirituality in the recovery process, the field has been quite reluctant to recognize the legitimacy and viability of strictly religious pathways to recovery. As a result, treatment professionals know very little about these religious pathways and why they are so viable for some persons and so seemingly inaccessible to others.

M. *The Politics and Theology of Abstinence*   Marie grew up around alcohol and alcoholism. Born on an Indian reservation and raised in an Indian boarding school, she had spent most of the first 30 years of her life, whether on the reservation or living in Indian ghettos in large cities, surrounded by alcoholism. She took to alcohol readily in her late teens, what seemed like a natural choice for one who was both beautiful and wild of temperament. She was surrounded by men, but looked on Indian and Anglo alike with contempt because of the ease with which she could manipulate them. The whole time the fiery liquid continued to flow. Her transformation began around age 25, sparked by a long series of drunken escapades that left her with a painful emptiness. She attempted contact with AA on the reservation, but they were all men and their lack of maturity and substantial sobriety repelled her. She had become increasingly preoccupied with her mother and her grandmother, both who had died prematurely of alcohol-related health problems. She began seeking out older women on the reservation who knew them, and it was through these contacts, that she became fully aware of her heritage as an Indian. Her growing racial consciousness drew her to Indian political organizations but she turned away due to the grappling for power and personality conflicts she found there. Unable to initially find strength in the present, she sought strength from the past. She became obsessed with Indian tradition which she began to learn through both oral and written history. Somewhere along the line she simply stopped drinking and within two years viewed alcohol as a symbol of the genocide which had been perpetrated upon her people. To drink alcohol was to participate in that genocide. Sobriety was an act of survival—an act of purification and an act of personal and racial pride. Sobriety for Marie was one component—not the end but a step—in her spiritual journey. It became a tenant of faith within a personal philosophy that drew strength from the past to create personal meaning in the present.

N. *The Risk-Driven Sobriety Decision* Rayburn, by his late twenties, was becoming increasingly concerned about his drinking and had begun to seek out information about alcohol abuse and alcoholism. Rayburn had particular access to such information since he worked at a family counseling agency. With his interest and concern intensified by his preliminary reading, Rayburn signed up for a formal course on substance abuse. Whatever doubts he may have had going into the course about his risks for alcoholism were completely erased by the time his classes were completed. According to the instructor's information, Rayburn had nearly all of the risk factors—familial history of alcoholism, a prior history of attention deficit disorder in childhood, mild conduct disorder in adolescence, euphoric recall of his first drink, and high tolerance from the onset of his drinking. The instructor's description of early stage alcoholism Rayburn experienced as a detailed description of his last ten years. Rayburn entered therapy about this time to explore a number of issues in his life. It was in further exploring his drinking with his therapist that Rayburn finalized his decision to stop drinking. Over the past five years of sobriety, Rayburn has completed therapy, become involved in an Adult Children of Alcoholics support group and continued his reading and training in addiction and recovery.

Comment: Is it possible that at least some early stage alcoholics, like Rayburn, could abort their addictive careers through the self-examination stimulated via substance abuse education? Under what conditions or with which particular persons can such educational experiences stimulate or enhance the decision to seek sobriety? Given Rayburn's story, every substance abuse trainer/lecturer should view every trainee/student as potentially drawn to such experiences to assess their own alcohol/drug relationship.

O. *The Health-Driven Sobriety Decision*   Gerardo began drinking
early, drank daily throughout his life and participated in episodes
of excessive and explosive drinking during times of ritual or
ceremony within his culture, *e.g.*, weddings, funerals. In spite of
the chronicity and intensity of his drinking, Gerardo would
experience no major identifiable consequences related to his
drinking until late in life. In his fifth decade of life, Gerardo was
diagnosed with alcohol-induced cirrhosis of the liver and was
referred into an alcoholism treatment unit. He denied having most
of the symptoms of alcoholism, *e.g.*, loss of control, radical
personality change while drinking, failed efforts to control, failed
promises and resolutions about his drinking. He was viewed as a
highly resistant client and given a poor prognosis for recovery.
Upon his return home, Gerardo failed to make contact with AA,
did not follow through with participation with aftercare groups
and returned daily to the local bar where he had drunk for the past
20 years.   What Gerardo didn't do in the years following his
treatment, to the great surprise of the treatment staff, was drink.
Gerardo, like others before him, simply stopped drinking. He goes
into a bar almost every day, drinks soda water and tells stories
from his days of glory. He also spends a lot of time talking about
his liver.

Comment: Gerardo experienced a cultural pattern of alcoholism
markedly different than the dominant pattern of alcoholism in the
United States, typified by the first stories of Robert and Lee. Just
as Gerardo's etiological pathway into alcoholism was different than
that of Robert and Lee's, his pathway of recovery would also
differ. Recovery for Robert and Lee hinge on their identities as
recovering alcoholics, their active involvement in a culture of
recovery, and their lifelong participation in a 12-step recovery
framework. The key for Gerardo was to find out how one could
maintain status and esteem in his culture as a non-drinker. In
Gerardo's culture, one such pathway involved a medical problem

that would no longer allow one to drink. One had to provide sufficient evidence to one's peers that to drink was to die. With such evidence, one's machismo could be sustained as a non-drinker.

P. *The Relationship-Driven Sobriety Decision* For Rene, cocaine had been an irresistible seducer over the past several months since her initial contact with the drug. Her impulsive choice to expose herself to the drug during a weak moment had been both blessed and cursed, exposing her terribly ambivalent feelings about the growing drug relationship. While using cocaine late one afternoon, she became oblivious to her interrupted meal preparations until the screams of her daughter pierced her drug-induced reverie. With horror, she would observe her daughter's hands, scalded from water boiling in a pan which she had tried to remove when her mother hadn't answered her calls. The daughters hands would heal within weeks, but the vision of those hands would be seared into Rene's soul forever. She has been sober since that day when she begged forgiveness and swore renewed love for her children. She prays daily in thanks, understanding that if her use would have continued a day could have come when the very lives of her children could have been sacrificed in the worship of her drug god.

Comment: How many Renes have veered off the addiction path as a result of the acute awareness of the pain they had caused a child, a spouse, a lover, a friend or a parent? Such choices are possible early in the addiction path. But Rene was right. A time could have come when, late on this path, the only escape she would have from her pain was flight back into the drug relationship, a flight precipitated by the shame that she would continue to value the drug relationship more than her own children.

Q. *The Emotion-Driven Sobriety Decision*   Rob took to alcohol naturally as a rite of passage into manhood, as did most of his peers in this rural community.   His drinking was explosive, unplanned and conducted without regard to its consequences upon self or others.   It's not that Rob did not care about self or others, it was simply that such concerns had not been raised to a level of conscious awareness.   At age 24, Rob was arrested for a DUI, having hit a parked vehicle while having a blood alcohol level of .24.   He entered the DUI remedial education classes with characteristic bravado and resistance.   In spite of hearing information that suggested he night be high-risk for future alcoholism, the classes had had no dramatic impact on Rob until the fourth session.   At this session, a woman whose son and his girlfriend were killed by a drunken driver spoke.   This powerfully emotional presentation penetrated the armor of smugness and defiance with which Rob had entered the classes.   Rob experienced himself as the driver that killed the woman's son and what it would be like to carry such pain and guilt.   Rob decided to stop drinking that night and has not had a drink in the seven years that have passed since then.   It's as if this woman's tear-stained face is permanently imprinted in Rob's mind and inextricably bound to the issue of his drinking.   This event would galvanize a number of decisions by Rob at this time which would move him toward increased maturity and a new construction of personal identity and values.

Comment: Was Rob alcoholic or at risk for future alcoholism? Perhaps in one thin moment of time, Rob experienced his future. Perhaps some element of his future fate became visible along with the knowledge that sobriety was the only vehicle through which that fate could be escaped.   There are other Robs out there whose relationship with alcohol or drugs will drive a pathway of destiny within which is premature death of self or death of others.   What interventions could expose them to experiences so that, like Rob, there is a sudden breakthrough in vision that allows them to abort such destinies? How does one leave the addiction pathway early before it becomes the main course of one's life? How can professional helpers intervene to terminate this person-drug (and person-drug-culture) relationship while the power and intensity of such relationships are at their weakest level?

R. *Recovery and Environmental Change: Vietnam* Henry doesn't talk much about Vietnam. It's not the primary source of his identity. It is not his obsession. Many would say he escaped without permanent scars. But Vietnam was insane—what he remembered of it. To Henry, Vietnam was death—ever present and incomprehensible—comradery with those in the field, and hashish and heroin. By the time his tour was up, Henry's relationship with heroin was completely out of control. In spite of knowing he'd have to drop urine to get out of Vietnam, Henry used right up until the day his dirty urine would delay his return home, via a detoxification center in Saigon. Detox helped—not as much for the heroin as for the emotional decompression. Henry left heroin behind him as he left Vietnam—a bad dream that couldn't be described or explained to outsiders. Like so many of his peers that "experts" feared would bring their addiction back to further infect the United States, Henry would never again use heroin. For Henry, heroin was of Vietnam and left in Vietnam.

Comment: Alcoholics and addicts alike are known for their attempts to blame addiction on physical settings and to escape addiction through geographical escape, only to find their addiction following them like a shadow. And yet is it possible that some patterns of addiction are environmentally shaped and sustained? Can addiction for some be an adaptation to an insane environment, that when changed, allows a flight to freedom?

S. *The Anti-script*   Jeremy can be found on a soapbox any day preaching the horrors of drug abuse. The experiences which would crystallize his path to sobriety would occur not in the milieu of a treatment center or self-help group, but in the isolation of a jail cell. Jeremy's pathway to recovery involves preaching the anti-drug message every day. By channeling his anti-drug passion into a variety of volunteer activities after his release from prison, Jeremy would eventually be hired to work full time as a drug abuse educator.   He has channeled his most visible skill—his ability to speak with passion and charisma against drugs—into a legitimate profession.   Jeremy has maintained uninterrupted sobriety primarily through his anti-drug crusades for the past decade.

Comment: Jeremy's story illustrates one pattern within the phenomenon of spontaneous remission. He turned the defense mechanism of reaction formation into a sustained lifestyle. Jeremy's story exemplifies the anti-script—the fighting off of one's unacceptable impulses by forcefully representing ideas and actions opposing such impulses. The treatment field knows very little about the incidence of this recovery pathway or the long-term prospects of this profile of recovery. In the author's experience, it may be some of the most successful within this profile who are at greatest risk of relapse. There is a high casualty rate for some of the most successful and most visible of the "super ex-dope fiend folk heroes" within the substance abuse field.   Like their counterparts in televangelism, the lack of a sustained recovery framework to contain and remove defects of character—narcissism, grandiosity, excessive risk-taking—can lead to eventual self-destruction.

T. *Methadone for Life*   Marcus' 12 years of heroin addiction was regularly interrupted by short periods of incarceration and both voluntary and involuntary efforts at treatment.   He has had repeated experiences with long- and short-term drug-free treatments and self-help involvement but has never been able to sustain sobriety outside of a treatment setting. Marcus doesn't like being on methadone but has painfully come to realize that it is only while on methadone that he has any reasonable chance of stability. As long as he is maintained on low dosages of methadone, he does not drink or use other secondary drugs, refrains from all contact with his previous criminal lifestyle, maintains regular employment, supports his family and sustains his own physical health. Every previous effort to detoxify and go off methadone, regardless of the intensity of his motivation, has resulted in heroin relapse. Marcus has now reconciled himself to the probability that he will need methadone for the rest of his life. History suggests that he can live a productive and meaningful life like anyone else, except in his case, this will require daily consumption of a drug that can quench his historically insatiable appetite for heroin.

Comment: Can persons who utilize methadone as a developmental stage of stabilization on the road to a drug-free lifestyle be considered in recovery? Does the field consider persons who, like Marcus, may need a maintenance drug like methadone for life, in a process of recovery? Some in the substance abuse field would deny persons in such categories this status. There are those for whom the admonition to not drink and use drugs and go to meetings forever may prove simplistic and inappropriate. If there are, in fact, some persons who may be constitutionally incapable of sustained, radical abstinence from all psychoactive drugs, then what alternative pathways are possible for such persons?

O. *Maturing Out* Matt's heroin addiction spanned 14 years of his life, hustling escapades through urban America and innumerable episodes of "doing time" and "doing treatment", none of which had any significant impact in deterring his addiction.   His disengagement from heroin and hustling spanned two years of his life, almost mirroring his early courtship with heroin. Between ages 28 and 30, his periods of drug abstinence became longer and his periods of "rippin' and runnin'" became shorter and shorter. By his 32nd birthday, he realized he had actually quit. No treatment. No great breakthrough of intellectual or spiritual awareness. No emotional crisis. Matt just got tired and bored being a dope fiend. Over the past ten years, he has not used heroin, has used marijuana probably a half dozen times a year and drinks a couple of times a year. In the years after his heroin use, Matt got involved with a steady woman whom he now lives with and fell into a straight job that he really enjoys. No paragon of virtue or radical sobriety, Matt would be the last to hold himself out as a role model. Yet, there is a pattern of maturing out clearly evident in Matt's history. Matt has broken his relationship with heroin and hustling and his rare or episodic use of other intoxicants is not producing any significant impairments in his life.

Comment: There are innumerable variations in maturing out stories. While maturing out is clearly a pathway out of addiction for some persons, treatment professionals know very little about the incidence of this phenomenon nor possible clinical interventions that could influence the timing or speed of such maturing out.

P. *Futurism and the Prevention of Addiction*   Erisa's parents had anxiously awaiting the Bioscreen test results which were now provided routinely to all 5 year olds entering the technical and non-technical academies. John and Marla were not surprised when Erisa tested positive on the ARS (Addiction Risk Screen). Ancestry from both families trees revealed the addiction risk. They were, however, particularly anxious to find out which pattern of risk was identified as there were still some patterns that were not medically curable. They were greatly relieved to discover that the risk was of the GMT (Genetic Maternal Type) pattern, which meant the risk was sex-linked— transmitted by Mary's genes in spite of her lifelong abstinence—and treatable. Erisa could be provided the new yearly chemical implants that would allow her to sustain control over available intoxicants. That genetic flaw which would make intoxicants so powerfully seductive could be chemically neutralized, allowing Erisa a physically normal relationship with these substances. Erisa would also be able to take advantage of new techniques of genetic engineering which would prevent her from passing on this GMT pattern of addiction risk to her children.

Comment: Who knows!!! Is it possible a day will come when treatment professionals look back on our understanding of alcoholism and addiction in 1990 as we now look back in history with pompous hindsight on the days when epilepsy was seen as possession by the devil and tuberculosis was treated by drinking elephant's blood or inhaling the smoke of burning cow dung?

15.2 *Styles of Recovery* Book I defined the culture of addiction and described different styles through which addicts related to this culture. Acultural, bicultural and culturally enmeshed styles of addiction were described. With the brief case studies catalogued above as a backdrop, the next section will examine parallel styles of recovery.

A. *Acultural Styles of Recovery* In acultural styles of recovery, recovering persons initiate and/or sustain their recovery from drug abuse or addiction in relative isolation from other recovering people. They do not affiliate with the major institutions in the culture of recovery, *e.g.*, treatment centers or self-help groups. There may be different milestones in their recovery process than those that characterize recovery within 12-step frameworks.

Persons in this style of recovery may not even embrace the identity of "recovering alcoholic/addict."

Several of the earlier stories in this chapter capture the possibility and essence of the acultural style of recovery. In the midst of their abuse/addiction, these persons experience some crisis (of health, identity, relationship, or sanity) that aborts the progression of their addiction. Included in this category are persons described within the professional literature under the rubrics of "spontaneous remission" and "maturing out."

The substance abuse treatment field needs to know a great deal more about acultural pathways to recovery. Isn't it significant that drug abusing and addicted persons—perhaps in substantial numbers—are reversing and eliminating this pattern without the aid of treatment or self-help group involvement? Isn't it important to understand how such sobriety decisions are made and sustained? Couldn't the study of acultural recovery have important implications? People are breaking their addiction to nicotine every day without treatment and self-help support. Isn't there a collective experience among these persons—and their alcohol and other drug counterparts—that should be studied and disseminated widely within the culture for others seeking to terminate their drug relationships? Shouldn't such pathways to recovery at least be openly recognized as possible and legitimized within the professional literature?

Within the broad category of acultural styles of recovery, there would seem to be some particularly cogent research questions regarding the phenomenon of spontaneous remission and maturing out.

- Who are these persons experiencing spontaneous remission/maturing out (SR/MO) and how do their

- characteristics differ from the current U.S. treatment population?
- Are there special populations more capable of SR/MO, *e.g.*, sex, ethnicity, personality characteristics, type and pattern of abuse/addiction?
- What commonalities exist in the constellation of experiences which stimulate the SR/MO response?
- Are there key developmental markers upon which the SR/MO response is dependent, *e.g.*, age, duration of use, intensity of use, intensity of drug-related consequences?
- Are there common methods utilized to initiate or sustain the SR/MO response?
- Given the facts above, are there educational or clinical interventions that could be designed specifically to speed the onset and enhance the durability of the SR/MO response?

If spontaneous remission and maturing out exist with any substantial prevalence, then it is a matter of some speculation why such phenomena have not been fully discussed and researched within the substance abuse field. After examining the resistance to consider the existence of the SR/MO response, four potential motivators of resistance appear to be in operation here: personal threat, clinical blindness, professional arrogance, and financial self-interest. In the first, it may be difficult for recovering professionals to openly consider alternative recovery pathways when their own sobriety and sanity may hinge on rigid adherence to one particular recovery path. In the second, some treatment professional simply fail to see the existence of patterns of addiction or recovery that cannot be explained and embraced comfortably within their current philosophies and paradigms. In the third, it may be difficult for some professionals to fully acknowledge the existence of addicted clients who may be able to recover as well without help as with it—and in fact without any professional or self-help process. In the fourth, it may be difficult for the substance abuse field to explore and bless pathways of spontaneous recovery that could compete and potentially remove persons from those pathways that generate millions of dollars of income for the substance abuse treatment industry.

The future understanding of addiction recovery—and the pathways and styles that can be reflected in this process—will extend dramatically beyond its current confinements. The future exploration of acultural patterns of recovery will constitute a field fertile with new and valuable insights and technology.

B. *Culturally Enmeshed Styles of Recovery* In the culturally enmeshed style of recovery, the person's addiction recovery is initiated and sustained within a social network that reinforces radical abstinence. It is often the case with this style that one trades the culture of addiction for an equally consuming and well-organized culture of recovery. With culturally enmeshed recovery, the person's identity is shaped by the culture of recovery, daily lifestyle is conducted primarily within this culture, and contact with outsiders is somewhat limited. Family life is shaped by the culture. Leisure is shaped by the culture. In short, one is fully absorbed in the culture of recovery. The vignettes at the beginning of this chapter illustrate such deep affiliation with a number of tribes within the culture of recovery, *e.g.*, 12-step programs, Women For Sobriety, religious groups. Perhaps an implicit assumption throughout this book has been that the intensity and duration of involvement in the culture of addiction must often be paralleled by the intensity of one's involvement in the culture of recovery. Culturally enmeshed addicts generally require culturally enmeshed styles of recovery.

The culturally enmeshed style of recovery—via alcoholism/addiction treatment and long-term 12-step program involvement—is the dominant and only pathway to recovery in this culture that has been widely legitimized within the professional community. The state of the art in addiction treatment today is defined primarily within this dominant pathway rather than through a broader framework that, while respecting the dominant pathway, legitimizes and individually directs treatment efforts with a view of multiple pathways, patterns and styles of recovery. This book has focused on culturally enmeshed styles of recovery primarily because it has focused on the treatment of culturally enmeshed addicts.   Changes within the culture of recovery are expanding the number of persons whose needs can be met within this style of recovery.   In the past twenty years, the field has seen:

- the creation and spread of 12-step programs to address drugs other than alcohol, *e.g.*, Narcotics Anonymous, Cocaine Anonymous, Pot Anonymous
- the increased specialization of 12-step recovery programs to meet the specialized needs of its members, *e.g.*, meetings for women, neophytes, old-timers, non-smokers, Gays and Lesbians, the young, and the ethnic
- the creation and spread of alternatives to 12-step programs for special populations of clients, *e.g.*, Women for Sobriety
- the creation and spread of new hybrid groups that blend characteristics of self-help and professionally directed groups for special clients, *e.g.*, the chronically mentally ill who abuse alcohol/drugs
- the growth of religious, political or special interest groups which provide both a philosophical rationale and substantial social support for radical abstinence
- a de-stigmatization of radical alcohol/drug abstinence that has lowered the deviance and increased the acceptance of recovering addicts in the culture at large

The culture of recovery is expanding in both size and diversity, ever extending its capacity to absorb new addicts seeking to break the drug relationship and to escape the culture of addiction which sustains that relationship. That alternative culture is becoming larger, easier to find, more specialized and more effective every day.

C. *Bicultural Styles of Recovery* In the bicultural style of recovery, recovering persons can move in and out of the culture of recovery with ease. They are involved with tribes from the culture of recovery but are also fully involved in the culture at large. Their social network is made up of both recovering and non-recovering persons and may be composed primarily of the latter. Their identity is not totally dominated by their addiction recovery status, but neither is such status denied. It is not unusual in this bicultural style that persons find themselves in occupational or social situations in which alcohol/drugs and active alcoholics/addicts may be present. In the bicultural style, the person is able or has learned to disengage emotionally (and at times physically) from such situations so that they do not constitute a threat to their continued sobriety.

Where in culturally enmeshed recovery one prevents and insulates oneself from exposure to drug stimuli; in bicultural recovery, one learns to keep such stimuli from triggering drug hunger and drug-seeking behavior. In culturally enmeshed recovery, one escapes from the outside world and lives essentially in a cloistered subculture of sobriety; in bicultural recovery one draws strength from the culture of recovery to sustain one's sobriety while fully participating in the outside world. Neither style has any inherent superiority over the other. It is simply a question of person-style fit.

D. *Style Preference and Evolution* The substance abuse field in the United States today consistently conveys the impression that alcoholism/addiction is of a singular—if unknown—etiology, responds to a narrow treatment philosophy and body of clinical technique and is arrested through a narrow scope of recovery practices. I hope this book which has teased out the numerous pathways into addiction and into recovery, and the cultures which surround these conditions, has helped stretch the reader's understanding beyond such a restricted view.

There is immense variability in the manner through which persons with abusive and addictive drug relationships reach the decision to terminate these relationships. There is equal variability in how such decisions are implemented and sustained over time. Just as the forces that initiated the drug relationship may differ from those which sustain it over time, the forces that crystallize the sobriety decision and get one through early recovery may differ from those forces which sustain the continued evolution of the recovery process. Long-term recovery may involve multiple pathways. Styles may evolve over time, *e.g.*, from culturally enmeshed in early recovery to bicultural in late recovery. The natural evolution of such pathways has occurred for generations but has not been clearly observed or charted.

Different pathways and styles of recovery fit different people. The very concept of "recovery" spans everything from the removal of a toxic habit from an otherwise unchanged life to a spiritual and life-transforming odyssey. The pilgrimage of the addict in search of recovery is to find that pathway and style through which one can escape self-destruction and then discover a meaning for living.

A wise yoga teacher once taught that the pathway to Heaven leads through Hell. If this adage is true, there must be a special place in

Heaven for those addicts whose tortuous pathways led through Hell on the way to recovery. And perhaps there is also a special place in Heaven for those who have served as guides for them along this journey to recovery.

APPENDIX A
SELF ASSESSMENT INSTRUMENT

This self assessment exercise is designed to help you assess how your alcohol/drug use has affected various areas of your life. Read each statement and think about whether the statement reflects an accurate description of your experience during the months preceding your start of treatment. Place a ✔ before each statement that *does* reflect your experience during this time period.

_____ 1. There are particular songs or types of music I associate with drinking/drug use.

_____ 2. I feel most comfortable when I am with other alcohol/drug users.

_____ 3. Alcohol/drugs help me get to sleep.

_____ 4. I spend more and more time preoccupied with drinking/drug use.

_____ 5. People I drink/use drugs with make me feel important.

_____ 6. Most of my leisure activities involve drinking/drug use.

_____ 7. I have friends who want me to drink/get high even when I don't feel like it.

_____ 8. There are friends who I think are no longer comfortable around me because of my alcohol/drug use.

_____   9.   I often spend more money on alcohol/drugs than I intended to.

_____   10.   There are things I have done while intoxicated that make me feel ashamed.

_____   11.   I feel special because of my alcohol/drug use.

_____   12.   I can name five famous people who are/were addicts.

_____   13.   I have changed when and what I eat as a result of my alcohol/drug use.

_____   14.   The language I use with my friends would not be understood by most persons who weren't users.

_____   15.   I don't think I take as good of care of my personal appearance as I used to.

_____   16.   There are times of the day or particular days of the week that I almost always drank/got high.

_____   17.   My friends and I are always telling "war stories" about our alcohol/drug escapades.

_____   18.   I have bought alcohol/drugs from lots of different people/locations.

_____   19.   I keep drug paraphernalia in my home.

_____   20.   My alcohol/drug use has changed my relationship with my family.

_____   21.   I have committed criminal acts related to my alcohol/drug use.

_____   22.   I believe there are lots of things I would have done with my life if it were not for my alcohol/drug use.

_____   23.   My alcohol/drug use has changed my sleeping schedule.

_____   24.   I think about running out of alcohol/drugs even when I have plenty.

_____   25.   There are a number of leisure activities that I no longer do because of my alcohol/drug use.

_____   26.   I use a lot more profanity when speaking than I used to.

_____   27.   I am very uncomfortable around people who don't drink/use drugs.

_____   28.   I have worn clothes (T-shirts, jackets, hats, belt buckles, etc.) that reflect my alcohol/drug tastes.

_____   29.   I think my values have changed as a result of my alcohol/drug use.

_____   30.   There are a lot of places in the city where I live that I associate with my alcohol/drug use.

_____   31.   I have had dreams/nightmares related to alcohol/drug use.

_____ 32. I am known by a nickname or other name assumed during the time of my alcohol/drug use.

_____ 33. I associate paydays or having cash with alcohol/drug use.

_____ 34. I have been alcohol/drug-impaired at work or school.

_____ 35. I sometimes feel I defy death by the way I use alcohol/drugs; I sometimes think it's only through luck that I'm still alive.

APPENDIX B
GLOSSARY OF CLINICAL
INTERVENTIONS AND TECHNIQUES

Aversive Techniques: pairing a prior conditioned stimulus (music, drug paraphernalia) with an unpleasant or painful stimulus (image of friend who died of overdose) to decrease the power of the conditioned stimulus to trigger drug hunger.

Biographical Techniques: structured exercises, such as writing one's autobiography or daily journaling, which are designed to enhance the recovering addict's self-perception and to speed the process of emotional thawing.

Centering Rituals: activities such as prayer or meditation which help keep one focused on daily recovery activities and values.

Confrontation Techniques: providing feedback from staff, family and treatment peers to the addict on behaviors that continue to reflect cultural engagement. Confrontation often focuses on incongruity between stated values and current behavior, "You say..., but do...."

Contingency Contracting Techniques: the negotiation of special agreements with clients that make specific pre-determined positive or negative consequences contingent upon certain actions of the client.

Contracting Techniques: negotiated individual and collective agreements for behavioral change. Behaviors are explicitly defined as are consequences for compliance and non-compliance.

Decompression Techniques: rituals whose mastery enables one to consciously lower his or her level of physical/emotional arousal.

Desensitization Techniques: the use of behavioral conditioning to extinguish the addict's response to cultural triggers (stimuli from the culture of addiction that have historically triggered drug hunger and drug-seeking behavior);   the previously conditioned response (drug hunger/drug seeking-behavior) is neutralized by pairing the trigger (music, sight of paraphernalia) with relaxation and the absence of drug reward.

Grieving Techniques: rituals to facilitate the expiation of emotion involved in the addict's loss of the drug relationship and his or her affiliation with the culture of addiction.

Humor and Parody Techniques: the use of humor or comic exaggeration to lower a client's defense structure, to confront inappropriate behavior and to engage the client in trying on new alternative behaviors.

Identification Techniques: structuring relationships and interactions within the treatment environment to enhance the addict's affiliation with the treatment process. Techniques include the structuring of symbols and initiation rituals to enhance the addict's identification and affiliation with the treatment milieu; by reflecting an understanding of the addict's personal and tribal (drug-specific) experience, we let the addict know that he/she is in the right place.

Isolation Techniques: the removal of the addict from environments and interactions in which cultural triggers (stimuli historically paired with intoxication) are likely to serve as a catalyst to drug hunger and drug-seeking behavior;

isolation techniques can range from placement of the addict in long-term residential treatment to actively structuring the addict's daily lifestyle as part of the process of outpatient treatment;   relapse prevention planning often involves identifying the most powerful triggers for drug consumption and altering daily patterns and rituals to create isolation from such stimuli;   isolation techniques buy time until other interventions can reduce the seductiveness and power of such cultural triggers.

Mirroring Techniques: the use of audiotape, videotape or another person to portray a client's presentation of self;   these techniques enhance the perception of self by allowing addicts to see themselves at a time when they are out of role and when resistance is lowered.

Modeling Techniques: specialized identification techniques that provide role models for cultural disengagement and for pathways and styles of recovery that uniquely fit each addict. These role models present new attitudes and behaviors that the addict can try on and they serve as a powerful source of hope.

Initial stage identification may require models that share key aspects of the addict's experience, *e.g.*, ethnicity, gender, drug choice, or milestones in the addictive career.   Second stage identification involves more uniquely personal attributes. The key is creating high levels of client interaction within a large pool of potential role models.

Paradoxical Techniques: the therapeutic manipulation of a client's resistance to break habitual patterns of responding and to get the client to try on new behaviors.

Reframing Techniques: changing a stimulus which has previously served as a trigger for drug use into a stimulus that reinforces drug abstinence.   Also used to describe the process of cognitively restructuring a client's experience within a framework supportive of long-term recovery.

Reinforcement Techniques: the use of rewards to encourage feelings, attitudes and behaviors congruent with the recovery process.

Replacement Techniques: the process of systematically exchanging core elements from the culture of addiction with core elements from the culture of recovery, *e.g.*, replacing "street" jargon and profanity with recovery jargon.

Role Disengagement Techniques: special techniques and strategies utilized to confront and alter addict styles of "doing treatment." They often encompass a number of the other catalogued techniques, *e.g.*, contracting, paradox, etc., that are aimed at disengaging the client from   compulsive and self-defeating patterns of thinking, feeling and acting.

Role Transference Techniques: the conscious planning and application of a client's knowledge and skills from the culture of addiction into a socially appropriate role in the culture of recovery, *e.g.*, the "Jailhouse Lawyer" is linked to volunteer work as an advocate for indigent senior citizens.

Satiation Techniques: a special type of desensitization technique in which the client is saturated with a cultural trigger to the point that the stimulus loses its power to elicit the previously conditioned response, *i.e.*, drug hunger.

Self-Assessment Techniques: providing structured times and methods that allow addicts to assess their level of cultural disengagement, to identify behaviors and attitudes that continue to reflect cultural identification, and to assess progress in new behaviors and attitudes reflecting increased affiliation with the culture of recovery. Based on areas of needed change clearly identified by the addict, self-assessment techniques provide feedback to self on congruency between stated goals and current attitudes and behavior.

Skill Building Techniques: providing clients with concrete skills required for full participation in activities and relationships outside the culture of addiction.

Teaching Interventions: any structured learning experience which provides addicts a cognitive framework for making sense out of the transformation in their life and enhances the identification of lifestyle changes required for long-term recovery. Teaching interventions serve to: 1) help addicts reconstruct and articulate their addictive history in a language that protects self-esteem and reduces shame and guilt; 2) provide a cognitive map for the recovery process; and 3) provide cognitive exercise to speed the pace of neurological healing. The design of teaching interventions must be based on adult learning principles.

Techniques for Milieu Management: special approaches to shaping the group process within the treatment milieu so that the culture of addiction brought into treatment by clients can be reshaped into a culture of recovery.

Thought-Stopping Techniques: rituals that allow one to consciously abort thoughts that are self-defeating and self-destructive.

Trigger Identification Techniques: the formal exploration and recognition of those precise stimuli—people, places, situations, feelings, objects, images, sounds—which trigger drug hunger and compulsive drug-seeking behavior.

Storytelling: the transmission of values from the culture of recovery through the sharing of tales, anecdotes, fables, allegories and myths.

Story Reconstruction: the conscious reformulation of the client's life story. Story reconstruction involves the reinterpretation of life events to replace those elements of the addict's life story that have served to justify and sustain addiction.

Values Clarification Techniques: structured exercises that force the client to explicit define values from the culture of addiction. These techniques provide clients a safe context within which they can begin the reconstruction of a personal, recovery-based value system.

Visualization Techniques: consciously controlled visual imaging which can be utilized: 1) as a decompression technique, 2) as a tool in identity reconstruction, or 3) as a tool for rehearsal of critical incidents in the recovery process.

BIBLIOGRAPHY

Agar, M. *Ripping and Running: A Formal Ethnography of Urban Heroin Addicts*. New York: Seminar Press, Inc., 1977.

Agar, M. Folklore of the Heroin Addict: Two Examples. *Journal Of American Folklore*, 1971; 84:175-185.

Bahr, H. *Skid Row: An Introductions To Disaffiliation*. New York: Oxford University Press, 1973.

Bales, R. F. The Therapeutic Role Of Alcoholics Anonymous as seen by a sociologist. *Quarterly Journal Of Studies On Alcohol*, 1944; 5:267-278.

Bateson, G. The Cybernetics of Self: A Theory of Alcoholism. *Psychiatry*, 1971; 34(1):1-18.

Becker, H. *The Outsiders*. New York: Free Press, 1963.

Biernack:, P. Junkiework, Hustles, and Social Status Among Heroin Addicts. *Journal of Drug Issues* 1979; Fall:535-551.

Black, C. *It Will Never Happen To Me*. Denver, Colorado: MAC Printing and Publication Division, 1982.

Blum, R. *The Dream Sellers*. San Francisco: Jassey-Bass Inc., Publishers, 1972.

Brown, S. *Treating the Alcoholic: A Developmental Model of Recovery*. New York: John Wiley & Sons, 1985.

Brown, G. *Manchild in the Promised Land.* New York: The MacMillian Company, 1965.

Burroughs, W. [Originally Written Under Pseudonym (William Lee)] *Junkie* Ace Books, Inc., 1953.

Campbell, J. *The Hero with a Thousand Faces.* Princeton, N.J.: Princeton University Press, 1949.

Casanave, J. Career Conversion: Illegitimate to Legitimate. Unpublished Paper, 1980.

Cheek, F. E., *et al.* Deceptions in the Illicit Market. *Science*, 1970, pp. 167, 1276.

Chein, I.; Gerard, D.; Lee, R; and Rosenberg, E. *The Road to H.* New York: Basic Books, Inc., 1964.

Conley, P. & Sorensen, N. *The Staggering Steeple: The Story of Alcoholism and the Churches.* Philadelphia, Pilgrim Press Book, 1971.

Courtwright, D., Joseph, H, and Des Jarlais, D. *Addicts Who Survived: An Oral History of Narcotic Use in America*, 1923-1965. Knoxville: University of Tennessee, 1989.

Covington, S.S. Facing the Clinical Challenges of Women Alcoholics: Physical, Emotional and Sexual Abuse. *Focus On Family*, 1986; 9(3):10-11, 37, 42-44.

Crothers, T.D. *The Disease of Inebriety.* New York: E. B. Treat Publishers, 1893.

Crowley, A. *The Diary of a Drug Fiend.* New York: Lancer Books, 1972.

Douglas, M. *Dealing: Or The Berkeley-To-Boston Forty Brick Lost Bag Blues.* New York: Knopf, 1971.

Dr. Bob And The Good Oldtimers. New York: Alcoholics Anonymous World Services, Inc., 1980.

Erikson, E. *Childhood and Society.* New York: Norton, 1963.

Feldman, H. Ideological Supports To becoming and Remaining a Heroin Addict. *Journal Of Health And Social Behavior,* 1968; 9:131-139.

Fiddle, S. Notes on the Heroin Addict and His Culture, in *Portraits From a Shooting Gallery.* Edited by Fiddle, S. New York: Harper and Row, 1967.

Finestone, H., ed. by H. Becker Cats, Kicks and Color, in *The Other Side* New York: Free Press, 1969.

Geertz, C. *The Interpretation of Cultures.* New York: Basic Books, 1973.

Goffman, E. *Stigma: Notes On The Management Of A Spoiled Identity.* Englewood Cliffs, N.J. Prentice-Hall, 1963.

Hanson, B. et.al., *Life With Heroin: Voices From the Inner City.* Lexington, Mass: Lexington Books, 1985.

Holiday, B. *Lady Sings the Blues.* New York: Doubleday, 1956.

Howard, J. and Borges, P. Needle Sharing in the Haight: Some Social and Psychological Functions, in *It's So Good, Don't Even Try It Once: Heroin In Perspective*. Ed. by D. Smith & G. Gay, Englewood Cliffs, New Jersey: Prentice-Hall, Inc., 1972.

Hughes, P. *et al.* The Social Structure of a Heroin Copping Community. *American Journal of Psychiatry*, 1971; 128(5):551-558.

Huxley, A. *The Doors of Perception*. New York: Harper & Row, 1954.

Iceberg Slim *Trick Baby*. Los Angeles: Holloway, 1969.

Iceberg Slim. *Pimp: The Story of My Life*. Los Angeles: Holloway, 1969.

Jacobson, M., Atkins, R., and Hacker, G. *The Booze Merchants: The Inebriating Of America*. Washington, D.C.: CSPI Books, 1983.

Jacobson, R. & Zinberg, N. *The Social Basis of Drug Abuse Prevention*. Washington, D.C.: The Drug Abuse Council, Inc., 1975.

Jellinek, E.M. *The Disease Concept of Alcoholism*. New Haven, Connecticut: College & University Press, 1960.

Johnson, B. *Taking Care of Business: The Economics of Crime by Heroin Users*. Lexington, Mass: Lexington Books, 1985.

Ketcham, K. and Mueller, A. *Eating Right To Live Sober*. New York: New American Library, 1983.

King, A. *Mine Enemy Grows Older*. New York: Simon and Schuster, Inc., 1958.

Kirkpatrick, J. *Goodbye Hangovers, Hello Life.* New York: Ballantine Books, 1986.

Larner, J and Tefferteller, R. *The Addict in the Street.* New York: Grove Press, 1964.

Leary, T. *Politics of Ecstasy.* New York: Putnam, 1968.

Ludwig, A. Cognitive Processes Associated With "Spontaneous Recovery" From Alcoholism. *Journal Of Studies On Alcohol,* 45: 228-236, 1984.

Lyle, D. The Logistics of Junk *Esquire* 1966; 65:59-67, 138-144.

M., Dr. Earle. *Physician, Heal Thyself!* Minneapolis, MN: Comp Care Publishers, 1989.

Malcolm X *The Autobiography of Malcolm X.* New York: Grove Press, 1964.

Mannion, M. The Joy of Recovery. *The Alcohol Quarterly,* 1988; I(1).

Morgan, W. *Drugs in America, 1800-1980: A Social History.* Syracuse, NY, Syracuse University Press, 1981.

National Household Survey on Drug Abuse: Main Findings, 1985. Rockville, Maryland: National Institute on Drug Abuse, 1985.

Neilson, L. Sexual Abuse and Chemical Dependency: Assessing the Risks for Women Alcoholics and Adult Children. *Focus on Family and Chemical Dependency,* 1984; 7(6):6, 10-11, 37.

Patridge, William C. 1973 *The Hippie Ghetto*. The Natural History of a Subculture New York: Holt, Rinehart, and Winston.

Pepper, A. and Pepper, L. *Straight Life: The Story of Art Pepper.* New York: Schirmer Books, 1979.

Polsky, N. *Hustlers, Beats, and Others.* Chicago: Aldine Publishing Company, 1967.

Powell, D. H. Occasional Heroin Users: A Pilot Study. *Archives Of General Psychiatry,* 1973; 28:586-94.

Preble, E. and Casey, J. Taking Care of Business - The Heroin User's Life on the Street. *The International Journal of the Addictions,* 1971; 6(1).

Prugh, T. Recovery Without Treatment. *Alcohol Health & Research World,* Fall, 1986; II(1): 24, 71.

Robins, L. N. A Follow-up of Vietnam Drug Users. *Interim Final Report: Contract No. HSM-42-72-75,* Special Action Office For Drug Abuse Prevention, 1973.

Rooney, J. Group Processes Among Skid Row Winos. *Quarterly Journal of Studies on Alcohol,* 1961; 22: 444-60.

Rubington, E. Drug Addiction as a Deviant Career in *The International Journal of the Addictions,* 1970; 2(3).

Rubington, E. The Bottle Gang *Quarterly Journal of Studies on Alcohol,* 1918, 29 (December), 943-55.

Rudy, D. R. Slipping and Sobriety: The Functions of Drinking In Alcoholics Anonymous. *Journal Of Studies On Alcohol*, 1980; 41 (7):272-732.

Sacks, O. *The Man Who Mistook His Wife For A Hat*. New York: Harper & Row, 1985.

Schmidt, J. *Narcotics Lingo and Lore*. Springfield, Illinois: Charles C. Thomas, Publisher, 1959.

Smart, R. G. Spontaneous Recovery In Alcoholics: A review and analysis of the available literature. *Drug and Alcohol Dependence*, 1975/1976; 1:277-285.

Soloway, I. Methadone and the Culture of Addiction *Journal of Psychedelic Drugs*, Spring, 1973; 6:2.

Spradley, J. *You Owe Yourself A Drunk: An Ethnography Of Urban Nomads*. Boston: Little, Brown & Company, 1970.

Stephens, R. and Levine, S. The Street Addict Role: Implications for Treatment *Psychiatry* 1971; 34(4):351-357.

Substance Abuse on Film and TV. *National Coalition on Television Violence*. 1989; 10(5-6).

Sutter, A. G. The World of the Righteous Dope Fiend. *Issues in Criminology*, 1966; 2(2):177-122.

Thomas, P. *Down These Mean Streets*. New York: Alfred A. Knopf, Inc., 1967.

Tournier, R. Alcoholics Anonymous as treatment and as ideology. *Journal Of Studies On Alcohol*, 1979; 40(3):230-239.

Trice, H. M. A study of the process of affiliation with Alcoholics Anonymous. *Quarterly Journal Of Studies On Alcohol*, 1957, 18 39-54.

Trice, H. M. Delabeling, relabeling and Alcoholics Anonymous. *Social Problems*, 1970; 17:538-546.

Trocchi, A. *Cain's Book*. New York: Grove Press, Inc., 1960.

Tuchfeld, B. S. Spontaneous remission in alcoholics: Empirical observations and theoretical implications. *Journal Of Studies On Alcohol*, 1981; 42:626-641.

Vaillant, G. E. and Milfsky, E. S. Natural History of Alcoholism, IV. Paths to Recovery *Archives Of General Psychiatry*, 1982; 39(2):127-133.

W., Bill *Alcoholics Anonymous Comes Of Age*. New York: Alcoholics Anonymous World Services, Inc., 1957.

Waldorf, D. and Biernacki, P. The Natural Recovery from Heroin Addiction: A review of the incidence literature. *Journal Of Drug Issues*, 1979; 9:281-289.

Waldorf, D. and Biernack:, P. The Natural Recovery From Opiate Addiction: Some Preliminary Findings. *Journal of Drug Issues* Winter, 1981; 11(1):61-74.

Waldorf, D. *Careers in Dope*. Englewood Cliffs, N.J.: Prentice-Hall, Inc., 1973.

Wallace, J. Tactical and Strategic Use of the Preferred Defense Structure of the Recovering Alcoholic. New York: The National Council on Alcoholism, Inc., 1974.

Wallace, S. *Skid Row as a Way of Life*. New York: Harper & Row, 1965.

Wegscheider, S. *Another Chance: Hope and Health For The Alcoholic Family*. Palo Alto, Science and Behavior Books, 1981.

Weil, A. *The Natural Mind*. Boston: Houghton Mifflin Company, 1972.

Wellisch, D. *et al*. The Easy Rider Syndrome: A Pattern of Hetero- and Homosexual Relationships in a Heroin Addict Population *Family Process*, 1970; 9(4):425-430.

White, W. and Godley, M. *Illinois Child Neglect Services Project: Program Handbook*. Springfield, Il: Illinois Department Of Children and Family Services, 1988.

White, W. *Incest In The Organizational Family: The Ecology of Burnout in Closed Systems*. Bloomington, Il: Lighthouse Training Institute, 1986.

White, W. Themes In Chemical Prohibition, in *Drugs in Perspective*. Rockville, MD: National Institute on Drug Abuse, 1979.

Wholey, D. *et al*. *The Courage To Change*. New York: Warner Books, 1986.

Williamson, H. *Hustler* New York: Avon, 1965.

Wilson, C. *The Outsider*. New York: Dell, 1956.

Winick, C. The Life Cycle of the Narcotic Addict and of Addiction *Bulletin On Narcotics*, 1964; 16(1):1-11.

Winick, C. Maturing Out Of Narcotic Addiction. *Bulletin On Narcotics*, 1972; 14:1-7.

Woititz, J. *Adult Children of Alcoholics*. Hollywood, Florida: Health Communications, Inc., 1983.

Zinberg, N. Nonaddictive Opiate Use *in* James Weissman and Robert Dupont, eds. *Criminal Justice and Drugs: The Unresolved Connection*. Port Washington, NY: Kennikat, 1982.

INDEX